Creating Web Pages FOR DUMMIES®

7TH EDITION

by Bud E. Smith and Arthur Bebak

WILEY

Wiley Publishing, Inc.

Creating Web Pages For Dummies®, 7th Edition
Published by
Wiley Publishing, Inc.
111 River Street
Hoboken, NJ 07030-5774

Copyright © 2004 by Wiley Publishing, Inc., Indianapolis, Indiana

Published by Wiley Publishing, Inc., Indianapolis, Indiana

Published simultaneously in Canada

For general information on our other products and services or to obtain technical support, please contact our Customer Care Department within the U.S. at 800-762-2974, outside the U.S. at 317-572-3993, or fax 317-572-4002.

Wiley also publishes its books in a variety of electronic formats. Some content that appears in print may not be available in electronic books.

Library of Congress Control Number: 2004107901

ISBN: 0-7645-7327-6

Manufactured in the United States of America

10 9 8 7 6 5 4 3 2

7B/SZ/QZ/QU/IN

WILEY

About the Authors

Bud E. Smith is a computer book author with over 12 years of publishing experience. *Creating Web Pages For Dummies,* 7th Edition, is one of over a dozen books Bud has written; his Wiley Publishing, Inc. titles include *Internet Marketing For Dummies* and *Web Usability For Dummies.* In addition to writing books, Bud has been a computer magazine editor and product marketing manager.

Bud got his start with computers in 1983, when he left a promising career as a welder for a stint as a data-entry clerk. Bud then moved to the Silicon Valley to join a startup company, followed by work for Intel, IBM, Apple, and AOL. His work and interests led him to acquire a degree in Information Systems Management from the University of San Francisco.

Arthur Bebak received a degree in Computer Engineering at the University of Illinois, which he attended on a fencing scholarship. He has designed mainframes, managed large engineering projects, and studied business administration. Arthur is founder of Netsurfer Communications, Inc., a highly successful electronic publishing company, and is an accomplished author.

At Netsurfer, Arthur oversees a large staff of people who create Web sites for numerous clients. They also write, edit, and publish several Web-based e-zines.

Authors' Acknowledgments

The authors thank Steve Hayes, acquisitions editor, and the staff that helped produce this book: Editors Paul Levesque, Rebecca Senninger, and Nicole Haims, Technical Editor Danilo Celic, as well as the many other people responsible for page layout, proofreading, indexing, and graphic art.

The Web was built more for love than for money, and that tradition was continued by the many people who generously gave their time and support for this book. We especially thank the providers of Web tools who supplied us with an excellent set of programs for the CD-ROM and the Web authors who agreed to let us use their sites for the figures in this book.

Publisher's Acknowledgments

We're proud of this book; please send us your comments through our online registration form located at www.dummies.com/register/.

Some of the people who helped bring this book to market include the following:

Acquisitions, Editorial, and Media Development

Project Editors: Nicole Haims, Paul Levesque

(*Colleen Williams Esterline*)

Acquisitions Editor: Steven H. Hayes

Copy Editor: Rebecca Senninger

Technical Editor: Danilo Celic

Editorial Manager: Carol Sheehan

Permissions Editor: Laura Moss

Media Development Specialist: Travis Silvers

Media Development Manager: Laura VanWinkle

Media Development Supervisor: Richard Graves

Editorial Assistant: Amanda Foxworth

Cartoons: Rich Tennant (www.the5thwave.com)

Composition

Project Coordinator: Maridee Ennis

Layout and Graphics: Andrea Dahl, Denny Hager, Joyce Haughey, Stephanie D. Jumper, Heather Ryan

Proofreaders: Laura Albert, John Greenough, TECHBOOKS Production Services

Indexer: TECHBOOKS Production Services

Publishing and Editorial for Technology Dummies

Richard Swadley, Vice President and Executive Group Publisher

Andy Cummings, Vice President and Publisher

Mary Bednarek, Executive Acquisitions Director

Mary C. Corder, Editorial Director

Publishing for Consumer Dummies

Diane Graves Steele, Vice President and Publisher

Joyce Pepple, Acquisitions Director

Composition Services

Gerry Fahey, Vice President of Production Services

Debbie Stailey, Director of Composition Services

Contents at a Glance

Table of Contents

Introduction

*I*t may be hard to remember, or it may seem like only yesterday, but some years ago, the personal computer was introduced. The rise and rise *and rise* of the personal computer — with maybe an occasional stumble but never a real fall — seemed certain to be the most important social and technological event at the end of the twentieth century. From Wozniak and Jobs's Apple II to Bill Gates's Windows 95, nothing, it seemed could ever be bigger, or more life-changing and important, than PCs.

But, people do talk. In fact, talking is one of the main things that people are all about, and in the beginning, the personal computer didn't let you interact with others. However, first with modems, and then with networks, and finally through their combination and culmination in the Internet, personal computers became the tools that opened up a new medium of communication. The most visible and exciting part of the Internet is the World Wide Web. Now communication, not computation, is the story. Computers are still important, but mostly as the means to an end; the end result is to enable people to interact.

If the most exciting channel of communication is the Web, the means of communication is the Web page. Ordinary people demonstrate amazing energy and imagination in creating and publishing diverse Web home pages. And although ordinary people have a *desire* to create Web pages, businesses have a *need* to set up shop on the Web. So the rush to the Web continues, often with the same people expressing themselves personally on one Web page and commercially on another.

So you want to be there, too. "But," you ask, "Isn't it difficult, expensive, and complicated?" Not any more. As the Web has grown, easy ways to get on the Web have appeared. And we discuss the best of them in the pages of this book.

About This Book

It's *about* 380 pages.

Seriously, what do you find here? Easy ways to get published on the Web for any kind of Internet user we could think of. Ways to make your first Web page rich with carefully arranged text, graphics, and multimedia. Plus the information you need to go beyond your first Web page and create a multipage personal or business Web site. And tools (tools that we describe in the book or provide as demos or in full versions on the CD-ROM) to help you go as far as you want to go in creating a Web site.

Foolish Assumptions

Lots of good information is in this book, but almost no one is going to read every word of it — except our long-suffering editor. That's because we cover Web page topics from beginning through intermediate levels, including how to publish a Web page via Web-based services and the major online services, how to use several different tools, and some Windows-specific and Mac-specific stuff. No one needs to know all of that! But anyone who wants to get a Web page up on the Web does need to know some of it.

But what do *you* need? We assume, for purposes of this book, that you have probably used the Web before and that you want to create a Web page. We further assume that you are not yet a Web author, or that you're fairly new to the process. To use the information in this book, you need access to a personal computer running Windows or Mac OS, and you need access to the Web — either through an online service or an Internet service provider (ISP). You should be running a Web browser such as Microsoft Internet Explorer, Netscape Navigator, or a browser provided by an online service. If you have a UNIX system and an Internet connection, much of this book works for you, but you don't have access to the online service or Web page creation tools that we describe, except those available directly on the Web.

If you don't have Web access from your personal computer, see Appendix B for a list of service providers who can help you get it. You should already have spent some time surfing the Web, or be willing to do so as you gather information and examples for your Web page. In other words, if you're wired, or willing to get wired, you're in. With that, the door to this book is open to you, whether you want to create your first Web page or add new features to one you already have.

The figures in this book show up-to-date Windows screen shots for a consistent appearance. We wrote the instructions and steps in this book to work equally well for Windows and the Macintosh.

Jump around in the book and go straight to information that you need. Later, you can back up and read something that interests you, page through the how-to sections, try using one of the tools on the CD-ROM, and then go look at something on the *Creating Web Pages For Dummies* home page (created by one of the authors) at the following address:

```
www.creating-web-pages.com
```

CD (-ROM) for Me, See?

The CD-ROM that comes with this book is a rich source of software for creating World Wide Web pages. You can find plenty of software for either

Windows or Macintosh. For details about what's on the CD-ROM, see Appendix E. For details about how to use specific programs, see the chapters and sections of this book. For information on how to install the software on the CD-ROM, see the instructions in Appendix E.

Conventions Used in This Book

When our publisher first told us that this book was going to have *conventions,* we got out our silly hats and our Democratic and Republican paraphernalia, but apparently she just meant that we had to be consistent. The conventions in this book are standard ways of communicating specific types of information, such as instructions and steps. (One example of a convention is the use of italics for newly introduced words — as with the word "conventions" in the first sentence of this paragraph.)

Here are the conventions for this book:

- Things that you, the reader, are asked to type are shown in **bold**.

- New terms are printed in *italics*.

- Information used in specific ways is formatted in a specific typeface. In this book, one of the most common kinds of information displayed this way is HTML tags; that is, formatting information used to create Web pages (see Appendix A for a more complete definition). An example of a tag is `<TITLE>`.

   We also use a special typeface for URLs (Uniform Resource Locators), which are the addresses used to specify the location of Web pages. For example, the URL for the For Dummies Web site is `www.dummies.com`.

- The Web is fast-paced and evolving. By the time you read this book, some of the URLs listed in it may have changed.

- Representative browser versions appear among the figures.

- Menu selections look like this: File⇨Save. This particular example means that you choose the File menu and then choose the Save option. The underlined letters represent Windows shortcut keys — hold down the Alt key and press the first shortcut key, and then press the second shortcut key (with or without Alt held down) to make the selection.

- Related, brief pieces of information are displayed in bulleted lists, such as the bulleted list that you're reading right now.

- Numbered lists are used for instructions that you must follow in a particular sequence. This book has many sequential steps that tell you just how to perform the different tasks that, when taken together, can make you a successful Web author.

To make the steps brief and easy to follow, we use a specific way of telling you what to do. Here's an example of a set of steps:

1. **Start your Web browser.**

2. **Go to the Web site** `www.tryfreestuff.com.`

   Note: This site is not real, just an example.

3. **Click the link that matches the type of computer you have: PC, Macintosh or UNIX.**

Part-y Time: How This Book Is Organized

We wrote this book to a carefully plotted, precise, *unvarying* plan, with the predictable and predicted result: the book you're holding in your hands now. And the CD-ROM? Same thing.

Wait a second. Isn't it true that the Web is changing every day, that Web sites appear and disappear like so many jacks-in-the-box — or whack-a-moles, if that's a more familiar example to you — and that Web companies can pop into and out of existence in a few weeks? So, what was that about a plan?

Well, okay, we did change things a little along the way. Maybe a lot. But we *did* have a plan behind the book, even if it was finalized in a conference call at 5:00 this morning. The following sections explain the parts that make up the book.

Part 1: Create a Web Page Today

You probably want to dive right into becoming a Web publisher. So we start the book with some ideas about what to do in your Web site, and then give some basics of HTML, the underlying language of Web pages, and specific instructions on how to get your first, simple Web page up. You can start with Yahoo! Geocities, a free service accessible to everyone, or built-in AOL or CompuServe features, if you use one of those as your ISP.

Part 11: Building Pages

The free, easy-to-use services in Part I are great for your first efforts as a Web publisher. But soon you'll want to use some "real" tools for managing and editing your Web pages. You'll also want to make your page richer with formatted text and links. You may even want to add META tags to allow someone using a search engine to easily find your pages. We tell you how to do all that and more in this part.

Part III: Better, Stronger, Faster Pages

Huge books have been written about Web graphics. We know — one of the authors co-authored one of them, *Creating Web Graphics For Dummies* by Bud Smith and Peter Frazier (Wiley). In this part, we show you the high points of how to create Web-friendly graphics and how to place graphics in your Web page. Then we show you how to publish your customized Web page where everyone can get to it.

Part IV: Getting Interactive

Most Web pages just sit there. But the fun ones interact with the user. We show you how to add animation, multimedia, Web logs, and more interactivity to your Web page. And we show you how to expand your "simple" Web page, which by this point may be quite large, into a multi-page Web site. Have fun!

Part V: The Part of Tens

A Top Ten list is a great way to make complex information fun and easy to remember. Our Top Ten lists show you key DO's and DON'Ts of Web publishing.

Part VI: Appendixes

Appendixes in books are usually like appendixes in people: funny little things that get taken out of the patient in a hurry if they act up. But for this book, we pack in great information that can really help you. In Appendix A, a complete glossary defines Web publishing terms that may be confusing to you. In other appendixes, you see information about Internet service providers and Web page developer resources, including a guide to the CD-ROM that comes with this book.

Icons Used in This Book

 Tells what is on the accompanying CD-ROM.

 Marks information that you need to keep in mind as you work.

 Warns you of effects that may make your page take a long time to appear.

 Points to things you may want to know but don't necessarily need to know. You can skip these and read the text, skip the text and read these, or go ahead and read both.

 Flags specific information that may not fit in a step or description but that helps you create better Web pages.

 Points out things (in addition to slow downloads) that may cause problems.

Part I

Create a Web Page Today

The 5th Wave — By Rich Tennant

"You know, I've asked you a dozen times not to animate the torches on our Web page!"

In this part . . .

*J*ump right in with HTML and simple Web page publishing. Use Web-based services or your ISP to get a page online today. Your reward: Telling your friends and colleagues your Web address tomorrow!

Chapter 1

Web Page Publishing Basics

*T*he Web is an incredibly easy way to get your message — any message — out to anyone in the world who's interested in it. By putting up a Web page, you can stay in touch with friends and family, entertain people, help yourself get a job, or help yourself do your job. You can start a business, grow a business, or just have fun expressing yourself.

Over half a million people have purchased this book since its first edition over ten years ago, and as far as we can tell, they've used every technique we describe in this book, and more, to get their first Web pages up. By reading this book you're starting on a path that many, many people before you have followed to Web page success.

Web Basics 101

You may have begun using the Internet and Web without really getting a chance to learn how they work. Knowing how they work can help you become a better Web publisher. Here's a brief, to-the-point description. For more information, you can search the Web; the World Wide Web consortium site at www.w3.org is a good place to start.

Understanding how the Web works

The Web, formally called the *World Wide Web,* is a collection of a bunch of text and graphics files (plus some other stuff) that make up *Web pages.* The base of the Web is the Internet. The Web depends on the Internet to connect its many files together and to allow people to get to the Web. E-mail is a separate function that also depends on the Internet.

The Web is defined by two specifications: HyperText Transfer Protocol (HTTP) and HyperText Markup Language (HTML). The underlying idea behind the Web is *hypertext* — text that can contain links to other pieces of text stored anywhere on the Internet. The Web got its name from the way all the links connect the pieces of text together like a huge spider's web.

You look at Web pages using a program called a *Web browser*. A Web browser uses HTTP to request a Web page from a Web server. The Web page, in turn, uses HTTP to request any other files, such as graphics images or ads, that are part of the Web page. After you request a Web page, your Web browser pulls the files that make up the Web page from one or more Web servers and assembles those files into one page on your machine.

The most popular Web browsers are Microsoft Internet Explorer, which you can use separately or as a built-in part of America Online software; Netscape Navigator; Opera, a standards-compliant Web browser from a much smaller company; and Safari, a relatively new browser for Macintosh computers.

At this point, HTML steps in. Each Web page includes a text file written in a format called *HTML* (for HyperText Markup Language) and usually one or more graphics files. HTML defines a Web page's appearance and functionality. Actually, HTML doesn't precisely specify the Web page's appearance: Different Web browsers display various HTML commands differently. Also, users can specify how they want things to look. So what one user sees when she looks at a Web page may be very different from what another user sees. (Chapter 4 goes into detail about HTML.)

Getting Webbed

This book talks a lot about the Web but doesn't discuss how to get on it. And even if you're on the Web already, perhaps through a connection at work, you may also want to get on the Web from home. How do you do that?

The most popular online service is America Online (AOL). AOL has robust Web publishing features, robust coverage around most of the world, and many other good features. Also popular are MSN (Internet access from Microsoft), Earthlink, and CompuServe (owned by AOL), which all have advantages. Because AOL has both robust Web publishing features and by far the most customers, we describe in detail how to publish your first Web page using AOL's publishing features in Chapter 3. If you have another Internet service provider, use the information on quickly publishing your first Web page using Web-based services in Chapter 2.

Web terms to know

We want to clear up how we define and use some Web terms:

✔ **Web page:** A text document that is published on a Web server, has HTML tags in it, almost always includes hypertext links, and usually includes graphics. When you click the Back button in your Web browser, you move to the previous Web page that you visited.

✔ **Web site:** A collection of Web pages that share a common theme and purpose and that users generally access through the site's home page.

✔ **Home page:** The Web page that people generally access first within a Web site. You let people know the URL (address) of your home page and try to get other Web page creators to provide links to it.

✔ **HTML tags:** Brief formatting or linking commands placed within brackets in the text of an HTML file. For instance, the <b> tag tells the Web browser to display text after the command in bold type; the </b> tag turns bolding off. See Chapter 4 for more on HTML.

Getting a Web page up on the Internet is surprisingly easy. In fact, if you're in a hurry, you may want to go straight to Chapter 2 (for GeoCities, a Web-based service) or Chapter 3 (specifically for AOL or CompuServe) and follow the instructions there to get your first Web page up in a few hours.

Getting up URLy

The *Internet* is the giant computer network that connects other computer networks around the world. At its base, the Internet is just a giant mechanism for moving files from one computer to another. It finds files using a kind of address called a *URL* (Uniform Resource Locator — which sounds like something the Armed Forces invented to track down clothes!). The acronym URL is usually pronounced "you are ell," though some pronounce it "earl."

The address that you type to get to a Web page is a URL. For example, www.netsurf.com is the URL for Arthur's Netsurfer Communications Web site. A URL consists of three parts (see Figure 1-1):

✔ **Protocol:** The name of the communications language that the URL uses: HTTP (used on the Web), FTP, Gopher, and so on.

✔ **Domain name:** The name of the server the file is on.

✔ **Pathname:** The location of the desired file on the server.

Figure 1-1:
URLy to
Web, URLy
to rise.

◄──Protocol──►   ◄──Domain name──►   ◄──Pathname──►
http://   www.server.com/   folder/filename.ext

The For Dummies Way to Web Publishing

Reading this book is going to make you a Web publisher — because anyone who puts up even a single, simple home page is a publisher on the World Wide Web. Congratulations in advance!

Putting up a Web page involves a few steps that are the same no matter which tools or techniques you use. The steps may have different names, or be intermingled with each other, but they're still basically the same. Here they are:

1. **Create the HTML text file that's the basis for your Web page (see Chapter 6).**

2. **Create or obtain the graphic images you'll use to spice up the appearance of your page (see Chapter 9).**

3. **Create a link to the graphics in your HTML text file so they appear where you want them to (covered in Chapter 10).**

4. **Preview your Web page on your own machine (see Chapter 6).**

5. **Find Web server space (see Chapter 12).**

6. **Transfer the HTML text file and the graphics files to the Web server (also in Chapter 12).**

7. **Check that your new Web page works correctly now that it's online (again, see Chapter 12).**

These steps are usually simple if you're creating a basic Web page. However, they do get more complicated sometimes, especially if you're trying to create a multi-page Web site. This book tells you several different, easy ways to create a Web page, and gets you started on expanding your Web page into a multi-page Web site.

When you create a Web page that has complex formatting, or that mixes text and graphics, you'll want to test it in all the popular Web browsers. See Appendix B for the Web addresses from which you can download Microsoft Internet Explorer, the America Online client, the Netscape browser, the Opera browser, the Safari browser, or other tools.

For an example of a good-looking Web page, check out the For Dummies Web page, shown in Figure 1-2. It has an attractive layout, interesting information, and links to a great deal more information on the For Dummies site and other sites. The For Dummies Web site is very well done, but you, too, can achieve similar results with a reasonable amount of planning and hard work. In this book we concentrate on helping you create a simple, individual Web page and combine several Web pages into a closely linked group of pages called a *Web site*.

Note: The For Dummies home page is shown in Microsoft Internet Explorer, the most popular Web browser. For consistency, we use Internet Explorer for most of the Web page images in this book.

Making simple things simple

If all you want to do is create a simple "I exist" Web page, either for yourself or for your business, you don't have to go through the rigmarole of figuring out HTML or learning a tool, finding server space, and so on. Chapters 2 and 3 show you two ways to get your first Web page up quickly and easily, using existing templates or simple HTML. Chapter 2 is for those who want to use GeoCities, a Web-based service; Chapter 3 is for those who want to use the built-in Web page publishing tools in AOL or CompuServe.

Figure 1-2:
The For Dummies home page shows Web publishing skill.

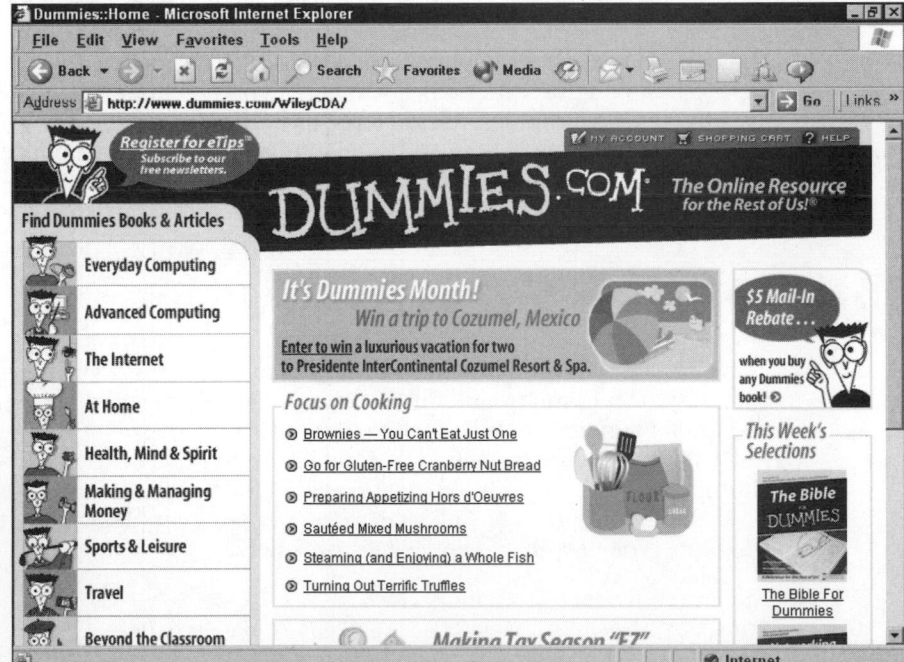

Seeing HTML

When Tim Berners-Lee invented HTML at CERN (the European particle physics research facility) in the early 1990s, he probably never imagined that so many people would be interested in seeing it. Today, most browsers include a command that enables you to see the actual HTML source that makes the page look and work the way it does.

For example, in Internet Explorer, choose View⇨Source to view the underlying HTML file. You see all the HTML tags that make the Web page look and act the way it does.

After you open the HTML file, you can edit the text and the HTML tags, save the file, and then open the file again in your browser to see how it looks with the HTML changes.

To see how easy publishing on the Web is, just turn to Chapter 2 or 3 and get started. You'll be a Web publisher with just an hour or two of effort.

Making difficult things possible

The free services and online services we describe in this book differ in how far they allow you to go without outgrowing what you can get for free. If your site gets too large or gets too much traffic, or if you want to use your site for business, at some point these services ask you to start paying for the site.

The rest of Part I describes what you need to know to get an initial, simple Web page up on the Web. Parts II and III tell you how to improve your Web page, by placing graphics, adding links, and making your layout look attractive. Part IV tells you how to add animation and interactivity, plus expand your Web page into a Web site.

Types of Web Sites

The Web offers examples of nearly every communications strategy known to humanity, successful or not. But not every example of a Web page that you find online applies to your situation. For one thing, the resources of different Web publishers vary tremendously, from an individual putting up family photos to a large corporation creating an online commerce site. For another, several different types of Web sites exist, and not every lesson learned in creating one type of Web site applies to the others.

The major types of Web pages are personal, topical, commercial, and entertainment sites. In the next sections, we describe some of the specific considerations that apply to each type of Web page and not to the others. Decide in advance what type of Web page you want to create, and look for pages like it online.

Personal sites

Personal Web sites can have many goals. Often, your goal is simply to share something about yourself with coworkers, friends, family, and others. Personal Web pages are a great way for people to find out about others with similar interests and for people in one culture to find out about other cultures. You can also use a personal Web site to share family photos and events — kind of like a holiday letter that's always up to date. Figure 1-3 shows part of the personal site of Jeff Lowe, who's piloting a remote-controlled blimp in the pictures. You can find the site at www.jefflowe.com.

Creating a personal Web site is a great deal of fun and great practice for other work. But personal Web sites are often left unchanged after the initial thrill of creating and publishing them fades. Be different — keep your Web site updated!

Figure 1-3: Jeff Lowe pilots the blimp (and posts his résumé too).

Are personal Web sites still relevant?

Most of the activity you hear about on the Web these days relates to large, commercial sites, political sites, and so on. Personal Web sites have gotten somewhat lost in the shuffle as better-funded sites belonging to organizations get all the attention. Never fear; personal Web sites are still fun and easy to create. And did we mention that they're fun?

Part of what's driving the continuing interest in personal Web pages is that more and more people all over the world have access to the Web. The chances are better than ever that a high percentage of your friends, family, and colleagues can visit and appreciate your site. So don't be put off by the tremendous growth of business on the Web. The personal and fun side is growing, too; it's just getting less media attention than the commercial side.

As personal Web sites evolve, their creators tend to add more information about a single key interest, in which case the pages may become topical Web sites (described later). In other cases, the Web site creator adds more information about professional goals and accomplishments, in which case the Web page becomes more like a business Web site.

Following a few simple rules helps make your personal Web site more fun and less work:

- ✔ **What's on first?** No, no. What's on second . . . The upper part of your Web page — the part that appears first when you bring the page up on-screen — needs to make the main point of the site clear. If the main point is "you," the first thing people see should be your name, your photo, and links to some of the things about "you" that are in your site. If the point of your site is a topical interest, business interest, or professional self-promotion, you should make that clear, too.

- ✔ **Keep it simple.** Start with modest goals and get something up on the Web; then create a "To Do" list of ways in which to extend your site. Consider spinning off commercial and topical pages that reflect your desires and interests — each page with its own access point — rather than creating a sprawling personal Web site.

- ✔ **Provide lots of links.** One of the best ways to share your interests is to share information about Web sites that you like, as well as books and other resources. You can put this list on your one and only Web page or make it a separate page that's part of a personal Web site. If you develop a thorough, carefully updated list of links for a specific interest area, you create a very valuable resource for others.

✔ **Consider your privacy.** A Web page is just like a billboard — except that 100 million or more people can see it, not just a few thousand. Don't put anything up on your Web page that you wouldn't want on a billboard. And think twice before putting up information about your kids and other family members; you might be willing to compromise your own privacy, but you shouldn't make that decision for other people.

Topical sites

That's "topical," not "tropical." (See the Kaua'i Exotix home page later in this chapter for an example of the latter.) A *topical home page* is a resource on a specific topic. A topic can be an interest or volunteer group to which the author belongs, in which case the page may grow over time into something much like a commercial Web site. (Creating a Web site for a group is a tremendous contribution that you can make, but it can be a lot of work; watch what you may be getting yourself into!) Or your topical Web page can be about any interest, cause, concern, obsession, or flight of fancy that you have. In this sense, the Web is like an out-of-control vanity press, allowing anyone to go on and on about anything — sometimes offering something of great value, oftentimes not.

Making a second career out of maintaining and extending a topical Web site is easy, but the pay is usually nil. Here are some things to consider when you create a topical Web site:

✔ **What's on first?** As with a personal Web page, the title of a topical Web page and the first screen that users see need to make unmistakably clear the topic that the page covers. And, to the extent possible, they must describe what resources the Web site offers about the topic.

✔ **Keep focused.** A topical Web site loses some of its value if it goes beyond a single topic. How many of the people who share your love for Thai cooking also share your abiding interest in rotifers? (Microscopic creatures which are too small to use in most recipes, Thai or not.) If you have two interests that you want to share on the Web, consider creating separate Web sites.

✔ **Create a succession plan.** If your Web site grows beyond your capacity to maintain and extend it properly, find someone to help out or to take it over. The first person you should ask about taking over is anyone who's complaining that you're not extending the site fast enough! Decide what role you can handle and then ask for help in doing the rest.

Getting personal with blogs

A *Web log,* or *blog* for short, is a sort of online diary that usually includes links to Web sites that the user has recently found interesting — thus the term Web log. *Blogging,* or maintaining a Web log, is a whole new form of Web publishing.

You can create a Web page or Web site that's nothing but a blog, or combine blog content with traditional content. Some blogs are extremely personal — sometimes uncomfortably so. Web logs are also used in big Web sites, such as major newspaper sites. In other words, Web logs cross the boundaries between personal,

topical, and business categories — and some of them are pretty entertaining as well!

We have the somewhat old-fashioned view that you probably would benefit from knowing about Web page creation in general, not just blogging, so we defer a detailed discussion of it to Chapter 16. But if your whole reason for wanting to create Web pages is to create a blog to call your very own, please skip ahead and read Chapter 16 now, and then come back here when you want to find more about Web pages in general.

Business sites

Business Web sites, also known as commercial sites, constitute the 50,000-pound gorilla of the Web, with a tremendous amount of time, energy, and money devoted to them. Business Web sites cover a wide range of styles because their goals and the expertise and resources behind them vary so much. This book provides enough information for you to create a competent "Web presence" site with several pages of contact and company information. But even these kinds of sites vary quite a bit, and you need to be sure that your company's page is well implemented.

Figure 1-4 shows the Netsurfer home page created by Arthur Bebak, one of the authors. (So now you can call him "Author" Bebak!) Go surf around the Netsurfer site to see what a site designed and implemented by one of us looks like: www.netsurf.com/nsd.

The first question to ask about a business Web site is "Who can access it?" Some sites are intended for the World Wide Web and everyone on it; others are on the World Wide Web but are password-protected or otherwise restricted in access; still others are on private networks and inaccessible to outsiders. These inaccessible networks are described as being "behind the firewall." Any Web page that isn't accessible to everyone is considered to be on an *intranet,* if access is limited to one company, or an *extranet,* if access is limited to a group of companies that are business partners.

Despite the wide variety of business Web sites, following just a few rules can help you create a page that meets your goals:

✔ **What's on first?** A business Web page should make the name and purpose(s) of your business immediately clear. Also, the site should provide easy-to-find information on how to contact your business and what products and services the business offers.

✔ **Get the right look.** Telling someone you don't like their Web site is like telling them you don't like their haircut — they're likely to take it personally. But an ugly Web site, like an ugly haircut, can make a permanently bad impression. Make sure that the look of your Web site is up to the professional standards set by other aspects of your business.

✔ **Get permission.** Unless you own the business, you should ask for permission before putting a company page on the open Web. You also need to make absolutely sure you have the permissions you need for any images or documents that you use before you publish your Web page.

✔ **Inside or outside the firewall?** Deciding who gets access is tricky. For example, a small amount of otherwise confidential information can make a site more valuable, but the presence of confidential information also prevents you from opening up the entire site to the broader public. Implementing access controls can also be difficult. Investigate how to password-protect a site, or ask a network administrator at your company whether you can physically control access. For instance, you may be able to selectively allow access based on what network the user connects from.

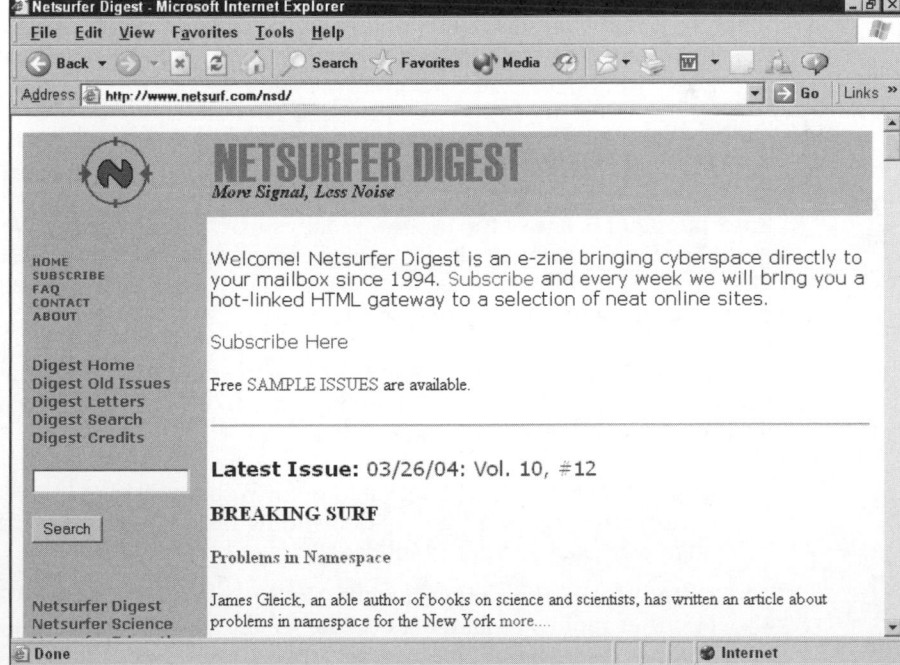

Figure 1-4: The Netsurfer Communications motto: More signal, less noise.

- ✔ **Find experts.** Businesses similar to yours — or even colleagues, if you're in a large company — likely have Web sites that have a purpose similar to yours. Look to the creators of those sites for guidance and inspiration.

- ✔ **Monitor usage.** Investing time, energy, and money in a business Web site requires a trade-off among the Web site and other things that those resources could go to. One of the crucial questions you may need to answer in order to justify Web site maintenance or expansion is how much use the site gets. Investigate ways to measure the use of your site. A good way to start is a basic hit counter, such as the free one you can find at the following URL: `www.bcentral.com/services/fc/`.

- ✔ **Seek out additional resources.** This book focuses on hands-on creation of single Web pages and simple Web sites. For a larger business site, you need access to additional information to help you with the planning, hosting, and maintenance of the site. Consider purchasing *HTML 4 For Dummies,* 4th Edition, by Ed Tittel and Natanya Pitts, for more information on the HTML specification, and *Internet Marketing For Dummies,* by Frank Catalano and Bud Smith (both books from Wiley), for more information on planning and creating a business Web site with a marketing bent.

Having a Web site that's too obviously "handmade," rather than professionally created, can be embarrassing for a business. However, many sites are going "back to the future" with a simple, clean look that's light on graphics. So how do you decide whether to make your look fancy or simple? The best way to get a quick reality check is to look at some competitors' Web sites and make sure that your initial site looks roughly as good as theirs. And remember that oftentimes the most embarrassing thing is having no site at all.

Entertainment sites

Entertainment is one of the top few reasons why people use the Web, and the number of entertainment sites continues to grow. Humorous pages and services such as multiuser dungeons (MUDs) and shared games on online services are now a major presence on the Web.

The high expectations that people have of entertainment sites can make these sites some of the most demanding ones to create. Here are a few suggestions for creating entertainment sites:

- ✔ **Don't start here.** Don't try to figure out Web publishing by creating an entertainment site. It's a very demanding task. Try another type first and edge your way into entertainment.

- ✔ **Keep it fresh.** How funny is a joke the second time you hear it? You have to either rapidly update the content or allow participants to provide the content through their interaction with one another — neither option is easy.

Is your page cybersmut?

For most Web page publishers, the best policy with respect to putting anything potentially offensive in your Web pages is to keep your site clean. The use of gratuitous sex and violence in your Web pages will simply put off many people and put you and your Web site in a bad light.

But what if the sex or violence is not gratuitous and is actually central to your point? Then send the authors your URL so that we can see it for ourselves. No, seriously: Be sure to make the first page a home page that warns readers that

they may find your content offensive. That lets them gracefully opt out before they view whatever you show.

Even that enlightened approach may not be enough, however. Some Web server owners will drop your page if it violates their rules, and several countries have laws that specify what can and can't be on a Web page. Be sure to find out about the rules and laws that apply to you before you put anything questionable on your Web page.

✔ **Push the technology.** Interactivity is also key to entertainment, which means going beyond HTML and static graphics. You probably need to figure out and use at least one advanced Web technology, such as Flash, to make a fresh and interesting entertainment Web site.

✔ **Let the technology push you.** The technology can give you ideas that are in themselves pretty funny. Try using Java to create a Three Stooges-type animated routine, or use ActiveX to create a virtual reality environment that includes fun-house mirrors. (We describe both Java and ActiveX in Chapter 14.)

Web Page Guidelines

A Web page or Web site is basically a publication, though an interactive one. Thinking through a few simple principles now, before you start, can help make your Web page much more interesting and useful to the people who see it. You can also revisit this section after you put up your initial Web home page; use these guidelines to revise your page and make it even more interesting and useful!

Asking "Why am I doing this?"

Ask yourself, as you're starting, "Why am I doing this?" (As you do more and more work on your page, your answer to this question may come to have some degree of profanity in it!) That is, why are you creating the page, and not having someone else create it for you? The answer helps you determine some important things about the page. The following list details the most common reasons for people to get involved in creating a Web page:

- ✔ **For work:** More and more people are being asked to create Web pages and Web sites as part of their jobs; for example, they use the Web to communicate with people inside or outside their companies. But unless you plan to be a full-time Webmaster, you need to balance the time you spend developing your pages with the time you spend on the other demands of your job. Be modest in your initial goals, and keep track of each step in creating and modifying your Web pages so that you — or the person who takes over for you — can refer to the records later.

- ✔ **For fun:** Fun sites are a good thing, and they are a lot of what makes the Web worthwhile. But if you create your site for fun, you may find time to work on it only after you spend time on other things, such as work, school, or time with friends and family. So don't be too ambitious in your initial plans, or you may take quite a while to finish and publish your page.

- ✔ **As a career move:** So you want to be a full-time, or nearly full-time, Webmaster; or you want, in some other way, to make the Internet or Web part of your career. In this kind of situation, you can afford to plan an ambitious Web site that uses advanced tools, tracks usage, and other-wise gets closer to the cutting edge of the Web. To gain experience, create your initial Web page by using the accessible and broad-based tools and approaches we describe in this book. Then take your page closer to the cutting edge by using the more advanced techniques described and taught elsewhere, such as JavaScript programming as described in *JavaScript For Dummies,* 3rd Edition, by Emily A. Vander Veer (Wiley).

- ✔ **Who knows?** As famous baseball manager Yogi Berra once said, "When you come to a fork in the road, take it." You may not have a specific reason for publishing on the Web, but that shouldn't stop you. You may figure out a good reason after you have a little Web experience under your belt. Start simple, so you can score an early success in getting a basic Web page up, and then go from there.

Don't spend too much time on design

Designing a Web page is unlike designing any other kind of publication, because you don't have as much control over the look and feel of Web pages as you do with other types of publications. Modem and network connection speeds, browsers, screen sizes, and font and other settings within a browser vary so much that users can have very different experiences with your Web page.

Big issues for big sites

This book focuses on the needs of people who create a single Web page or a small Web site, and who do so on their own. Larger sites, or sites that need to be put up quickly or changed rapidly, need to have additional people working on them.

If you want to create a larger site down the road, start thinking now about what resources may be available to put into it. How many people in your company or other organization work on advertising, public relations, and marketing? How many people question whether those jobs are real work? (Just kidding — the lead author, who's a marketer, wrote that!)

You may reasonably expect your company to re-target some fraction of its advertising, marketing, and PR resources to support a presence on the Web. And what about sales? As Web-based business transactions take off, some portion of a company's sales effort becomes Web-based, necessitating a suitable up-front commitment to bring returns down the road.

Or your company may already suffer from Web burnout. Classic symptoms of Web burnout include massive early investment to create a beautiful site, months of failure to update or maintain the site, followed by finger-pointing about who wasted all that money. Usually the problem is that no one set goals for the site, so no one managed the site's design and construction with those specific goals in mind. Companies often designate too few financial and human resources for maintenance and improvement of the site. If this scenario has happened in your company, you know the problems that result, so be sure to establish clear goals for your own Web efforts.

The most important element in adopting any new technology for business is a successful pilot project. As someone creating a smallish Web site, you're developing important skills and knowledge about the all-important convergence of your business's needs with the Web's opportunities. Set specific goals, strive to meet them, and record both your problems and your successes. By doing so, you position yourself to justify further investment of resources as the Web grows in importance for your company.

With the latest versions of HTML, controlling more aspects of your Web page's appearance is possible. Advanced sites, such as amazon.com, use many different aspects of HTML, as well as programming languages such as JavaScript, to create dense, rich layouts more like a magazine than a typical Web page. However, some aspects of the newest versions of HTML are not yet standard across different Web browsers. In this book we stick with HTML 4.0, which works the same way for nearly all Web users.

Keep your design simple and don't spend too much time on it initially. Then improve it, as you find out more about Web publishing and more about how people use your page.

Putting the good stuff first

Imagine the Web as a giant magazine rack and the person surfing the Web as someone scanning the front covers of all those magazines. People who see your Web page decide whether to stay at your site — or go elsewhere — based largely on what they see when your page first comes up.

If your purpose is to provide information or links, put that information first or, at most, one click away. For example, to create a site that provides information about a company, make getting the contact information — your company name, address, phone number, and fax number — very easy to find. To create a personal site that is attractive to potential employers, make clear what employment field you're in right at the top of your Web page and make your résumé easy to access.

If your purpose is to draw people into your site to entertain them, educate them, or expose them to messages from advertisers — or to do all of these things at once — then the first part of the page should make a strong impression and invite the user to go further into your site. Figure 1-5 shows the Kaua'i Exotix Web page, certainly one that catches your attention, located at the following URL: `www.kexotix.com`.

Figure 1-5:
Buds for
your buds.

But, like the Kaua'i Exotix Web page, your home page also should help people who seek a quick "hit" of information; they're more likely to come back later if you don't waste their time during their first quick visit.

Thinking twice about download times

Putting lots of graphics in your pages is time-intensive for you because creating or finding good graphics and placing them appropriately in your Web page can take a great deal of time and effort. Graphics are also time-intensive for those who surf your site because they can take a long time to download. So plan to use spot graphics (small images that download quickly) at first. Think twice before creating large clickable image maps or attractive opening graphics like those you find on the sites of large companies, such as General Motors or Apple. If you do use an opening graphic, keep it under 20K or so. (See Chapter 9 for details.)

You may find a good deal of coverage in the computer press, and even in mainstream newspapers and newsmagazines, about ongoing efforts to make faster access available to ordinary users. But for all the talk about cable modems, Digital Subscriber Line (DSL), and other advanced techniques, about half of home users in the United States are still on 56 Kbps or slower modems — more in most other countries. (Business users are typically on faster connections.) So ignore the hype — the speed at which the average person accesses the Web is still moving upward gradually, not leaping ahead. For now, be conservative in how much data you put in each page, and test the download times of your pages over a modem-based connection before you publish them.

Knowing your audience

According to Web researchers, Web users overwhelmingly speak English as either a first or second language. Consequently, the great majority of Web content, Web creation tools, and Web browsers use the English language. Even ten years after the birth of the Web — which happened in Switzerland — North America is still the "center of gravity" for Web access. This situation will gradually change as other countries catch up to Web penetration in the United States.

Why are people online? Surveys indicate that the top reasons people use the Web are for information-gathering, entertainment, education, work, "time-wasting," and shopping. Which of these purposes do you intend for your site to serve? How do you appeal to people who are online? How do you help them find you? The answers to these questions can help you enhance the appeal and usefulness of your site.

Finally, what kind of browsers are your users running? Surveys indicate that over 90 percent of Web users run Microsoft Internet Explorer; most of the rest use Netscape Navigator. Both of these browsers, and most others that make up the remaining user base, support graphics and tables, and nearly all users run their browsers with graphics turned on (which doesn't mean that they appreciate waiting for complex images to load — unless those images are pretty cool!).

For more details about who's online, what they do there, and what it means to you if you're creating a business Web site, see *Internet Marketing For Dummies,* by Frank Catalano and Bud Smith (Wiley).

Using text bites

As we mention earlier in this chapter, when preparing a Web site, less is more. Saying something with less text makes users more likely to read and remember it. A *text bite* is like a sound bite — it's a short, clearly written piece of text that makes a single point.

Although you can overuse text bites, they are very important in Web page design. Text bites help you convey as much information as possible in the limited amount of time users spend looking at each Web page. And they help you balance the basic elements of Web page design: text, links, and graphics.

If you want to put long documents on the Web, consider rewriting them as a series of text bites. If rewriting them is too much work to be practical, at least create short, punchy text for navigation and for introductory paragraphs to the long documents. Within a long document, add headers to break up the flow of text and provide pointers on your Web site to key areas within the document. Without such guidance, users may well give up in frustration without reaching the information they're looking for.

Looking at sites you like

Look at sites you like and at sites whose purposes are similar to your own. What's good about them? What's not? Imitate successful elements — without copying, which would be a violation of ethics as well as copyright laws — and avoid unsuccessful ones. As the development of your site progresses, keep checking it against the sites you previously identified and widen your search to get additional ideas — on what not to do as well as on what to do.

Few original ideas exist on the Web, and your initial site is likely to contain one or two new ideas at best. The rest of your site may echo things readers have already seen, and you're better off if your site brings to mind other good sites, rather than bad ones. (But be careful. If you start yelling "Bad site! Bad site!" at your computer screen and swatting it with a rolled-up newspaper, you may not be allowed to have a working Internet connection much longer.)

Planning for ongoing improvements

As you plan and implement your initial Web page, you will, no doubt, find yourself creating a "To Do" list of things that you can't fit into the original site but want to add later, when time allows. (Creating this list for later use is great protection against trying to create a supersite right off the bat, getting stuck in the creation process, and never getting to a point where you can actually publish your first Web page.) This list is the start of a plan for ongoing improvements.

Some things that you put in a Web site need to be kept current. For example, if your business Web page shows your company's quarterly results, be ready to update it quickly when the next quarter's results come out. If it lists company officers, update it as soon as a change takes place. (Unless you're one of the people changed — then it's your successor's problem!)

Web site information that is obviously out of date is one of the best ways to leave a bad impression of you or your organization/company and to steer visitors away from your Web site.

Not only do you want to update the Web site, you want to avoid using "Under Construction" signs and otherwise apologizing for things that aren't there yet. Everything on the Web is under construction, which is half the fun of using the Web and creating pages for it in the first place. You get only one chance to make a first impression, and an "Under Construction" sign doesn't count in your favor.

Deciding how you define success

Before you design and create your Web page, define what you believe can make it a success. For an initial effort, simply putting up something on the Web that clearly conveys basic information is probably enough. For follow-up work, get more specific. Are you trying to reach a certain number of people or type of people? Will measuring *page views* — the number of times that people look at one page from your site — be enough, or do you need some other measure of response, such as having people send e-mail or call an 800 number? Do you want to create a cutting-edge site in terms of bell-and-whistle features like fancy graphics and animation — and if so, are you willing to invest the time and money to make this site happen? Talk to people who do advertising and marketing in the real world, as well as to people who work on the Web, and get a sense of what goals they set and how they measure success in meeting their goals.

Chapter 2

Going Worldwide with GeoCities

Getting your first page up on the Web seems like a tall order. So you may not believe just how easy getting started is. With the free Web-based publishing services we describe in this chapter, you can have your first Web page up within a couple of hours — at no cost. You don't have to figure out everything about HTML, you don't have to deal with typical publishing complexities, and did we mention that you don't have to pay anything?

If you're a member of America Online (AOL), you can use free AOL Web publishing tools to get a Web page up quickly and easily, as we describe in Chapter 3. AOL has the advantage of built-in support for your Web page efforts from the same help resources — including your fellow online service members — that you're already familiar with. So if you're a member of America Online, consider starting your Web page creation effort with Chapter 3.

If not, though, you have an alternative that's just as good: Yahoo!'s GeoCities site. GeoCities is the most popular site for free personal Web page publishing and has offered this service for many years. Since its inception, GeoCities has hosted the creation of more than 5,000,000 — yes, that's 5 *million* — personal Web page sites, with thousands of new sites added each day. And now that Yahoo! has acquired GeoCities, it has the resources to keep on growing for quite a while to come.

GeoCities' high level of popularity means that its service is extremely popular with visitors as well as publishers. It also means that its advertising-supported, self-publishing model is so successful that GeoCities is likely to be around for a long time to come. (Other services featured in earlier editions of this book have since disappeared, a testament to the rapid rate of change on the Web.)

Follow the instructions in this chapter to become a Web page publisher on GeoCities. You can be a Web publisher in less time than most people take to start thinking about how to get their first home page published on the Web.

Starting with a GeoCities Web Page

Putting up a personal Web page accomplishes a lot of things. For one, it's fun. Millions of people have gotten a real kick out of sharing information about themselves and their interests by putting up a Web page. Many personal Web pages that initially start out quite simple evolve into large and popular Web sites focused on topics of every imaginable sort. As the number of Web users increases, more and more of your colleagues, family, and friends can see your Web page, as can (of course) millions and millions of complete strangers.

Creating a personal Web page is also very valuable in helping you find out how to publish on the Web. Until you publish something on the Web, you may find the notion that you can actually do it hard to believe. After you put up your first Web page, you may find the notion that anything can stop you from doing it again hard to believe! The initial success of getting up your personal Web page will spill over into all your future Web efforts.

Now, you may feel that you should start out with a business Web site, a home page for a nonprofit organization, or something similarly serious. But the business or serious approach has a couple of problems:

- ✔ The "barriers to entry" — if we may use a marketing term — for a site that represents an organization are much higher because you're taking on a more complex task, and many people need to be involved.

- ✔ For a more serious site, the quality of your work has much more impact because you're representing a larger cause than just your personal interests. So your fear of failure is greater. And you're undertaking this important task with no background and no experience, which can make getting anything worthwhile done hard.

- ✔ Finally, Web space for business sites almost always costs money. So you have a buying decision to make before you can even get started — yet another barrier.

So get on the Web first with a simple, personal Web page. Discover something new, have some fun, and prepare now for more ambitious endeavors later. And GeoCities is just the place to do it.

Checking out Yahoo! GeoCities

To see what other people have done with their personal Web sites, visit GeoCities right now at `http://geocities.yahoo.com`.

Figure 2-1 shows the initial home page for GeoCities. Yahoo!, after buying GeoCities, put its name on the pages too. Don't be alarmed if you see something slightly different for the home page; GeoCities, like any popular Web site, often updates its home page. Even if the GeoCities home page has changed, the instructions in this chapter are likely still valid.

GeoCities initially organized the Web pages that users created into *neighborhoods,* with each neighborhood hosting home pages from people with a specific set of shared interests. However, Yahoo! has stopped supporting the neighborhoods idea; only people who created Web pages on GeoCities in the 1990s can still use them. As a new GeoCities user, you get a Web address based on the Yahoo! user ID that you get when you first visit GeoCities.

Your Web page's Web address is in the following form: `www.geocities.com/youruserid`. This address is simpler than the Web addresses that GeoCities used to give people, which included the name of the neighborhood the user chose as well as a specific site number. If you look at existing GeoCities Web pages, many of them still have neighborhood addresses.

Figure 2-1:
GeoCities is the home of more than 5 million personal Web pages.

Web tools versus Web services

A *Web publishing tool,* such as Netscape Composer, is a program that helps you prepare content for the Web. A *Web publishing service* is a support function that handles part of the process of Web publishing for you, such as hosting your Web page(s) on a server. The Web publishing services we describe in this chapter and Chapter 3 also include online tools for preparing your Web page(s), but the free Web page hosting service they provide is most notable, so we refer to them as services rather than tools.

When you first visit GeoCities, use the Search function on the GeoCities home page to find GeoCities Web pages on topics of interest to you. See what other people have done; look at some pages that are still initial efforts, and then see what others have done with their Web pages to spruce up the place after they first arrived!

Tear out the Cheat Sheet at the front of this book and tape it to the wall! Although you don't need to know HTML to use the services we describe in this chapter, knowing a little bit of HTML can help you make your initial page look better. See the Cheat Sheet for a list of tags that can spruce up your initial Web page.

Following the city ordinances

You can use the GeoCities easy-to-use editing tool to create a simple home page quickly and easily. You can then use HTML, FTP (see Chapter 12), and other tools to create and transfer more sophisticated pages to build almost any kind of Web site you want, up to 15MB in size. But you have to keep in mind the restrictions listed in Yahoo!'s Terms of Service:

✔ **Not for your business:** You can't use this free Web page service for a business home page, although you can mention your business on your free personal home page. (Some people use their free personal Web pages to "mention" their businesses an awful lot.) That means you can't sell products or services, advertise, conduct raffles, or display advertising or sponsorship banners. You can, however, use Yahoo!-supported partnership programs that allow you to get paid for books, music, and other goods sold on your site. For details on what you can't do, check the Terms of Service at docs.yahoo.com/info/terms/geoterms.html.

GeoCities or online service?

If you are a user of an online service such as America Online, you have the option of creating a free personal Web page on GeoCities, on your online service, or on both. We recommend that online service users put their first Web page on their online service. Why?

The first and foremost reason is support. Online services are great sources of help for all kinds of online concerns, not least of which is getting your first Web page up and running. You can easily get a lot of help from your fellow members and from the support personnel of your online service.

Second is familiarity. You're already familiar with your online service. You're more able to take advantage of its free services than the

services in any other kind of setup, even one as friendly and open as GeoCities.

Third is community. Online services try to foster a sense of community, as does Yahoo! with GeoCities. If you're a person who values this feeling, you probably have already developed it within your online service; you may as well take advantage of the community that you're already paying for!

So if you're an AOL user, consider going to Chapter 3 and following the instructions for creating and hosting a free Web page. If not, you don't need to join an online service just to get free Web hosting service; GeoCities is fast, easy, and fun.

If you do want a business Web site, try Yahoo!'s premium Web site programs. You can access them from the GeoCities home page at geocities.yahoo.com.

✔ **No monkey business:** Yahoo! imposes restrictions on what you can publish; obscenity, harmful or abusive content, libel, and invasion of privacy are prohibited, among other things. Check the Terms of Service at the previous URL for details.

✔ **No more than 15MB space:** All your Web files together must occupy no more than 15MB of disk space; that's about 15,000 pages of text, or about 100 large, quarter-screen graphics. This restriction is not a problem for single Web pages, because only one Web page is almost certainly well below the limit. If you expand your Web page into a multi-page site and the limit becomes a problem for you, you can get more disk space and other goodies from Yahoo!'s premium Web site programs, which are mentioned on the GeoCities home page.

✔ **No more than 3GB data transfer:** The amount of information uploaded to your site and downloaded by users must not exceed 3GB in a month, or GeoCities suspends service for a period of time. This maximum bandwidth is a lot for the average Web page — but if you post, say, a 10MB movie file, having it downloaded 300 times puts you over the limit.

✓ **No guarantees:** Yahoo! doesn't guarantee that it will continue to provide free Web page service in the future. (The company has to include this disclaimer to protect itself from unanticipated events, but all indications are that it does indeed plan to continue this free service for quite a while.) If Yahoo! does stop offering GeoCities, or even if you just find another hosting site you like better, you can always set up shop there instead. For now, the point is to take advantage of a valuable opportunity.

Planning Before You Begin

Putting up your home page on GeoCities takes only an hour or so — not bad for getting a free Web page set up, hosted, and published! Even so, doing a few things before you begin makes the process easier, more pleasant, and more productive:

✓ **Visit GeoCities Web pages.** GeoCities does a good job of helping you get your initial Web page up, but don't you want to see what others have done before you get started? Use the Search function and the categories of Web sites to find Web pages related to your interests.

✓ **Find out more about GeoCities in general by clicking and navigating around GeoCities-related Web pages in the Yahoo! Web site.** You can discover a lot about GeoCities by clicking around and reading press releases, the Terms of Service, and so on. One thing you may not discover is how Yahoo! can afford to give away free Web space through GeoCities. The answer is that free Web pages are a powerful way for sites such as Yahoo! to attract and retain users for its other services. Also, Yahoo! places advertising on Web pages built in GeoCities; Yahoo! makes a few pennies every time someone (including you) looks at your home page.

✓ **Look for the URLs of your favorite Web sites.** Many GeoCities templates let you list links to several of your favorite Web sites — but to link to them, you need the URLs. Recall some of your favorite sites — they may be listed in your Web bookmarks — and write down the site names and URLs for use in creating your Web page. (Doing this research in advance is much easier than at the time you're creating your Web page.)

✓ **Look for the URLs of Web sites of friends and family members.** The Personal Page template that we use in the example later in this chapter gives you space to list the descriptions and URLs for one to four Web sites of friends and family members. Get the URLs before you start.

✓ **Plan your initial Web page.** In a word processing program or on paper, rough out the text and Web links for your initial Web page. This way you're ready to go when it comes time to actually get your page up.

✔ **Scan a picture.** Get a picture or other image onto your hard disk, in GIF or JPEG format, so you can easily upload it as part of your Web page. The picture could be of you, or be related to the topic you're interested in. You can get a film photo scanned into a digital file, take a picture with a digital camera, or even capture a digital image with a mobile phone. Kinko's and other copy shops have computers and software you can rent for scanning purposes if you don't have everything you need at home. Chapter 9 tells you a great deal about Web graphics.

Getting Registered

The steps you need to follow to sign up for a GeoCities Web page may change after we complete this book. If so, go to www.dummies.com and look up the update page for this book to get the latest instructions.

The first step in setting up your GeoCities Web page is to apply for a Yahoo! user ID number. This user ID enables you to use a variety of services on Yahoo! and, if you're not careful, to receive e-mail solicitations you don't really want. If you don't already have a Yahoo! user ID, follow these steps to set up your Yahoo! user ID and start using GeoCities:

1. **Open your Web browser.**

   The GeoCities Web site works with any browser.

2. **Go to** geocities.yahoo.com.

   The screen shown in Figure 2-1, or something very much like it, appears.

3. **If you are currently signed in as a member of Yahoo!, your user name appears on the Web page you see. Skip the rest of the steps in this section.**

   If you're a Yahoo! member, sign in. Then skip the rest of the steps in this section.

   Enter your Yahoo! ID and Password in the Sign In to Yahoo! section, and then click the Sign In button.

   If you are not yet a member of Yahoo!, click the Sign In button in the upper-right corner of the browser window; when the Welcome to Yahoo! screen appears, click the Sign up now link.

   If you click the Sign up now link, the Sign Up for Your Yahoo ID! screen appears, as shown in Figure 2-2.

4. **Enter your desired Yahoo! ID and password. Retype your password.**

Welcome to Yahoo! - Microsoft Internet Explorer

File   Edit   View   Favorites   Tools   Help

Back ▼   ×   🗘   Search   Favorites   Media   ▼   W ▼

Address   http://edit.yahoo.com/config/eval_register?.intl=us&new=1&.done=http%3a//us.rd.yahoo.com/geoho   Go   Links »

YAHOO!   Yahoo! - Help

Sign up for your Yahoo! ID   Already have an ID?   Sign In

Get a Yahoo! ID and password for free access to all personalized Yahoo! services.

Yahoo! ID: [   ]

Examples: "dairyman88" or "free2rhyme"

Password: [   ]

Must be six characters or more

Re-type Password: [   ]

Choosing your ID
You will use this information to access
Yahoo! each time. Capitalization matters for
your password!

Activate Yahoo! Mail: ☑ Create your free Yahoo! email address for this ID and
begin using Yahoo! Mail.

Free Yahoo! Mail
Your email address will be the Yahoo! ID
you've chosen followed by @yahoo.com.

If you forget your password or need help with your account, you'll need to confirm the
following information:

Security Question: [Select a Question to Answer] ▼

Your Answer: [   ]

Birthday: [Select One] ▼ [ ] . [ ] (Month DD, YYYY)

Alternate Email: [   ]

Account notices will be sent to this email address, including new

Recalling your password
This information is our only way to verify
your identity. To protect your account,
make sure "Your Answer" is **memorable**
for you but hard for others to guess!

Done   Internet

Figure 2-2:
Get your
Yahoo! ID
so that you
can use
GeoCities.

Reproduced with permission of Yahoo! Inc. © 2000 by Yahoo! Inc. YAHOO! and the YAHOO! logo are trademarks of Yahoo! Inc.

Any Yahoo! ID you find desirable, like most first name and last name combinations (such as "budsmith" for one of the authors), or your favorite sports team ("sfgiants," for instance), is likely to be unavailable — one of Yahoo!'s existing tens of millions of users probably already has it. To save yourself a bunch of retries, pick a user name that makes sense, but is likely to be unique, such as your first and last name followed by the name of your state or hometown ("budsmithsf," for instance). Try to make it memorable, too — your home page's URL is in the form `www.geocities.com/`, followed by your Yahoo! ID.

For your password, use six or more characters.

5. Clear the check box if you don't wish to have a Yahoo! Mail account. Then enter information in case you forget your password.

Use the pull-down menu to select a question that Yahoo! prompts you with if you forget your password. Enter your answer, your birthday (with a four-digit year, such as 1978), and your current e-mail address. Use an e-mail address that you'll have immediate access to, so you can complete the process of activating your account. (And enter your real birthday — "Always tell the truth, so you don't have to try to remember what you told people.")

"He tried, but he couldn't do it" — despite our best efforts, we were unable to get GeoCities to accept a Yahoo! e-mail address as the contact e-mail address for a GeoCities Web page. You have to use a different e-mail account, not a Yahoo.com account. You can use an existing personal or work e-mail address or a friend's e-mail address. Or you can get a new, free e-mail account at `www.hotmail.com` (the most popular source for free e-mail), or any of several other sites on the Web.

6. **Enter your personal account information. Clear the Send Me Special Offers. . . check box if you don't want advertising from Yahoo! in your e-mail.**

   Choose your language-country combination, such as English - United States. Enter your zip code or postal code, your gender, your occupation, and the industry you work in. Clearing the "Send Me Special Offers. . ." check box tells Yahoo! that you *really* don't want a bunch of advertising stuff sent to your e-mail account.

   Be sure to clear the check box unless you want to receive advertising e-mail from Yahoo! and its partners. Many Web sites have agreed to present boxes such as this one with the option unchecked, so only people who make the effort to click the check box get signed up, but Yahoo! makes you do the unchecking yourself. See the sidebar, "Yahoo! for privacy?" for more.

7. **If you want to, indicate areas of interest to you.**

   You have the option of clicking areas of interest to you by putting a check in each relevant check box. Like the pull-down menus for customizing Yahoo!, the Interests check boxes help Yahoo! customize news and information for you on the Yahoo! site. The information also helps Yahoo! and its partners target e-mail they send you (if you don't uncheck the check box), ads they put on Web pages that you view, and otherwise personalize their marketing efforts to you.

8. **Type in the word shown on-screen.**

   Type the word shown on-screen. This step is to make sure a real person is filling out the registration.

9. **If you want to read the GeoCities Terms of Service, the Yahoo! Privacy Policy, or Yahoo Privacy Information, right-click the link to open them in a separate window. Otherwise, or after you finish, click the Submit This Form button.**

   If you click this link with a regular mouse click, the GeoCities' Terms of Service replaces your current browser window contents. If you click the Back button in the browser window to return to the signup screen, everything you entered so far is gone! If you make this mistake — which is all too easy to do — repeat Steps 4 through 8.

   After you click the Submit This Form button, you are sent an e-mail message with steps to follow to access your account. Follow the instructions in the e-mail message, and sign in to Yahoo. Then go to the next section to see how to begin working on your site.

Yahoo! for privacy?

Yahoo! follows certain policies relating to your privacy. Some of the highlights:

✔ **No opt-in guarantee:** Some Web sites now promise not to put you on e-mail lists unless you opt in — take some affirmative action, such as checking a check box, to put yourself in spam's way. As of this writing, Yahoo! doesn't do this. So accidentally putting yourself on an e-mail list that then is used to send you advertising when signing up for a Yahoo! service is easy.

✔ **TRUSTe-certified:** Yahoo! is TRUSTe-certified. This certification means that Yahoo! has submitted a privacy statement to TRUSTe, an industry privacy organization. TRUSTe is not a strong organization at this point, but at least Yahoo!, through TRUSTe, has committed itself to putting its policy statement in writing and letting you see it.

✔ **Use of information:** Yahoo! uses the information you give it, and the information it gathers from the choices you make in using Yahoo!, to customize your Web-surfing experience to your interests and to send you customized e-mail.

✔ **Sharing with partners:** Yahoo! doesn't actually transfer data about you to partners without your permission. However, partners' agreements with Yahoo! may include access to you through Yahoo!.

✔ **Changing your information:** To change your account information, log into Yahoo! with your user ID and password, and then go to `edit.my.yahoo.com/config/eval_profile`. There, you can change your account preferences to stop receiving e-mail offers or update your personal information and preferences.

You can reach the GeoCities Web site by typing the URL `www.geocities.com` into your browser's address window. The address is automatically remapped to `geocities.yahoo.com`. Web sites often give simpler Web addresses to the public, but remap them to other internal Web addresses for their own convenience. You can continue to use the `www.geocities.com` address as a starting point for your own ease of use.

Begin Building Your Web Site

After you sign in, the Way to Build a Better Web Site page reappears. (Refer to Figure 2-1.) Follow these instructions to get started.

1. **Under the Get Started heading on the left side of the screen, click the** <u>Free</u> **link.**

   The Free: Highlights page appears.

2. **Click the** <u>Sign Up</u> **link.**

The Free Web Site option gives you a free home page with the URL `www.geocities.com/`*yourname*, where *yourname* is your Yahoo! User ID. You may want to use one of the paid options later, but you probably want a free Web site to use for practice in any case.

After you click the Sign Up link, the GeoCities Free page appears.

3. Choose a topic for your Web page.

Carefully choose a topic for your Web page. Yahoo! displays advertising relating to this topic on your Web page, so choose carefully. (The right kind of advertising can actually "ad" value to your page — pun fully intended.)

4. Click the Continue button.

A Welcome to Yahoo! GeoCities Web page appears, as shown in Figure 2-3.

5. Write down your Yahoo! ID and password and your new home page's Web address.

6. Click the Build Your Web Site Now! link.

The front page of the Yahoo! GeoCities Web site appears, but this time with your user name in the upper-left corner and your Web page's URL in the upper right. Follow the steps in the next section to begin building your Web page.

Figure 2-3: When you see this Web page, you're in.

We're Off to See the Wizard

GeoCities has recently introduced a new feature, Yahoo! PageWizards, for creating an initial Web page quickly and easily. Wizards are an easy way to get your Web page off the ground.

Unlike many other Web page tools, you cannot enter HTML tags in the text within Yahoo! Wizards. However, you can edit your Web page later and add HTML tags, as we describe in Part II.

Use the Yahoo! PageWizards to quickly create your initial Web page:

1. **From the home page of GeoCities, at** www.geocities.com, **make sure you're signed in and then click Yahoo! PageWizards.**

   If you have not done so already, you have to become a registered Yahoo! user to proceed. To do so, see the instructions at the beginning of this chapter.

   If you're a registered user, the Yahoo! PageWizards page, part of which is shown in Figure 2-4, appears.

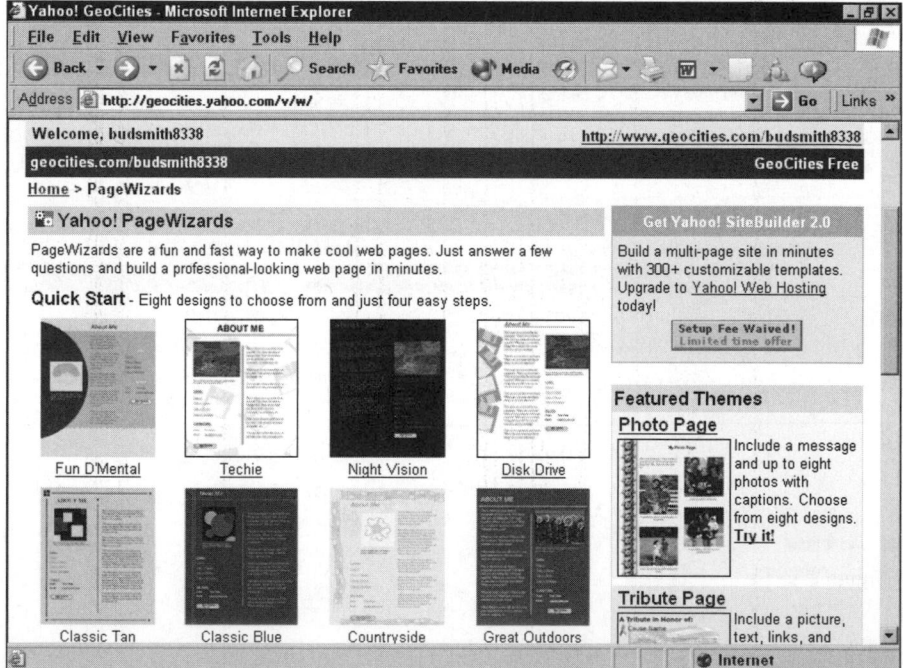

Figure 2-4:
We're off to
see the
(Page)
Wizards.

2. **Scroll down and click the <u>Personal Page</u> link.**

   Getting the right wizard can save you a lot of time, so looking at as much information as possible before choosing is worth your time. For the purposes of this chapter, we describe how to use the Personal Page Wizard; if you want to try a different wizard, roughly the same steps apply, but you need to work around the differences.

   The choices, at this writing, include

   - **Photo Page:** If you have a few digital photographs handy — or can get your local photo processor to convert your next roll to digital format — this wizard is a fun choice to start out with.

   - **Quick Start:** A group of page templates with roughly the same information about you but each with a distinctive look.

   - **Sanrio Themes:** Copyrighted cartoon graphics liven up these simple page designs. These are great for kids to use.

   - **Baby Announcement:** Great if you just had a little one; not much use otherwise. If you do this, make sure to include a picture! See Chapter 9 for details.

   - **Birthday or Party Invitation:** This is fun to do, but online invitation services such as eVite (www.evite.com) also help you put up an event Web page, plus help you handle the inevitable e-mail messaging back and forth. Either this wizard or the eVite-type approach is a good option.

   - **Personal Page:** This wizard is the best choice for most people who want to quickly create their own page. You have four choices of color — and yes, you can replace the little stick figure with a picture.

3. **Click the <u>Launch Yahoo! PageWizards</u> link.**

   The Build Your Personal Page screen, shown in Figure 2-5, appears. It shows the six areas that you are customizing: Your name and e-mail address, your image (or you can keep the stick figure!), a brief personal description with your hobbies and interests, a list of favorite links (up to four), and a list of friends and family links.

4. **Click the Begin button.**

   A screen that allows you to choose a look for your page appears: green, blue, yellow, or pink. Choose one.

5. **Choose a color and then click Next.**

   Now you're ready to actually create your page. The next section tells you how.

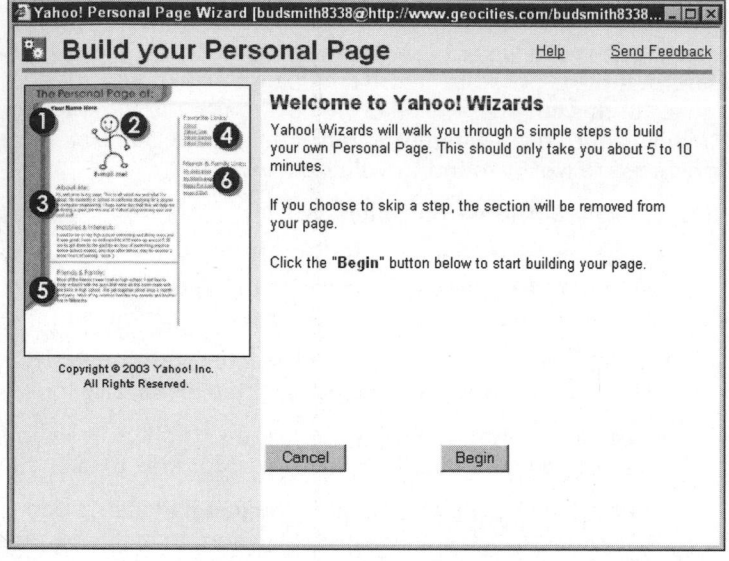

Figure 2-5:
Six items,
six minutes,
one home
page.

The Steps to Success

After you launch Yahoo! PageWizard, as described in the previous section,
you're just a few quick-and-easy steps away from having your own Web page.

1. **Enter your name and (optionally) the e-mail address you want to have
   appear on your Web page, and then click Next.**

   If you don't want to publish your work e-mail address, or heavily used
   personal e-mail address, on the Web — where it might be copied into
   spammers' lists — consider creating a Yahoo! e-mail account for the purpose of publication. Go to mail.yahoo.com to sign up; if you do create a
   new address, remember to check it. Or, just don't enter an e-mail
   address at all; you don't have to.

   At any point in the wizard process, you can preview your page as you
   build it. Just click the Preview button where it's available. You can close
   the preview when you finish with it; just don't close the underlying
   Personal Page Wizard browser window!

   After you click Next, the Pick Your Picture Web page appears.

2. **Choose a picture — a picture you upload, the default stick figure
   image, or no picture. Then click Next.**

   If you want to upload a picture, GeoCities allows you to pick any image
   from your hard disk in any of the following Windows formats: .jpg
   (JPEG), .gif (GIF), .tif (TIFF), .bmp (Windows Bitmap), or .png

(Portable Network Graphics). See Chapter 9 for more on these formats and on obtaining images. (After you upload one or more pictures, you can use them by choosing them from the Pick from your account drop-down menu.)

Don't publish an image you don't have rights to on your Web page. No sense in inviting a call from someone's lawyer.

After you click the Next button, the Describe Yourself Web page appears.

3. **Enter a description to appear in the About Me section and a list of your hobbies to appear in the Hobbies and Interests section and then click Next.**

In the description of yourself, leave out hobbies and interests; they're in the next section. You may want to include where you were born and live, what kind of work you do, and similar information. Don't give too much information, though; a scam artist can get credit in your name with just a few pieces of data such as your full name, address, and mother's maiden name.

In the Hobbies and Interests text box, keep it brief, for now, but make it interesting; your hobbies and interests may be as individual to you as your fingerprint.

After you click Next, the Enter Your Favorite Links Web page appears.

4. **Enter a description and the URL for up to four of your favorite Web links and then click Next.**

Enter several favorite links. And don't worry about the small number of links; you can change the links later, or add more links using other tools.

After you click Next, the Describe Your Friends and Family Web page appears.

5. **Type a description of your friends and family and then click Next.**

Say something about your family — the one you came from, as well as your spouse and kids, if you have such. Emphasize anyone who has a personal Web page that you can link to — or anyone who will be especially thrilled to see their name on the Web, such as kids. Again, be careful about giving too much detail, such as a full name, that scam artists could use.

After you click Next, the Enter Your Friends and Family Links Web page appears.

6. **Type in links to friends and family members' Web pages. Then click Next.**

You can link to family members' Web pages. If you don't know of any, just leave all the entries blank.

After you click Next, the Name Your Page Web page appears.

7. **Enter a page name for your personal page. Then click Next.**

The name you enter becomes part of your Web page's Web address. For instance, if you use the default name, "personalpageblue," the Web page's complete address is `www.geocities.com/`*yourname*`/personal pageblue.html`. We suggest you rename it something shorter, such as "mybluepage."

If you want to make this your site's home page, name it `index.htm`. (Not a bad idea; if you do this, the URL someone needs to type to reach your page is simpler: `www.geocities.com/`*yourname*). You can always move the page around within your site later if needed. When you click Next, the wizard tells you that a page already exists by that name, and asks if you want to replace the page. Choose Yes.

After you click Next, the Congratulations! page appears.

8. **Click the link to view your new Web page.**

   Your new Web page appears in a window, as shown in Figure 2-6.

9. **Write down or save your Web address and return to the wizard and click Done.**

You probably want to improve your Web page quite a bit from here (don't forget to check your spelling!), but you're off to a great start. Send your new Web address to your friends, and take a well-deserved break!

Figure 2-6: Houston, we have a Web page.

Chapter 3

Web Publishing with AOL and Other ISPs

Although the easy-to-use, open, ungovernable World Wide Web may seem as though it is going to wipe out traditional, closed, monitored online services such as America Online (AOL), circumstances are not really working out that way. The online services are adapting quickly. They have become gateways to the Web, and in some cases offer easy-to-use Web publishing services that include hosting your Web page for free.

If you already use AOL, it's probably the best place for you to start experimenting with Web publishing. You already know the interface, you can find online forums and discussion boards for Web publishing, and you can take advantage of the easy-to-use Web publishing features that AOL has scrambled to provide.

If you aren't an America Online or a CompuServe user, the quickest and cheapest way to get your first page up on the Web is to use GeoCities, the Web-based service we describe in Chapter 2. But if you are, you may well be better off using your online service for Web publishing. America Online, in particular, has strong features for intermediate Web publishing, including support for both Windows and Macintosh, several megabytes of free server space, and (at the time of this writing) no restrictions on using free Web pages for business.

Note: Just like the Web, online services are always evolving. The information in this chapter is accurate at the time of this writing, but you need to check online for the latest info. See the updates page for this book at www.creating-web-pages.com for more information.

The Best Internet Service Provider

You certainly have freedom of choice when choosing the best way to get online. You used to have to choose between an online service such as AOL or CompuServe, which offered limited Internet access, or an Internet service provider, which had little online community or other online service features. Now you can get a range of online service-type and ISP-type features from a range of providers, all referred to as ISPs. And your choice truly is free, at least for a while — most ISPs offer free sign up and a free trial period. You can try two or three different services before making a long-term choice. Just remember to resign from any service that you stop using, or the $20 or so a month charge to your credit card may go on forever!

You also have the option of using a traditional Internet service provider (ISP), such as Earthlink. Earthlink has more and more built-in content and services, like America Online or CompuServe, but is really focused on open Internet and Web content and tools. Other ISPs vary in the amount of built-in content and services they offer.

In many areas you also have the ability to use a free ISP service, such as Netzero. A free ISP service gives you a fast, free connection to the Internet and a few additional frills. But who needs frills? If you like using the Internet and the Web for your information, chat, and so on, and a free ISP service is available in your area, you should seriously consider it.

With any ISP, you can use GeoCities (described in Chapter 2) or other free Web page publishing services to create your first Web page. With AOL or CompuServe, you also get the option of using built-in Web publishing services.

America Online is the biggest and best traditional online service. Because it's far bigger than any other online service — over 30 million users, about five times the number of the next competitor — it has more people to chat with online, more areas with existing content, and more people to support you.

America Online owns CompuServe; CompuServe has been positioned as the "value" service — a little less content, a little less service, for a little less money. You can get basic service using CompuServe 7.0, the latest version of CompuServe, for $19.95 a month. You may have received CompuServe service as part of a bundled deal with your computer.

MSN Internet Access is a Microsoft offering that's positioned as a value alternative to AOL. For $21.95 a month you get Internet access and use of Microsoft services such as Hotmail and the Microsoft Network (MSN). This deal may not seem too good because much of what you get as part of MSN Internet Access is free to any Web user, but MSN Internet Access is popular, with millions of users and growing steadily.

As for more general concerns, all three interfaces have a modern, relatively attractive GUI *(graphical user interface);* CompuServe 7.0, the latest version, incorporates many features of America Online. It also includes something new, however; the browser in CompuServe 7.0 is based on the Netscape browser, rather than the version of the Internet Explorer browser built into AOL. You find little difference in using the program, however, and you can still run any browser you want to in parallel with either AOL or CompuServe.

Figure 3-1 shows the clean and attractive interface of America Online. Figure 3-2 shows the improved interface of CompuServe 7.0; Figure 3-3 shows the revamped interface of MSN 9 Dial-Up, which is simply a Web page available to any Internet user.

The examples show the versions for Windows. The Macintosh offerings on the Big Three tend to lag behind the versions for Windows, and MSN Internet Access doesn't work with the Macintosh or even with Windows 3.1. Many Macintosh owners choose America Online, which got an early start with Macintosh users. (America Online's software is based on work Apple did for its own, now-defunct online service.)

Figure 3-1:
America Online is easy for everyone to use.

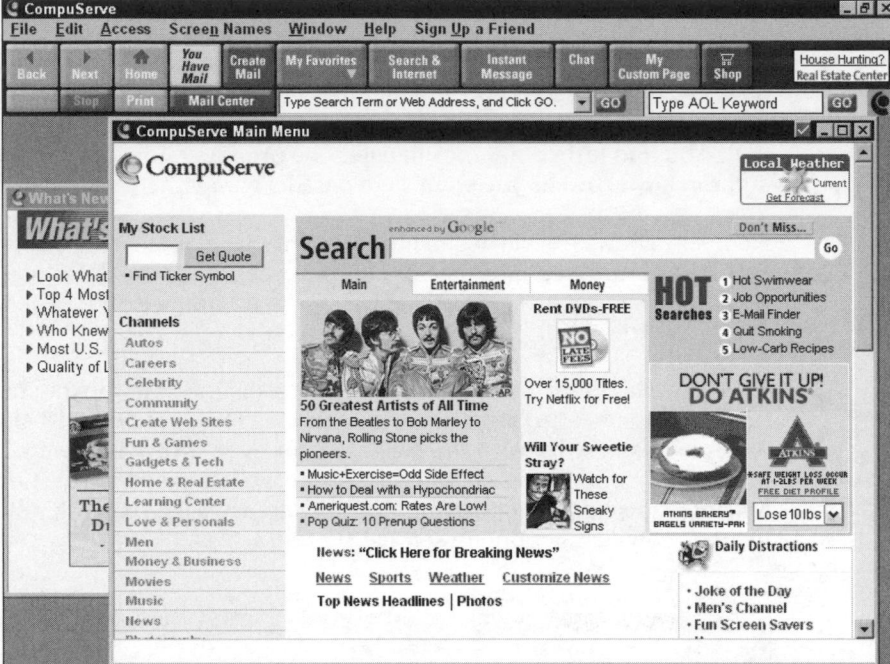

Figure 3-2:
CompuServe
gets more
GUI with
time.

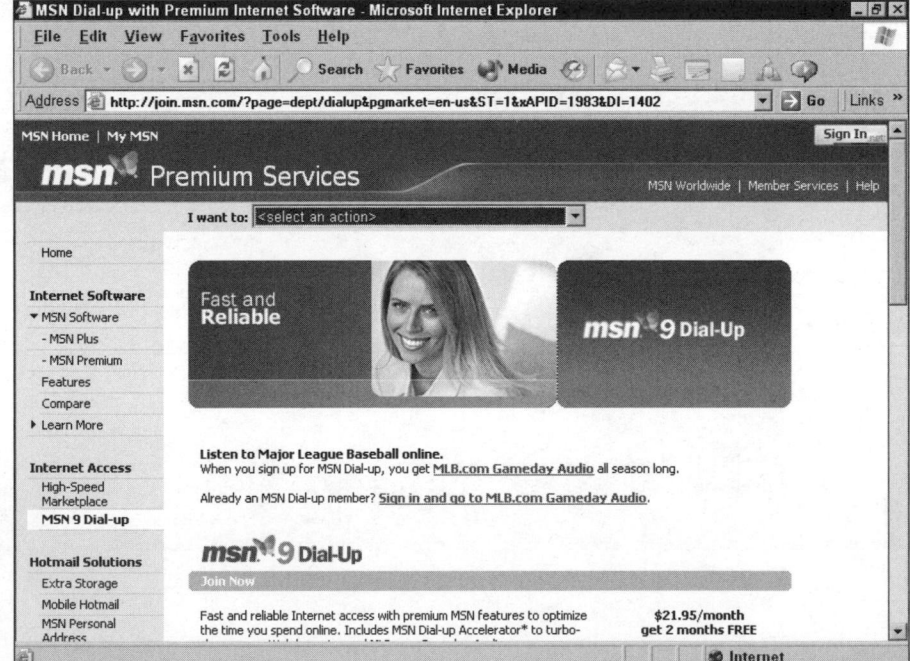

Figure 3-3:
MSN
Internet
Access —
Microsoft's
ISP.

If you have not yet chosen an online service, or have been considering switching, here are the high points — and low points, where applicable — of each service:

- ✔ **America Online:** So far, the market consistently votes most strongly for America Online, now with over 30 million users. It has recently launched Version 9.0, which adds faster Web browsing, better parental controls, and other features to its familiar mix of Internet access, chat, e-mail, and Web publishing. America Online also has the most Macintosh users and Mac-related content of the major services. You can find current information about the services and download client software from www.aol.com.

- ✔ **CompuServe:** For business, CompuServe may still be a good choice. It has a vast array of business-oriented services and millions of business-oriented users, who help each other with both general and industry-specific questions, as well as robust offerings in other areas. However, more and more such support is moving to the open Web. With CompuServe being repositioned as a value service, price may be its main attraction. You can find current information about the services and download client software from www.compuserve.com.

- ✔ **The Microsoft Network/MSN Internet Access:** Microsoft basically gave up on the full-featured online service market and relaunched The Microsoft Network as MSN Internet Access. MSN Internet Access only works on Windows 95 or later versions of Windows. It uses the Internet Explorer browser — renamed MSN Explorer — and the msn.com Web site as its user interface. It also limits extra services to free Hotmail accounts (which are also free to anyone else!) and a few special offers. See www.msn.com for details.

- ✔ **Earthlink:** Earthlink is the winner of the wars among "pure" ISPs, having acquired the second-place contender, MindSpring, some years ago. Earthlink offers dial-up, broadband, and wireless Internet access, with your choice of browser software. Visit www.earthlink.com to learn more.

- ✔ **Netzero:** Netzero got into the online services game late, with free Internet access as its claim to fame. The company now gives away up to 10 hours a month of access — about enough to receive and upload e-mail — and charges $9.95 a month for unlimited use. You can find out what's offered at www.netzero.com.

So what's the best online service for budding Web publishers? AOL is the most expensive, has the most users, and sports the most Web publishing features. If you already use one of the services, you should probably stick with it when pursuing your Web publishing efforts. Figuring out a new service is a big hassle, and CompuServe and AOL both have decent Web publishing support. You always have the option of using GeoCities or a competing Web-based publishing site (see Chapter 2), no matter what your ISP is.

Checking newsgroups for the real deal

For user feedback on online services, you may want to check Usenet newsgroups, which you may have access to at school or at work. Newsgroups are discussion groups, hosted on the Internet, that allow people to discuss shared interests. Web browsers often include the capability to read Usenet newsgroups, and the online services offer Usenet access along with Web access. (You choose the name of the newsgroup from within a Web browser window, not by entering it as a URL.) Try the following newsgroups:

- `alt.online-service.america-online`
- `alt.online-service.compuserve`
- `alt.online-service.microsoft`

The Web sites of America Online, CompuServe, and MSN are among the most popular sites on the World Wide Web. You can even use these sites to check your AOL, CompuServe, or MSN e-mail using a Web browser. You can also find many smaller national services and dozens of local online services around the world, though the number is gradually dropping through mergers, acquisitions, and bankruptcies. Each online service has its pluses and minuses, its fans, and its specific appeal. You may even discover a worthwhile local ISP by searching online or asking friends.

Broadband access is, of course, increasingly popular. If you plan to host multimedia content such as music or movies on your Web site, it's simply a necessity; even if you don't plan to do this, you may well value broadband access for faster Web surfing. Broadband also enables you to quickly download programs you can use in creating content for your Web site.

Most of what we tell you about online services in this chapter applies to broadband services as well, but details vary considerably depending on precisely where you live. Some areas may not have any broadband access; some may have access via fast DSL phone lines; others may have access via cable TV, or both. Check the sites of the major players (`www.aol.com`, `broadband.msn.com`, and `www.earthlink.com`) to see if you can get broadband access from them at your home or office.

Also check with your local cable and satellite TV companies to see what they offer.

Some services offer language-specific support. If you want to work in a language other than English, ask others who speak your language and who live in the same city or region about available services.

Traditional online services: Pros and cons

The ISPs that started out as traditional online services, before the Web was created — AOL, CompuServe, and Prodigy — all offer Web access, but what's offered varies dramatically. In general, if all you want is Web access, you may be better off with an Internet service provider (ISP), a company that provides direct access to the Internet and that may well be cheaper, inflict less advertising on you, have better browser support, or offer more reliable access than the major online services.

The best news for a new Web publisher about these services is that you can find plenty of Web publishing support. Given the difficulties you may encounter in figuring out how to use the Web and publish on it, who wouldn't want a few million friends online to help out? All the online services offer support for Web use and Web publishing. Online forums can tell you what to do, point you to good sites, and more. Online technical support helps you get beyond Web problems and problems with the online service itself.

However, the online services also share some Web access problems. The default browser is usually an older version of Microsoft Internet Explorer. If you want to use Netscape Navigator, or the latest version of Internet Explorer, you may be able to, but only by running it separately — and then you have a harder time getting questions about how to use your browser answered by your fellow online service users, who tend to be users of the built-in version of Internet Explorer.

Using one of the online services can be a bit like using training wheels. Remember how free you felt when your parents finally took the training wheels off of your first bike? Having the interface of your online service take screen space away from your Web browser, having access to online newsgroups restricted by the online service, and switching back and forth between the "look and feel" of your online service and your accustomed browser may irritate you when compared to feeling the open air of the unregulated Internet.

The Best Web Publishing Support

Online services are a good place to start your initial Web publishing efforts: low prices, good tools, lots of support — kind of like running downhill with a tailwind. Now that America Online, CompuServe, and The Microsoft Network are increasingly integrated with the Web, Web publishing is an attractive feature for the services to offer. America Online and CompuServe offer the following:

✔ **No extra charge for Web page authoring:** America Online and CompuServe both offer free support for Web page authoring; you pay only the normal access charges for creating and viewing your page and other Web pages.

✔ **Easy Web page authoring tools:** America Online and CompuServe offer easy-to-use, fill-in-the-blank tools that help you quickly create an initial Web page. AOL has several levels of Web page tools and support for additional features; CompuServe offers some, but not all, of the same features as AOL.

✔ **Free Web server space:** One of the biggest problems in creating an initial Web page is getting space on a Web server. America Online and CompuServe both offer free Web server space for personal and business home pages.

✔ **No file transfer hassle:** Getting your files onto a Web server is often a pain; the online services' easy-to-use Web page authoring tools can make getting your information online easy.

✔ **Upgrading to HTML tools:** The online services enable you to use separate HTML tools to create your own custom Web page and then to transfer your files to their server for free hosting.

The online services are rapidly developing their Web support in general and their Web publishing support in particular, so check updates on Web services before making a final decision about which online service to use.

Each online service has different specific features and restrictions on your Web pages. At this writing, the policies and offerings of the top online services are as follows:

✔ **America Online:** Several megabytes of free Web server space. More good news: AOL has a very easy-to-use tool called 1-2-3 Publish, and a more capable tool called Easy Designer, both integrated into the service. America Online also offers step-by-step instructions for using HTML and free add-ins to your Web pages, and allows you to use your free server space to put up business Web pages.

✔ **CompuServe:** CompuServe gives you free access to 1-2-3 Publish, the same built-in Web publishing tool offered by AOL. CompuServe offers free templates and the ability to upload your own HTML files and graphics to a free, 20MB space. You can also add counters and other cool features, and you can use your Web page for your business. (No business transaction capability is supported, though, and you aren't allowed to add your own.)

✔ **MSN:** MSN doesn't really do anything special for you when it comes to Web publishing — and if you look around the Web, you find that many Web pages on free, Web-based services such as GeoCities (see Chapter 2) are created by MSN members. Basically, as an MSN user, you're on your own.

All the publishing services we describe in this book enable you to include HTML commands in your text. For a description of key HTML commands, see the Cheat Sheet and Appendix C. (Feeling restless? Tear out the Cheat Sheet and tape it to the wall in front of you, where you can see it!)

What's a Mac user to do?

Two words: Get AOL. America Online has robust Macintosh support, including full cross-platform support for easy Web publishing. CompuServe doesn't support an easy-to-use Web publishing tool on the Macintosh, only on Windows. (Mac users have access to free Web server space, but no easy-to-use publishing tool.) The Microsoft Network doesn't support the Macintosh at all! So if you are a Mac user who wants an online service that supports your Web publishing efforts, get America Online.

Getting Your Web Page Up with AOL or CompuServe

America Online is an amazing success story — and by far the leading Internet service provider in the world. It also offers solid Web publishing services, backed by a strong online community that can help you publish your first Web page and then steadily improve it.

America Online is such an amazing success story that it acquired its biggest rival, CompuServe. (This was a couple of years before it acquired something even larger — the media company Time Warner.) The 1-2-3 Publish tool, which we describe in this chapter, works in both AOL and CompuServe.

If you're not an America Online or a CompuServe user, GeoCities (described in Chapter 2) is an excellent choice. Anyone with Web access can use Geo-Cities. But if you're an America Online or CompuServe user, you have a choice between America Online's built-in services — available in CompuServe as well — and GeoCities. We suggest that you start with AOL's tools if you have that choice.

Why? The answer isn't really that AOL's tools are better; they're roughly equivalent to the GeoCities tools. The difference is community. Most AOL users spend more time in AOL's online forums than on the open Web. And in those open forums you can quickly get answers to your questions about using AOL's tools to get your initial Web page up, and then improve it from there. The same goes for CompuServe.

If you're already an America Online user and are still on an early version of the service, do upgrade to the latest version before proceeding. All it costs you is a little time, and you get access to all the Web publishing capabilities we describe in this chapter.

Use this chapter to get started with the America Online tools and create your first Web page. Then use the more advanced information later in this book and the online forums in America Online to push your page to the next level.

Looking into What AOL Offers

America Online has several parts to its Web publishing service:

- ✔ **1-2-3 Publish:** 1-2-3 Publish lets you use a template to quickly create your first Web page. It removes most of the initial barriers of getting a Web page up quickly and easily. However, it doesn't let you create your own custom Web page design or work in HTML. 1-2-3 Publish is also available on CompuServe.

- ✔ **Easy Designer:** Easy Designer is the next step up from 1-2-3 Publish. It lets you drag and drop text and images and use HTML to extend the capabilities of your page. (Easy Designer replaces the Personal Publisher and Personal Publisher 3 services from previous versions of the AOL software.)

- ✔ **Verio services:** For a really big site, AOL has integrated Web hosting services from Verio, a major Web hosting provider, into its offering. The good news for you is that you get some Verio services free, and others at a discount, by accessing them through AOL.

We recommend that you use 1-2-3 Publish to get that all-important first Web page up, and then continue editing your Web page with Easy Designer. The next section tells you how to create your first Web page with 1-2-3 Publish; it should take 30 minutes or less. You can follow the instructions for 1-2-3 Publish in CompuServe as well. If you already know something about Web page creation and want to go straight to a more challenging environment, try Easy Designer first. (At this writing, you don't have access to Easy Designer from CompuServe.)

Planning Before You Start

Putting up your first home page using AOL's 1-2-3 Publish tool takes only a few minutes, because you skip so many hassles that normally come with Web publishing. But, as with the GeoCities process in Chapter 2, you can help yourself by doing a few things in preparation:

- ✔ **Visit AOL Hometown Web pages.** To see other users' Hometown Web pages, click the Keyword button at the top of the AOL screen. Type **Hometown** in the window that appears at the top of the page, and then click Go. You see the AOL Hometown main page, which allows you to search for Web pages by keyword, or to visit Web pages in various communities.

✔ **Find out more about AOL Hometown by looking at Hometown-related Web pages.** You can find more about Hometown by looking at the instructions for beginners; clicking the Create, Edit, and similar links at the bottom of the Web page; or examining all the templates. Return to the Hometown main page to get started.

✔ **Look for the URLs of your favorite Web sites.** Many AOL Hometown templates let you list links to several of your favorite Web sites — but to link to them, you need the URLs. Surf around the Web and find the URLs of several sites that reflect your interests, or of sites of friends or family members. (The more obscure your favorites are the better!)

✔ **Plan your page.** Use a word processing program or a few pieces of notebook paper to plan your initial Web page. (Use the paper for drawing only — neither origami nor paper airplanes translate well to the Web.) Rough out what text you want to put in and what URLs to include. Then you can be ready to focus on the mechanics of getting the Web page right.

✔ **Scan a picture.** Many personal Web pages look much better with a picture — of you, or of something relating to the topic you're interested in. Scan a picture of yourself and use an image editing program such as Photoshop to save it in a Web-ready format such as GIF or JPEG. (For more on graphics for the Web, see Chapter 9.) If you lack appropriate software, go to a copy shop, such as Kinko's, that rents scanners and time on personal computers with appropriate software. You can also ask your photo developer to put your pictures on disk; several nationwide chains do this.

For users' convenience, try to reduce the file size of the picture to 30K or less before adding it to your Web page. (A 30K image takes about 10 seconds to download when a user is viewing your page with a 56K modem.)

Getting a Start with 1-2-3 Publish

Beginning Web publishers can choose 1-2-3 Publish, the very easy-to-use tool that helps you put a Web page up fast, or Easy Designer, a more flexible tool that helps you do more with your Web page. Easy Designer can work with Web pages that you create initially in 1-2-3 Publish.

You can get to 1-2-3 Publish in CompuServe by typing **ourworld** in the Web address bar at the top of the CompuServe application window and then pressing Return. Then click the 1-2-3 Publish link in the upper-right corner. (The text link says 3 Steps to Happiness.) You can skip to Step 5 in the following steps.

1-2-3 Publish offers the best of both worlds: an easy-to-use tool that isn't limiting, because you can use Easy Designer, or add-ons that AOL makes available, to improve your initial page. Follow these steps to create your first Web page with 1-2-3 Publish:

1. **Start America Online.**

   The Welcome screen appears.

2. **Click the Technology channel.**

   The AOL Technology channel, consisting largely of CINET content, appears. (CINET is a major Web site for computing content and a partner of AOL.)

3. **Click the Web Building button in the lower-left area of the screen.**

   The AOL Technology: Web Building screen appears, as shown in Figure 3-4.

4. **From the Web Building screen in AOL, click the <u>Create Your Own</u> link in the upper-right corner.**

   The 1-2-3 Publish starting screen appears, as shown in Figure 3-5.

5. **Scroll down and examine all the different templates to see what options are available.**

   You can use one of the top-level templates or one of the more specific templates farther down for your first Web page. However, for the purposes of these steps, we avoid the other templates and use the "All About Me" template.

6. **Click the <u>Personal Pages</u> link.**

   The Personal Pages screen appears.

7. **Click the <u>All About Me</u> link.**

   A page with a series of steps appears, as shown in Figure 3-6. The next section describes how to follow these steps.

Figure 3-4:
AOL gives
you a
toolbox full
of ways to
start.

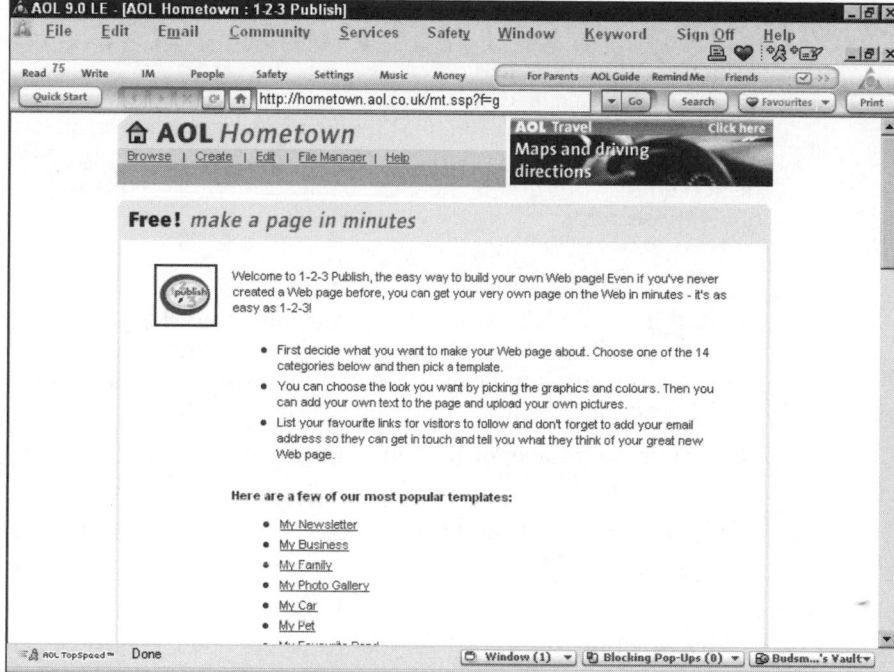

Figure 3-5:
1-2-3
Publish
gives you
scores of
choices.

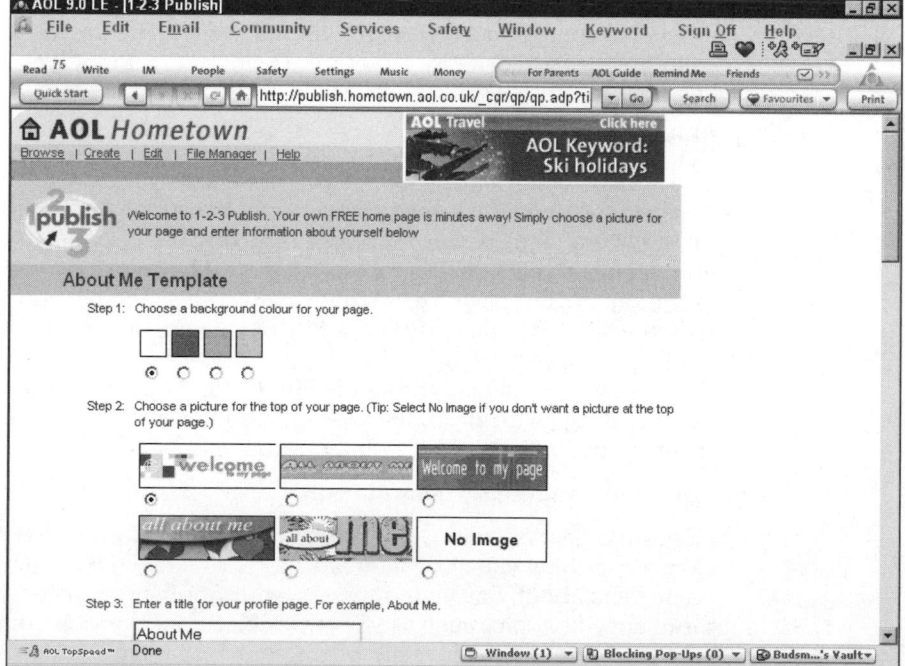

Figure 3-6:
You're just a
few steps
away from
your Web
page.

Publishing Your First Home Page

Use the template called My First Home Page Template to create your first home page. (If you use a different template, the steps are basically the same, but you have to adjust to fit different details as you go along.) After you reach the screen for your first home page, as described in the previous section, follow these steps:

1. **Set up the overall look of the page.**

   The first step is to select the background color for your page. The choices are white, light green, light pink, and light yellow. A white background gives you the most flexibility in choosing other graphics, adding pictures, and so on.

2. **Choose an image for the top of your page.**

   The choices are My Favorites, My Quick Bio, Blue Asterisks (no words), Welcome to My Page, I Recommend, and Blank. Pick the picture that best fits the content you plan to put on your Web page.

3. **Add a title and a picture to your page.**

   Enter a title that describes your page. Include a keyword that people can search with — if your page includes information about your interest in horses, put "horses" in the title. Or put your name in the title to allow your friends to search for your site easily.

   You can also upload a picture for your site. Click the Browse button to search your hard drive for a picture. To find more about Web graphics, see Chapter 9.

4. **Choose a divider style.**

   Choose one of the six divider styles. This is a very important choice because the divider between sections has a surprisingly strong effect on the overall look of your Web page. The first style, greenish dots, has a color scheme that matches the first picture, My Favorites, which appears at the top of your page. The second style, orange and blue dots, goes with the second choice, My Quick Bio, or the fourth choice, Welcome to My Page. The third choice, a bar of pastel colors, the fourth choice, a blue and white leaf design, and the fifth choice, a set of purple curlicues, don't really go with any of the top-of-page images. The final choice, no divider, goes with anything — but doesn't help break up your page.

5. **Enter one to three sections of text.**

   Here's the beef of your page. Enter a title and text for up to three sections describing you, your interests, hobbies, and so on. Enter a title and basic facts about you, your interests, your hobbies, your friends, or more specific topics such as your work history. Take some time with this step; this information is really where your Web page stands or falls in terms of being interesting to other people.

Unlike in other entry-level Web publishing services, HTML tags do not work within 1-2-3 Publish. You can't use HTML tags to format your Web page.

6. **Add links to your page.**

Enter the name and URL of three links that you want to put in your Web page. Your favorite links are like your gift to the Web community, giving people who share your interests quick access to the most valuable resources you've found. Enter Web pages that you like and use a lot and that other people might not already be familiar with. Also, choose links that relate to the text you entered. (You can add to this list later, using other tools.)

7. **Decide whether to add special features to your page.**

Choose whether to allow AOL to run ads on your page — you're more likely to irritate people than to make big bucks — and whether to let your Web page visitors reach you via Instant Messenger (IM for short). If you like IM, this addition might be fun.

8. **Click the Preview My Page button.**

Your Web page appears! It has a special box at the top that allows you to go back and change the page (by clicking Modify) or save It to the Web (by clicking Save). Figure 3-7 shows the very simple Web page one of the authors created as an example.

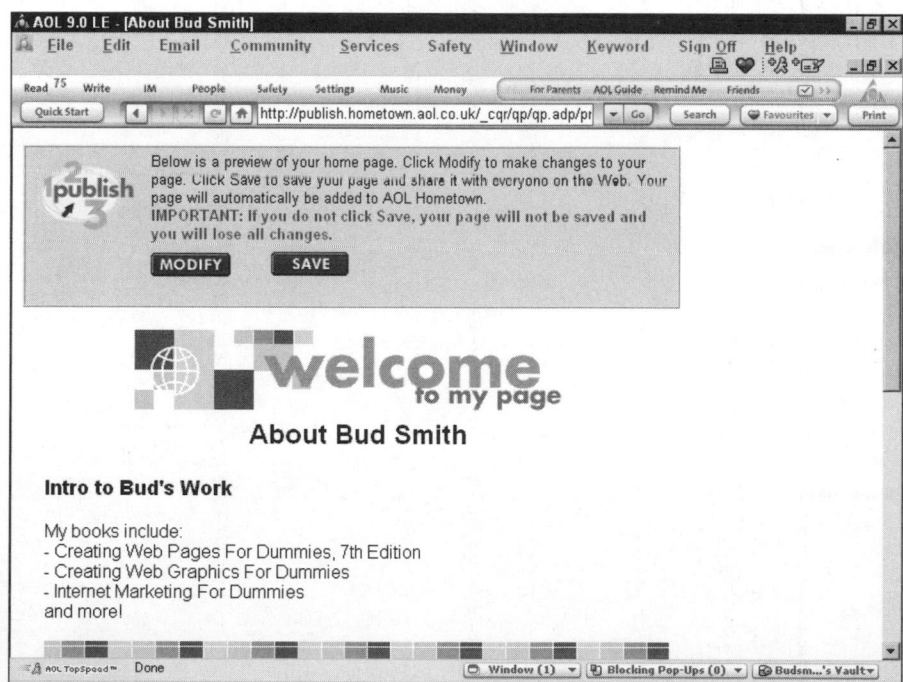

Figure 3-7: Bud's sample 1-2-3 Publish Web page.

9. **Continue to modify and preview your page until it's ready, and then choose Save.**

   Your Web page now is published on the Web! You see a Congratulations page, as shown in Figure 3-8, and the Web address of your new page. Write it down or save it in a safe place, and tell your friends!

   You can also make other changes, such as moving your Web page to a different area within AOL's home page categories. Click around on the Congratulations page and investigate the different options.

   Use the link, <u>Send This Page to Friends and Family</u> link to get the word out. When you click this link, you can enter the e-mail addresses of several people, who receive a link back to your home page.

   To be able to see your Web page quickly, click the link for your home page to make it appear in a Web browser window. Then click the Favorites icon at the top of the AOL screen. Choose Add Top Window to Favorite Places, and you can always return to your Web page again.

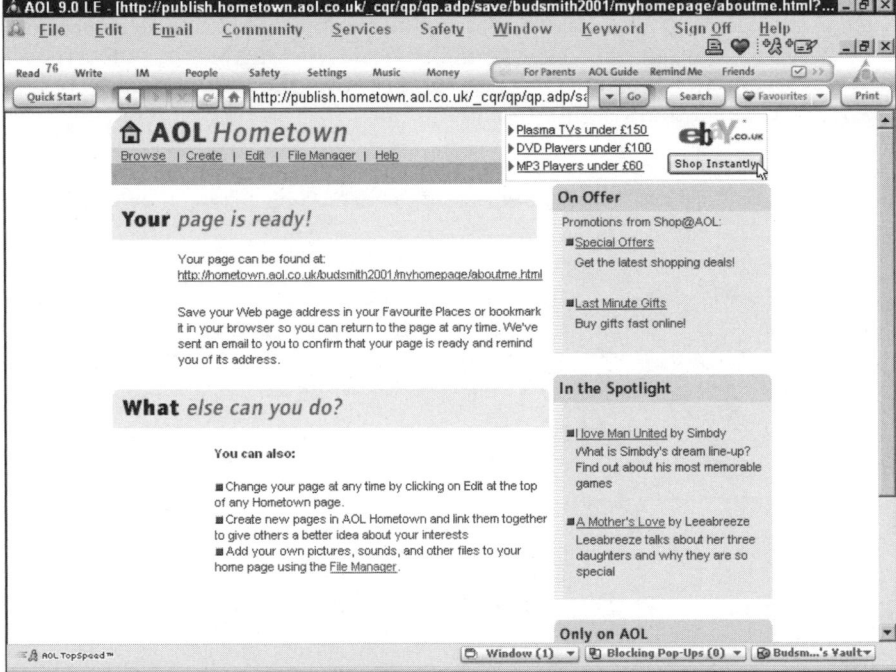

Figure 3-8:
AOL gives you your URL and offers ways to change your page.

All about the Andrews?

AOL offers you the opportunity to make money for including an AOL ad banner in your page. The idea is that, whenever someone visits your Web page, they see an ad banner inviting them to join AOL. If they do so, and stay 90 days or more, AOL pays you "up to" $15. (That's almost a U.S. $20 bill, which has Andrew Jackson's picture on it.) Don't do it! Don't add to the clutter and annoy your friends and family — who probably are your first Web page visitors — by including an ad with your first Web page.

After you take your page as far as you can with 1-2-3 Publish — which may take a while because the tool is pretty capable — you can move up to Easy Designer. Easy Designer allows you much more flexibility in the content and layout of your Web page, with drag-and-drop editing and placement of text and graphics.

Just use the steps at the beginning of this chapter to choose a tool, but choose Easy Designer instead of 1-2-3 Publish. You can choose the Web page you developed with 1-2-3 Publish as your starting point for work in Easy Designer.

After you edit a page in Easy Designer, you can no longer edit it further in 1-2-3 Publish. So be sure you take your Web page as far as you want to in 1-2-3 Publish before editing it with Easy Designer.

Chapter 4

Introduction to HTML

Knowing the basics of HTML is a *good* thing. HTML is the code that connects the text content of your Web page with the graphics, links, and appearance users see in a Web browser. If you know the basics of HTML, you'll understand why Web pages look and work the way they do, and you'll understand how you can create and improve your own Web page.

Trying to figure out a lot of HTML right away is a *bad* thing. Spending hours and hours going over all the details of HTML is likely to slow your quest to become a Web publisher. And becoming a Web publisher quickly can, again, be a *good* thing. So don't let a bad thing get in the way of good things; use this chapter to find out just enough about HTML to help you create some basic pages and get them on the Web.

Why bother with HTML basics?

Most Web authoring tools try to hide HTML from the user; you can use one of these tools to create a Web page without knowing a thing about HTML. But here are several reasons to figure out the basics of HTML:

- **Because everyone else is:** Bad reason. Next!

- **To understand how the Web works:** This understanding is pretty valuable if you're a heavy Web user (or a light one), especially if you plan to publish on the Web. Some of the Web's limitations, such as "what you see is not what you get," are hard to understand if you don't know something about HTML.

- **To use free Web tools:** Many free Web tools enable you to enter HTML tags directly to

jazz up your text. Knowing a few tags can go a long way.

- **To work directly in HTML:** Many Web pros tire of managing HTML tags by hand and start using a tool that hides the tags. Others swear by HTML. Everyone swears at HTML, at least some of the time. But the only way to have a choice is to know some HTML.

- **To do better work using a tool:** When you're using a tool that hides the gory details of HTML from you, knowing enough HTML to understand what's going on "behind the scenes" is an advantage. In fact, tools that hide the HTML almost all have a mode that lets you see and work in HTML when you choose to, for just that reason.

Get Ready: A Refreshingly Brief Description of HTML

HTML (HyperText Markup Language) is a specific way of adding descriptive tags to regular text so that all the formatting, linking, and navigational information you need in a Web page is contained in the same file with the regular text. HTML is designed to be something that humans can read *and* that machines can process, a kind of common ground for human-to-machine communication.

Suppose you want to add bold to a word in your text, such as:

```
You can use HTML to specify that a word is bold.
```

To add formatting to a sentence using HTML, just take the regular sentence and add a couple of tags to specify where bolding starts and stops. Here's the previous line in HTML:

```
You can use HTML to specify that a word is <b>bold</b>.
```

When you display the sentence with the HTML tags in a Web browser, the browser displays all the words, but not the *tags* — the information between angle brackets. The Web browser uses the tags to do extra things to the text, such as add formatting to it. In this case, the formatting is simple: Start using bold text after the word "is," and stop using bold text after the word "bold."

Because HTML tags exist alongside the text that users see on your Web page, a document with HTML tags in it is called *HTML-tagged text.* That simply means text with HTML tags in it. A file with HTML-tagged text in it is called an HTML file and usually has the extension .htm or .html at the end of the file-name. If you look at HTML-tagged text in a text editing program, you see the angle brackets and HTML commands; if you look at it in a Web browser, you see a Web page with formatting, links, and so on.

A document with no formatting — such as italics and other formatting added by a word processor — is called a *plain text* document. HTML-tagged text documents are considered plain text documents because the characters you see on-screen are the only characters in the document. Word processing documents that aren't plain text documents have additional formatting codes embedded in them to tell machines how to display and print the text.

You can add HTML tags to regular text to create your own Web documents in any text editor or word processing program. Or you can use a Web editing tool that hides the gory details of HTML tags.

This chapter gives you enough background to know what you're seeing when you look at text that includes HTML tags and to make a few changes in HTML-tagged text if you need to. We don't burden you with hundreds of pages of HTML tags, tips, and tricks. You can find some of the more technical details and background in the sidebar called "The helter-skelter growth of HTML." (Try it; you'll like it.) After you publish a few Web pages, you can take the time to find out more about HTML. At that point, you may want to buy your-self that 400-page HTML book.

 If you like to know everything that's going on before you roll up your sleeves and plunge into things, you may want to start by looking at *HTML For Dummies,* 4th Edition, a comprehensive guide to HTML by Ed Tittel, et al (Wiley).

Viewing HTML documents

You can see HTML anytime you use the Web. Just pull up a Web page in your browser and choose View⇨Source for Internet Explorer, or a similar command for other browsers. A new window opens, the contents of which are the HTML source code that underlies the Web page. Figure 4-1 shows the home page of the For Dummies site and its HTML source code as an example.

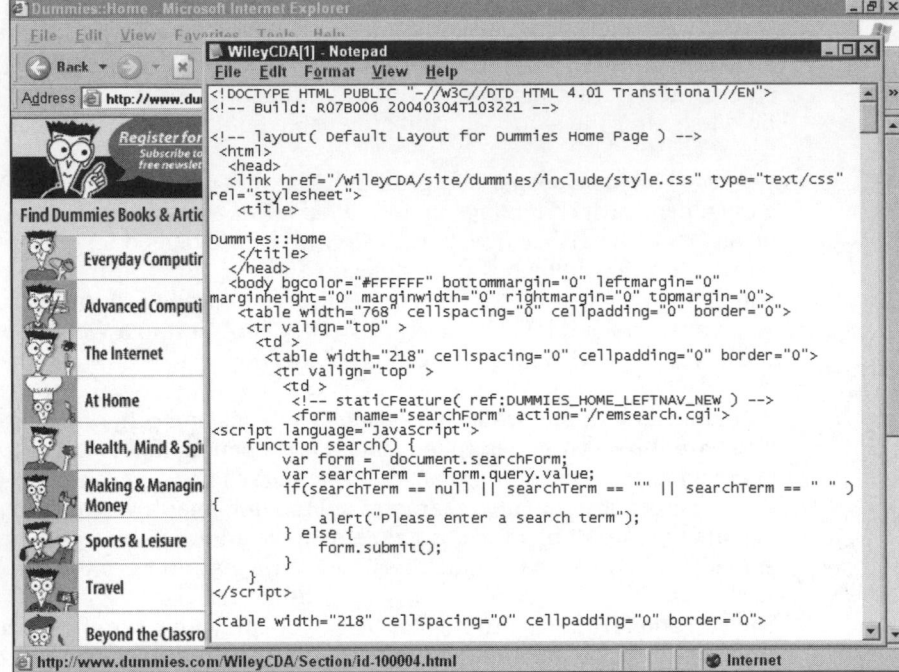

Figure 4-1:
The For
Dummies
site is made
of HTML-
tagged
text and
graphics.

Having the ability to instantly view a document's HTML code naturally leads to the temptation to borrow attractive documents from the Web, save them to your disk as HTML files, and then use them as templates for your own work — kind of a magpie approach to Web page building.

The helter-skelter growth of HTML

HTML is a markup language that follows rules set out in a more complex specification — SGML (Standard Generalized Markup Language). HTML has evolved to Version 4, and most, but not all, browsers and Web authoring tools support all the features of HTML 4. Many users never upgrade the browser they get with their computers, so old versions of browsers stick around for a long time. And some users

access the Web through devices like WebTV, which don't support advanced features such as frames and Dynamic HTML (DHTML). For the widest possible audience, stick with older tags, such as those in the HTML 3.2 specification or earlier. Nearly all the capabilities we describe in this book are from the most widely supported, early versions of HTML; we point out the few times we use more advanced features.

Examining the HTML script

Take a closer look at the term for which HTML is an acronym, HyperText Markup Language. You may already know that hypertext is text that has links in it. A *link* is just a connection to another file. So far so good. But what's a *markup language*? (It's not that confusing language that car dealers speak when they decide how high to jack up the price!) A markup language is simply a way to put information about a document — for example, information about hypertext links and formatting — in the document itself. Markup languages often use tags — labels placed within text that give display instructions. So HyperText Markup Language — HTML — is a specific way of using tags to convey information about a document.

Most tags in HTML come in pairs: One starts a change and the other ends it. In the following sample sentence, the first tag, <b>, means start displaying text in a **bold** typeface; the second tag, </b>, means stop using bold.

Here's how the sentence looks when "marked up" with HTML tags:

```
That's a <b>good</b> idea.
```

Here's how the sentence looks when displayed on-screen:

```
That's a good idea.
```

The browser reads the original, text-only sentence — That's a <b>good</b> idea. — and says to itself, "I display That's a, turn bold on, display good, turn bold off, and display idea." The person who created the original sentence puts in the HTML tags, the browser interprets them, and the user only sees the effect — in this case, the word good displayed in boldface type.

The <b> and </b> tags are *formatting tags* that describe how a browser displays text. Another kind of tag in HTML is the *linking tag.* Linking tags specify outside information brought into a document. Here's some complicated-looking HTML text that shows examples of formatting and linking tags:

```
To learn about <i>Pokemon</i>,
the "pocket monsters" that
were so popular with kids,
go to the official Web site
for <a href="http://www.
pokemon.com">Pokemon</a>.
```

The text appears on-screen as follows:

```
To learn about Pokemon, the
"pocket monsters" that were
so popular with kids, go
to the official Web site
for Pokemon.
```

The <I> and </I> formatting tags specify that the first occurrence of the word *Pokemon* is displayed in italics. The <a> and </a> linking tags specify that second occurrence of the word Pokemon is displayed as an *anchor* — that is, the starting point of a link. On most browsers, as here, anchors are underlined. So what does the extra text — href="http://www.pokemon.com" — inside the <a> tag mean? href is short for *Hypertext REFerence.* If you click the anchor, your browser looks for the URL that serves as the hypertext reference, which in this case is the Pokemon Web page address that appears after the equal sign.

The idea of a machine or procedure that reads a piece of input, uses that input to make a decision, carries out the decision, and then reads some more input is centuries old and has been thoroughly studied. Such a machine or program — a browser, for example — is called a *finite automaton.* (Pronounced to rhyme with "fly night oughtomaton.") Try dropping that term into your conversation the next time the Web comes up!

Borrowing someone else's material is okay for basic HTML formatting, but for more sophisticated formats that are distinctive and embody a great deal of work, get permission before you use them — or don't use them. Simply contact the Webmaster at the site you admire, describe how you want to use the format, and request permission. You may be surprised how many people say yes — without even exacting a promise from you that you hand over your firstborn.

Creating HTML documents

You can create HTML documents in a word processing program, in a text editor, or by using an HTML tool. Each method has its advantages:

- **Word processing program:** Most new versions of popular word processing packages include "save as HTML" capability. You can open and edit a document in the word processing program and then save it as HTML-tagged text that makes up a Web page. However, the conversion process between the many features that a word processor supports and the smaller range of features supported by HTML is less than perfect. Ironically, you can only use your familiar word processing program to edit HTML documents effectively if you understand what formatting HTML supports directly, which you find out about in this chapter.

- **Text editor:** A text editor is a program that edits regular text, such as the dull, boring, plain text that many people send e-mail messages in — no fonts, no bold or italic text, and no styles. You can use a text editor to create a file with HTML tags in it. When you save a file from a text editor, it saves as plain text, with no added, hidden codes for formatting. (But save it with the extension .htm to distinguish it as an HTML file.) Although most text editors lack the advanced features found in word processing programs, many HTML experts swear by them. (You can also create a file in a word processing program and then save it as a text file to achieve the same effect, but you have to remember not to save it as a word processing file.)

- **HTML tool:** An HTML tool hides some of the details of HTML from you. However, you have to go through a learning curve for any HTML tool, and few tools completely hide HTML. So the basics we present in this chapter help, even if you plan to use a tool. By knowing the basics, you can make better use of the tool and have some alternatives if the tool doesn't do everything you need it to. (And what tool does?)

After you create an HTML file, save it with the .htm extension. The extension enables the Web browser to recognize the file and interpret it correctly. If you use the .html extension instead, not all systems can recognize it as an HTML file.

Every computer allows different kinds of filenames. But for your Web pages to work on the widest possible range of systems, keep your Web filenames short, and within the 8 x 3 filename limits of DOS. (FILENAME.EXT is an example of an 8 x 3 filename; up to 8 characters before the period, up to 3 characters after.) HTML files end in the characters .htm Also, leave spaces and special characters such as colons or apostrophes out of the name. This way, your filenames are valid regardless of the type of computer that ends up being the Web server for your pages.

One of the most frustrating problems that beginning HTML authors run into is the fact that word processing programs now try to function as HTML editors and make working directly with HTML tags hard. These programs want to hide the tags from you and "let" you work in a formatted document where you don't see the tags directly, which is easier at first but gives you less control. If you work in Microsoft Word or WordPad (which comes with Microsoft Windows), and save the file in text format each time, you can have direct access to the HTML tags. You must be persistent, though; Word or WordPad asks you repeatedly if you want to save the file as a formatted document. Just say no!

Previewing HTML documents

However you create your HTML file, you need to see what it's going to look like on the Web. Some HTML tools offer special preview modes, but you can get the best idea of how your HTML file will look on the Web by using your Web browser.

While working in your text editor or word processing program or while using an HTML tool, simply save your file to disk. (Remember to save the file using the .htm extension.) Then open your Web browser. In Netscape Navigator, choose File⇨Open Page to open the file you just saved. In Internet Explorer, choose File⇨Open, click the Browse button to find the file, and then open it.

The file appears in your browser just as it does when the file is posted on the Internet. If you're connected to the Internet, you can even click links in your document to see the appropriate graphic or Web page. However, what you see may not be what other people see when they open the file; other people may use different browsers, and they may specify different fonts for displaying Web pages. And accessing a file from your hard disk is much faster than accessing the same file from the Internet. But at least you get an idea of how the page looks.

If you can run your editing tool and your browser at the same time, all the better. (In Windows, use the Alt+Tab key combination to shift quickly between applications. On the Mac, use the application pull-down menu in the upper-right corner of the screen.) You can change the document in your editing tool, save the file, and then use the Reload command or similar command in your browser to see the changes. (Kind of like those bumper stickers you may have seen on the freeway that say "Keep Honking, I'm Reloading.") This way, you never need to be surprised by what you see after something you created is published on the Web.

If you're tricky, you can size and arrange the windows on your screen so that you can see both the HTML file you're editing and the browser window that displays the resulting Web page at the same time!

But don't stop there. See what your document looks like on different browsers before you publish on the Web. You can get copies of the top browsers from the Web sites of the main browser companies, as described in Chapter 5, and preview your document in them as well.

Get Set: HTML Horse Sense

People used to refer to common sense as "horse sense." Most things about HTML fall under the realm of horse sense. After you see HTML tags a few times, most of the rules "feel right," and you have little trouble remembering or using them most of the time. You will occasionally make mistakes, though; don't be surprised *to see that most of a document's text is in italics because you forgot to add a </i> tag to end italics.* (Having these last several words in italics was the authors' idea of a joke.)

Basic HTML rules

Here are a few basic HTML rules and some "gotchas" to watch out for:

- **Most HTML tags work in pairs.** (Does that make these dynamic duos "tag teams"?)

  For example, if you want some text to appear in bold, you have to put <b> at the front of the text that you want to have appear in bold, and you have to put </b> at the end of the text. (The slash, /, indicates that a tag is being turned off.) If you forget the </b> at the end, you can easily end up with a document that looks fine at the start but then switches to bold somewhere in the middle — and this bold continues all the way through to the end.

  So remember to use paired tags and to check your document for unpaired tags before you publish it. If you still end up seeing italics or bold all over your document, you know what to look for.

✔ **HTML tags are written in lower case.**

Convention says to put HTML tags in ALL CAPS so that they stand out from the text they're embedded in. However, newer standards specify lower case for HTML tags. Inside an anchor, put the hypertext reference (such as a URL) in the case it normally has (upper or lower) if you're using it elsewhere. The following example illustrates this use of capitalization:

```
<a href="textver.htm">Text version.</a>
```

The parts of the tag that are predefined HTML tags, such as `<a>`, `</a>`, and `href`, are in ALL CAPS. The filename is in all lowercase letters, a convention used by UNIX (a type of operating system) that may save you some problems if your Web page ends up on a UNIX server. You can capitalize the text between the tags, which appears on the Web page as link text, in whatever way makes sense for your Web page's readers.

UNIX machines are case-sensitive: If you call one file MyFile.txt and another file myfile.txt, they are saved as separate files. The Macintosh and PC are case-insensitive and treat the names MyFile.txt and myfile.txt the same. Because you may end up putting your Web files on a Web server that's a different kind of machine from the one you create them on, you need to pay attention to the use of upper- and lowercase. The easiest rule is the one followed by UNIX users: Always use lowercase letters for filenames. (Some UNIX users go to extremes and use lowercase for everything, including all the text in personal e-mail messages they send.)

✔ **HTML ignores paragraph symbols and tabs in your text.**

One of the most confusing things about HTML is that it ignores the paragraph markers created in your text when you press Enter, as well as tab characters. When displaying HTML, the browser automatically breaks lines to fit the current window size. And the browser makes a paragraph break only when it sees the paragraph tag, `<p>`, or some other tag that implies the start of a new line (such as a top-level heading tag, `<h1>`).

✔ **HTML needs you to put paragraph tags (`<p>`) between paragraphs.**

No matter how many times you hit Return while typing your text, you don't prevent the text from showing up as a big blob on your Web page unless you put paragraph tags (`<p>`) between paragraphs.

✔ **Basic HTML looks different on different types of browsers.**

Basic HTML doesn't give you much control over the appearance of your document. (Newer versions of HTML allow more control but aren't supported by older versions of popular browsers, so we suggest that you avoid the new stuff.) Different browsers handle the same tags differently. For example, a top-level heading (specified by the `<h1>` and `</h1>` tags) may look much larger in one browser than in another browser.

✔ **Some tags don't work on some browsers.**

Some browsers (such as Netscape Navigator) support tags that other browsers can't handle. We recommend that you stick with basic tags to avoid the chance of giving users nasty surprises when they view your documents. We use only those tags in this book.

✔ **Users configure their browsers differently.**

As if the differences among different browser versions weren't enough, users can configure their browsers differently. Users who have bigger monitor screens tend to look at documents in a bigger window. But because these users sit farther back from their big screens — remember your mother telling you always to sit at least six feet from the TV? — they may also use larger font sizes to display text. Some users set their browsers to display all graphics as the page transmits; a few turn off graphics. All these idiosyncrasies can make your document look different to different users. Figure 4-2 shows the Web page for the For Dummies site, displayed with different option settings. As you can see, the figure doesn't look like the normal Dummies page.

Figure 4-2:
The Dummies home page with different font settings.

Ten key HTML tags plus one

The Cheat Sheet at the beginning of this book shows an example of an HTML document, which is just regular text plus tags — those funny things with the angle brackets around them. If you haven't already, tear out the Cheat Sheet so you can look at the sample HTML document while you read this section. Table 4-1 summarizes the tags we use in this chapter.

Table 4-1	Key Tags to Use
Tags	*Tag Location*
`<head>`,`</head>`	Put these tags around the `<title>` and `</title>` tags at the start of the document.
`<title>`,`</title>`	Put these tags around a short title that describes the document, which appears at the top of the browser window. (For more information about the `<head>`, `</head>`, `<title>`, and `</title>` tags, see the section "Head users your way to win" in this chapter.)
`<body>`,`</body>`	After you add the `</title>` and `</head>` tags to end the title and header area, you surround everything below them in the document with the `<body>` and `</body>` tags.
`<h1>`,`</h1>`, `<h2>`,`</h2>`,…	Put the initial heading at the top of your document between the `<h1>` and `</h1>` tags. Then use higher-numbered tags for progressively lower heading levels. You can go down six levels (`<h6>`, `</h6>`), which is a lot — this whole book uses only three heading levels. If a book that weighs in at 350-plus pages needs only three levels, you have to create something pretty detailed before you need five or six.
`<b>`,`</b>`	Surround text you want to display in bold with these tags.
`<i>`,`</i>`	Surround text you want to display in italics with these tags.
`<p>`,`</p>`	You don't need to place the paragraph-break tag at the end of headings and in some other places, such as within a list, but you do need the tag everywhere else. Besides the anchor tags (`<A></A>`), `<P>` may be the easiest common tag to misuse. The end paragraph tag, `</P>`, is basically optional for beginners.

(continued)

Table 4-1 *(continued)*

Tags	Tag Location
`<hr>`	The horizontal rule tag displays a horizontal line that is good for separating sections of documents.
`<a>,</a>`	The anchor tags define hypertext links and contain hypertext references, somewhat complicated information about where the link goes to. Link text — the text that gets underlined to indicate a hypertext link — goes between the tags. When the user clicks the underlined link text on a Web page, the display changes to show the Web page indicated by the hypertext reference.
`<a href="http://www. aSite.edu">My kid's site.</a>`	The `<a>` and `</a>` tag pair defines an anchor. href indicates a hypertext reference — in this case, a pointer to a Web site's URL. The link text is `My kid's site`; the user sees this text, underlined, as part of the Web page. See the section on anchors near the end of this chapter for details on these and other kinds of hypertext links.
`<img src="budpic.gif">`	The `img` tag brings in an image in a format that the browser understands, either GIF or JPEG, and displays it as part of the Web page. The `src` part of the tag tells the browser where to find the file. In this example, the filename is `budpic.gif` and is in the same directory or folder as the HTML file that the `<img>` tag is in. (You can tell it's in the same directory because the filename doesn't have any pathname information in front of it, such as `/images/budpic.gif`.)

For an example that uses these tags, see the Cheat Sheet. For a list of basic HTML tags, see Appendix C.

Go: Creating a Web Page with HTML

Yes, you are just about ready to create a Web page with HTML. However, the whole secret of using HTML is knowing what tags to use and when. So now that you know what a tag is, what more do you need to know? Well, tags are divided into three kinds:

✔ **Tags that contain meta-information about your document:** *Meta-information,* such as the title in the header section of your document, doesn't affect what shows up within the body of the Web page; instead, this information is used by various Web tools, such as search engines, that look at the title to see what your document is about. (And we never "meta" Web tool we didn't like!)

✔ **Tags that format characters in your text:** These tags (`<b>`, `</b>` and `<i>`, `</i>`, for example) do nothing but modify the way your text looks when the browser displays it.

✔ **Linking tags:** These tags connect the user to different kinds of information and even to other documents. The section "Look back (and forward) in anchor," in this chapter, explains linking tags in detail.

After you create and save an HTML file with text and these different kinds of tags, pat yourself on the back. You've just created a complete HTML document, and you're well on the way to being a tagger yourself! (Not the kind that puts graffiti on buildings, but the kind that expresses himself or herself electronically on the Web.)

Creating a blank file for your HTML

HTML files include only plain text — no hidden formatting codes from your word processing program. And the name of the document always end with `.htm`. So start by creating a text-only file to hold your Web page's text and HTML tags.

To create a blank plain-text document that you can insert HTML code into, follow these steps:

1. **Start your text editor or word processing program.**

2. **Open a new document.**

   Some programs automatically open a new document when you start them. In that case, you can skip this step.

3. **Start the process of saving your document so that you can name it.**

   If you use a word processing program, use the Save As or similar command and choose Text as the type of file.

   Don't choose the Text with Line Breaks option; line breaks make the document harder to edit. The good ol' Text option does the job.

4. **Name the document.**

   Put `.htm` at the end of the name.

5. **Save the document.**

   In most programs, you click a Save button or press Enter.

The steps enable you to create a blank HTML document — which isn't very interesting if you put it on the Web! So now you want to start filling in your document by adding heading information.

Recent versions of Microsoft Word and other word processing programs may try to "help" you in a way that interferes with what you're trying to accomplish. For instance, when you tell Word to save your file as a text file, it automatically changes the suffix to `.txt`. Change it back to `.htm` and save the file normally.

Head users your way to win

First, some bad news: You start your HTML documents with some tags that don't really do much for the appearance of your Web page. In fact, the tags add a few more things to worry about. And you thought that you could finally start getting some real work done!

Now, the good news: These tags make the Web a better place. They contain introductory *meta-information* — descriptive information about your document that doesn't affect how the user sees your document. But although the user doesn't see these tags directly, the tags support search tools and other tools that make finding a Web page — hopefully, finding *your* Web page — so quick and easy that users can get to it straight away. (Of course, looking at a lot of other things in between can be half the fun of using the Web.)

- `<html>`, `</html>`: These tags surround everything in your document and identify the document as being in HTML. As the Web supports more and more different types of files, these tags become increasingly important.

- `<head>`, `</head>`: These tags go around the title of your document and any other information that doesn't appear within the Web page itself. For now, that just means the title.

- `<title>`, `</title>`: These tags go around the title of your document. The title is a short phrase that describes your document and doesn't appear within the body of your Web page. It does appear, however, within the strip at the top of the document window when your Web page is viewed.

- `<body>`, `</body>`: These tags go around everything in your document that isn't part of the head. The `<body>` tag goes just after the `</head>` tag, which goes just after the `</title>` tag.

If you use a tool that creates a Web page for you, such as the free services described in Chapters 2 and 3, or Netscape Composer, described later in this chapter, you don't need to put these introductory tags in because the tool does it for you. However, you may need to add the `<title>` and `</title>` tags, and put the title of your Web page in between them yourself.

Look at this well-mannered, albeit nearly empty, HTML document to see what the top of a Web page looks like:

```
<html>
<head>
<title>A Brief Introduction to Electric Guitars</title>
</head>
<body>
Some introductory information about electric guitars.
</body>
</html>
```

Popular Web tools use these tags. The Advanced Search option of the AltaVista Web-searching service enables users to search specifically by words in the title; just enter the phrase **title:** followed by the text you want to search for in the title. To access the AltaVista search engine, go to www.altavista.com.

Microsoft Internet Explorer and Netscape Navigator use the title of your document — the phrase between the <title> and </title> tags — as the document description in their Favorites or Bookmarks menu. The title also appears in the title bar of the browser window when the page displays.

To give yourself a head start each time you want to begin a new HTML document, create a text-only document in your word processing program or text editor with the head, title, and body tags already in place. When you're ready to begin a new HTML document, start by making a copy of this document.

Follow these steps to create a text-only document that contains the introductory tags:

1. **Open a new document.**

2. **Save your document as a text-only document with the name you want, ending with** .htm.

3. **On the first line of the document, enter the** <html> **tag.**

4. **On the second line of the document, enter the** <head> **tag.**

5. **On the third line of the document, enter the** <title> **and** </title> **tags.**

   Don't enclose anything within the <title> and </title> tags for now. After you copy this text-only document to create an HTML document, you can enter the material that you want to use as the "title."

   When you are deciding what to include between these tags, remember that many Web tools use the information between these tags when searching for documents.

6. **On the fourth line of the document, enter the** </head> **tag.**

7. **On the fifth line of the document, enter the** <body> **tag.**

8. **Leave the sixth line of the document blank.**

   The main content of the document goes here.

9. **On the seventh line of the document, enter the** `</body>` **tag.**

10. **On the eighth line of the document, enter the** `</html>` **tag.**

    Whatever else you do in your document, `</html>` is always the last tag.

11. **Save the document.**

Getting a heading and some body

Underneath the headings, your document needs some content — just plain old words, maybe highlighted with **bold** and *italics* where needed.

Don't overuse the bold and italic tags. Like early desktop publishers, who put *three* different fonts on every **line** of text, HTML novices tend to put **lots of bold** *and italics* in their documents. (The formatting in the previous sentence was meant to be funny, please don't blame the printers!) When you preview your document in your Web browser, look for areas where you overuse bold and italic formatting. And when in doubt, don't use bold and italics. Your Web page's visitors will thank you.

Here's how to put a top-level heading and some basic text into your Web document:

1. **After the** `<body>` **tag, and before the** `</body>` **tag, put in your top-level heading. Surround the heading with the** `<h1>` **and** `</h1>` **tags so that the browser knows that the text is a level-1 heading.**

   You may also use the text of your top-level heading between the `<title>` and `</title>` tags, as many Web publishers do.

2. **After the heading, type some text.**

   For optimal use by Web search tools, the first paragraph in your document should be a brief summary of the document's contents.

3. **At the end of each paragraph, put in a** `<p>` **tag.**

   No matter how many times you press Enter in your document, your dense browser doesn't get the message. It only understands that you want to end a paragraph and start a new one when it sees the `<p>` tag.

4. **Surround text with the** `<b>` **and** `</b>` **tags to make it bold.**

   Don't overdo the use of the `<b>` and `</b>` tags! Starting out, use bold once or twice just to get a feel for it.

5. **Surround text with the** `<i>` **and** `</i>` **tags to make it italic.**

   Don't overdo italicizing, either! Use italics a few times in your first document or two for practice.

6. Try adding a horizontal rule.

Add the <hr> tag in one or two places to create horizontal rules. (Not to start an argument with those who think that vertical or diagonal rules.)

As with headings and other elements of your document, put the <hr> tag on a line by itself so that you can find it easily later to move or remove it.

7. After you're done, check your tags.

Be sure paragraphs end with a <p> tag to start the next paragraph, all <b> tags have a matching </b> tag, and all <i> tags have a matching </i> tag.

The most effective way for many of us to check tags, believe it or not, is to print out the document and then cross out pairs of tags with a pencil. In the old days, computer programmers called this kind of exercise "desk-checking."

8. Save your document.

If you use a word processing program rather than a text editor, be sure to save your document as text-only, with .htm as the end of the filename.

The Cheat Sheet at the front of this book shows a simple sample Web page.

Adding a little list

One of the best ways to "break up" your Web page is to insert lists. HTML supports bulleted lists, numbered lists, and lists of definitions or descriptions. Although HTML makes creating lists easy, it doesn't give you direct control over how lists look. (Repeat after me, "Trust your browser, trust your browser. . . .")

- **Unnumbered lists (often called bulleted lists):** Unnumbered lists display as lists with bullets next to them and are "appropriately" indented (the indentation varies with different browsers and browser settings). The list you're reading now is a bulleted list, but it uses check marks in place of the bullets.

- **Ordered lists (often called numbered lists):** These lists are similar to bulleted lists, but with — you guessed it — numbers in place of the bullets. You can rearrange the items in the numbered list as much as you like. The browser automatically keeps things in order by putting in the right numbers when it displays the list.

- **Definition lists:** These lists usually alternate terms and their — duh — definitions. The term goes where the bullet goes in a bulleted list, and the definition goes next to it or on the line immediately below.

You create all lists in basically the same way: You start the list with a beginning tag, such as ⟨ul⟩ for an unnumbered list. You then tag each item separately to let the browser know that it's a separate item. You use the tag ⟨li⟩ at the beginning of each item in both unnumbered and numbered lists; you don't use an end tag for individual list items. The list finally ends with a closing tag — ⟨/ul⟩ to end an unnumbered list, for example.

The formatting in HTML lists often looks different than how you want it to look. For instance, many browsers display a bulleted HTML list with a blank line before the list items, but no blank lines between them. You can't change this formatting with standard HTML commands — and trying to change it by using tricky HTML is a very difficult process. Better to get used to the way HTML displays lists.

The following steps show you how to create an unnumbered (bulleted) or ordered (numbered) list:

1. **Put in a tag to start the list: ⟨ul⟩ for an unnumbered list, ⟨ol⟩ for an ordered list.**

2. **Put in an ⟨li⟩ tag to indicate a list item.**

3. **Starting on the same line, enter the text for the list item.**

   "Red Hot Chili Pepper Potato Chips" is a good way to start.

4. **For the remaining items in the list, enter the ⟨li⟩ tag followed by the item text. Press Enter at the end of each line to visually separate the items on-screen as you edit.**

   You don't need to use an end tag for list items. Also remember that hitting Enter at the end of a line causes the cursor to move to a new line on-screen but doesn't cause line breaks in the HTML-tagged text; the browser starts a new line when it sees a new ⟨li⟩ tag or a ⟨/ul⟩ tag. The ⟨li⟩ tag is one of those rare tags that doesn't come as part of a pair.

5. **Enter a tag to end the list — ⟨/ul⟩ to end an unnumbered list or ⟨/ol⟩ to end an ordered list.**

To create a definition list, follow these steps:

1. **Enter the ⟨dl⟩ tag to start the definition list.**

2. **Enter the ⟨dt⟩ tag to indicate a definition term.**

3. **Enter the text for the definition term.**

4. **Enter the ⟨dd⟩ tag to indicate definition data — the description of the definition term.**

5. **Enter the text for the definition data.**

6. **For the remaining items in the list, enter the <dt> tag followed by the definition term and then enter the <dd> tag followed by the description of the term. Press Enter at the end of each line to visually separate the items on-screen as you edit.**

As with other list items, you don't need to enter an end tag for definition terms or definition data.

7. **Enter the </dl> tag to end the list.**

Figure 4-3 shows an example that includes the three kinds of lists. Because people use the Web to find out new things and to look things up, lists are among the most important formatting elements in HTML.

Looking back (and forward) in anchor

Remember that HTML stands for HyperText Markup Language? Well, applying all those tags is the markup part. Now hang on to your hat: Here's everything you need to know about the hypertext part. In this section, we demonstrate how to use hypertext to create links between information in your document and information in other documents. This stuff is a bit confusing at first, but after you understand it, you'll think of many exciting ways to use hypertext in your Web pages.

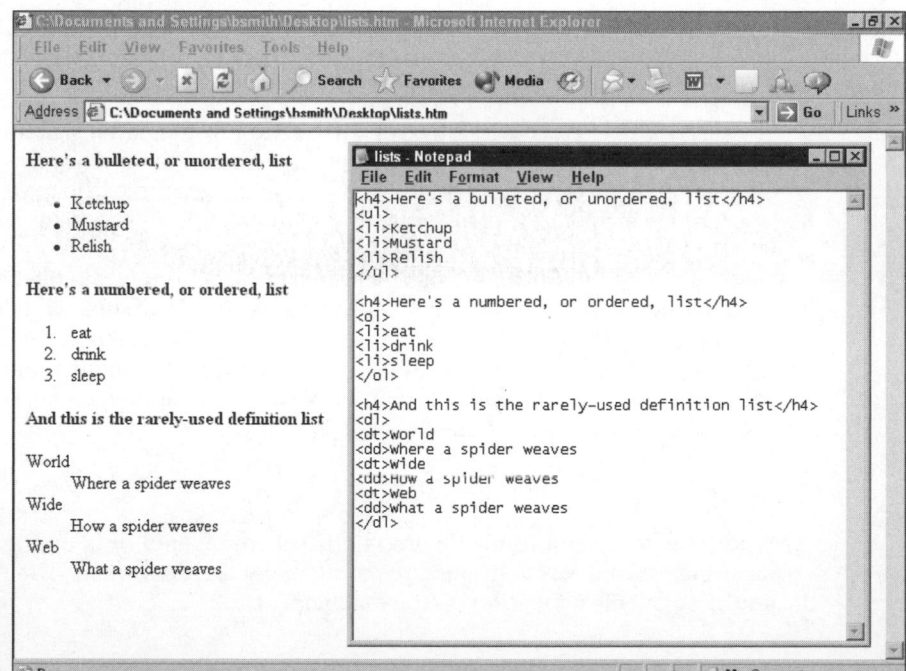

Figure 4-3: Using lists in your Web page.

In HTML, every hypertext link has two ends, which are called *anchors*. (Some people think that putting anchors into a Web page makes them anchorpersons — but sorry, no seven-figure salary.)

When you define an anchor, you use tags to specify two things:

- ✔ The text or image that is highlighted as the place you click to follow the link
- ✔ The other anchor that you want to go to when you click the link

Anchors are among the most complicated tags in basic HTML. But you don't want to say "Anchors away," as the old movie had it, because anchors expand the possibilities of your Web page tremendously. The following is an example of an anchor:

```
<a href="http://www.listentoyourdog.com">How to train
        dogs</a>
```

Here are the parts of an anchor:

- ✔ `<a>`, `</a>`: These tags go around text that you want highlighted as a hypertext link (`How to train dogs` in the preceding example). Try to use text that represents the thing that you want to link to, such as "Adobe Corporation" or "my résumé." The better this text describes the thing that you link to, the more helpful the text is to the user.
- ✔ `href`: This information falls within the `<a>` tag. When the user clicks the hypertext link, the browser brings up the Web location indicated by the pathname that appears after `href`.
- ✔ **Hypertext reference:** These characters follow the equal sign in the `href` part of the anchor and are enclosed in quote symbols. They are the pathname of the document that you link to. In the example, the hypertext reference is the name of a Web site: `"http://www.listentoyourdog.com"`.

When you post an HTML file on a server, some anchors in the file can point to Web documents on the same Web server as the HTML file, while other anchors point to Web documents on other Web servers. When the document is on another server, the anchor contains the document's full URL, in the same form as you type it in your browser. For example, an anchor pointing to the For Dummies Web site looks like this:

```
<a href="http://www.dummies.com">"For Dummies"</a>
```

When the document that's pointed to by the initial anchor is on the same machine, the anchor contains the pathname of the document. The pathname specifies the file's location on the machine.

For simple Web sites that you create, put all the documents in the same directory or folder so that you have simpler anchors. Then you don't have to worry about pathnames!

The pathname looks different depending on where the second document is in relation to the HTML document that contains the link. If the two documents are in the same directory or folder, the pathname is simply the filename. But if the second document is in a different directory, you can use two methods to specify how to reach it: absolute addressing and relative addressing. In *absolute addressing,* you use the path from the lowest-level, or *root,* directory of the server to the second document. In *relative addressing,* you start with the location of the HTML file that's currently being viewed. You then use the path from the HTML file to the second document.

To specify an absolute address, start with a forward slash (/) to indicate the root directory of the Web server. Then specify the full pathname from the root directory to the file. The following example shows an absolute address:

```
/photoshp/samples/sunrise.gif
```

To specify a relative address, start with the directory of the HTML document that the anchor is in and then enter the path that leads to the desired file from there. A pair of dots (..) specifies the directory one level above the current one.

For example, if you have an HTML file called `sunset.htm` in the directory `/mysite/html`, and you need a GIF graphics file that is in `/mysite/html/pix`, a subdirectory of the current directory, the relative address is the following:

```
pix/sunset.gif
```

If you also need a file that is in `/mysite/trial/pix`, you use the .. characters to specify the subdirectory above this one and then go back down the directory tree to the needed file. Put a slash after the dots. In this case, the relative address is as follows:

```
../trial/pix/moonrise.gif
```

Starting at the beginning of the path, ".." means "the directory above the current one." The words separated by slashes, "/trial/pix/," are the names of the directory and subdirectory in which the file is stored. And "moonrise.gif" is the filename.

Usually, you create your Web site on one machine, and then publish it by copying the files to another machine, the Web server. Forgetting to copy all the files needed to the Web server is very easy. If you keep all the files in one overall folder — that doesn't have any files in it that aren't part of the Web site — you have a fighting chance of making the transfer successfully.

Table 4-2 shows examples of anchors.

Table 4-2	Examples of Hypertext Links (Anchors)
Destination	**Sample Anchor**
Web page on same server, same directory	`<a href="mydoc2.html">link text</A>`
Web page on same server, different directory; relative addressing	`<a href="personal/resume"> link text</A>`
Web page on same server, different directory; absolute addressing	`<a href="/maya/personal/ resume">link text</A>`
Web page on a different server	`<a href="http://www.mycorp .com/job requirements"> link text</A>`

The simplest way to handle addressing, and the one least likely to cause errors, is to put all documents in the same directory or folder. The next simplest way — best used for more complex Web pages or Web sites — is to use relative addressing. Relative addressing allows others to easily bundle up all the files needed for your Web pages and move them around on a Web server. Absolute addressing is the most error-prone.

Quotes and the space race

One question about HTML that gets asked a lot is about quotes: When do you need to put quotes around information in HTML?

There are three answers to this: What you are *supposed* to do, what you *can* do, and what you *should* do.

You're *supposed* to put quotes around every *argument* you provide in HTML — that is, any data you enter in HTML code, such as a filename or a number. But things work fine if you follow a different strategy.

What you *can* do is only use quotes when a space is in the data, such as a space in a filename. With this approach, you never need to put quotes around numbers, for instance, because they never have spaces around them.

But what you *should* do is get in the habit of always putting quotes around arguments, such as filenames, that sometimes have spaces in them and sometimes don't. That way you're not caught out by a problem when you use a filename with a space in it.

(Using short filenames with no spaces is always a good idea, just in case.)

Linking for yourself

Absorbing all this knowledge about hypertext links is pretty useless if you don't actually use the knowledge yourself. Here's a description of how to create a link; note how we cleverly work several different types of links into the steps:

1. **Open an existing HTML document.**

2. **Move to the place in the document where you want to insert a link.**

3. **Start the link by entering the opening tag, including the hypertext reference that you want the link to lead to.**

   For a link to a Web page in the same directory, enter the filename in quotation marks, as in `<a href="anotherdoc.htm"></a>` ("anotherdoc.htm" is the filename).

   As described previously in this chapter, you can enter a relative or absolute address for a document that's in a different directory within your Web site.

   For a link to a file in the graphics subdirectory of the current directory, enter the pathname: `<a href="graphics/dancers.gif">Dancers</a>`.

   For a document that's on a different server, enter the document's URL (for example, `<a href="http://www.ACoolSite.com"></a>`).

   If you don't enter a specific filename, the browser looks for the default file: `index.htm` or `index.html`.

4. **After the opening tag, enter the link text.**

5. **Don't forget the closing tag!**

   After the opening tag and the link text, enter the closing tag.

Linking from within

That's a lot of stuff to absorb! Just one more thing to consider: What if you want to link to a specific spot *within* the same Web page?

To link to a specific spot, you need a pair of anchors. The first is at the spot from which you want to link, just like we describe in the previous section. This first anchor is just like the external links, but it has one more element — the name of a second anchor that's at the spot to which you want to link. You have to put the second anchor into the Web page you're linking to, at the spot where you want the link to go. For example, the following anchor links to a spot that's named "Bebak," within the same file as the first anchor:

```
<a href="#Bebak">Bud's coauthor</az>
```

The pound sign, #, denotes an anchor within a Web page. The second anchor, also called the link, is at the spot to which you want to link. The second anchor exists only to specify that spot and doesn't cause the link text to show up as underlined on the user's screen. Here's the link for the second anchor:

```
<a name="Bebak"></a>Arthur Bebak<p>
```

The link doesn't need a pathname, but the anchor that links to it needs a pathname if the anchor and link are in different files. And you don't need any text between the anchor's beginning and ending.

Try using internal links in an HTML document on your own machine, and test the links in your browser. Experiment with different kinds of relative addresses, or pathnames. Trying different links and pathnames gives you the experience you need to easily use these features in your "real" Web pages.

Linking to specific spots in your own Web page is common. Many Web sites have long Web pages that include clever internal links that move the user around in the page. Linking to specific spots in other people's Web pages is less common. Why? Because controlling where the other page's author chooses to put link anchors is hard — and harder still to make sure that link anchors don't get moved around on you unexpectedly, rendering your anchor invalid. How would you like it if, for example, you defined a link to a serious essay on home wine making and later discovered that the essay had been replaced by a discussion of Greek philosophy? (Though much of the latter may have been inspired by consumption of the results of the former.) Sheesh!

Browsing your own Weblet

Here's the moment you've been waiting for: Whether you've followed all the previous steps, or just some, you now have a ready-to-use little HTML document. To see whether you did it right, all you have to do is try it in your Web browser. That's right — you can view your very own HTML document in your very own browser!

Can your browser handle it?

An anchor can link the current document to another HTML file or to some other type of file, such as a graphic, a sound, a video clip, or almost anything else. Most browsers know how to handle HTML files and GIF or JPEG graphics files automatically. Different browsers may handle other types of files in different ways — automatically, or by the user's specifying a program to handle them. So for these examples, we stick with links to HTML files and GIF and JPEG files because we know that those files work with just about any browser.

Not only can you view your HTML document from your browser, but you can even follow the links to other HTML documents on your local system and from your system out onto the Web. (We assume that your browser is connected to the Web at the time. If not, following a hypertext link to a Web URL is a short trip!) Using the Back command in your browser, you can even return to your own document.

There's only one limitation to this testing: Other Web sites can't link to your HTML document because it's only saved on your local machine, not on a Web server. And that's the one thing that's stopping your HTML document from being a Web page: It's not hosted on a Web server. Details, details — we take care of that little omission in Chapter 12.

For now, you need to figure out how to view your HTML document in your browser. This is something you do every time you work on HTML documents. Start a document; view it in your browser. Change the document; view it in your browser. And on and on . . . (Maybe it's finally time to buy that 20-inch computer monitor you've been thinking about so that you can see both documents at once as you switch back and forth.)

To view your HTML document in your browser:

1. **Start your browser.**

2. **Choose File⇨Open File (for Netscape) or File⇨Open (for Internet Explorer). In the Open dialog box that appears, click Browse.**

3. **Find your HTML document on your hard disk and open it.**

4. **View your own HTML document in your own Web browser.**

   You can even follow links by clicking them. Use the Back command in your browser to return to your HTML document.

5. **Look for problems in your HTML document or things you want to add.**

   So half of your document is in *italics* and the rest <u>is underlined as if it's all part of a link</u>. Who cares?! Go fix it!

6. **Open the HTML document in your text editor or word processing program and fix it.**

   You don't need to close your browser to work on the HTML document. Note that the earlier sections of this chapter may be of some help here.

7. **Save the changed HTML document.**

   If you forget to save the document, your changes don't show up in your browser, and you wonder whether your changes "took" or whether you're losing your sanity.

8. **Use the Refresh command or a similar command in your Web browser to reload the fixed HTML document.**

If you forget to reload the document, your changes don't show up in your browser, and, again, you wonder whether your changes "took" or whether you're losing your sanity.

If you forget to save the document after you make changes, or forget to reload the document in your browser, the changes you just made don't show up. Anytime you think that this may have happened, just go back to your text editor or word processing program, save the document, return to your Web browser, and reload. The changes appear.

9. Repeat Steps 5 through 8 until you're done.

(*Done* can mean until the HTML document is done, as in finished, or until the HTML document's author is done, as in toast!)

Don't forget to use the Refresh command when you're done modifying your document and want to look at it again in the browser.

Looking to the next HTML steps

The parts of HTML that we cover in this chapter represent just the basics. As you create, test, and deploy your own Web pages, you may want to understand more about HTML.

If you use Netscape Composer, which we describe in Chapter 5, or an online Web page service such as the ones we describe in Chapters 2 and 3, you may be protected from the gory details of HTML. But you never know when you may end up back in "raw" HTML to add a feature or fix a problem. You can find lists of HTML tags on the Web at sources such as www.w3.org. And don't forget that *HTML 4 For Dummies,* 4th Edition, by Ed Tittel et al (Wiley) is an excellent source for more detail on HTML.

Advances in HTML

Since the Web first became widely (and wildly) popular in the mid-1990s, several advances in HTML have taken place. These advances build on the solid base of the original HTML specification and add new capabilities. However, they also make HTML much more complicated and add many more issues for those who design Web pages.

The biggest changes are the additions of tables, frames, and Dynamic HTML. Tables not only display information in table form, but also are widely used to help precisely position text and graphics. Frames allow a Web page to be divided into independently controlled sections. They are somewhat widely used, but not as popular as tables.

We describe how and when to use tables and frames in Chapter 11. However, you can go far with the basic HTML specification that is usable by all browsers, so we stick with that version throughout most of this book.

Part II
Building Pages

The 5th Wave — By Rich Tennant

"It's a site devoted to the 'Limp Korn Chilies' rock group. It has videos of all their performances in concert halls, hotel rooms, and airport terminals."

In this part . . .

It's time to tackle a couple of tools that let you do anything you want with your Web pages. Learn how to enrich your page with formatting and links. And now, META tags are an arcane art no longer. Help Web searchers find your pages!

Chapter 5

Choosing Your Tools

ou can use online tools, such as those we discuss in Chapters 2 and 3, to create your initial Web page using a template. However, at some point, you will want to go further with your Web page than a template allows. To go beyond templates, you have to move away from the online tools and create your own Web page on your own hard disk. Then you can upload tried-and-tested Web pages to any number of different Web hosts, including Yahoo! GeoCities and AOL.

This chapter describes how to create your initial Web page locally, on your own hard disk. The next few chapters describe how to improve your Web page and how to extend your Web page into a multi-page Web site. Chapter 12 tells you how to publish one or more Web pages that are on your own machine onto the Web.

This chapter helps you choose the approach you want to use and then shows you how to create your initial Web page.

Yahoo! GeoCities and AOL each have advanced tools that let you go pretty far with your Web page. However, these tools lock you into having your hosting done on the service that provides them. If you feel comfortable keeping your Web page on the same host for a long time to come, you may want to continue using these advanced tools. The approach we describe in this book, however, gives you more opportunities to keep costs low and flexibility high.

Choosing Between WYSIWYG and Plain Text

You can use a couple different approaches to create and edit Web pages on your own computer. One approach is to use a WYSIWYG Web page editor. WYSIWYG is pronounced "whizzywig," and stands for What You See Is What You Get. A WYSIWYG Web page editor is like a word processing program — what you see on-screen is at least close to what you get when you publish your Web page and look at it online.

The problem with this is that WYSIWYG doesn't work perfectly on the Web. As we describe in Chapter 4, different Web browsers can interpret the same HTML tags differently. Also, users can have different browser settings, which means the same page can take on a different look for different users. This variability undermines your efforts to make your Web page look just so. To work around these problems, and to create Web pages that work well on the widest possible range of different kinds of computers and different browser versions and settings, knowing what's going on with the underlying HTML really helps.

For this reason, many Web page publishers work directly with HTML tags. Others work with a WYSIWYG editor, but frequently check what the underlying HTML-tagged text — usually just called "the HTML" — looks like.

We recommend that you either work directly in HTML or use a simple WYSIWYG tool that doesn't try to do too much for you, and look frequently at the underlying HTML. If you do want to use a tool, we recommend Netscape Composer.

Pluses and minuses of text editors

The reasons in favor of editing HTML directly in a text editor are fairly simple. You work directly in HTML — never anything else. You're always looking directly at the HTML tags. Any time you want to add a feature to your Web page, you're forced to learn the HTML tags for that feature and use them, which means you're gradually learning the underlying language of Web pages.

The reasons not to work directly in HTML using a text editor are fairly simple as well. Imagining what your Web page is going to look like is quite difficult when you're just looking at text and tags. You can easily make mistakes in the construction of your Web page when you're working directly with the tags — and easily get lost in looking at the HTML-tagged text when you're trying to remember where to make an addition or change.

Figure 5-1 shows a simple Web page as it appears when being edited in a text editor and the Netscape Composer editing window. You may be able to tell just from looking at the picture which kind of environment you prefer to work in. If not, try both, using the instructions in this chapter, and see which one you prefer.

Pluses and minuses of Netscape Composer

Using a WYSIWYG editor such as Netscape Composer has its trade-offs too. WYSIWYG editors shield you from the underlying HTML, so you can see what your page is likely to look like on the Web. But the underlying HTML tags are hidden from you, so you don't know exactly what's going on. The more capable WYSIWYG editors support newer, more advanced HTML functionality as well — which is good if you want to use those functions, but makes creating Web pages that don't work well on all Web browsers all too easy.

Netscape Composer has most of the advantages of an HTML tool, with few of the disadvantages. Here are its six key advantages as an HTML tool:

✔ **Netscape Composer is free.** Netscape makes Composer available for free along with Netscape Navigator, the first widely popular browser for the Web.

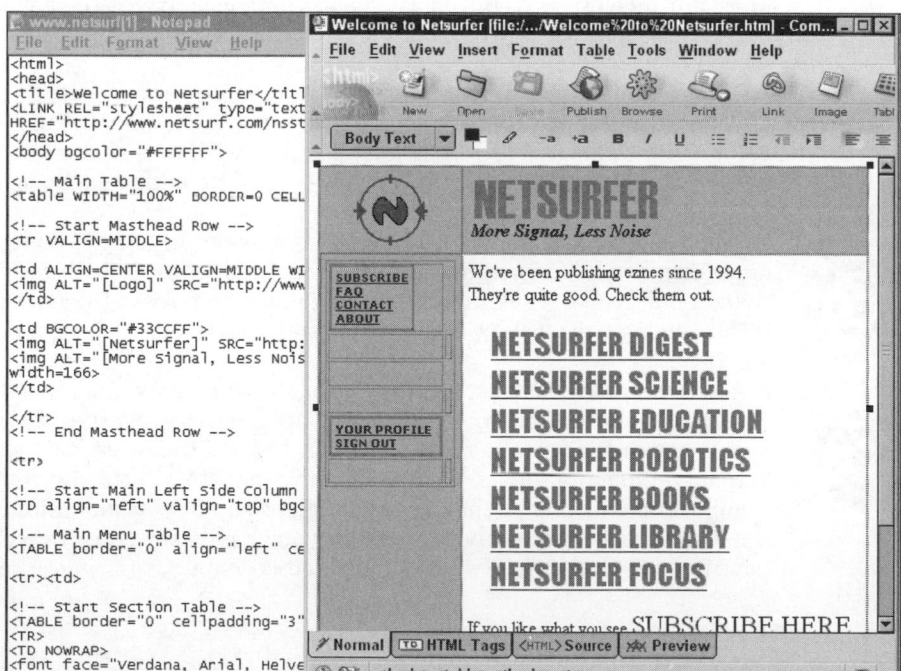

Figure 5-1: You can compose in a text editor or Composer.

✔ **It's easy.** Netscape Composer is very easy to use. It leaves out some complex editing functions in favor of drop-dead simplicity.

✔ **Its functions match HTML tags.** The functions available in Composer are the functions available in HTML — and only those functions. So you don't try to do things in your Web page that aren't supported by Web browsers.

✔ **It uses "generic" HTML.** The only functions available in Composer are those supported by all widely used versions of HTML. Web pages that you create with Composer are likely usable by all major Web browsers.

✔ **It lets you see and edit HTML.** Netscape Composer gives you one-click access to the HTML tags underlying your Web page. You get ease of editing in WYSIWYG mode but can still always see and edit the underlying HTML-tagged text.

✔ **It's part of Netscape Navigator.** Composer comes with Netscape's browser, the second-most-popular browser for the Web. You need to have the Netscape browser, along with Internet Explorer, available on your system anyway for testing your Web pages before you publish them. Because you need the Netscape browser anyway, it's convenient that Composer comes with the Netscape browser.

These features of Netscape Composer place it comfortably between using a text editor and working directly with HTML tags, which can be frustrating and lead you to make mistakes in the look and layout of your page, or the more advanced HTML editors, such as FrontPage and Dreamweaver, which may overwhelm you with functionality.

So we recommend that most beginning Web publishers use Composer, and check the underlying HTML frequently to see what's really going on. As you get more knowledgeable with HTML, you may wish to buy and use a more advanced HTML editor — or go the low-tech route and use a basic text editor.

We recommend that you consider using Composer initially even if you own a more advanced HTML editor such as Dreamweaver or FrontPage. The functionality of Composer is simpler, making it easier to learn the core features of HTML, and you can follow along better with this book.

If you already have Netscape software installed, you may already have Netscape Composer on your computer. Check Start⇨Programs⇨Netscape 7.1⇨ Composer, or similar folder and filenames, to see if the Netscape browser, with or without Composer, is installed on your system. If so, check to see if Composer is available, either as a separate program or as an option within the Netscape browser. If Composer is there, you can run the software you already have or upgrade using the instructions in this chapter.

What if you use AOL or Compuserve?

AOL and CompuServe each have built-in Web browsers that run within the program, somewhat muddying the distinction between the online service itself and the open Web that anyone can access.

It used to be that if you ran AOL, you could only use the Web browser built into the program. However, with recent versions of AOL software, you can run a regular Web browser alongside the AOL client software. (You've been able to do this for years with CompuServe.) We recommend that you do use a "real" Web browser alongside the AOL or CompuServe client software.

Simply install the latest versions of Internet Explorer and Netscape software. (This chapter describes how to install Netscape software; for general instructions about installing Internet Explorer, see the sidebar "What if you need IE?" later in this chapter.)

Start your AOL or CompuServe software and connect to the Internet. Then start your Web browser. (You can even start one browser, then the other; recent versions of IE and Navigator can both run at the same time.) The following figure shows AOL and Internet Explorer running at the same time. Use your Web browser to look at Web sites, including for testing your own Web site under development. And use Netscape Composer to create Web pages.

You can also test the Web page(s) you're developing in the built-in AOL or CompuServe browser to make sure you don't have problems. However, testing with AOL or CompuServe is less important than testing in the IE or Navigator browsers, which are more widely used.

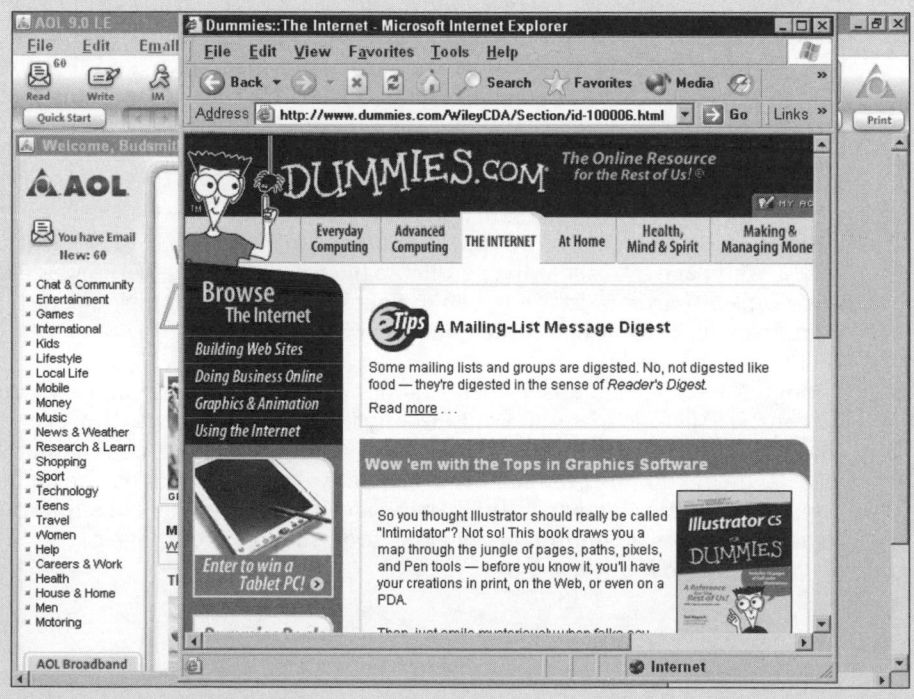

Working with Netscape Composer

Netscape Composer has all the important basic features that you need to build basic Web pages. Using these features, you can

- ✔ Create and edit Web pages without seeing HTML tags.

- ✔ Drag and drop links to other Web locations without typing the URL or pathname.

- ✔ Cut and paste graphics into your Web page, resize graphics, and add alternate text.

- ✔ Create and edit tables.

- ✔ Create and edit *forms* — interactive data entry fields commonly found on Web pages.

You can also insert multimedia files and computer programs into your Web page. However, not all users can play back those files or run those programs because they may not have the appropriate browser or the right plug-ins installed. If you add advanced elements, such as multimedia files or computer programs, into your Web page, be prepared to test your pages with several different browsers and to tell your Web visitors what to expect.

Netscape Composer supports forms, but it can't give you the CGI scripts, also known as CGIs — short for Common Gateway Interface scripts — that you need to make the forms work. These CGI scripts process the data that the user enters into a form; if you can create CGI scripts, you're probably ready for a more advanced tool than Netscape Composer. However, if you don't want to mess with creating these scripts, you can get CGIs from others on the Web.

Netscape Composer doesn't support *frames* — advanced HTML elements that split a Web page into separate, scrollable pieces. Designing Web pages that work well with frames isn't easy, so it makes some sense that Netscape Composer, as a free tool, doesn't support frames.

Though Netscape Composer doesn't support frames, it does enable you to add any HTML tags that you want directly into your Web page. However, the whole point of using a tool is to reduce the amount of HTML coding that you have to do; if you find yourself coding directly in HTML to avoid the limitations of Netscape Composer, such as the aforementioned lack of support for frames, consider buying a more capable tool, such as FrontPage or Macromedia Dreamweaver.

What to call Netscape software

If you're considering using Netscape's software — which has been known by many names over the years — you might want to know a bit about the history of this famous company. Netscape was launched by Jim Clark, who brought a small fortune from his co-founding of Silicon Graphics, and Marc Andreesen, a leader of the team that created Mosaic, the first popular Web browser. Netscape brought out a new browser, Netscape Navigator, which quickly replaced Mosaic as the best way to surf the Net.

Netscape Navigator was wildly popular for several years, until Microsoft brought out Internet Explorer. The first versions of Internet Explorer — "IE" for short — were not very good, but gradually, Microsoft's software caught up. Microsoft also got advantageous distribution deals for IE from many computer manufacturers, and got a version of IE built into America Online's software as well.

Netscape expanded Navigator into a suite of related applications (such as e-mail, an address book, and a calendar) and named the suite Netscape Communicator. The last version of the Communicator suite was Netscape Communicator 4.7. Communicator remained popular for a while, but Internet Explorer gradually gained market share.

Now Internet Explorer is the most-used browser with over 90 percent of the market, and Netscape has most of the remainder. Netscape was purchased by America Online, but it remains a separate company within AOL.

Now Netscape calls its software "Netscape," followed by the version number — the current version is Netscape 7.1. The Netscape software includes all the functions of the old Netscape Communicator, except for the calendar, but you can pick and choose which pieces you want. The Netscape browser remains the core of the package, and at this writing Netscape Composer — the program we recommend for Web authoring — always downloads with the browser.

When you hear someone talk about "Netscape," "Navigator," "Communicator," or "Netscape 7.1," they're usually talking about the same thing: Netscape's browser software, with or without add-on tools.

Where Netscape 7.1 runs

At this writing, the current version of Netscape software is called Netscape 7.1. (See the sidebar "What to call Netscape software" for details.) You can choose which parts of the suite to download; you can get all the pieces that used to be in the Netscape Communicator suite, such as the e-mail application, or just the browser (including Composer), or any mix you want. For more about Netscape 7.1, go to the Netscape Browser Central page at `channels.netscape.com/ns/browsers/`, shown in Figure 5-2.

In this chapter, we tell you how to get the basics that you need for Web authoring: the Netscape 7.1 browser and Composer. You can download more pieces of the suite if you choose. Follow the instructions in the next section.

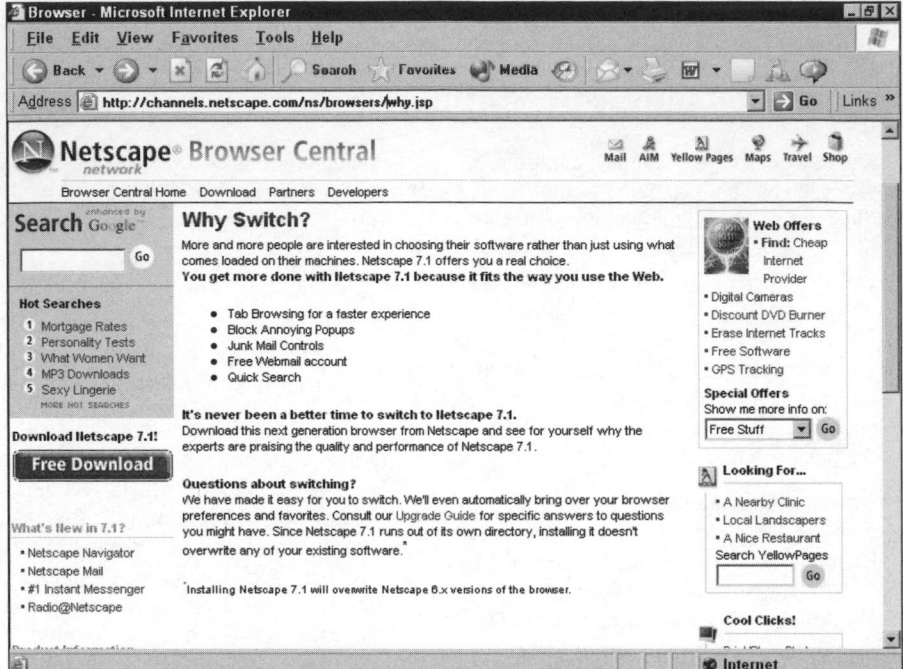

Figure 5-2:
Find out
about
Netscape's
benefits.

In order to run Netscape 7, you need one of the following system setups:

✔ **Windows:** You can run Netscape 7.1 on Windows 98 or any later version of Windows — Windows 98 SE, Windows ME, Windows NT 4.0, Windows 2000, or Windows XP. You need a 233 MHz or faster Pentium, 64MB of RAM, and 52MB of free hard disk space. (You can actually run Netscape 7.1 on a somewhat lesser system configuration — as long as you have, or can clear off, enough hard disk space to install the parts of Netscape 7.1 that you download — but performance does suffer.)

✔ **Macintosh:** For the Mac you need a fairly recent version of the operating system: Mac OS X 10.1.*x* or Mac OS X 10.2.*x* or later. Hardware requirements are similar to those for the PC: A 266 MHz or faster PowerPC 604e, G3, or G4 chip, 64MB of RAM, and 72MB of hard disk space.

✔ **Linux:** Netscape 7.1 runs on Linux on Intel-architecture machines (usually called PCs). You need Red Hat Linux 7.0 or later — or the Linux kernel 2.2.14 with #glivc 2.2.4, gtk+ 1.2.0 (1.2.5 or greater preferred), and XFree86-3.3.6. Hardware requirements are the same as for Netscape running on Windows — a 233 MHz or faster Pentium, 64MB of RAM, and 52MB of free hard disk space. As with Windows, you may be able to get by with a slower Pentium or less RAM, but performance is slow.

If you have a UNIX workstation (not using an Intel microprocessor and Red Hat Linux), or a PC or Mac that doesn't meet the requirements, you can probably get an earlier version of Netscape software that meets your needs. Find the older software at `wp.netscape.com/browsers/4/index.html`.

If you need to use an older version of Netscape software, follow the on-screen instructions for installation. They are similar to the instructions for installing Netscape 7.1, but not exactly the same.

Getting Netscape Composer

You may already have Netscape Composer, Netscape's free Web authoring software, on your system. You may have the old Communicator suite, which includes the Netscape Navigator Web browser plus an e-mail package, AOL-compatible Instant Messenger functionality, an address book, and other software. Or you may just have the stand-alone Netscape Navigator browser without the other parts of the Communicator package. In either case, you probably want to upgrade to the current version of the software, which at this writing is called Netscape 7.1.

The instructions in this section tell you how to get the newest version of Netscape software (including Composer) only, not the remaining pieces of what used to be called the Netscape Communicator suite. That's because getting Navigator only makes the download quicker and means you have a simpler software package that takes up less hard disk space. We show you where to click a different button if you want the other parts of the suite as well.

Be sure to upgrade your software if you have Netscape Composer or Netscape Navigator Version 6.0. Netscape 6.0 was widely disparaged as buggy, slow-loading software. Later versions, such as 6.1 and 6.2, don't have the same problems.

If you're in a networked business, organizational, or school environment, check to see if your company, organization, or school has a preconfigured, approved version of Netscape software available for you to install. Doing so saves you configuration hassles that you might otherwise have relating to the interaction of Netscape software and the network.

Download procedures for Netscape software may change due to changes in the Netscape Web site. If the following steps don't match what you see on-screen, check for updates on the Web page for this book at

`www.creating-web-pages.com.`

Follow these steps to get the current version of Netscape Navigator:

1. **Go to the Netscape Web site at** www.netscape.com.

   The Netscape Web site appears — slowly, if you're not on a fast connection, because it's a complicated page with many small graphics. This site is the default home page for the Netscape Navigator browser. And this is just the beginning — as we'll describe in a later step, the complete download takes over an hour on a modem-based connection.

2. **On the Netscape home page, click the <u>Netscape 7.1</u> link in the Tools area on the left-hand side of the window.**

   The Browser Central page appears.

3. **Click the Free Download button.**

   The Download page appears, as shown in Figure 5-3.

4. **Click the Download Now button.**

   The File Download dialog box appears.

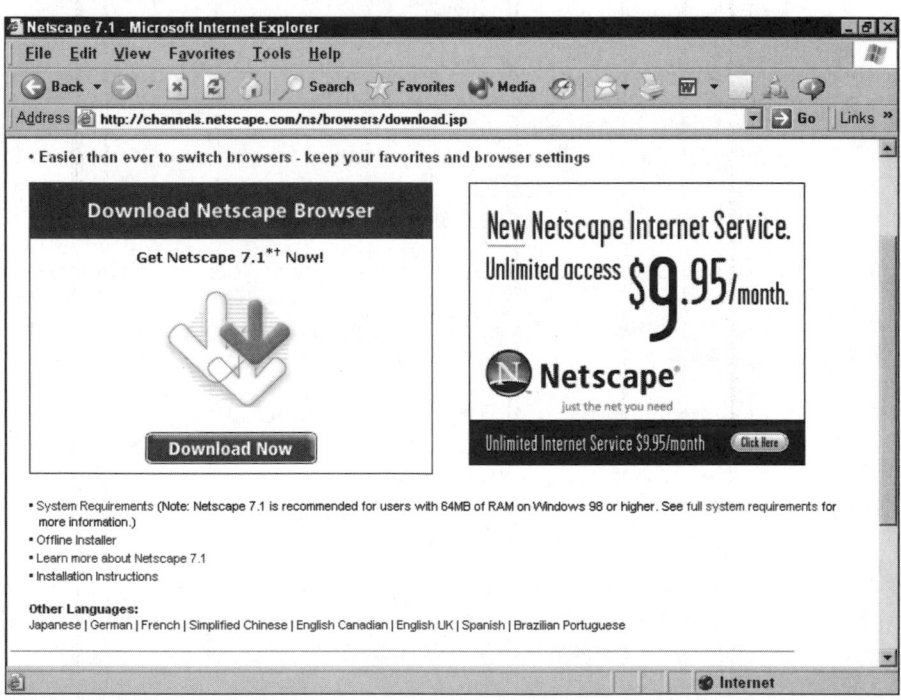

Figure 5-3:
Get ready to download Netscape software.

5. **Click Open.**

   Missing this button is easy, because the default option for the File Download dialog box is Save, which saves the program to disk. If you keep this option, you go through an unnecessary step of erasing the installation program.

   The installer program downloads into a temporary folder, which takes about a minute over a modem connection, and then the Netscape 7.1 Setup Welcome dialog box appears.

6. **Click Next.**

   The license agreement appears.

7. **Click Accept to accept the license agreement.**

   The Setup Type dialog box appears.

8. **Choose Custom and then click Next.**

   The Select Typical Components dialog box appears, as shown in Figure 5-4.

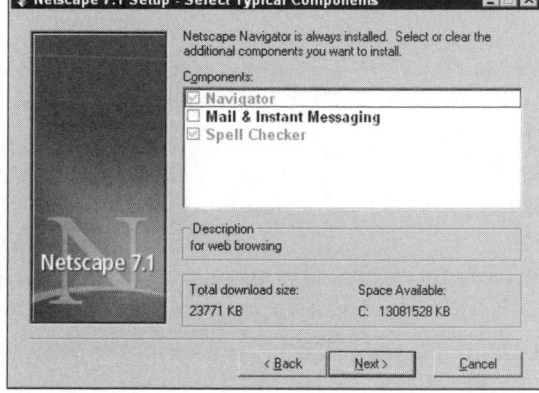

Figure 5-4:
Just get
Navigator
and the
spell
checker.

9. **Clear the Mail and Instant Messenger check boxes, unless you need these programs for reasons other than Web page authoring. Click Next.**

   The Mail program and Instant Messaging option adds about 2.5MB to your download size and hard disk requirements.

   The Select Additional Components dialog box appears, as shown in Figure 5-5.

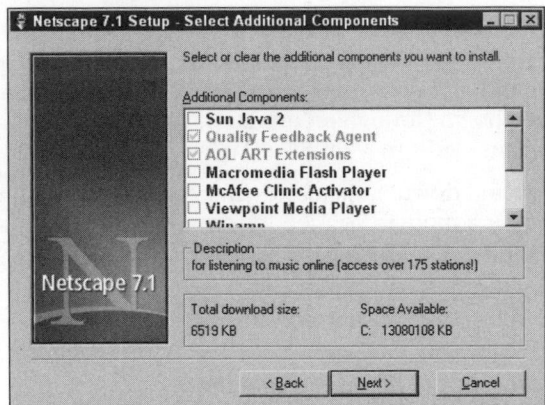

Figure 5-5:
Clear most
or all of the
Additional
Components.

We recommend that you don't download additional components unless you are sure you need them for Web sites you plan to visit using Netscape Navigator, or unless you plan to add the relevant media type to your own Web site and therefore need the component for testing. The additional components are

- **Sun Java 2 (9.9MB):** Fewer and fewer Web sites use Java, partly because it's prone to security problems. So unless you plan to use Java in your own Web site, and therefore need the component for testing, don't add nearly 10MB to your Netscape download.

- **Macromedia Flash Player (420K):** Some sites do use Flash, so you may want to keep this relatively small player. (This download doesn't help you create Flash animations; go to the Macromedia Web site at www.macromedia.com for tools to do that.)

- **McAfee Clinic Activator (40K):** If you use McAfee VirusScan, you may want this tool, which helps you track updates to the program.

- **Viewpoint Media Player (2.2MB):** An alternative player to QuickTime or RealPlayer that few people have ever heard of; supports new styles of online advertising.

- **Winamp (2.2MB):** Winamp is good for playing back MP3 files, so include this player if you plan to play MP3s or put MP3s on your Web site. More on MP3 is in Chapter 13.

- **Radio@Netscape Plus (1.9MB):** An add-in that supports playback from scores of radio stations.

- **Canadian Region Pack (60K):** You only need this if most people using your Web page are likely to have it, so you can see what they see. But because this option is so buried in the installation dialog box, your users will unlikely have it, so we recommend you skip it.

- **Developer Pack (500K):** If you want to debug JavaScript, this add-on is a good thing to have. Otherwise, unless you need the Chatzilla IRC client or DOM Inspector — if you don't know what these are, you probably don't need to — then skip it.

Several pieces that used to be optional are now included in the download whether you like it or not: the Quality Feedback Agent, which makes filling out a bug report possible if Netscape software crashes while you're using it; AOL ART extensions, which allow you to view AOL-formatted graphics in your Web browser; and the Classic Skin, which gives your browser an old-fashioned look. You see these pieces selected and grayed out in the Additional Components list, meaning you can't remove them from the download. But don't worry — they only take up about 1MB of download and hard disk space.

When you click Next, the Select Program Folder dialog box appears.

10. **Keep Netscape 7.1, the default choice, and then click Next.**

When you click Next, the Quick Launch dialog box appears.

11. **Enable Quick Launch by leaving the check box checked if you plan to run Netscape Navigator as your everyday browser; otherwise clear the check box. Click Next.**

Quick Launch moves part of the Netscape Navigator startup code to your computer's startup process, which means some of the work of loading the program is already done when you launch Navigator itself. This short-cut costs you a few seconds every time you start up, and uses system resources that other programs might need, but saves you a few seconds every time you start Navigator. The tradeoff is worthwhile if you plan to use Netscape Navigator as your daily browser, and isn't worthwhile if you plan to use Internet Explorer or another browser, such as the built-in browser in AOL or CompuServe software, instead.

The Download Options dialog box appears.

12. **Clear the Make Netscape.com My Home Page option, unless you really want this somewhat busy and slow-loading page as your home page when using the Netscape browser. Leave the Save Installer Files Locally option unchecked. Click Next.**

If the installation works properly, you don't need to run it again, so you have no real need to save the installer files, right?

The Start Install dialog box appears.

13. **Review the choices you've made. If you need to make a change, click Back as many times as needed, make the changes, and then work your way back to this point. Then click Install.**

When you click Install, the Download dialog box appears. If you chose the minimal download we recommend — Netscape Navigator plus the spell checker — the downloaded file is about 9.1MB in size, and takes a minute or two to download over a fast connection, about 45 minutes to download over a 56K modem, or about an hour over a 28.8K or 33.6K modem.

After the install is complete, the Netscape 7.1 folder opens on your desktop, and both Netscape Navigator and Composer are available from the Start menu.

Using Netscape Composer

Throughout the remainder of the book, we describe how to use Composer to make specific kinds of changes in your Web site. But before that, follow these steps to start Netscape Composer and get oriented to using it:

1. **Start Netscape Navigator.**

   Start Navigator from the Start menu by choosing Start⇔Programs⇔ Netscape 7.1⇔Navigator.

   The Navigator window opens. The Netscape home page is shown in Figure 5-6.

   You can also start Composer directly, by going straight to Step 2, but you'll generally find having the Netscape browser running as well as Composer convenient. You can use it for finding content or links for your Web page and for testing your page as it develops.

   The Netscape Navigator browser starts and the Netscape Web site appears — slowly, if you're not on a fast connection, because it's a complicated page with many small graphics. This site is the default home page for the Netscape Navigator browser. (You can change it by navigating to the page you want, and then choosing Edit⇔Preferences. Choose the Navigator category, and then change your home page address by clicking the Use Current Page button.)

2. **Start Composer by choosing Window⇔Composer.**

   The Composer window opens, as shown in Figure 5-7.

3. **Pull down the menus and look at the flyout options and buttons to see what options are available.**

Figure 5-6:
Navigator gives you a busy home page.

Composer's options are only those supported by HTML, so you can get a good idea of what you can do on a Web page by looking carefully through Composer's menu options. The remaining chapters in this part of the book go into detail about how to create a Web page using Composer.

What if you need IE?

Over 90 percent of Web users these days use Internet Explorer as their first-choice browser. However, you may be one of the few who doesn't have Internet Explorer, or you may have an old version that needs updating. If so, go to the Microsoft Web site at www.microsoft.com and click the Downloads link. Use the instructions to download and install the current version of Internet Explorer; the process is similar to the process for downloading and installing Netscape Navigator described in this chapter.

One caveat: You may not wish to upgrade your version of Internet Explorer if you have an older version that includes FrontPage Express. FrontPage Express is a Web page editor that Microsoft offered with old versions of Internet Explorer, but no longer offers with newer versions. If you have a version of Internet Explorer with FrontPage Express, you'll probably have to avoid upgrading if you want to keep it — some newer versions of Internet Explorer don't coexist on your computer with some older versions.

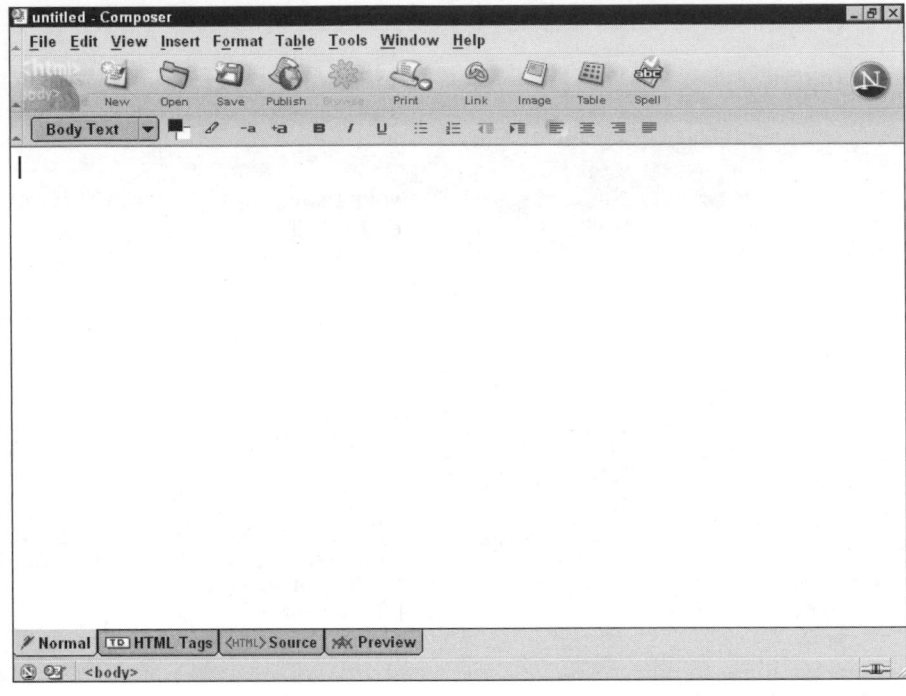

Using a Text Editor

If you want to use a text editor, you have the following choices:

✔ **A "pure" text editor such as Notepad (Windows) or BBEdit (Macintosh):** "Pure" text editors don't add any formatting to text, so you don't have to worry about hidden formatting getting added to your file. Windows WordPad, which comes free with Windows, is a simple word processing program, not a true text editor — use Notepad instead.

The CD-ROM for this book includes NoteTab Lite, a Notepad replacement with HTML capabilities, and BBEdit, a Macintosh text-editing program, along with a set of BBEdit extensions for Web-page editing.

For the PC, you may want to see if you can find a freeware or shareware text editor with Web editing features; a good place to look is C|NET's download.com at www.download.com.

✔ **A word processor:** You can use a word processing program such as Windows Microsoft Word, WordPerfect, or some other full-featured word processor. However, you have to be sure to always save your Web page files as HTML files, and to add the extension .htm to the end of the file-name. Also, the plethora of features in your word processor can be confusing, because most of them aren't supported by HTML and therefore don't appear in your Web page.

When using either a word processor or a text editor, you should save your Web page files with the suffix .htm. When using a word processor, you additionally have to use a pull-down menu or other option setting to tell the word processor to save your file as a text file — that is, with none of the normal word processor formatting.

We can sum up the trade-off between using a pure text editor versus a word processor as the trade-off between two different kinds of convenience. A pure text editor never adds word processor formatting to your document — the file is always a text file. And the pure text editor is simple — it doesn't offer you a bunch of formatting options that may or may not be supported by HTML.

A word processor, on the other hand, is familiar. You know exactly how to work with features such as the spell checker (which already has any words you've added to the dictionary), formatting, and print options. This familiarity can be a real plus when you're working with a long and complicated Web page file.

Many spell checkers choke on HTML tags, so they aren't very usable for Web pages. Composer's spell checker works on the text that appears in the Web page, so it doesn't have this problem.

You can use either a text editor or a word processor, but our experience is that the text editor is a better choice. Almost every serious Web page pro we know uses a text editor for some of their work, and a full-featured Web page creation tool such as FrontPage or Dreamweaver for the rest.

If you do use your word processor for editing Web pages, you may find that it has an option for working directly on Web pages. In our limited experience, this option is more confusing than helpful. However, you may wish to try this option if you feel most comfortable in the word processing environment.

Chapter 6

Creating Your Home Page

· ·

In This Chapter

▶ Deciding what to put in a home page

▶ Starting your page

▶ Getting your META tags right

· ·

Creating your Web home page is a lot of fun — and may be the occasion for some anxiety. After all, your home page will be published on the World Wide Web — it's like putting something you wrote onto a billboard on the busiest street in town!

Knowing what to say on your home page can be hard, but we give you some ideas in this chapter. Luckily, the mechanical part — creating your first Web page and putting it on the Web — is fairly easy. This chapter tells you how to create the page itself; the next chapter tells you how to add graphics. Other chapters tell you how to improve your page further. And in Chapter 12 we tell you how to publish your page on the Web.

What to Put in a Home Page

Many people think the most important thing about publishing their first Web page is learning HTML. They may take an HTML course, or pick up a book like this one, and feel ready to create their first Web page. Only then do they find out that the real problem in creating their first Web page is knowing what to say!

The "what to say" problem is easier to solve if you think of your Web page as a set of blocks of content. Each block covers a specific thing you want to describe on your Web page. For instance, a set of links relating to your hobby is one block of content; your résumé can be another block. By figuring out which blocks of content you want to put up first and then figuring out what to say in each block, you cut the overall problem of what to put on your Web page into easier-to-manage pieces.

Using blocks of content also helps you move smoothly from having a single Web page to having a multi-page Web site. Your first Web page might be a long page with several blocks of content. When you're ready to move to a multipage Web site, as described in Chapter 15, you can take the blocks of content and move several of them onto separate Web pages.

The great thing about Web publishing is that you can always change your Web pages later. "Just do it" — get something up that you're at least sort of proud of — then continually improve your Web page as you learn more.

You may have your own ideas for what to put on your initial home page, and if so, that's great. But in case you're stuck, the next few sections offer a few ideas to get you started.

Me and my interests

The easiest and most fun thing to put on your first Web page is a description of yourself and the things you're interested in. This type of Web page is put up for fun, and also works well for certain specific purposes, such as applying for college or online dating (don't laugh, it's a big deal — at least here in Silicon Valley). Figure 6-1 shows an example of this kind of personal Web page.

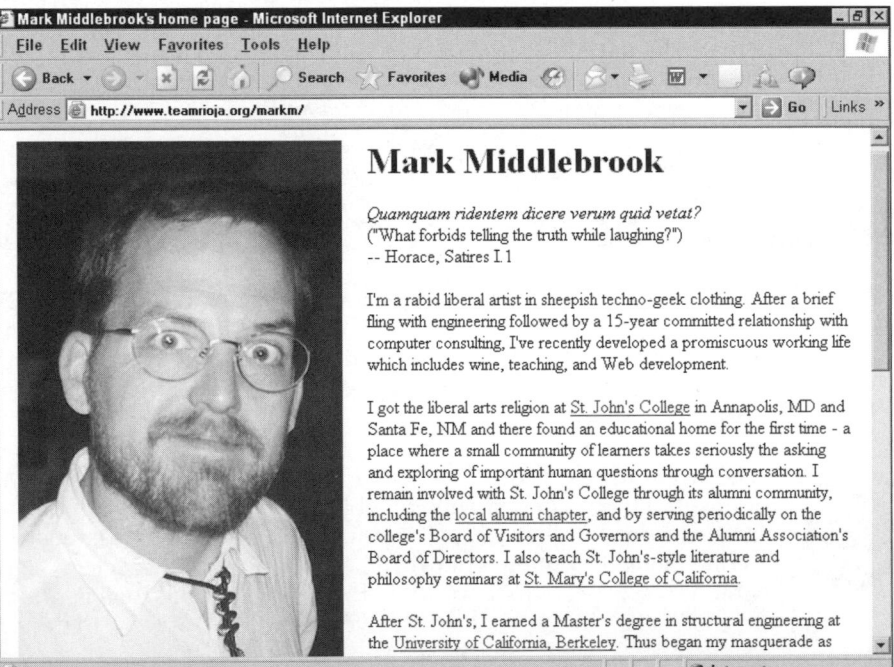

Figure 6-1: Get personal with your first Web page.

Here are some of the blocks of content you may want to include in an interests page:

- **A brief description of yourself:** Briefly describe yourself — name; age or age range; what you do; where you work, go to school, and live; and a bit of your personal history.

  Don't give too much detail about yourself, or you may become a victim of identity theft. See the sidebar, "Maintain your identity," for details.

- **A photo of yourself:** You can use a photo of yourself as part of your self-description. We tell you much more about how to get a photo of yourself onto the Web in Chapter 9.

- **A description of your interests:** Your Web page may focus on one or two of your interests, but having a brief list of all your major interests is nice — this section makes someone visiting your Web page feel like they really know you.

- **A description of your work or school:** Describing how you spend your days is an interesting part of a rounded picture of you. Include a link to the Web site of your company or school, if there is one. (We tell you how to create links in Chapter 8.)

- **Favorite links, by interest:** (One or more blocks.) Many people put their favorite links on their Web site, but the list tends to be both obvious and confusing — a mish-mash of things thrown together and including obvious sites such as Yahoo! or Amazon, which almost all Web surfers know about already. Create short lists of your favorite sites on one specific interest at a time — and precede it with a brief description of why you have that interest.

- **Detailed link descriptions:** For each link you provide, give a description of the site and what you find valuable about it. Link to specific pages in the site with the best stuff, rather than just linking to the site's home page.

You can create this kind of Web page as a simple, long, scrolling page with no navigation — just one block of content after another. For this kind of Web page, whether the formatting and look of the page are kind of rough around the edges doesn't matter — interesting content is enough to make the Web page stand on its own.

Me and my family

A popular use of a Web page is to put up photos of yourself, your spouse or significant other, your kids, your pets, and other important people in your life. (We know pets aren't people, but many pet lovers don't.) This kind of Web site helps families and friends keep in touch. See Figure 6-2 for an example.

Figure 6-2:
Make the
Web a
family affair.

Such pages can grow into fairly large Web sites as additional pages are put up for each family member and each birthday party or vacation that gets memorialized on the Web site. For your initial, simple home page, though, consider the following content:

- ✔ **A brief description of yourself and other family members:** Have each person in the family briefly describe themselves — name, age or age range, work or school details, where he or she lives, and a bit of personal history.

  See the sidebar, "Maintain your identity," for some caveats about how much personal information you should put on your site.

- ✔ **A photo of each person:** Include a group photo or a photo of each person. Don't use too many photos, or photos that are too large, or your Web page loads very slowly. See Chapter 9 for more on photos and other graphics.

- ✔ **Descriptions of everyone's interests:** A brief list of each person's major interests is a nice touch on a family Web page. This section can also give relatives a clue as to what to get each person in the way of birthday and holiday gifts, without anyone being too obvious about saying what they want.

> ✔ **A description of each person's work or school:** Seeing — or being reminded — how each person in your family spends his weekdays is nice. Include a link to the Web site of each person's company or school, if available. (We tell you how to include links in Chapter 8.)

> ✔ **Favorite links, by person:** (One block per person.) A list of each person's top five or seven sites gives visitors an idea of each family member's interests without making the page too lengthy.

Like a personal page, a family page can be a simple, long, scrolling page with no navigation, and the look can be whatever you want it to be — no professionalism needed. This kind of page is more fun the more you put into it, without worrying too much about appearances.

Me and my work

You can put up a brief Web professional page describing your professional background and interests — kind of an illuminated résumé. You can tilt this kind of page toward sharing your professional interests, or more narrowly focused on helping you get a job.

Maintain your identity

When creating your personal Web page, avoid giving out specifics that a thief could use to steal your identity. Another person needs surprisingly little personal information to fill out a credit application in your name and get credit while posing as you. The identity thief can then run up thousands of dollars of charges against your credit in a few days, all without your knowledge. Cleaning up after this kind of attack on your credit can be very difficult, expensive, and time-consuming.

The main thing to avoid is giving specific names and numbers: Your driver's license number, your Social Security number, and credit card numbers are strictly off limits, which may seem obvious. But you should also avoid giving other numbers: Your street address and your personal phone number are good things to leave out, as are your exact age and your birth date. You might even want to leave these details off an online résumé; just include your name and e-mail address for people to use in making an initial contact with you.

Don't give a lot of details about family members, and specifically avoid giving your mother's maiden name — a bit of information that's commonly used to verify identity. Staying vague about family members protects them as well as you.

Be especially careful to avoid giving details about kids, especially information that could allow someone to identify and find a child. For instance, you may decide to go ahead and put your address and phone number on your site — but don't also include a picture of one of your kids and his or her name, or your kids may get the attention of the wrong kind of people.

Some blocks of content you may want to include in a work-related page:

- **A brief description of yourself:** As in a personal page, described in the previous section, a brief description of yourself is interesting. Talk about yourself — leave your professional interests to their own section.

- **A photo of yourself?:** A photo of yourself is a nice addition to a professional site. But if you're going to be using your professional page for getting a job, you may want to leave the photo off. Why? Because employers who are concerned about discrimination issues don't accept a résumé with a photo in the early screening stages; they simply ignore any such résumés. So leave the photo off your professional site if you're actively looking for work.

- **A description of your professional interests:** A professional Web page should list your major professional interests. You should probably leave personal interests for your personal site, unless you have a leadership role in a volunteer organization or some other work-relevant personal involvement.

- **Favorite links, by interest:** (One or more blocks.) A well-organized list of links to areas of professional interest to you can be a real resource for others with similar interests. Create a separate list for each of your major areas of interest.

- **A formatted, printable résumé:** If you are considering using your professional site as a resource for a job hunt, or if you just want people to be able to see all the work experience that's summed up in your résumé, then add a formatted résumé to your Web page.

A work-related site can be a single Web page at first, but you'll probably want to have your résumé as a separate page before too long. We describe how to add additional pages to your Web site in Chapter 16. As for appearance, making sure your professional page looks sharp isn't too important, but you don't want it to be out-and-out ugly either. See Chapter 11 for details on creating an attractive site.

We suggest that you not create a Web site for your business — even a small business — as your first Web publishing effort. A business Web page needs to have an attractive look, a good balance of text and graphics, and correct spelling and grammar. This is a lot of requirements to meet in your first Web publishing effort. We suggest you create a personal Web page — either for yourself as an individual, for your family, or for your work interests — to start. Later you can use your newly acquired skills to tackle the tougher job of creating a business Web site. (We describe how to in Chapter 15.)

Starting Your Page

Okay, so you're ready to create your first personal Web page. How do you actually do it?

Just fire up your Web page editor — whether it's a text editor or a Web page editing program such as Composer — and start writing. Use HTML commands, if in a text editor, or the commands that your Web page editor makes available to format your text as you go along.

 One way to make Web publishing easier is to separate the "what do I say" part from the Web publishing part. Consider creating a mock-up of your home page first in your favorite word processing program. Get the text right, insert a picture, and so on. Then, when you actually create your Web page, copy and paste the text from your word processing program into your Web page editor.

 When you bring content from a word processing program into a Web page editing program, be ready to redo your formatting — and to rewrite some of your text to make it more Web-friendly. Short, punchy text with lots of headings, bulleted lists, and numbered lists is the recipe for easy-to-read Web writing.

Creating your initial page using HTML

In this section, and the following sections, we tell you how to create your Web page using HTML in a text-editing program. This allows you to really get to know the HTML tags by using them directly.

In alternating sections we describe how to do the same thing using a Web page editing program such as Netscape Composer. This allows you to concentrate more on your content and less on the mechanics of HTML.

 The steps in this section are for Windows Notepad, but a similar process works for any text editor — or even for a word processing program, if you're careful to save the file as text, and then add .htm to the end of the filename to indicate that it's an HTML file.

In this section, we describe very specifically how to get your HTML file started — if you do it right, life is easy, but if you make even a small mistake, editing and previewing your file is hard. Follow these steps to create an initial Web page in HTML:

1. **Open your text-editing program. For instance, to use Windows Notepad as your text editor, choose Start⇨Programs⇨Accessories⇨Notepad.**

   Your text-editing program opens a new document.

2. **Add the required header and other tags to your document: The**
   `<html>` **and** `</html>`, `<head>` **and** `</head>`, `<title>` **and** `</title>`,
   and `<body>` **and** `</body>` **tag pairs.**

   Enter the following lines in your HTML file:

   ```
   <html>
   <head>
   <title>Bud Smith's Personal Web Page
   </title>
   </head>
   <body>
       <!--The main content of your Web page goes in the body
           section.-->
   </body>
   </html>
   ```

   See Figure 6-3 for a display of these HTML tags in a Notepad document.

   The main part of your Web document goes between the `<body>` and
   `</body>` tags. The tag with an exclamation point, `<!-- The main con-`
   `tent... -->`, contains a comment. The browser ignores this tag and its
   contents, and doesn't display them in your document, but using this tag
   allows you to make notes to yourself in the HTML text.

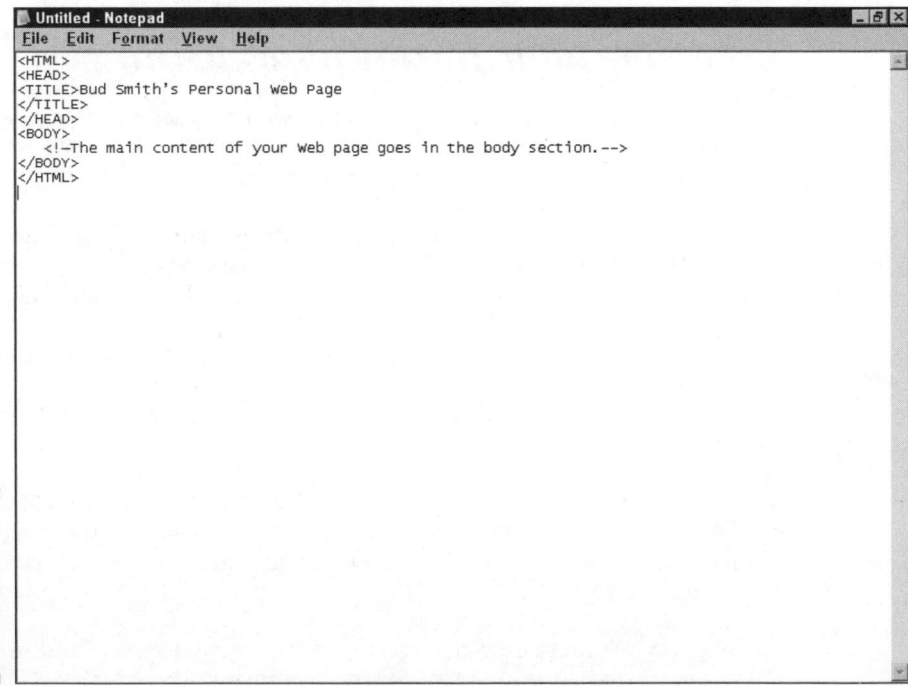

Figure 6-3:
Get the
HTML
into your
document.

The text between the `<title>` and `</title>` pair of tags is the title of the document. A Web browser displays the title in the top of the file window.

3. **Begin the process of saving the file by choosing File⇨Save.**

   The Save As dialog box opens.

   Both the Save and Save As commands open the Save As dialog box when you're saving a file that you haven't previously saved.

4. **Create a new folder for your Web page files. Use the pull-down file menu at the top of the Save As dialog box to navigate to the spot where you want to create your new folder. Then use the Create New Folder icon — the folder with the star on it — to create the new folder. Name it according to the rules in the sidebar, "How to make Web filenames." Then open the new folder to save your file into it.**

   See the sidebar, "Files of a feather," for details on why keeping all the files that make up your Web page or Web site in one place is important.

5. **Use the Save as Type pull-down menu to save your file as a text document.**

   Get in the habit of saving your HTML files as text documents. That way, even if you work on the file in a word processor, your file saves in text format, without any word processor formatting codes.

6. **Enter the filename you want to use, followed by the suffix `.htm`. For example, you can call the file `mypage.htm`.**

   See the sidebar, "How to make Web filenames," for details on why saving your file as a text file is important, and to end your HTML files' filenames with `.htm`. Using the `.htm` suffix allows you to easily open the file in a Web browser program to review it.

7. **Click the Save button.**

   Notepad saves your file as a text document with the filename you give it, including the suffix `.htm`.

8. **To preview your Web page in a Web browser, open a browser such as Internet Explorer.**

   Now's a good time to get in the habit of having a browser window open so you can check your HTML work as you go along. Every time you save your HTML document, you can open the saved document in your Web browser to see how it will look as a real Web page.

9. **In your browser, choose File⇨Open to bring up the Open dialog box. Click the Browse button to open a dialog box that allows you to find your file. Navigate to where your file is and click its name to select it. Then click Open.**

10. **Your file opens in the browser. Figure 6-4 shows the text file and the browser open next to each other. Note that the title specified in the HTML document is shown in the Web browser's file window.**

    Web page authors commonly use this way of working, with the HTML document and a Web browser open at the same time, to keep track of the changes they're making in a document.

To see changes you're making in your HTML document, you have to save the HTML file and then click the Refresh or Reload button in your browser. Refreshing the contents of your browser makes the browser get a new copy of the page from the Web server — or, in this case, from your computer's hard disk.

Title in HTML document   Title displayed in Web browser

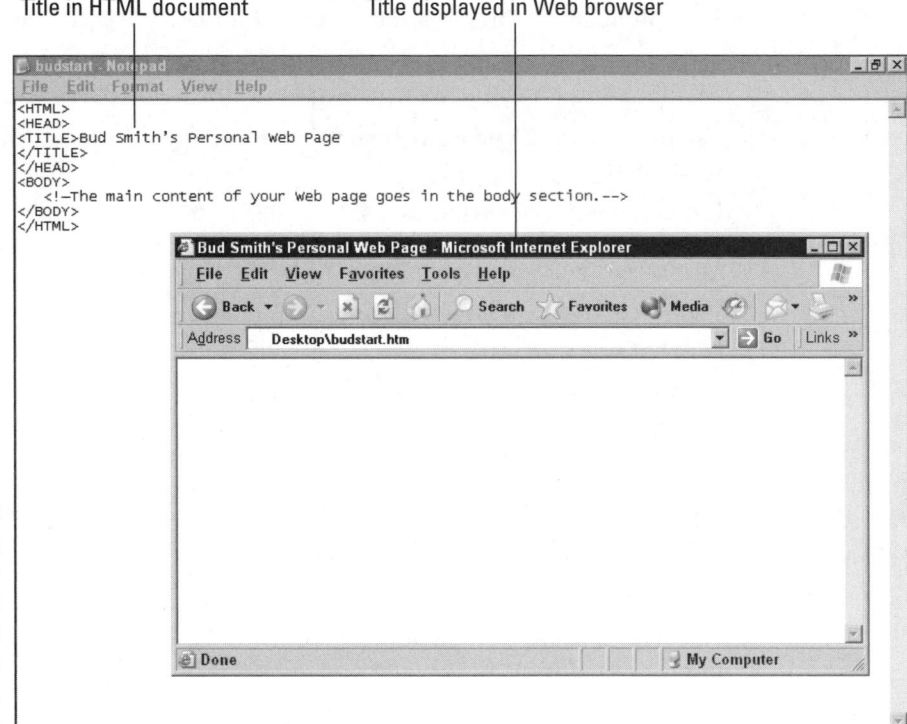

Figure 6-4:
Only the title is changed to protect the emptiness.

Creating your initial page using a Web editor

Using a text editor, as described in the previous section, allows you to get up close and personal with HTML tags. Using a Web editor such as Netscape Composer, as described in this section, allows you to worry less about HTML tags and more about your actual content. (Don't worry that you won't learn HTML — we have you look at the HTML-tagged text underlying your document frequently.)

The steps in this section are for Netscape Composer, but a similar process works for other Web page editors, such as Microsoft FrontPage or Dreamweaver. These full-featured editors have all the features of Composer, and then some, so you can follow the steps given here in the more capable programs.

How to make Web filenames

Here are a few things to keep in mind when naming your files for the Web:

✔ When you tell a Windows program to save your file as a text document, it saves just the actual text characters that you see on-screen, without any formatting commands. The Windows program also assigns the suffix .txt to the file, unless you tell it otherwise. The filename's suffix, which is usually hidden from you by Windows, helps Windows figure out what kinds of programs the file "belongs" to. When you name your file with the suffix .htm, it overrides the .txt suffix.

✔ When your file ends in .htm, Windows recognizes it as an HTML file. This extension allows you to easily open the file from a Web browser program such as Internet Explorer. By doing this, you can preview your file as you work on it — and, more importantly, other people can open your file as a Web page when you put it on a Web server.

You may also see some Web pages with filenames ending in .html; this suffix works on some servers. However, you should not end the filenames of your Web pages with .html because some programs that you may use to edit your file or to transfer it to a Web server truncate the suffix to .htm. This breaks any links you have to the document, because they refer to the file using its original suffix, .html. Save yourself potential headaches and always use .htm as the suffix for your HTML files.

✔ Not putting spaces in your Web filenames, keeping them eight characters or less in length, and using only lowercase letters in the filenames is also important. Why? Because your Web page might be published on a UNIX server, or on a server that runs an old version of Windows. Different servers have different filename rules. Only a filename with its main part eight characters or less, with .htm as its suffix, and with no uppercase characters are sure to stay intact and accessible when you publish your Web page onto a Web server.

You should also keep your folder names all lowercase and eight characters or less, for the same reasons. If your folder name changes when you transfer your Web page to a server for publication, links to the Web pages and graphics files in the folder can be broken. There's not much that's more frustrating — or embarrassing, especially if you're creating a Web page for a company or other organization — than having your hyperlinks break when you move your Web site from your own machine to a Web server.

Follow these steps to create your initial Web page in Composer:

1. **Open Composer. First open Netscape Navigator by choosing Start⇨ Programs⇨Netscape7.1⇨Navigator. Then choose Window⇨Composer.**

   Netscape Composer opens with an empty window.

   After you open Composer, you can close Navigator, and Composer still stays open.

2. **Give your document a title by choosing Format⇨Page Title and Properties.**

   The Page Properties dialog box opens.

3. **Enter the title for your document. (A Web browser displays the title in the top of the file window.) Optionally, you may want to enter your name and a file description in the Author and Description areas. Click OK when you finish.**

   The Author and Description fields are most useful if you're working with others on the same machine or on the same Web site. They help identify who on a team is working on a document and what each HTML file is for.

4. **Preview your document's HTML by choosing View⇨HTML Source or clicking the <HTML> Source tab at the bottom of the editing window.**

   Your document's HTML source appears, as shown in Figure 6-5. Note that you have no actual content in your document, but already you have almost a dozen HTML tags! These tags are automatically generated by Composer. Don't worry, most of the work you do from here on has results that are directly visible in your Web page.

   Note the sets of tag pairs that are standard in any HTML document: the `<html>` and `</html>`, `<head>` and `</head>`, `<title>` and `</title>`, and `<body>` and `</body>` tag pairs.

   Also note the META tags. For a brief description of META tags, see the section "I Never META Tag I Didn't Like" later in this chapter.

   The main part of your Web document goes between the `<body>` and `</body>` tags. The tag with an exclamation point, `<!-- The main content... -->`, contains a comment. The browser ignores and does not display this tag and its contents in your document, but the comment tag allows you to make notes to yourself in the HTML text.

   The text between the `<title>` and `</title>` pair of tags is the title of the document. The Web browser in the top of the file window displays it.

5. **Return to a normal view of your Web page by choosing View⇨Normal Edit Mode or by clicking the Normal tab at the bottom of the editing window.**

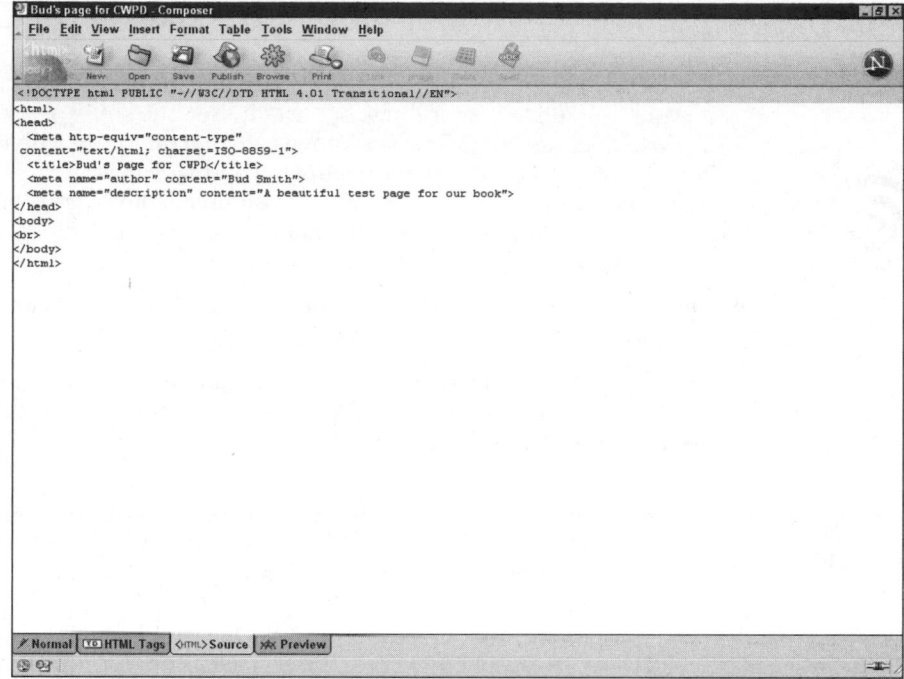

Figure 6-5:
Composer
lets you go
to the
(HTML)
source.

Your empty editing window appears. Note, however, that your Web page's title appears at the top of the editing window.

If you don't give your document a title before you save it, Composer prompts you to enter a title before saving.

6. **Begin the process of saving the file by choosing File⊅Save.**

The Save Page As dialog box opens.

Both the Save and Save As commands open the Save Page As dialog box when you're saving a file that you haven't previously saved.

7. **To create a new folder for your Web page files, use the pull-down file menu at the top of the Save Page As dialog box to navigate to the spot where you want to create your new folder. Then use the Create New Folder icon — the folder with the star on it — to create the new folder. Name it according to the rules in the sidebar, "How to make Web filenames." Then open the new folder to save your file into it.**

See the sidebar, "Files of a feather," for details on why keeping all the files that make up your Web page or Web site in one place is important.

8. **Use the Save as Type pull-down menu to save your file as an HTML files document.**

   Composer saves your document with the suffix .html to indicate that it's an HTML document. (You don't usually see the suffix of a Windows filename, but it's how Windows knows which icon to use when displaying a file, and what programs can open it.) However, in the next step we'll change the suffix to .htm. See the sidebar, "How to make Web filenames," for details on why ending your HTML files' filenames with .htm is important.

9. **Add .htm to the end of the filename to make sure it is given the .htm extension and not .html. Then Click the Save button.**

   Composer saves your file as an HTML document. Because it has the suffix .htm in the filename, you can easily open the file in a Web browser program to review it.

Files of a feather

Keep all the files for your Web page, or for a small multi-page Web site, in a single folder. The Web publishing process is much easier.

✔ **For a Web page:** Keeping the HTML file for your Web page and all the images that are used in your Web page in a single folder is important. Why? Because the hyperlinks are much simpler if you just have to give the filename. If you put image files in a separate folder, the hyperlink (see Chapter 4) has to name the folder and its relationship to the folder. Trust us, you don't need the hassle.

There's yet another reason to keep your HTML file and your image files in one folder. When you publish your Web page, you move your HTML file and the image files onto a different machine — the Web server that hosts your Web page. If you keep all your files together in a single folder, doing this transfer correctly is much easier.

✔ **For a multipage Web site:** Hyperlinks to images and to other Web pages in your site are easier to specify, and transferring the site to a Web server is easier, when you keep all your files in a single folder.

This reasoning breaks down, though, when a Web site gets larger and more complicated. When you have more than a couple of dozen files, keeping them all in one folder becomes difficult to manage. At that point you have to break your site into a group of folders, one per Web page, plus a folder for shared graphics. And then you get to change all your hyperlinks so they work across the new folder hierarchy (see Chapter 4 for more about hyperlinks).

You should also keep extraneous files that aren't part of your Web page out of your Web page's folder. Why? You'll most likely move these extra files, along with your Web page, to a Web server when you publish your site. And who needs the extra files?

If you want search engines to easily find your Web page, put key information — like your full name, for a personal page, or your business name, for a business page — in the title, in the first heading within your document, in the first 20 or so regular-text words of your document, and in META tags (described in the next section) in your document. When a *spider* — a program that moves across the Web looking at the content of pages and sites — indexes your page, it looks in some or all of these places, and people searching for your name or your business name are very likely to see your page in the search results.

1 Never META Tag 1 Didn't Like

One of the most interesting, and controversial, tags in HTML is the META tag. That's because META tags affect how your Web page appears in search engines, and some people go to great lengths to have their pages rank high in search engine lists. The META tag is used for *meta-information* — information about your Web page, rather than information that displays in your Web page.

The META tag is used only in the header area of your site. The header area is all about meta-information, so that makes sense. (The ⟨title⟩ tag is sup-posed to be meta-information, for use only by spiders, but Web browsers also display the title in the top of the file's window.)

The META tag has one main purpose: To better describe your Web page to the spider programs that gather Web information for search engines. Some search engines depend heavily on the contents of META tags to decide how to index pages for use in search results, and to find a description of the page to use in the search results themselves.

In some cases, if a user is searching for Ukrainian Frisbee teams, and the words in your META tag include "Ukrainian" and "Frisbee," your page comes up first in the search engines! Other search engines, though, largely ignore the content of META tags. For more on how to place your site high in search engine results, see Chapter 15.

META tags consist of three pieces: The word META, a field that describes the content of the META tag, and the information that goes in the field. Here's the META tag that Netscape Composer puts in all your Web pages:

```
<meta http-equiv="content-type" content="text/html;
          charset=ISO-8859-1">
```

What a bunch of junk! But this tag is simply three fields of data. The first tells a Web spider that this is a META tag. The second says that it's the "content-type" version of a META tag. The third says that the content of this Web page is text, in HTML format; it uses the character set ISO-8859-1, or standard English-language ASCII characters. You can add this META tag to any docu-ment you create.

There are three other META tags you really should put in your Web page: the author, description, and keyword versions of the tag. Examples follow:

✔ `<meta name="author" content="Bud Smith">`

The author version of the META tag simply states who created the page. This tag is mostly useful for internal purposes — so someone who knows you, or who works in the same organization you do, knows who to go to with questions or comments about this particular Web page.

✔ `<meta name="description" content="Bud Smith's own Web page">`

The description version of the META tag is simply a brief description of the Web page. Put this META tag in any Web page that you want to have show up in search results. Some search engines use the DESCRIPTION version of the tag as the actual description that shows up in the search engine listings, so write the content carefully.

✔ `<meta name="keyword" content="Bud Smith, Web authoring, Dummies, For Dummies">`

The keyword version of the META tag is a list of keywords that you want search engines to associate with your page. Your results are better, overall, if the keywords listed in your META tag are also within the title, first header, or first 20 or so ordinary words of your Web site.

For additional information about META tags, check out Search Engine Watch at `searchenginewatch.com/webmasters/meta.html`. This Web site has the latest and greatest information about Web search engines. Its information about META tags is written in an understandable way, and it has a lot of other great search engine information as well. We also think the same applies to *Search Engine Optimization For Dummies* by Peter Kent (Wiley).

Adding META tags with HTML

You can easily add META tags to your HTML document:

1. **Open your Web page in your text-editing program.**

   For instance, to use Windows Notepad as your text editor, choose Start➪Programs➪Accessories➪Notepad, and then choose File➪Open to choose the file to open.

   Your Web page opens in Notepad or your text editor of choice.

2. **Add the author, description, and keyword META tags to your document in the header area, between the `<head>` and `</head>` tags:**

   ```
   <meta name="author" content="xxx">
   <meta name="description" content="yyy">
   <meta name="keyword" content="z1", "z2", "z3"...>
   ```

Replace *xxx* with your name; *yyy* with the description of your Web page that you want to have appear in a search engine's results; and *z1, z2, z3,* and so on, with the keywords related to the content of your page. For a personal Web page, good keywords are your first name, last name, your full name, and keywords relating to the interests described on your page.

3. **Save your document, and then exit your text-editing program.**

   You can't preview this change in a Web browser, because META tags don't appear in your Web page. So simply save your document and exit.

Adding META tags with Composer

Most changes to your Web page are easier with Composer than with HTML in a text editor. However, because adding META tags involves adding HTML code directly to your document, it's actually a bit complex to do this in Composer:

1. **Open your Web page in Composer.**

   Choose Start➪Programs➪Netscape 7.1➪Navigator to start Netscape Navigator. Then choose Task➪Composer to start Composer. Finally, choose File➪Open to open your Web page file. Your Web page opens in Composer.

2. **Within Composer, choose Format➪Page Title and Properties.**

   The Page Properties dialog box opens, as shown in Figure 6-6.

3. **Enter or modify the contents of the Author and Description fields. Don't be afraid to write a long description, even though the dialog box doesn't have much space for it. (You can also take this opportunity to modify the title of your Web page if you want.) Click OK when you finish.**

   Composer automatically generates the author and description META tags for you and places them in the Header area of the HTML document you're creating.

   The description you enter may show up as the description of your Web page in the results page of a search engine.

   The good news is, that was easy. The bad news is, you're not done yet. You still need to enter the keywords for search engines to associate with your Web page, and you have to work directly in HTML to do that.

4. **In Composer, click the HTML Source tab, or choose View➪HTML Source.**

   The HTML source for your Web page appears. Note that the META tags for author and description are there, just as you entered them.

Page Properties ☒

Location:	[New page, not saved yet]
Last Modified:	Unknown

Title: `Bud's Home Page`

Author:

Description:

Advanced users:
To edit other contents of the <head> region, use "HTML Source" in the View Menu or Edit Mode Toolbar.

[OK]   [Cancel]

Figure 6-6:
Paging all
properties.

5. **Copy and paste the META tag for your Web page's description into the HTML source. (You should now have two identical DESCRIPTION lines.) In the second line, change `"description"` to `"keyword"`. Then change the words after `"content="` to the keywords you want to associate with your Web page for search engines.**

Editing a copy of existing HTML is often much easier than creating new HTML code yourself.

6. **Go back to the normal viewing mode by clicking the Normal tab, or by choosing View⇨Normal Edit Mode.**

The content of your Web page appears, with HTML tags hidden.

7. **Save your document and exit Composer.**

Your Web page now has appropriate META tags — many commercially created Web pages don't. Congratulations!

Chapter 7

Filling In Your Home Page

*T*he previous chapter shows you how to get your Web page started. This chapter shows you how to put some text in it and get the text formatted so it looks good.

Along the way, we also talk about how to write for the Web. Web writing is a bit different than other kinds of writing. It's also kind of fun, after you get used to it.

Writing for the Web

Every new medium develops its own style. Magazine articles are often wordy and literary in style. Newspaper articles are brief, to the point, and written in a "pyramid" style that puts the most important information first. The Web has its own style. Learning to use it, even a little bit, can make your Web page much more interesting and effective.

Web realities

The new style of writing found online is based on three underlying realities about the Web:

✔ **The capabilities of HTML:** HTML allows you to specify some simple text formatting, headers, and lists. Newer versions of HTML also allow you to specify fonts and specific text sizes, but a user can override these specifications.

What it means for you: Don't count on complicated formatting and specific layout to get your message across. Keep it simple.

- ✔ **The difficulty of reading from a computer screen:** A computer screen is a much lower resolution than a printed page — about 100 dpi versus anywhere from 300 dpi on up for most print. People's eyes get tired when they try to read long blocks of text on-screen. Figure 7-1 shows how far on-screen letters are from the smooth lines of printed text.

What it means for you: Shy away from long blocks of text. Write briefly, and break up what you write using headers, lists, quotes, and other devices. Then cut what you write down to the fewest words that do the job.

- ✔ **The ease of clicking away:** One of the most fun things for Web users is one of the most vexing for Web publishers: Clicking away to another site is very, very easy. Web content is free and voluminous, so users are always enticed to go elsewhere.

What it means for you: In addition to keeping your text brief and broken up, you need to make it as interesting as possible. Take advantage of the ease of clicking away: Include relevant hyperlinks in your Web text.

To further illustrate these difficulties, Figure 7-2 shows a PDF file from the For Dummies site at `www.dummies.com`. It shows content from the previous edition of this book. It's very well laid-out online, but the amount of content displayed is only about half of one printed page (remember, a book reader sees two pages at a time). The comparison to the Web is even more unfavorable for magazines or newspapers, which fit even more information on a page than a typical book does.

The point is that the reader gets far more content for a given amount of effort from print than they do from online content. So when writing for the Web, you need to keep your text short, your layout simple, and your content interesting.

If you have something dense and detailed that you really want people to read, put it on a separate Web page and encourage people to print the page out. Printing allows them to carefully read the text rather than scan it, as most people tend to do with text on the computer screen.

Figure 7-1: Zooming in shows how "chunky" on-screen letters are.

chunky

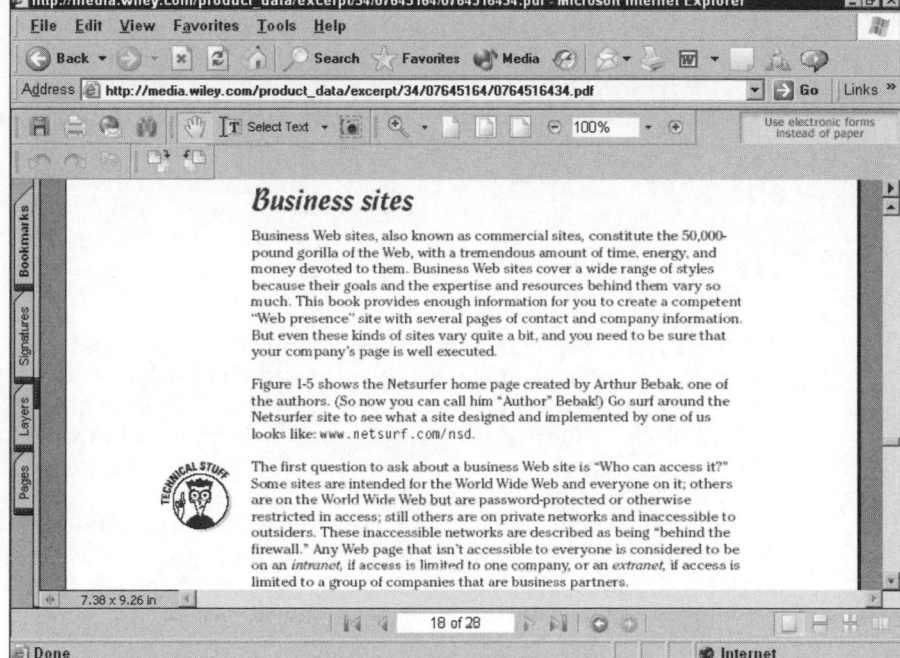

Figure 7-2:
An on-screen page has fewer words than a printed one.

Web style

Some characteristics of Web writing are based on physical realities. Others evolved because of the way the Web evolved — beginning as a network for rapid communication among scientists and researchers, both civilian and military. As a result, Web writing has a couple of other characteristics that are interesting:

- **A lack of hype:** In the early days of the Web, commercial use of the Internet was expressly forbidden — though some business activity did sneak in. In the early 1990s, the Internet and the Web were opened to commercial activity. Even so, a calm, informative tone still dominates on the Web. Enthusiasm is encouraged, but hype, overly broad claims, and hucksterism seem odd and out of place on the Web.

- **An informal tone:** Web writing, like e-mail, tends to be casual in tone — like writing to a friend. Formality stands out like a sore thumb, but so does too much cuteness. The Web is a "cool" and informative medium. Figure 7-3 shows a page from Netsurfer Digest, published by Arthur Bebak, one of the authors of this book. It's cool, low key, informal, and informative.

✔ **A need for correctness and accuracy:** Informal doesn't mean inaccurate. It's true that early use of the Web was partly a way of connecting friends — people in the scientific and military communities who knew each other from school, through conferences, and via e-mail. However, they were highly educated and extremely literate friends. You need to be accurate in order to show people that you're one of the voices on the Web worth listening to.

Have fun

Writing for the Web is actually fun, once you start to get used to it. You can be informal, and you don't need to go on and on to belabor every obscure point you're trying to make. Just make your point, perhaps add links to a couple of Web sites that give relevant facts or support what you're trying to say, and move on.

Do check over what you've written before you publish it, though. People will feel like you're wasting their time if you don't make sure your spelling is correct, your grammar is passable, and your facts are accurate. (If you're not sure of your information on a given point, just say so.)

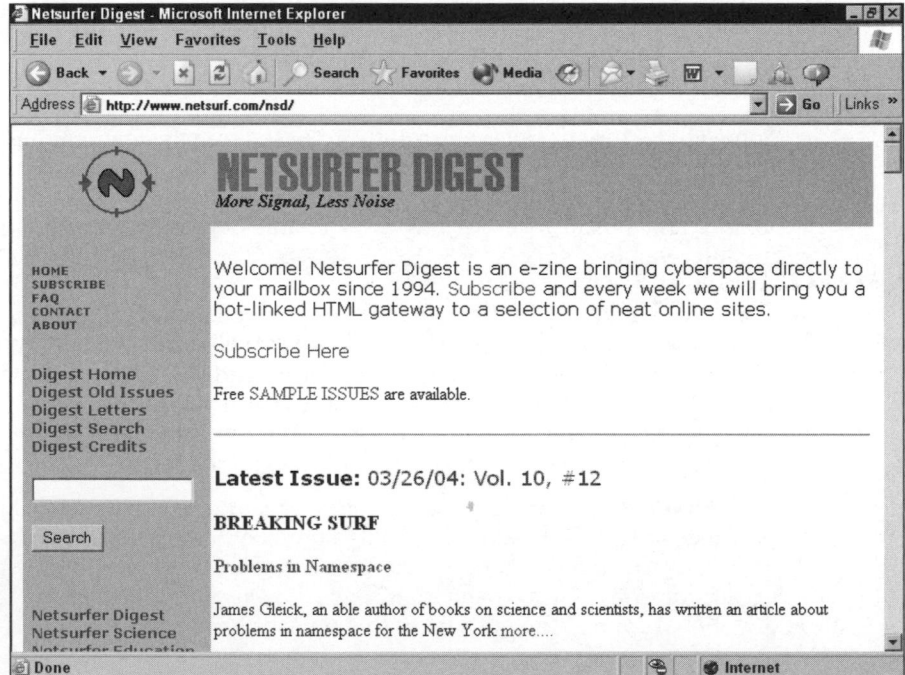

Figure 7-3:
Netsurfer
lacks hype.

Many unhappy Returns?

One of the most disconcerting things about Web page editing when you work directly in HTML is the way HTML handles carriage returns and line breaks.

We're all used to pressing the Enter or Return key when we want to create a line break in a word processing document or an e-mail message. If we want more blank space, we press Enter or Return more times. However, it doesn't work that way when you're creating a Web page.

First is the issue of getting a carriage return into your document when you're working directly in HTML. (Netscape Composer and other Web page editors handle this problem for you.) When you press Enter or Return when entering text in HTML, HTML doesn't notice the end-of-paragraph marker that gets placed in the text. So, if you enter several paragraphs of text, pressing Enter or Return after each, you end up with one big blob of text in your Web browser.

What's the solution? When working directly in HTML, you have to insert a <p> tag at the start of each paragraph and a </p> at the end. Every time HTML sees a new <p> tag, it starts a new paragraph. (The </p> tag at the end of the paragraph isn't strictly necessary, but it's better to be safe than sorry.)

So if you need more white space between paragraphs, you just add a few more <p> tags, right? Well, no. Different browsers handle multiple <p> tags differently, but most ignore the second and succeeding <p> tags. No matter how many <p> tags you put in, you just get one paragraph break. (The same goes for the <br>, or break, tag. The <br> tag creates a line break without starting a whole new paragraph. This can be useful when you're working in a list, for instance, and want to insert a line break without starting a whole new paragraph, which might be indented differently.)

The solution is to insert a special character called a non-breaking space in each blank line you want. The tag for a non-breaking space is #nbsp;. Just put this tag after a <br> tag and, in most versions of the major browsers, you get a full line break.

Formatting Web Text

The mechanics of formatting Web text are actually pretty simple. Later in this section, we show you how to use these capabilities either when using a text editor, working with HTML directly, or using a Web page editor such as Netscape Composer. First, here's a brief list of the text capabilities available for Web publishers, based on the HTML tags found in the most widely used versions of HTML:

✔ **Headings:** You can specify six levels of headings in HTML, using the tag pairs <h1> and </h1> for the largest, top-level heading; <h2> and </h2> for the next level; and so on down to <h6> and </h6>, the lowest level of headings.

What it means for you: The ideal way to use headings is as intended — <h1> for the most important heading and so on, down to <h6>. However, you may notice the heading you're using seems too large in comparison to the text beneath it. Many people use <h4>, for instance, for a second-level heading, or use text size commands and bolding to create their own header styles. Try using the intended headings first, and then use your own formatting if you really need a specific look.

✔ **Font sizes:** HTML allows you to specify font sizes that are larger or smaller than medium, or standard, size. You can go two sizes smaller or three sizes larger than medium. This formatting works even if users specify a font size or style in their browser setup or in Windows. (As people get older, and their eyes weaken, they resort to various tricks to make using the computer easier — as one of the authors knows from experience.)

What it means for you: You don't want your Web page to look like a hostage note, but font sizes can be a good way to make a point (with a larger font size) or fit a lot of text into a small space (with a smaller size). Using relative font sizes is one of the few formatting tricks that almost always work well on Web pages.

✔ **Character formatting:** You can make text bold or italic using the <b> and </b> tags to start and stop bolding and the <i> and </i> tags to start and stop italics. You can also underline text, but we don't recommend it, because users can easily get confused — because HTML links are usually underlined.

What it means for you: You should feel free to use bold and italic to emphasize your point, but don't overdo it. Structured use of bold and italics, such as the bolding used to highlight items in this list, is one good solution. As for underlining, avoid using it on the Web — people confuse it with the underlining (and use of a color, usually blue) used for hyperlinks. See the "What color is your hyperlink?" sidebar for details.

✔ **Advanced character formatting:** Using tags that aren't supported by all browsers currently in use, you can specify the fonts used in your Web page, as well as font colors. There are problems with doing this, though. Some users have older browsers that don't support this kind of formatting. And some folks have their browsers set to use specific fonts, regardless of what you specify. Yet others have specified large fonts in Windows, which make some parts of your Web look much different than you intended.

What it means for you: We don't recommend using advanced character formatting because it's complicated and because, just when you start to depend on it, you find it doesn't work for some of your users. Using font and link colors can cause problems because users are accustomed to seeing only standard colors used for text and for links. Stay away from this kind of formatting unless you're working at a professional level, with the design help and testing resources needed to make it work well for all your users.

What color is your hyperlink?

HTML allows you to use colored text on your Web page. We generally don't recommend this.

Why not? (This book is about all the things you can do on a Web page, after all!) The reason is that people are very used to monotone text, usually black, on a contrasting background. People have adjusted to the use of colored text on Web pages, but mainly in the form of standard hyperlink colors: blue for a link the user hasn't clicked yet, and purple for a recently visited link.

Some Web page authors customize these colors to fit better with the color scheme of their Web pages. The problem is, research into making

Web pages easier to use and less confusing has found that users subconsciously count on blue underlined text to indicated unvisited links and purple underlined text to indicate visited links. Any change in these colors, or any use of underlining or blue or purple text for other purposes, causes deep confusion.

So we recommend that you don't use colored text, don't change link colors, and don't use underlining except in links. The people who visit your Web page will have a better time using it as a result.

Figure 7-4 shows these options for Web text formatting in a single example. Use it as a resource when deciding what formatting to use in your own Web page.

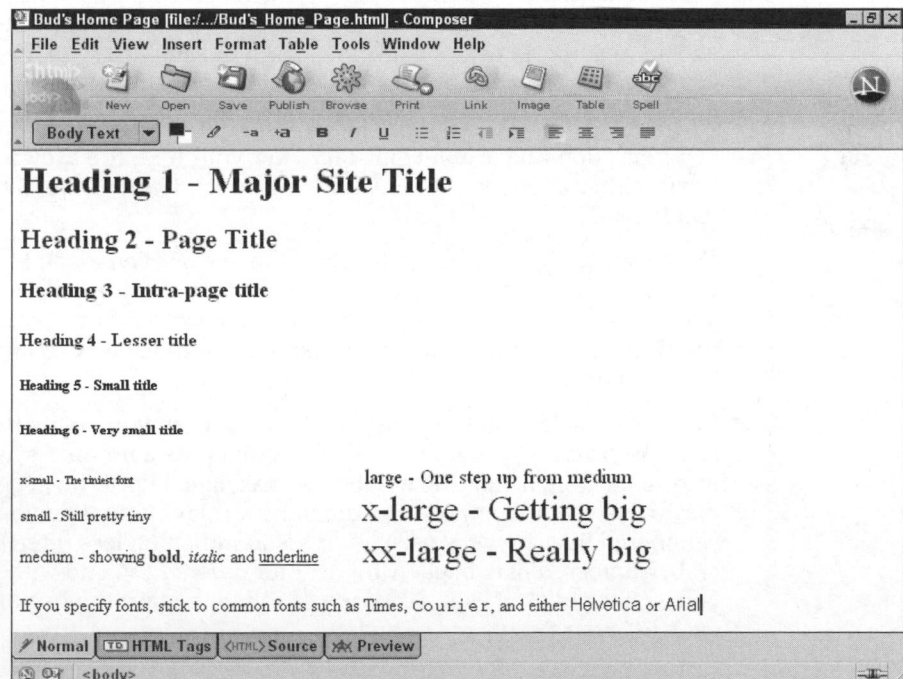

Figure 7-4: Take advantage of Web formatting options.

Using HTML Lists

People really like lists. David Letterman's Top Ten lists are the highlight of his *Late Night* show and have been the subject of several books. Everywhere you look, you see lists. Here are our top three reasons why — in a list, of course:

- ✔ **Lists are interesting to look at.** Writing pros are always telling people to use lots of white space to vary the appearance of their pages so they're not just featureless blobs of text. Lists do this; they break up text.

- ✔ **Lists are easy to scan.** As we mention earlier in this chapter, people are more likely to scan text on the Web than to read it carefully. Lists are very easy to scan. With the key points highlighted, people can go in depth by carefully reading the points that interest them, then skim the ones that don't.

- ✔ **Lists make the writer get to the point.** When you write a list, you have to cut and condense what you're trying to say. You may end up editing a page of boring, monotonous text down to three or four points in a half-page bulleted list. All this extra work you have to do greatly benefits the reader, especially the reader who's reading from a computer screen.

HTML and Web page editing programs based on HTML (such as Netscape Composer) offer three kinds of lists, but only two are used much.

- ✔ **Bulleted lists:** Bulleted lists are by far the most widely used kind of list on the Web. And why not? Bulleted lists are flexible and fun, both to write and, more importantly, to read. You start a bulleted list with the `<ul>` tag, which stands for *unordered list.* You end it with the `</ul>` tag. Each list item is preceded with `<li>`, which stands for — you guessed it — *list item.*

  List items don't have an ending tag. After your text, the browser expects to see either another `<li>` tag, for the next list item, or the `</ul>` tag to end the list.

  What it means for you: You can convert many, or even most, long blocks of text into a bulleted list — and make the text shorter, easier to read, and more interesting in the bargain. If you have to move existing text to the Web, consider "bulletizing" parts of it as a quick way to make it more Web friendly.

- ✔ **Numbered lists:** Numbered lists look weird when you create them in some Web editing programs — the program puts a number symbol (#) next to each item, and the number isn't assigned until the page displays. (Netscape Composer, fortunately, displays actual numbers.) Numbered lists are very useful, but are found much less often on the Web. Numbered lists begin with `<ol>` for *ordered list*, end with `</ol>`, and — like bulleted lists — use the `<li>` tag to mark the beginning of each list item.

What it means for you: Anytime you have a list that has an order in terms of importance, sequence in time, or any other reason, make it a numbered list. Putting your list items in order makes them even easier to scan than a regular, bulleted list.

✔ **Definition lists:** *Definition lists* give a term and then a definition for the term. They're rarely used, though finding a use for them in your Web page is a good exercise. A definition list starts with `<dl>` and ends with `</dl>`. Each term is preceded by `<dt>`, for *definition term,* and each definition is preceded by `<dd>`, for *definition data.*

What it means for you: The appearance of definition lists in your Web page is a bit funny — most Web browsers put the term on one line and then the definition, indented farther in, on the next line. You can help the reader who's scanning easily find the terms by making them bold, as in the list you're reading here. People like definition lists, but not necessarily formatted the way most Web browsers do it. Use definition lists where you can, or use bolding and bulleted or numbered lists to create your own definition-type list.

Netscape Composer or a free trial package?

Although offerings change with time, you can usually get a free trial version of excellent Web page editing software such as Microsoft FrontPage or Macromedia Dreamweaver from the companies' Web sites or an online download site such as C|NET's download.com (at `www.download.com`, natch). Why use Composer instead of a free trial version?

✔ **Truly free:** Composer is truly free for as long as you want to use it. You don't need to worry about paying anyone money when your trial version expires, which is usually just when you're getting going as a Web publisher.

✔ **Truly easy:** Because it's designed as an introductory program, Composer has only basic features — not too much complexity, which you don't need most of the time, to make things confusing.

✔ **Truly HTML-compatible:** As an introductory program, Composer only supports features that work on just about any Web browser

out there. By contrast, using all the features in FrontPage or Dreamweaver often means you add things that don't work in older browsers or within AOL or CompuServe.

And, of course, our argument is that you can better follow along with the instructions in this book if you're using the software that we use for many of our examples and figures — either straight HTML or Netscape Composer.

If you're sure that you're going to be using FrontPage or Dreamweaver soon, or if you already have a copy, you may want to use a trial version of the program that's in your future. Even then, you may want to use Composer for easy work, and the full-featured program for advanced features. If you do work in a full-featured Web page editor, most of the steps in the sections of this book dedicated to Composer still work for you — you just need to substitute the specific commands for your program in place of the instructions and illustrations for Composer.

✔ **Lists within lists:** You can insert or *nest* one list inside another. The nested list can be the same kind of list, or a different kind, than the list that contains it.

What it means for you: Users have a hard time keeping track of where they are in the overall list if you start throwing sublists at them as well. We believe that putting one list within another is usually a case of something that's technically possible, but not editorially desirable. (We look forward to one of you proving us wrong by coming up with a good use for nested lists.)

Figure 7-5 shows different list options. Pick and choose the right ones for you when creating your Web pages.

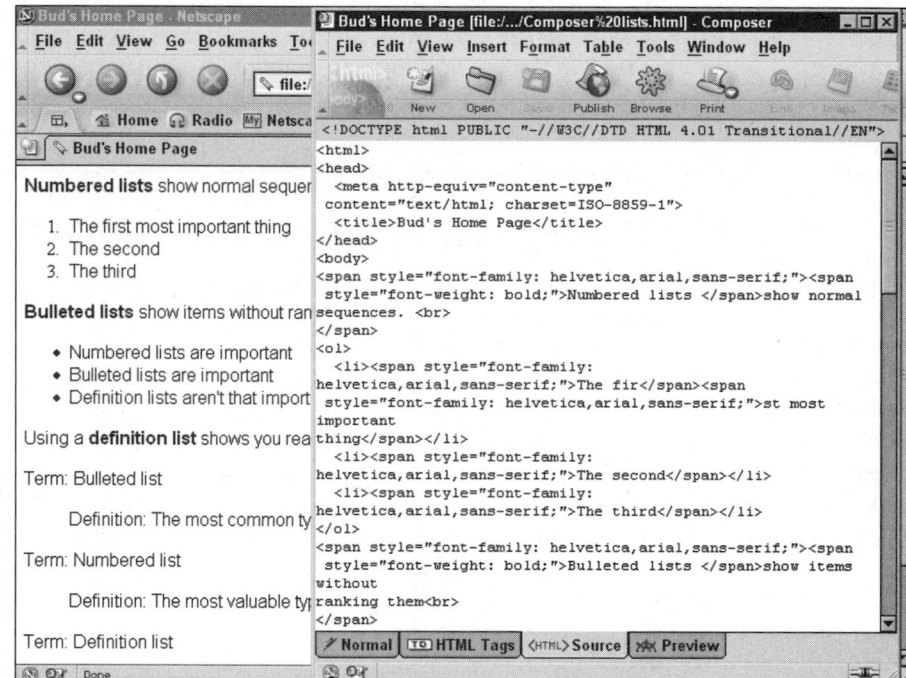

Figure 7-5:
List all your options and then choose one.

Entering Text in HTML

Entering text directly in HTML is a challenge at first because you have to spend a lot of time thinking about HTML tags instead of about what you want to say. After a while, though, you get used to it, and working with the HTML tags — while still tedious — becomes routine. The good news is that working this way gives you hands-on control of what your HTML is doing.

This section shows you how to use HTML to accomplish the following simple Web authoring tasks and fill in your initial Web page:

✔ Enter some text.

✔ Format the text.

✔ Make some of the text into a list.

✔ Check out how the text looks in a Web browser.

The rest of this section shows you how to accomplish these tasks with HTML in a text-editing program; in the next section, we show you how to accomplish the same tasks with Netscape Composer.

Entering and formatting text

The best way to get used to working with HTML is to jump right in:

1. **Open or create an HTML document in a text editor. Give your document a title and then add META tags, as described in Chapter 6.**

2. **In the editing window, enter some text.**

   The example in this chapter's figures includes the following text:

   ```
   I just got a new portable computer.
   I'm extremely happy with it.
   My favorite things about it are:
   1.4 GHz Intel Centrino processor
   30GB hard disk
   256MB of RAM (I wish it had 512MB though)
   It's much faster than my old portable computer.
   ```

3. **Start by surrounding lines of regular text with the paragraph tags (`<p>` and `</p>`).**

   In the sample text, we placed the paragraph tags before and after the first three lines and the last line.

4. **Find the text that you want to format.**

   In the sample text, we selected "extremely" in the phrase "extremely happy."

5. **Put formatting tags, such as `<b>` and `</b>` or `<i>` and `</i>`, around the text to format it.**

The tags appear around the text. It shows up as formatted when you look at it in a Web browser. In the sample text, we made the word "extremely" bold.

Be sure to apply the closing tag, where one is needed, for each new tag you start.

Making a list

Making text into a list works in much the same way as applying paragraph formats, such as Heading 1, but you have to work with several lines at once:

1. **Identify the lines of text that you want to make into a list.**

   In the sample text, we make a list out of the lines about processor, disk, and RAM.

2. **Surround the selected lines with the <ul> and </ul> tags for a bulleted list, or the <ol> and </ol> tags for a numbered list.**

3. **Precede each item in the list with the tag <li> to identify it as a list item.**

   Here's how the example looks now:

   ```
   <p>I just got a new portable computer.</p>
   <p>I'm <b>extremely</b> happy with it.</p>
   <p>My favorite things about it are:</p>
   <ul>
   <li>1.4 GHz Intel Centrino processor
   <li>30GB hard disk
   <li>256MB of RAM (I wish it had 512MB though)
   </ul>
   <p>It's much faster than my old portable computer.</p>
   ```

   The text immediately appears as a list.

   See Figure 7-6 to see how the screen appears at this point in the example.

   For more on HTML terms, such as numbered list or bulleted list, see Chapter 4 for HTML basics, and the sections earlier in this chapter for details about when to use which kind of list.

Looking at the Web page

When working in a text document using HTML, which allows you to be constantly reminded of the HTML tags you're using, being reminded of what the actual Web page will look like — and to look for any problems as you go along is also useful. Here's how to keep an eye on what your final Web page will look like as you work in HTML:

1. **Choose File⇨Save to save your document.**

2. **Open a Web browser, such as Internet Explorer.**

3. **Choose File⇨Open in your browser to open a file. In the Open dialog box, navigate to your saved file, and select it. Click Open to open the document.**

   Your Web document appears in the browser window as a Web page.

4. **In your text editor, make a visible change in your text.**

   Try adding a new sentence, with or without formatting.

5. **Save the file.**

   If you don't save the file to your hard disk, you can't see the changes when you look at it in your browser.

6. **Click the Refresh or Reload button in your Web browser.**

   The updated Web page appears in your browser.

7. **When done, save your document and exit Windows Notepad or the other text editor you're using.**

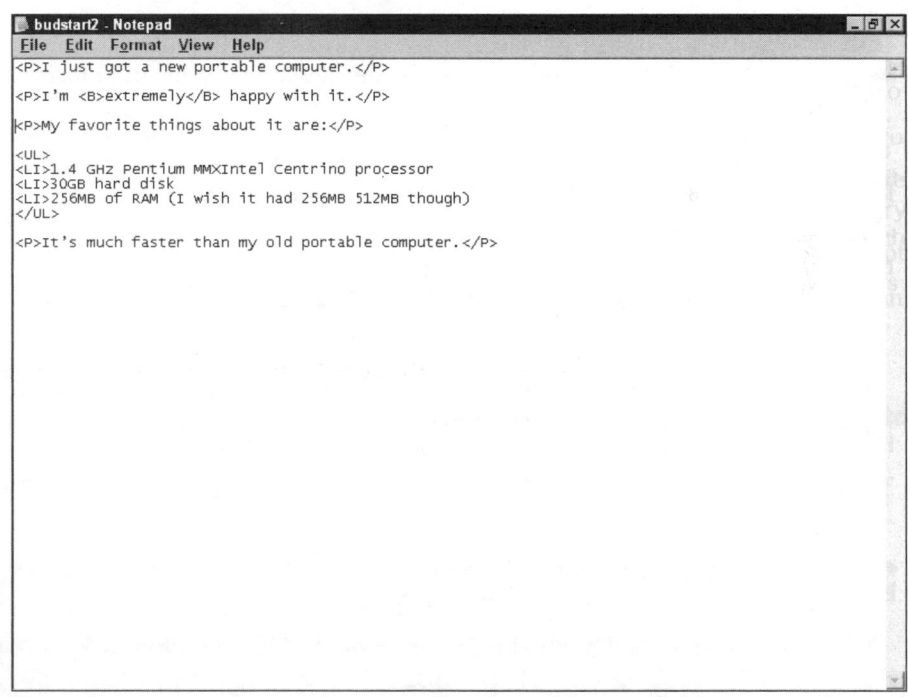

Figure 7-6:
Use tags to get your list right.

Entering Text in Netscape Composer

Filling in your initial Web page with Netscape Composer is fun because you can easily do most of the things that you may want to do with a Web page, though Netscape Composer doesn't let you do much beyond the basics. As you experiment with Netscape Composer, you'll find that you can use all the basic text features of HTML, without having to worry about HTML tags.

This section shows you how to accomplish the following simple Web authoring tasks and fill in your initial Web page:

- ✔ Enter some text.
- ✔ Format the text.
- ✔ Make some of the text into a list.
- ✔ Look at the underlying HTML-tagged text.

This section shows you how to accomplish these tasks with Netscape Composer; in the previous section, we show you how to accomplish the same tasks with HTML tags in a text editor.

See Chapter 5 for information about how to get Composer, and Chapter 6 for information about how to create your initial Web page in Composer.

You can learn HTML quite quickly by working in Composer and then clicking the HTML Source tab periodically to see the actual HTML tags that Composer puts into the HTML-tagged text that makes up your Web page.

Entering and formatting text

Editing text for Web pages by using Netscape Composer is easy and fun because you can use the formatting options that are allowed on Web pages — and only those options. That means you're instantly seeing just about the same thing your Web page visitors see — and not wasting your time with options that don't translate to the Web. Follow these steps to type and format some text:

1. **Open or create a Web document and give it a title. Then add META tags, as described in Chapter 6.**

2. **Type in the heading that you want at the top of your Web page.**

   For example, we entered Sierra Soccer Club as the first heading.

3. **Move the cursor to the same line as the heading text. (You don't need to select the text.)**

4. From the far-left pull-down menu, choose Heading 1.

The heading text reformats into Heading 1 style.

Any HTML styles — paragraph-level formatting commands — that you choose affect the entire paragraph of text in which the cursor rests.

5. Move the cursor to a new line.

6. Type some text introducing your Web page.

When someone searches for your Web page by using a search engine, the search engine may display the Web page title, as described in Chapter 6, and the first few words that appear in the document. So make the first few sentences of text that follow the title an introduction to the entire page or Web site.

In the document we created for this chapter, we typed:

```
Sierra Soccer Club is a boys' soccer club that practices
and plays at the highest altitude of any in the United
States. If you meet the following qualifications, you
may be eligible to become a member of Sierra Soccer Club:
Born in 1993 or 1994. Sierra Soccer Club has played
together since its founding members were 5 and 6 years
old and will stick together as they grow up. All our
club members must be born in 1993 or 1994.
Some soccer experience. If you have played in organized
leagues before, or if you're a skilled school player,
we may be able to help take your game to new levels.
Good academic record. We are proud that our club members
maintain good standing in school as well as in soccer.
```

7. Highlight any text that you want to format.

In our document, we highlighted the words Sierra Soccer Club at the beginning of the first sentence.

8. Click the button for the formatting style that you want: the B button for Bold, the I button for Italic, or the U button for Underline.

In our example, we made Sierra Soccer Club bold. The highlighted text takes on the formatting you choose.

Making a list

Formatting items into a list works in much the same way as applying paragraph formats, such as Heading 1. Just select the lines of text and then pick the effect that you want:

1. Highlight the lines that you want to make into a list.

In our document, we highlighted the lines that begin:

Born in 1993 or 1994

Some soccer experience

Good academic record

2. From the pull-down menu, choose the list style that you want: Bulleted List or Numbered List.

The text instantly reformats into the list style that you choose, as shown in Figure 7-7.

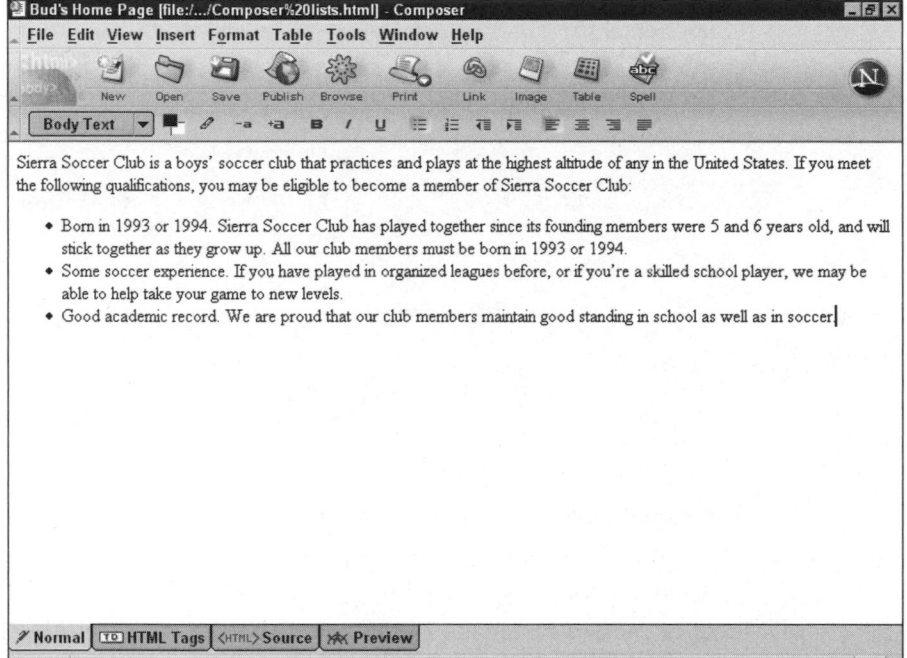

Figure 7-7: Composer makes listing easy.

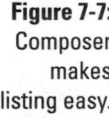

For more on HTML terms, such as numbered list or bulleted list, see Chapter 4 for HTML basics, and the sections earlier in this chapter for details about when to use which kind of list.

Looking at the HTML

When working in a WYSIWYG (What You See Is What You Get) tool such as Netscape Composer, you often want to look at the underlying HTML code.

Doing so enables you to find out how HTML works and gives you the chance to make adjustments in the HTML tags that affect the way your page looks and works on the Web. Here's how to check out your page's HTML code in Netscape Composer:

1. **Choose View⇨HTML Source, or click the HTML Source tab at the bottom of the window.**

   The HTML source for your page appears.

2. **Make any changes that you want in the HTML.**

   You can change the HTML directly — the changes are reflected when you go back to normal editing mode.

3. **Choose View⇨Normal Edit Mode, or click the Normal tab at the bottom of the window.**

   The Netscape Composer window displays the formatted Web page, reflecting any changes you made in the HTML code that cause visible differences in your Web page.

4. **Save your document and exit Netscape Composer.**

Chapter 8

Adding Links to Your Web Page

*W*eb *hyperlinks* — the connections that let you go from one Web page to another with a single click — are the key to what makes the Web great. They're also a bit complicated to create, test, and maintain. We show you how to do it right in this chapter.

Hyperlinks, known as *links* for short, have a long and honorable history. They are the underlying concept behind *hypertext,* a kind of writing that takes advantage of computer and network capabilities to connect a spot in a piece of text to other information that supports, gives detail on, defines, describes, relates to, or even contradicts the information at the spot where the link is.

Hypertext was discussed and implemented in smaller systems long before the World Wide Web was invented. Ted Nelson invented the term in about 1960 and promoted the idea for decades. He wrote a famous book called *Computer Lib/Dream Machines* that described many different types of hypertext and uses for it. (The book is currently out of print.)

The idea of hypertext became popular within the computer industry throughout the 1980s, as more and more computers were getting connected to networks. The reason for the growth of interest in hypertext was simply the truth behind a rule called Metcalf's Law: The value of a network rises exponentially with the number of computers connected to it.

So it is with hyperlinks. Using a hyperlink, you can connect your Web page to any information on any other Web page out there. As the Web has grown, the total number of available hyperlinks has grown rapidly with it, to the point that now the number of links is seemingly infinite. Clicking around the Web via hyperlinks is so much fun that the term "surfing the Web" is used to describe it.

Hyperlinks also work to bring information into your Web page. The graphics that appear embedded within a Web page are really separate files; hyperlinks in the HTML document that defines a Web page point to each graphic. It really doesn't matter to the Web whether the graphics within your Web page are on the same machine or scattered across the Web, though download time for your Web page might be inconsistent if the various files are scattered around.

We describe these different kinds of hyperlinks separately, and show you how to use each type in your own Web page. And we tell you how to avoid some of the problems that all too often arise with hyperlinks in your Web page.

Linking Basics

Before you plunge into specific kinds of links, as described in this chapter, getting an overview of how links work is helpful. The basic idea, remember, is for your HTML document — the core of your Web page — to refer to another file. The user is either going to see that file in your Web page, or click something in your Web page to leave it and link to the other file.

One of the biggest problems users have on the Web is broken links. Encountering a broken link is very frustrating, and you, as the Web page publisher, may not find out about the problem for a long time. Create and test your links carefully and repeatedly, fixing any problems, to avoid broken links.

How links work

The basic mechanism for creating a link from one Web page to another is simple. You use the <a>, or anchor, tag to begin the link. Within the anchor tag, you can specify where the link goes to, using the HREF attribute to specify the Hypertext REFerence, or destination, of the link. Some text within your document usually follows the anchor tag. An </a>, or end-of-anchor, tag then follows that text.

Here's an example of a typical anchor tag within a sentence of text:

```
Visit the <a href="http://www.dummies.com">For Dummies
          site</a> for more information.
```

Here's how this tag displays in a typical Web browser:

```
Visit the For Dummies site for more information.
```

In a typical Web page, the underlined text — called the *link text,* because it's where the user clicks to follow the link — displays in blue as well as being underlined.

Mouseover and out

Current Web browsers support a feature many users take advantage of: mouseover support. When your mouse moves over a link, the destination of the link shows up in the lower-left corner of the browser window. (Some versions of Internet Explorer have the status bar, where the destination appears, turned off by default; choose View➪Status Bar to turn it on and see link destinations.) You can use this mouseover support to check your own links when you're testing your site, both before and after you publish it. Rest assured that your savvier users will take advantage of the mouseover feature to check out where a link is going before they decide to click it.

The other kind of link you commonly create in your Web page is an image link. You begin this kind of link with the image tag, `<img>`. You use the `src` attribute, which nearly always appears within the `<img>` tag, to specify where the image lives. For simple sites, store the image in the same folder as the HTML file that links to the image. Then the `src` option is very simple:

```
<img src="myuglymug.jpg">
```

For more complex sites, you can consider putting images in one or more separate folders, and use more complicated links to refer to them.

The next chapter gives many important details about graphics and graphics links. In this chapter, we focus on how to link to the image file that you want, whether it's on your Web server or another machine.

Links and URLs

Links usually fulfill one of two main purposes: to help your user go to another Web page, or to bring in a graphics file to display in your Web page. Whichever kind of link you're creating, you need to know how to specify where the file is located.

Most linking mistakes are made due to misunderstandings about the way URLs work when you're linking from the HTML file that is the core of your Web page to another Web page or to a graphics file. Understanding how URLs work can help you create more interesting Web pages and experience much less frustration as you create and test your page. Table 8-1 summarizes how you create the different kinds of links.

Table 8-1	URL and Web Page Examples		
Location of target	*URL*	*Web Page Example*	*Graphics Example**
Same folder	*filename*	`<a href=" mycv.html"> text</a>`	`<img src=" myface.jpg">`
Subfolder at a lower level of the same path	*pathname/ filename*	`<a href=" subpages/ mycv.htm"> text</a>`	`<img src=" grfx/myface.jpg>`
Folder on a different path	*pathname/ filename*	`<a href="../ theotherpage/ otherpage. htm>text</a>`	`<img src="../ sharegfx/ proface.gif>`
Different server, home page (index.htm or index.html)	*domainname*	`<a href=" www.large domain.com"> text</a>`	`<img src=" www.largedomain. com/goodface. jpg">`
Different server, interior page	*Domainname/ pathname*	`<a href=" www.largess. com/files/bud. htm">text</a>`	`<img arc= "www.largess. com/gifs/ icon27.gif">`
Link within a page	*Any of above + # anchorname*	`<a name="my anchor"></a>; <a href="www. largess.com/ #myanchor>Go to my anchor </a>`	Doesn't apply

* This example leaves out the ALT option and other important graphics options, which Chapter 9 describes.

Linking to a file on another server

The easiest kinds of links are actually links to a spot on another Web server. That's because you can easily get the URL for the link — it's the same as the URL you see when you go to the site using your Web browser. When you're linking to a file on a different server than your HTML file, you can link to two kinds of URLs:

- ✔ **Different server, home page:** This is the easiest kind of URL: You just give the same domain name that you use to go to the home page of the Web site, preceded by `http://`. For instance, if you know of a racing fan's Web site with the domain name `http://www.mygreenhorse.com`, you simply give that URL as the hypertext reference. (The home page does have a filename — either `index.htm`, `index.html`, `home.htm`, or `home.html`. However, you only have to spell out the home page's filename if it's something different.)

✔ **Different server, not the home page:** This kind of URL is easy too; it's just the URL, but the URL is a little longer, because it includes the `http://` prefix and the domain name as well as a path down to the specific file you want. There's a twist, though: When you're linking to a file on a large site, the URL is often a bunch of gobbledygook.

For instance, here's a URL from a search for Gumby on the Google search site:

```
http://www.google.com/search?hl=en&ie=UTF-8&oe=UTF-
    8&q=gumby+show
```

Figure 8-1 shows this search and its results.

The URL is not really a file location; it's a database query stored in a URL. Still, this isn't something you need to worry about. Just find the page you want, copy and paste the URL into your Web page, and you have an accurate link. (At least, until something on the site you're linking to changes.)

Figure 8-1:
A typical search can generate a long URL.

You usually don't need to include the filename in the path for a Web page if the filename is `index.htm` or `index.html`. Most Web authors only use this filename for their site's home page, but others use it for major navigational pages deeper within the site as well.

Don't worry if you don't see `index.htm` or `index.html` when you visit the Web site's home page; the site is automatically remapping the filename your browser expects to the one it wants to use. Try typing the URL without a specific filename; if that works, you don't need to include the filename in your link.

Linking to a file on the same server

Linking to a file on the same server is harder than linking to a file on another server. That's for two reasons: Getting the path wrong when you are linking to a local file is easier because you can't just copy and paste a Web URL; and, the path you specify while testing on your own machine may change when you publish your Web site by moving it to a Web server. This can make the URLs you've been using wrong, breaking the links within your site.

When linking to a file on the same server, don't give the name of the server — just leave it off. Your Web browser knows to look on the same server as the Web page if no server name is specified in the path.

If you're linking to a file on the same server as your HTML file, the kinds of URLs you can link to include the following:

✔ **Same server, same folder:** If a file is on the same server, and in the same folder as the HTML file, you don't need any path information. The pathname is simply the filename. To link to a Web page called `myresume.htm` that's in the same folder as your Web page, the pathname is just `my resume.htm`.

✔ **Same server, subfolder:** If a file is in a subfolder below the HTML file that has the link in it, you need to include the path from the HTML file to the folder holding the other Web page or graphics file. For instance, if you have a folder containing your Web page and a subfolder, called `grfx`, with graphics files, the path to a graphic called `myface.jpg` is `grfx/myface.jpg`.

✔ **Same server, not on same path:** Things start to get really tricky if you want to link to a Web page or graphics file that's on the same server, but on a different path. You can either give the absolute pathname that describes the path from the beginning of the server's directory structure to the file, or the relative pathname from your Web page to the file. An example of an absolute path, on a machine whose main hard disk is called `maya`, is `maya/mypage/grfx/yourface.jpg`. An example of a relative path to the same file, from an HTML file stored at `maya/mypage/webpages/index.html`, is `../grfx/yourface.jpg`.

Use the characters . . / to indicate going up one level in the current folder hierarchy. It's not very user-friendly, but simple enough once you get used to it.

Linking within a page

There's one more intricacy to pathnames that is easy to miss, but important: You can link to a destination within a Web page, as well as to the top of the page.

The only trouble is, HTML doesn't allow you to specify a location within the page using normal language — you can't say "link to the spot just below the picture of Britney Spears and just above the picture of Madonna." Instead, you need to create a special marker, called an *anchor,* to link to.

Technically, any link you create is an anchor, but people typically call them HREFs if you're linking out to a Web page, or image references if you're linking in a graphics file. The term *anchor* is used most often to mean a special marker you create in an HTML file to give other HTML files a specific spot to refer to.

To create an anchor, you simply put the <a> and </a> tags into your Web page. For example:

```
<a NAME="aboveMadonna"></a>
```

You don't need to enclose any text between the <a> and </a> tags, because the anchor you are creating goes to the start of the next line of text below the anchor. There's no visible sign to the user of this kind of anchor — no blue-colored text or underlining, for instance.

To link to the anchor, you add the symbol # and the anchor name to any other kind of URL. Say you put in ten anchors into a Web page, one above each major header, and number them 1 through 10. Then a link to the third one, from within the same Web page, looks like this:

```
Check out the <a href="#three">third</a> wonderful reason to
              vote for me.
```

You can now link to the area in the Web page where this line appears by adding /#three to the end of the URL given after the HREF attribute.

Avoiding mistakes

Making mistakes in your Web site when you're specifying links is easy, and "good" links can easily become broken because of changes in the Web site you're linking to. Here are some ways to prevent problems, and to manage problems when they do come up:

✔ **Keep your whole Web page in one folder.** When your whole site is just one Web page, your only links are to the graphics images that display as part of your page. Put the graphics images in the same folder as the HTML file that defines your Web page. That way, your links to graphics files are simple — just the filename — and when you publish the site, you just move a single folder from your machine to the Web server.

✔ **Keep your whole Web site in one folder.** When you grow your Web page into a multi-page site, you can keep all the HTML files that define your Web pages, as well as all the graphics files they use, in a single folder, again simplifying links. This method does get crowded after a while, though.

Here's an alternative for sites with more than a couple of dozen files: Create a very simple hierarchy in which each HTML file is in a folder with the same name as the HTML file, shared graphics are in a separate folder, and graphics used only by a specific page are stored with that page. This method is still a whole new level of complexity, but at least you have some rules to operate by.

✔ **Avoid internal links to Web pages on other sites.** Linking directly to a spot within a Web page on another site is fun, but you're depending on an anchor that may go away as the Web page is updated. Try to only use internal links within your own site; that way you at least know who to blame if the anchor you're linking to is deleted or moved.

✔ **Check all links before you publish.** Before you publish your Web page or Web site, try every single page to make sure that graphics load properly, and try every single link to make sure it works correctly. If you find a problem, make the change while it's still easy — and then recheck to make sure you got it right.

✔ **Check all links after you publish.** Some of your Web links — both links to graphics within the Web page and links to other sites — quite possibly break when you publish your site. Check to make sure. If you do find problems, fix them, test on your local machine, and then re-publish and re-check.

✔ **Check all links every couple of weeks.** Other Web publishers can easily make changes in sites you depend on — and it's a sure bet that the minute you decide that the site you link to will never change, it does. Keep checking your links every couple of weeks to make sure they're all good. (And update any out-of-date content in your site while you're at it.)

Linking to a Web Page

Here we summarize the different kinds of links you can create and show you how to implement them in both straight HTML and in Netscape Composer. Actually, adding a link is quite different when working directly in HTML versus working with Netscape Composer or other tools.

Adding Web page links in HTML

To link to a Web page, just create an anchor tag and provide the path to the page you want (and any anchor that applies). Following are some examples:

- Linking to the home page of a site with its own domain name:

```
<a href="http://www.greatdomain.com">Go to the great
    domain.</a>
```

- Linking to a page within a site, giving the pathname and filename:

```
Read my review of <a href="http://www.greatdomain.com/
    reviews/budspeaks.htm">the great domain.</a>
```

- Linking to a page on the same server, and in the same folder, as your Web page:

```
I've created a <a href="gdlikes.htm">Web page</a>
    summarizing what I like about the great domain.
```

- Linking to a page on the same server, in a subfolder below your Web page:

```
I've created a <a href="/opinions/gdlikes.htm">Web
    page</a> summarizing what I like about the great
    domain.
```

- Linking to a named anchor within a Web page:

```
Now I don't like some things about <a href="http://
    www.greatdomain.com/news/policies.htm#payupnow">
    the great domain</a>.
```

In this last example, an anchor called #payupnow has to be on the policies. htm page in the News folder of the Web site www.greatdomain.com. If not, the user's Web browser takes him or her to the right page, but brings up the top of the page, not the desired spot within the page.

Adding Web page links in Composer

Creating a link in Composer can be a bit confusing. Follow these steps carefully to create a link in Composer without problems:

1. **Open Composer and your Web page, as described in Chapter 5.**

2. **Enter the text in which you want the link to appear.**

   Enter the text first, before you specify the link.

3. **Select the text you want to use as link text so that it's highlighted.**

   Don't select the space before or after the text you want to use; it looks odd to have leading or trailing empty spaces in a link.

4. **Bring up the Link Properties dialog box by choosing Insert⇨Link or pressing Ctrl+L. Click the Advanced Edit button to make all the options show.**

   The Link Properties dialog box appears. The text you highlighted displays at the top of the dialog box as the link text.

   You can also enter the link text by bringing up the Link Properties dialog box with no text highlighted and then entering link text in the Link Text box. When you're done, the link text appears on your page. However, anything you type immediately next to it becomes part of the link text, which can be a hassle.

5. **For a link to another site, enter the URL that you want to link to. For a link to your own site, enter the URL manually, or click the Choose File button, navigate to the file you want to link to, and then click Open.**

   Use a relative URL for most links to a Web page on the same server as the page that contains the link. See the section "Linking to a file on the same server" earlier in this chapter for details on how to compose the URL.

   The URL is Relative to Page Location check box automatically becomes checked or unchecked depending on which link location you enter. This option helps you confirm that the link location you enter is absolute or relative (as described in Chapter 2 and earlier in this chapter), whichever you are trying to use.

6. **If you want to use an existing named anchor within the file you're linking to, select it from the Link Location pop-up list. For local files only: If the anchor doesn't exist, but you want to create one next to a heading, select a heading from the Link Location list. Netscape Composer opens the file and creates an anchor next to the heading.**

   This is a lot for a free program to do for you!

   Note: If you want to add additional attributes to the link, click Advanced Edit to access the Advanced Property Editor dialog box, as shown in Figure 8-2. When you're done setting your attributes, click OK to return to the Link Properties dialog box.

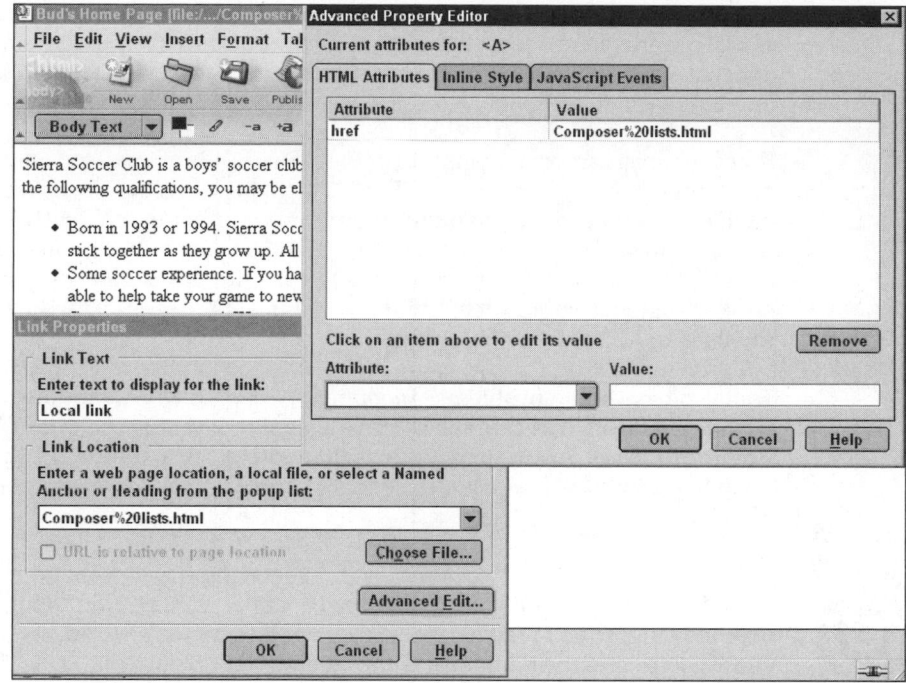

Figure 8-2:
Use the Link
Properties
dialog box
to set up
links in
Composer.

7. **Click OK in the Link Properties dialog box to accept your settings.**

   The appropriate HTML code is added to your Web page.

8. **Choose View⇨HTML Source or click the HTML Source tab to check the underlying HTML.**

   The HTML code for your page appears. Check it, using the information about links earlier in this chapter, to make sure it's okay.

Every so often, save your Web page to your hard disk, open it in a Web browser and test your links. Testing links is one of the most important kinds of testing you can do.

Creating a Mailto Link

Mailto links are a favorite trick on the Web. The good news is, they're fun to set up and fun to use. The bad news is, they don't work for all users.

A *mailto link* is a link that is supposed to automatically bring up the user's e-mail program and create a new mail message addressed to the e-mail address specified in the mailto link. The user only has to fill in the subject line of the e-mail message and the content, and then click Send.

However, many users encounter problems with this scenario. Some older browsers don't support mailto URLs. Also, many users don't realize that they have to be a bit proactive and have their systems set up correctly in order for the mailto link to actually trigger their e-mail package. And finally, some users have multiple e-mail programs connected to different e-mail accounts; the e-mail program that automatically comes up is not necessarily the one that the user wants to use at that moment.

You also have some problems. *Spammers* — people who send unwanted e-mail — get e-mail addresses by creating spiders that search the Web for e-mail addresses. Any e-mail address that you put in a mailto link might end up being harvested and used to send you spam. (This has happened to both of the authors.)

Create a separate e-mail account just for receiving e-mail from your Web site. That way, your personal or professional e-mail accounts aren't clogged with user mail and spam. Free services such as Hotmail (at `www.hotmail.com`) allow you to create and use an e-mail account at no cost.

Users can get quite touchy if you ignore their e-mail messages. Make sure to check for user mail once a day or so — even if you have to wade through a bunch of spam to find it.

One solution to all these problems is to not use mailto links and therefore not allow any user communication at all. However, we prefer two alternatives:

- ✔ **Create a form.** When asking for input, feedback, and so on regarding your Web site, consider using a form. A form allows you to structure the input from the user, if needed. And with a form you still get an e-mail message, but the user doesn't have to worry about what e-mail program (if any) gets launched, and you don't have to worry about spammers getting your e-mail address. There is work to do in getting the form to work, however. (See Chapter 10 for a discussion of forms.)

- ✔ **Spell out the e-mail address when using mailto.** Users whose systems are set up in such a way that the mailto link doesn't work usually know it. If you spell out the e-mail address, as well as provide a mailto link to it, then users who can take advantage of the mailto link can click it; users who can't take advantage of the mailto link can copy and paste the e-mail address into their e-mail program of choice. Figure 8-3 shows an example, with the e-mail address `budsmith2001@aol.com` marked as a mailto link. The following instructions show you how to do this.

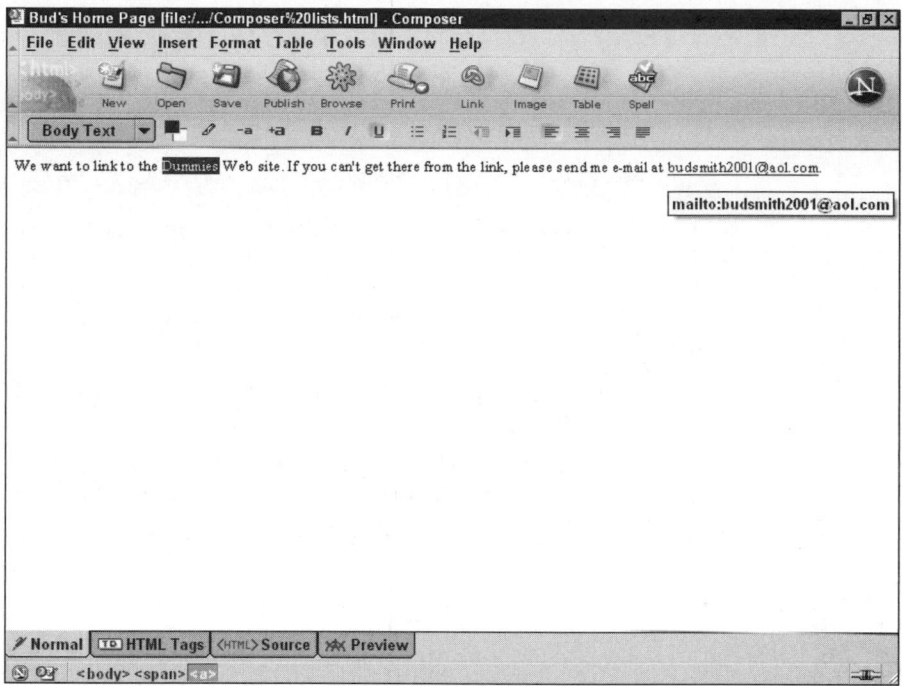

Figure 8-3:
Look to the
side to see
the mailto
URL.

Creating a mailto link in HTML

Creating a mailto link in HTML is easy; it's just like creating a regular link, but you don't have to worry about pathnames or local files versus files on other Web servers. Just add a line of text and HTML like the following:

```
If you'd like, send e-mail to Bud Smith, one of the authors,
      at <a href="mailto:budsmith2001@aol.com">
      budsmith2001@aol.com</a>.
```

Just as with a normal hypertext link, you use the anchor tag and the HREF attribute. Also like normal hypertext links, you surround the text that you want to highlight with the anchor tag in front and the anchor-end tag in back.

Notice that in this example we give the author's e-mail address explicitly, along with a link to it. Not only does this allow the user to cut and paste the e-mail address into the e-mail program of his choice, it also lets him see exactly where he's sending e-mail to before he clicks. In this case, users might appreciate seeing what looks like someone's personal e-mail address, instead of a generic address like `feedback@budsmith.com` or a Hotmail address that the author might not check very often.

Creating a mailto link in Composer

Creating a mailto link in Composer is just like creating a regular link, only simpler. Follow these steps:

1. **Open Composer and your Web page, as described in Chapter 5.**

2. **Enter the text in which you want the mailto link to appear.**

   Enter the text first — before you specify the link.

3. **Select the text that you want to use as mailto link text so that it's highlighted.**

4. **Bring up the Link Properties dialog box by choosing Insert⇨Link or pressing Ctrl+L.**

   The Link Properties dialog box appears. The text you highlighted displays at the top of the dialog box as the link text.

5. **For the link location, type** mailto: **and the e-mail address you want to link to, with no spaces.**

   This creates a link to the specified e-mail address.

   You don't need to look at the other properties for a mailto link; they're only needed for links to an anchor within a document.

6. **Click OK to accept the link properties.**

   The appropriate HTML code is added to your Web page.

7. **Choose View⇨HTML Source or click the HTML Source tab to check the underlying HTML.**

   The HTML code for your page appears. Check it, using the information about links earlier in this chapter, to make sure it's okay. Then pat yourself on the back — you've successfully created a mailto link!

Part III
Better, Stronger, Faster Pages

The 5th Wave   By Rich Tennant

"Well, shoot — I know the animation's moving a mite too fast, but dang if I can find a 'mosey' function anywhere in the toolbox!"

In this part . . .

Web graphics don't have to be hard to create; nor do they have to be large and slow to download. And with our help, you can place your graphics in your Web pages like a pro with text flowing artfully around them. When you have your page looking perfect, we show you how to get it onto a Web server.

Chapter 9

Creating and Adding
Web-Ready Graphics

· ·

· ·

*H*aving graphics as part of the Web seems like an obvious winner now —
after all, magazines and newspapers wouldn't work well if you took
away photographs, drawings, and the little graphical page design elements
that give each publication its own "look." In fact, including graphics in your
Web pages is such a winning strategy that one of the authors of this book
(Bud Smith) has coauthored a companion volume to this one, *Creating Web
Graphics For Dummies* (Wiley). You can refer to that book if you need more
graphics-related details than you find here.

In the 1980s and 90s, before the Web, the Internet was almost entirely a text-
only world. E-mail, Usenet newsgroups, and online service forums were all
text-only environments, running mostly on text-only computer systems like
UNIX and DOS.

Graphics made the Web take off — and they are also the most difficult aspect
of getting your Web pages right. You can use graphics to convey a thematic
"look and feel," to accent certain portions of a Web page, or even to convey
the main content of a Web site. Some use of graphics is necessary for just
about any site.

In this chapter, we look at the nitty-gritty of using graphics and explain how
to create the most common graphic special effects.

To succeed in the somewhat complex task of adding graphics to your Web
pages, you need to know some basics of HTML and of Web pages in general.
Create your basic Web page by using the information in previous chapters
before trying to add any graphics but the simplest. And if you aren't yet familiar with HTML tags, review Chapter 4 before reading this chapter.

Using Graphics in Your Web Site

Graphic images take up a lot of space on a computer's hard disk. (See the sidebar, "Text space versus graphics space," for details about why this is so.) And when graphic images are part of a Web page, they take a long time to be sent from the Web server to your computer over the Internet, especially if users are browsing your site with a dial-up modem.

Because you can't control the speed of users' Internet connection, the best way to make graphics show up faster for everyone is to use images that have small file sizes. You have two ways to do this. The first way is to use images that are small in display size — that is, in the amount of size they take up onscreen. The second is to use images that are small in file size — that is, they have been compressed to reduce the number of bytes needed to store the image.

You can use two kinds of compressed images in your Web pages: GIF and JPEG images. The next section explains these two kinds of images and how to use them.

Using GIF and JPEG graphics formats

A graphics program saves files in its own *proprietary graphics format* — the specific arrangement of data that the program uses to save its files. For instance, the popular graphics program Photoshop saves files in the PSD format (for Photoshop Document); Paint Shop Pro, another popular graphics program, saves its files as PSP files. (You guess what "psp" stands for!) Web browsers typically don't know how to display files stored in these formats.

Fortunately, for the purposes of using graphics in HTML, you need to concern yourself with only two formats for graphics files, GIF and JPEG — and even then you don't really need to know a lot about the gory details of these formats to use them.

  ✔ **GIF, or Graphics Interchange Format:** The file format used by most people to exchange most graphics that aren't photographs. Originally made popular by CompuServe, GIF spread to other online services and then to the rest of the Internet, including the Web. Any browser that supports graphics supports GIF.

  GIF images may contain up to 256 colors, so GIF formatting works effectively for images that have anywhere from a few colors to a few hundred colors. Most simple images and most images created on a computer fall into this category. If an image has more than 256 colors, it loses some color information when you convert the image to GIF. You have to look at the image before and after you convert it to GIF to see if the conversion noticeably affects the image's appearance.

✔ **JPEG, or Joint Photographic Experts Group format:** Compresses complex images, such as photographs, with many color variations. This capability makes JPEG the image format of choice for displaying photographs and other natural-looking images on your Web page. (What makes the image look natural is the way different shades of a color appear as light falls differently on various parts of an object.) These images retain their appearance well when compressed with JPEG.

Figure 9-1 shows a Web page from the NASA Web site to graphically illustrate (pun intended) the difference in GIF and JPEG photo file sizes. Another site you might find useful shows various versions of the same photo of Marc Andreessen, one of the founders of Netscape, to illustrate the various file types and compression options. Here's the URL:

```
cgi.netscape.com/assist/net_sites/impact_docs/e-jpeg.html
```

Use this GIF/JPEG test page to test the speed of your own Internet connection. The total size of the page with graphics is about 70K.

For images with lots of large blocks of solid color, GIF file sizes tend to be small. Thus, most people prefer GIFs for banners or images with large areas of solid color, such as bar graphs or icons. In other words, the simple drawings that most of us create work best with GIF. Dense artistic graphics and photos work better with JPEG.

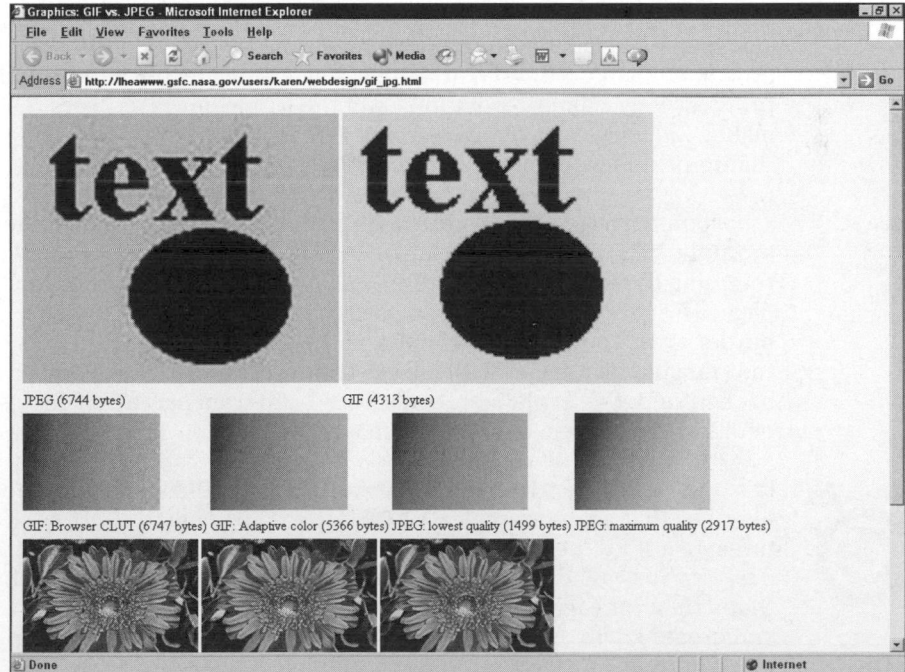

Figure 9-1:
Get an idea
of how
different
graphic file
formats
look.

Text space versus graphics space

Text files are much more efficient for computers to store and transmit across the network than graphics files. Why? Text is very tightly coded; you can fill a typical Web page with solid text using about 1,500 characters, which can be represented in 1,500 bytes, or 1.5KB, of space. Graphics, on the other hand, require a lot of storage. An uncompressed full-page, full-color image takes up about 1.5MB of space — roughly 1,000 times more space.

Large files take a long time to transmit over the Internet, making the Web page take a long time to download. So most Web pages are made up of lots of text, fairly large areas of white space, and small, highly compressed graphics. A Web page made up of only a 2K HTML file takes about 1 second to download over a modem, but is boring. An uncompressed full-page, full-color graphic takes about 12 minutes, which is way too long.

In order to transmit quickly, the best Web graphics are small in size and then compressed even further — mainly by using fewer colors. Graphics packages such as Adobe Photoshop allow you to save images in a compressed format, with a smaller number of colors used to convey almost all the original image. That's why some Web images are too small and have jaggy edges.

However, there are times when choosing a GIF format for a photo is a good idea. The GIF format gives you some Web page display options that you don't always get with JPEG files. For example, you can make the colors around GIF images transparent to whatever is in the background of the image, and you can save GIF images in *interlaced* format. Images saved in this way, and then downloaded by a browser, first appear at a very low resolution, and then in progressively clearer resolution, until the whole image appears. This feature makes GIF images preferable for quickly displaying a rough-looking graphic that improves with time and for creating fancy special effects.

Transparent images have a clear area surrounding the object of interest. For example, in a photo of a watch, you may not want any background color surrounding the watch, just the watch itself seeming to sit directly on the Web page. To achieve this effect, you use a transparent GIF, an image with a clear border area. The background color of the overall Web page shows through the transparent area, and the object of interest appears to "float" over the background. (We explain both interlaced and transparent GIF images in more detail, with pictures, later in this chapter.)

In some cases, the advantages of using GIF for photos outweigh the smaller file sizes that are more typical of JPEG. Use GIF if you need its special features; use JPEG the rest of the time. When you feel more confident in your design skills, you can play around with both formats and choose the one that's right for each photographic image. Read on to find out how to obtain and create graphics for your Web pages and how to save your graphics in either format.

Newer versions of JPEG that support GIF-like features are now available. However, not as many graphics tools or as many browsers support these new JPEG features as support GIF. Stick with GIF for these features until your expertise grows.

Using Web-safe colors

Making your Web page look good on all the computers out there is a big issue. One of the trickiest things that you need to concern yourself with is the issue of Web-safe colors.

Some computer users have display systems that only allow what's called an 8-bit color display, which supports 256 colors, at a fixed resolution, such as 800 x 600. Almost all Windows and Macintosh computer systems in use today support this relatively low resolution and basic palette of colors.

Other computers have more options. They can display thousands or even millions of colors. And they can display the computer desktop in higher resolution — 1024 x 768 and, increasingly, 1280 x 1024 are fairly common. Some computers support even higher resolutions. Usually, though, going to higher resolutions means you lose the choice of displaying as many colors at once as when you use lower resolutions.

However, even these more capable systems can also run at 256 colors and 800 x 600 resolution — and they run fastest in this mode. So, many users run at 256 colors and either 800 x 600 resolution or 1024 x 768 resolution for good performance. Also, some programs, such as games, force the computer into one of these setups, and don't tell the user they're doing so. Nor do they restore the previous setting when the user goes back to Windows. So, without being aware of it, users may be running in lower resolution, and with fewer colors, than their computer is capable of running.

To make sure your graphics will look good for all your users, they have to look good on a system running only 256 colors. Making matters worse, the PC and Macintosh have different 256-color palettes. Only 216 colors work in common on the low-color modes of both the Mac and the PC.

If you use a color that's not one of the 216 Web-safe colors, you may find that the color displays oddly on some systems. (These non-safe colors display as blends of other colors, making an odd and ugly effect.) A graphic that looks good on your computer may look awful on someone else's, though this is more of an issue for GIFs than for JPEGs). If you stick to the Web-safe colors, you won't have this problem.

Several online sources allow you to mix and match different combinations of the Web-safe colors to find ones that look good. Go to this Web site to find Web-safe colors: www.bagism.com/colormaker.

Standards for graphics

Any up-to-date Web browser can display three types of data: text with HTML tags, GIF graphics, and JPEG graphics. (Some people pronounce GIF as "jiff," others as "giff" as in "gift." We prefer "giff" as in "gift.") A typical Web browser displays HTML-tagged text appropriately, although not all browsers understand all the same tags. A browser also displays GIF and JPEG graphics inline — that is, embedded within the Web page. A Web page with inline graphics looks like a page in a magazine, with text and images mixed seamlessly together. However, each graphics file is stored separately from the HTML-tagged text that makes up the underlying Web page. This makes the Web work better overall, but contributes to some of the problems — such as the difficulty of keeping all your Web files together for proper display — that we describe later in this chapter.

Obtaining and creating graphics

So you want to put various graphics on your Web page. Great! But how do you create them and get them in the right format (GIF or JPEG)? Fortunately, creating the graphics you want, or finding some to use, is pretty easy.

The easiest way to obtain graphics is to get access to a clip art collection. Computer stores sell many inexpensive collections of business and recreational graphics on CD-ROM. You can also access a number of royalty-free graphics and icon collections online.

 If you're doing a business or professionally focused Web page, it's important that it have a clean, professional look. To get this kind of look, you have to use attractive graphics and lay out your page carefully. Chapter 11 tells you how to design your page appropriately for various purposes.

You can spend endless hours looking for art online. In fact, just this search alone may make you glad to be creating a Web page. You may not get a lot done for a few hours while you're looking, but you'll see a lot of neat stuff!

To get you started, here's a listing of sites we find especially cool:

- ✔ For a large number of different kinds of resources, go to the main WebReference site at www.webreference.com.

- ✔ For images, go directly to the images area at www.webreference.com/ authoring/graphics/backgrounds.html.

- ✔ For backgrounds, visit www.webreference.com/authoring/graphics/ backgrounds.html.

✔ For photographs, try a site with preexisting stock photos — `www.image state.com` is one we can recommend. Another choice, popular with professionals, is `www.gettyimages.com`.

✔ For a site offering all kinds of graphics options, check out `www.eye wire.com`.

You can find many more sites that offer images and image conversions. Start with the sites that we mention and expand your search until you find what you need.

Using the Image Search feature on the AltaVista search engine is one of the best ways to look for suitable graphics. Be careful, though: Most of the graphics you find are copyrighted; for your Web site, you should only use images that are explicitly made freely available. Visit AltaVista at `www.altavista.com`. Google also has an image search feature; check it out at `www.google.com`.

In addition to searching online, another way to get graphics is to whip out any paint program and draw the graphics that you want. For example, Windows includes a free graphics program (Windows Paint) that you can use for your initial graphics work. Even inexpensive paint programs today enable you to create some stunning graphics; you're limited mostly by your imagination and artistic ability (which for some of us can be quite limiting!).

For big-bucks commercial work and fine art, people regularly use high-end programs such as Adobe Photoshop and Adobe Illustrator. If you lack talent, you can always ask one of your artistically inclined friends to help you, or you can even recruit a starving art student.

Another technique is to use a scanner. You may already have one at home, or have use of a scanner in your office. If not, head to your favorite copy shop and rent some time using its scanner. Scanning is a perfect way to put photos online. Simply scan your graphic or photo, save it in GIF (for graphics) or JPEG (for photographs) format, and slap it on your Web site. Or work with a photo developer, such as a suitably equipped local developer, a chain store such as Wal-Mart or Rite Aid, or a mail-order and Internet operation such as PhotoWorks (`www.photoworks.com`), that can develop your film right to diskette or Photo CD.

More on graphics

The Graphics File Formats FAQ (Frequently Asked Questions page or area on a site) can answer almost any conceivable question about graphics. For a wide array of information, visit `www.dcs.ed.ac.uk/~mxr/gfx/utilshi.html`. Links from this site lead to detailed technical information about GIF, JPEG, and other file formats. For a detailed description of how to use images well, see `cgi.netscape.com/assist/net_sites/impact_docs index.html`.

The fourth way is to take photographs with a digital camera. Digital cameras come with cables that connect the camera to your PC to download the photographs onto your computer. They also come with software that enables you to edit the photos on your PC and save them, usually in JPEG format.

But how can you make sure that your graphics are in the proper format? That turns out to be easy, too. Many paint programs and most scanning software let you save a graphic in either GIF or JPEG formats. If your program doesn't save in these formats, it may be for one of two reasons:

- ✔ During installation, you may have chosen not to install converters for GIF and JPEG. Haul out your original install disks and see whether you can reinstall the program with the correct translators.

- ✔ If converters are not the problem, call your program's manufacturer or visit its Web site and see whether it has an update that enables the program to save to GIF and/or JPEG formats. If your software vendor can't sell you a program that handles GIF or JPEG, you can easily find one that does.

No matter what format your graphic came in originally, you can convert it to GIF or JPEG by using software that you can easily obtain from the Web. Mac users can run GIFConverter (available at `www.kamit.com/gifconverter/`), and Windows users can run the excellent LView program to convert between multiple formats (find LView at `www.lview.com`). Save your graphic as a GIF or JPEG file, and you're ready to incorporate the graphic into your Web page.

 Save your image in the program's default format in addition to saving it as a GIF or JPEG. When you save as a GIF or JPEG, the image can lose information. Every time you reopen the GIF or JPEG image, edit the file, and then save it again, you lose even more information. So save your file in its default format to preserve the data in it for later editing, and save a separate copy in GIF or JPEG to use on the Web.

Dealing with Graphics

The most difficult aspect of including graphics in your Web pages is resolving all the design issues that accompany the use of graphics. Creating effective graphics and placing them properly in relation to your text is not as easy as boiling water. This book doesn't cover all the complexities of graphic design. However, we can tell you the additional concerns that arise when you use graphics on the Web so that you can effectively apply your own graphics skills — or those of people who work with you — to your Web pages.

Speeding up slow pages

One of the Web's ongoing problems is *download speed* — the amount of time a Web page takes to appear on the user's screen. Download times are especially slow for graphics-rich pages, which, although more interesting to view, can be more frustrating because they appear more slowly. And the trade-off is not simple; lots of variables intervene. For example:

✔ **Access speeds:** Different users access the Web through connections that run at different speeds. And the same server can serve up a Web page at different speeds, depending upon how busy the server is. When you test your brand-new, graphics-rich page on your local machine, everything may run fast. But when you upload that same page to a server and access the page over a 56 Kbps (kilobits per second) modem, the page loads much more slowly.

✔ **Good and bad graphics:** If you plan to spend your users' time on downloading big graphics, invest some of your own time and money upfront to make sure that the graphics are as high-quality as possible. People don't mind waiting for a good graphic nearly as much as they mind waiting for a bad one. A good graphic may be a product shot that shows a Web surfer exactly what he or she is going to get. A bad graphic may be a banner that says "HELLO!" in six fluorescent colors.

✔ **Frustration levels:** The same users who enjoy watching your page appear in the morning while drinking a cup of coffee may be tempted to scream at their browser when they try to quickly check out your page just before heading home from work — especially if they had a bad hair day, a bad boss day, or even a bad browser day. The better the job you do with your graphics, the more your page will please people.

What on earth can you do to address all these factors, especially when they combine to make your page slow and your users grumpy? Be clever:

✔ Limit the number of colors in your graphics to make the files smaller so that they download more quickly.

✔ Get expert advice — from someone you know or a book — or look at cool sites online to help you make the graphics you do use more interesting to look at.

✔ Lightly sprinkle your page with small graphics, rather than burdening it with several big ones.

Table 9-1 shows the time necessary to download 60K (kilobytes) of data. A text-only page is usually just 2 or 3K, but pages with graphics are much larger. A complex, quarter-screen GIF image, for example, may be about 50K. Compare the total size of all the elements in your page to the times shown in Table 9-1 to get an idea of how quickly your page loads for the most speed-deficient user, and then design with that person in mind.

Table 9-1	Slowest Download Times	
Access Speed	*Description*	*Time to Download 60K File*
28.8 Kbps	Low-end Internet modem	35 seconds
33.6 Kbps	Mid-range Internet modem	30 seconds
56 Kbps	Fast Internet modem	20 seconds
DSL	Special phone line, modem	4 seconds
Cable modem	Special cable hookup, modem	1 second
Ethernet	Standard network	Less than 1 second

Avoiding three big mistakes

Don't make these three big mistakes relating to graphics on the Web:

- ✔ **No graphics:** Having no graphics on your Web pages means having boring pages. Because you're reading this chapter, we assume that you're trying not to make this mistake.

- ✔ **Too many graphics:** Using too many large, slow-to-download graphics may be the biggest newbie Web author mistake. (A lot of old hands make this mistake as well.)

- ✔ **No text alternative:** Some users don't have graphical capability at all, and many others run around the Web with graphics turned off, only turning graphics capability on when absolutely necessary. You need to accommodate these users by creating your page in a way that supports text-only access as well as graphical access.

Try an experiment: Go into your browser, turn off the graphics display, and load your Web page. If you can't tell what is on the page or what links go where, then you need to redesign your page. (Then, just to blow off steam, or if you don't have a Web page up yet, try the same experiment on some other people's pages and send them a note if you have problems.)

The usual way to redesign your page for text-only access is to include a textual menu linking to the same places as your graphical menu. Some sites provide a whole parallel set of Web pages that are purely textual rather than graphical. Providing parallel, text-only pages lets the user choose whether to go for the attractive, bandwidth-sucking graphical pages or for the very fast text-only pages, and enables those with visual impairments to enjoy the benefits of the Web.

What about rights?

You can find a number of great graphics in books and magazines and on Web sites. Can you just scan or copy these graphics and use them in your own Web site? Should you?

Yes and no. Yes, you can, but no, you shouldn't. Publishers either own the images that they use or obtain a license for them. You can't legally use most images on your own Web site without either buying or licensing them.

For some images on the Web, simply sending a note to the Webmaster gets you a quick okay. But for most Web images and for nearly all images in print, permissions may be very hard to get. Creating a new image that serves the same purpose is often easier than negotiating permissions. And then maybe you can make a little money licensing your own images to other people!

In the past, many have chosen text-only access because of slow download times. However, because this percentage of users continues to drop, providing a complete set of text-only pages may be overkill. Consider providing a *text-mostly* version, with limited use of images, simpler layout, and alternative text for images. This option may be just the ticket for users with visual impairments. Above all else, consider carefully all the issues as you handle graphics versus text on your Web pages.

Here are the most important rules for supporting text and graphical access:

✔ As you design and create your page, think about how your page will look with all graphic access turned off as well as on.

✔ Test your page with graphics turned off.

✔ Test your page in different browsers.

✔ Include ALT tags — actually, the ALT attribute within the IMG tag — in all images so that explanatory text appears whenever a graphic isn't displayed. (See this chapter and Appendix C for details about HTML tags used in graphics.)

✔ Provide text-only menus in addition to icon-based selections and image maps.

✔ If you want to make everyone very happy, consider creating a separate, text-only version of your site.

If you're considering creating a Web site that's accessible by portable devices such as the PalmOne or RIM Blackberry line of handheld devices, creating a text-only version of your site makes a great deal of sense. The text-only version of your site will make a good starting point for handhelds.

Using Graphics in HTML

The <IMG> tag is the HTML tag that causes an image to appear embedded in your Web page. (See Chapter 4 for more on HTML.) Here are the HTML tags for a page that displays the image menugraphic.gif by using the <IMG> tag, and then a text menu as an alternative:

```
<IMG SRC="menugraphic.gif" ALT="Menu Graphic"> [ <A
HREF="about.html">About</A> | <A
HREF="home.html">Home page</A> | <A
HREF="links.html">Fun Links</A> | <A
HREF="map.html">Site Map</A> | <A
HREF="search.html">Search Map</A> ]
```

It's good to know some HTML even if you are using a Web authoring program that allows you to drag and drop images, specify compression options, and so on. Why? Because you may need to make changes in options like the ALT text for the image or the directory that a file lives in. Your Web authoring program, or a text editing program, allows you to change the HTML directly, quickly, and accurately — if you know a little HTML.

With that in mind, here are three useful graphical effects for your Web pages:

- **Accents:** Small graphical images that serve as labels or highlights ("New," "Top Ten," and so on).
- **Icons:** Small graphical images that serve as links to another page. Click the icon, and you move to a different Web page.
- **Thumbnails:** Small graphical images that serve as previews of larger images. Click a thumbnail to download the larger image.

Accents use the <IMG> tag to link to a small graphic — an inline graphic that appears as part of the page, unless graphics display is turned off.

Icons and thumbnails combine the <IMG> tag, which makes the icon or thumbnail image appear, with the <A> (or anchor) tag. (Don't start singing "Anchors Aweigh" on this one — you need anchors here!) The anchor tag establishes a link to the Web page or larger graphic that appears when you click the inline graphic. For more on the anchor tag, see Chapter 8.

The steps in the following sections describe how to use the image tag, the anchor tag, and the ALT option separately and together. With these tags, you can combine graphics and navigation to create all kinds of effects.

Review the HTML tag definitions in Appendix C to find out about other options for these tags. You may also want to check out more advanced books, such as *HTML 4 For Dummies,* 4th Edition, by Ed Tittel and Natanya Pitts, and *Creating Cool HTML 4 Web Pages,* 2nd Edition, by Dave Taylor (both from Wiley) for more details and how-to information on advanced HTML options.

Use the <IMG> tag for inline graphics

To use the `<IMG>` tag to link to an inline graphic that appears as part of your Web page, along with the `ALT` option to specify "alternate" text, follow these steps:

1. **Create or find a graphic that you want to use.**

   Inline graphics that are embedded in the page should be small for fast display — about the size of a business card or smaller. Use the sources we describe in the "Obtaining and creating graphics" section earlier in this chapter to find or create graphics.

2. **If you're using Netscape Composer, choose Insert⇨Image. Type the URL of the image in the text entry box, or choose a file from your hard disk with the Choose File button. If you're working directly in HTML, add the `<IMG>` tag with the `SRC`, or "source," option to specify the image's pathname.**

   For a graphic that's in the same directory as the HTML file, use the `<IMG>` tag and `SRC` option like this:

   ```
   <IMG SRC="new.gif">
   ```

   For a graphic that's at a different Web site, use the `<IMG>` tag and `SRC` option like this:

   ```
   <IMG SRC="http://www.grafixsite.com/new.gif">
   ```

3. **Add the `ALT` option to specify text that appears if the graphic can't be viewed — for example, if the user is running a text-only browser or has graphics turned off. In Netscape Composer, put the text in the Alternative Text text entry box. If you're working in HTML, add the `ALT` option and text within the `<IMG>` tag, like this:**

   ```
   <IMG SRC="http://www.grafixsite.com/new.gif" ALT="New!">
   ```

 Don't depend on someone else's site being up at all times and always staying unchanged. If possible, copy the graphic that you need into your own site's directory and refer to it there. Make sure, though, that you're not violating copyright laws in doing so.

Add an A for anchor to create a graphical link

As we note in the first part of the section on graphics and HTML, one of the best ways to jazz up a Web page "cheaply" — that is, without slowing down the page a lot for everyone — is to use graphical elements as icons that link to outside information, such as a larger image or a different Web page. This technique is a great way to make your page appear graphically rich without burdening your users with long download times.

To add an anchor to create a graphical link, use the ⟨IMG⟩ tag between the beginning and ending anchor tags. If you also embed a word or phrase between the beginning and ending anchor tags, you give the user a choice between clicking the image or the phrase. The following steps demonstrate how to create a graphical link:

1. **In Netscape Composer, use the Insert⇨Image command to bring in an image. In a text editor, use the ⟨IMG⟩ tag to bring in the inline image that you want to use as a thumbnail image or icon:**

   ```
   <IMG SRC="minibud.jpg">
   ```

2. **In Netscape Composer, click the image and choose Insert⇨Link. In a text editor, add an anchor tag (⟨A⟩) to specify the link.**

   To display a larger image when a user clicks the small image, specify an anchor with an HREF, or *Hypertext REFerence,* that points to an image file:

   ```
   <A HREF="maxibud.jpg"> <IMG SRC="minibud.jpg"> </A>
   ```

   Figure 9-2, from Boojum Expeditions, shows a thumbnail graphic and the larger image that appears when the user clicks the thumbnail. John Forrester's travelogue can be found at http://boojum.com/ photographs.html.

   For a link to another page, specify an anchor with an HREF that points to an HTML document:

   ```
   <A HREF="bebakpg.htm"> <IMG SRC="bebak.jpg"> </A>
   ```

An HTML option not only allows you to resize an image, but also speeds up page displays. Add the HEIGHT= and WIDTH= options within the ⟨IMG⟩ tag to specify, in pixels, the height and width of your image. In Netscape Composer, use the Dimensions area within the Image Properties dialog box (which appears when you choose Insert⇨Image). Browsers use this information to fill in the rest of the page around the image first, allowing the user to scroll up and down in the page and read it while the graphic builds on-screen.

The height and width options can stretch or squeeze an image to make it appear different than its actual size. However, these options don't change the actual image. You must keep the height and width options proportional with the original image to avoid having the image stretched in one dimension. Also, if you put a small image in a large area, it will be stretched out to fit and appear odd. If you put a large image in a small area, it will look good, but the file size will be large compared to the amount of space the image takes onscreen. To prevent these problems, use an image editing program such as Paint Shop Pro to edit the image to the correct size, rather than using the height and width options to resize the image.

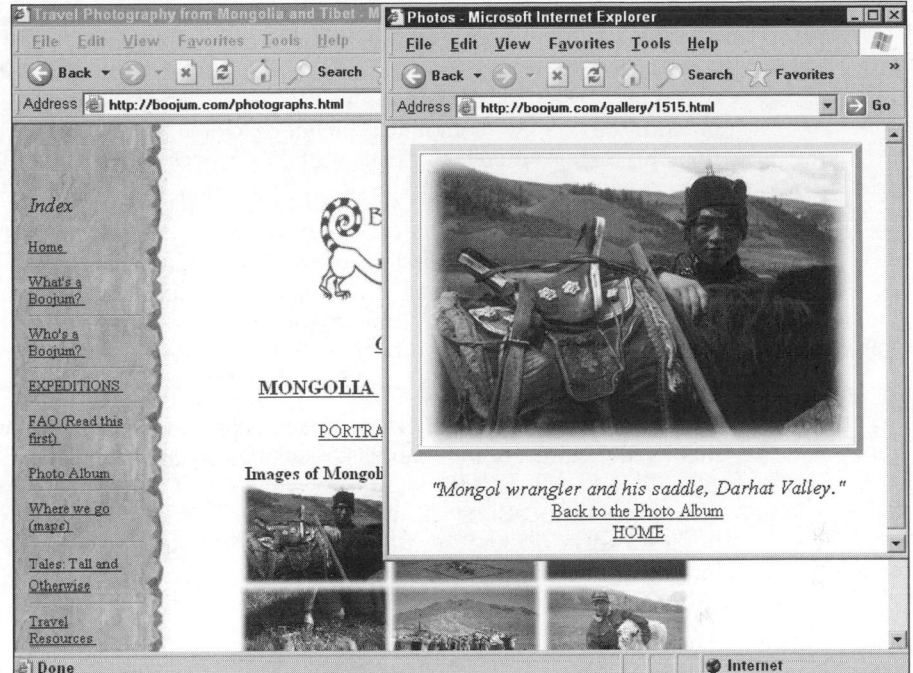

Figure 9-2:
Combining
mini-
and maxi-
graphics.

One of the most important ways for intermediate and advanced Web authors to organize their pages is by using invisible tables to position text and graphics relative to one another. Chapter 11 has a brief description of tables. This method is tricky! For example, a table-structured page that looks great at one monitor size can easily look terrible on a larger or smaller screen. Find some well-laid-out Web pages and view the Web pages' HTML source to see how other Web publishers use invisible tables. To see one expert's work, visit Creating Killer Web sites at www.killersites.com/.

Experimenting with Advanced GIFfery

GIFs are widespread on the Web, and download times are important; therefore, we recommend four advanced techniques for doing fancy things with GIFs:

  ✔ **Transparent GIFs:** Everyone needs to know this one. All GIFs are rectangular, but many of them seem to float over the background with no obvious border. These GIFs are *transparent* — the images' backgrounds are invisible — so they blend seamlessly into the browser's background. If this doesn't make sense, look closely at the example in Figure 9-3, which is from the For Dummies Web site — you see two For Dummies logos with black backgrounds and one with a transparent background.

✔ **Interlaced GIFs:** Not everyone needs to know about this one, but we mention it (again!) because if you use large, complex graphics, interlaced GIFs are worth knowing about. An interlaced GIF depends on an HTML feature that paints every fourth line of an image, then every second line, and so on until the image is complete. The image seems to appear at a low resolution and then gradually sharpens until the process is complete.

✔ **Animated GIFs:** The basic GIF specification, GIF89a, supports animation as well as static images. All you need to do is create a series of images that, when viewed in sequence, form an animation (like an old-fashioned flip book). Then you package the images together as a single GIF, using readily available tools, and include the GIF file in your Web page. Voilà! Instant animation. (But at a big cost in file size — the file size of a four-image animation can be as large as having four separate images.)

✔ **Clickable image maps:** Clickable image maps are very common in big-money sites and even in many smaller ones. A clickable image map is a graphic with different *hot spots* that, when clicked, take you to different Web pages or locations within a Web page. This kind of graphic is cool, but it's YABG (Yet Another Big Graphic), and you need design skills to make a good one.

Transparent GIF

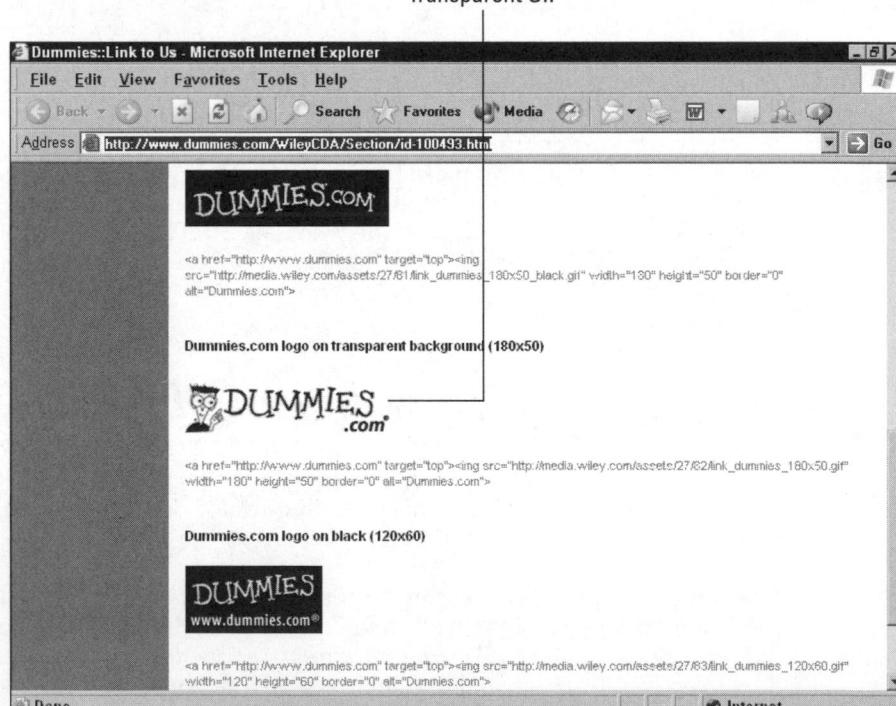

Figure 9-3:
Now
you see it
(the black
rectangle
around the
graphic);
now you
don't.

Graphics can be a time sink

We spend a lot of time in this chapter discussing how much time the user can spend downloading graphics. But what about the demand that using graphics places on your time as a Web developer?

Creating and editing graphics is fun! But creating even a simple business graphic, such as a bar graph, can consume hours of fooling around with fonts, colors, and image sizes. Getting your

images Web-ready and testing them takes up even more time. Working with graphics can easily become the most time-consuming part of creating and updating your Web site.

What to do? Use small graphics (and use them sparingly) while you gain experience. After you have experience, or after you hire someone who does, you can develop and deploy those knockout graphics that distinguish the best Web sites.

Transparent GIFs

Here are the steps to create a transparent GIF:

1. **Choose a color in the image's background to make transparent.**

   Every pixel in your image that's of the selected color becomes transparent. Choose a color that's used only in the area around the image, not in the image itself, since every pixel of the selected color becomes transparent. You may need to edit the image's surrounding area — the area that you want to be transparent — so that it's a different color from the rest of the image. The usual choices for transparency are white or the light gray background color most browsers use.

   For details on the procedure for choosing an area to make transparent, see the Web 66 Web site at `members.chello.at/Michael.donoho/xparent.html`.

2. **Use your graphics package or a tool to make the image transparent.**

   For the Macintosh, use Transparency, which you can find on the Web at CINET's download.com Web site and elsewhere.

   For Windows, use Paint Shop Pro. You can find an evaluation version on the CD-ROM that comes with this book.

   For any platform, you can use a Web-based package called TransWeb on the Massachusetts Institute of Technology (MIT) site at `www.mit.edu/tweb/map.html`. This package reads the image, converts it, and displays the result. You can then right-click on the image to save it to disk.

   To use TransWeb, you have to move your image to a Web server, as we describe in Chapter 12. (You can also do this as part of the process of creating a simple GeoCities Web page, as described in Chapter 2.) Then go to the TransWeb Web and follow the instructions.

3. **Add the image to your page, as we describe in the "Use the <IMG> tag for inline graphics" section, earlier in this chapter.**

4. **Test to be sure that the image remains transparent with several different backgrounds.**

   Bring up the image in your browser and then change the browser's default background color. Make sure that the background stays invisible throughout.

Animated GIFs

Animated GIFs are also supported online. You can find out how to use them and start putting them in your Web pages by using info out on the Web. To read the true and fascinating story of how animated GIFs were invented, and to link to many supporting examples and resources, go to these Web sites:

```
http://members.aol.com/royalef/gifmake.htm
http://builder.com.com/5100-31-5078158.html
```

Clickable image maps

To create a clickable image map, you must first create the graphic. (See the University of California, San Diego Web site at www.ucsd.edu for an example of an attractive, clickable image map.) Then you have to create a special file that maps regions of the image to specific URLs. A program that is available on the CD-ROM that comes with this book, Mapedit (see Appendix E), maps image regions for either Macintosh or Windows. Just load the image, click and drag over it to define clickable regions, and then enter the URL you want to link to.

The complication arises during the final part of this process. The original form of image maps, called *server-side image maps,* require that the map file be in a special place where the server can find it. Unfortunately, to use this kind of image map, you may need to talk to the server administrator, because no universal standard exists about where this file should be.

Netscape 2.0 and higher (and Netscape is up to version 7.1 now), Microsoft Internet Explorer, and all other up-to-date browsers support what are known as *client-side image maps* that don't require server involvement in any processing when the user clicks an image. Browsers are now smart enough to map the image, click to a URL, and fetch the URL directly without going through the server. See the Netscape 2.0 documentation or the Netscape site at http://wp.netscape.com/assist/net_sites/html_extensions_3.html for more information.

Chapter 10

Placing Graphics Right (And Left)

Chapter 9 shows you how to insert graphics into your Web page. When you start getting your Web page to look good, though, you have to worry about not just the image itself, but about how it's placed on the page.

In this chapter we show you how to make your graphics work well within your Web page by adjusting the size of the image; by flowing text smoothly around the graphic; and by putting a border around the graphic. We then show you how to actually implement the changes in HTML and in Netscape Composer.

Adjusting Graphic Size

You can specify the size of an image when you insert it into your Web page. Within the IMG tag, you add two options to specify the image's size: WIDTH and HEIGHT. If you're using Netscape Composer or another WYSIWYG Web page creation tool, you enter the width and height as options within the program you're using. The program then stores these values in the WIDTH and HEIGHT options for you.

Every graphic has an actual size — a height and width in pixels. When displayed at this size, the graphic looks as good as it's going to look. However, graphics can be stretched or shrunk to fit into an available space.

There are two very different reasons for specifying the size of your graphic — one excellent and one questionable:

- ✔ **To tell the Web browser what size the image is:** This is the excellent reason. When you specify the height and width of your image in the Web page, the user's Web browser sets aside just the right amount of space for the image to load on-screen while it continues displaying text. Because text can be transmitted so much faster than graphics, this often allows the user to see all of the text in a page and start reading it without having to wait for the image to appear.

- ✔ **To stretch or squeeze the image:** This is the questionable reason. If you enter a height or width that is different from the image's actual size, then the user's Web browser will stretch or squeeze the image to fit. This has no effect on the text, and can produce some very odd-looking results in terms of the appearance of the image.

If you are going to stretch or squeeze the image, you can set the height and width options four different ways:

- ✔ **Scaled smaller than the original image:** You can reduce the height and width by an equal proportion — say, one-third less, or 10 percent less — than the original image. The image will be smaller and still look good. However, it will still take up the same amount of file space as the original and take just as long to download and appear on-screen. It's better to edit the original image so it actually is smaller and then display it at its new actual size — the file will be smaller and download quicker.

- ✔ **Scaled larger than the original image:** You can stretch the image by increasing the height and width in equal proportions. The image is stretched evenly. It doesn't look too odd, but you can usually see some "breaks" in the image as a result of its being stretched. This option gives you a quick way to get a small image to fill a large space, but you're usually better off adjusting the image size in an editing program like Adobe Photoshop, which lets you fix any problems that come up. That way, you can use the new, edited image at its actual size.

- ✔ **Scaled out of proportion to the original image:** For most images, the worst thing to do is to set the height and width disproportionately. Let's say you have a 50 x 50 image but you need to fill a 100 x 50 space (that's 100 pixels tall by 50 pixels wide). You can simply set the height to 100 and the width to 50, and the user's Web browser will stretch the height of the image accordingly. However, the result is likely to look awful.

Figure 10-1 shows an image and the results of scaling the image smaller and larger, both out of proportion. It wasn't such a great a picture to begin with, but you can see that the changes have made it even worse. You can use any of these options as needed, but *caveat artifex* — let the artisan beware — the results aren't likely to be great.

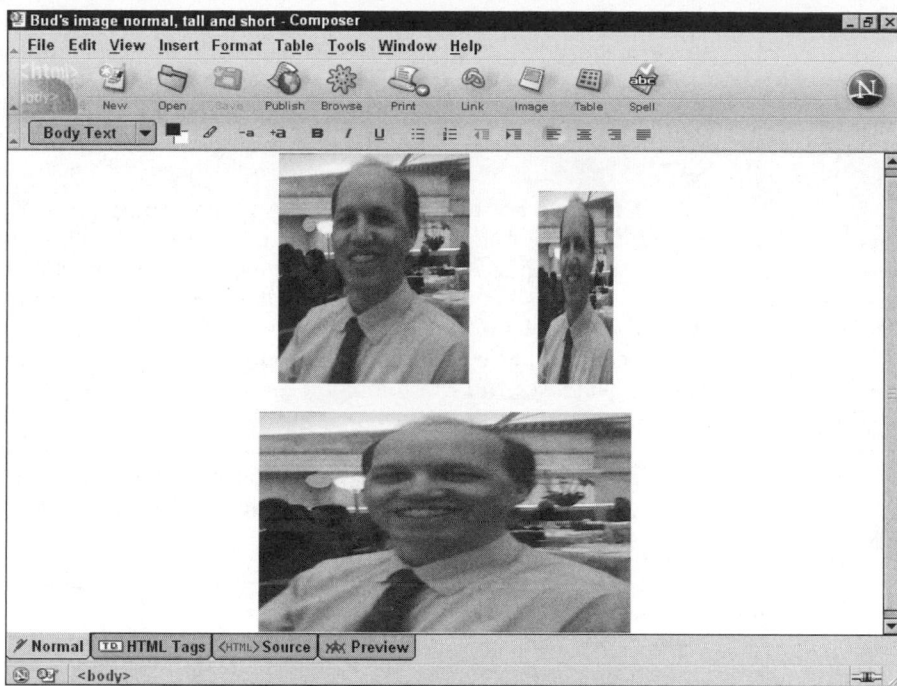

Figure 10-1:
A scaled image can look — well, scaly.

Flowing Text around Graphics

One of the trickier things to do on your Web page is to get graphic images and text to work well together. You have several choices for placing an image, from simplest to trickiest:

- **Putting text above and below — but not beside — the image:** You can create a clear area in the middle of your text and put the image in the middle of it. You can also put a caption below the image. This solution wastes the area to the left and right of your image, but it's the easiest to implement in HTML and creates the simplest layout. Your readers also don't have to adjust, as they're reading, to the "bump" in the text around where the picture is.

- **Putting one line of text beside an image:** You can put text beside your image and align the line at the top, middle, or bottom of the image. Figure 10-2 shows an example. This used to be the only way that HTML allowed you to position an image relative to text, and it produced some ugly layouts.

- ✔ **Wrapping text around an image:** A command that allows text to actually wrap around an image — in the manner we're all used to from magazines — was added to HTML several years ago. (The command in question is the HTML `ALIGN` attribute within the `IMG` tag.) By now, almost everyone out there has a browser new enough to support this feature.

- ✔ **Using a table to control precisely where everything goes:** You can use the HTML `TABLE` command to create a grid into which you can then place text and images, just like you might if you were laying out a newspaper page. This is difficult to do, and it can force you to redo the table every time you want to make even a small change in your image or your text. Because it allows such precise control, this option can produce the best-looking — or the worst-looking — results.

The most popular approach to placing graphics with modern Web browsers is to wrap text around the image. We show you how to do that, directly using HTML tags or by using Netscape Composer, later in this chapter.

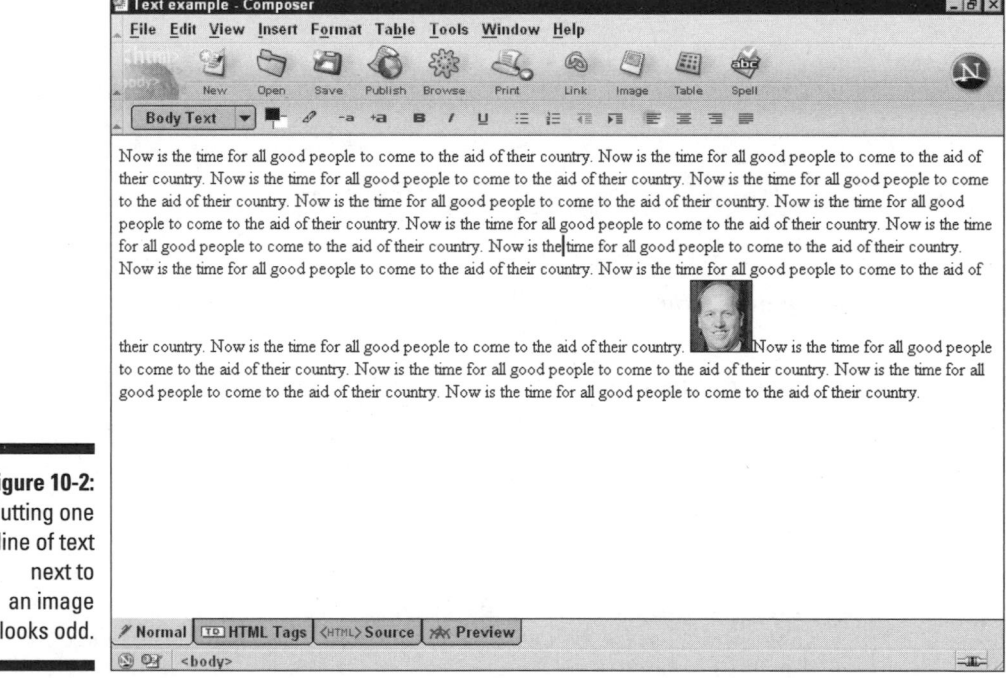

Figure 10-2:
Putting one line of text next to an image looks odd.

Putting a Border around a Graphic

One of the more important elements in designing a page to look good is *white space* — "empty" space that separates different parts of the page from one another. If content is crowded together too closely, the page as a whole looks chaotic.

White space is especially important when you flow (or wrap) text around a graphic, as we describe in the previous section. You can specify the amount of white space that surrounds a graphic, add a solid border to set the graphic apart, or both.

Most photos look better with a thin black border around them. We describe how to add such a border, either directly in HTML or in Netscape Composer, later in this chapter.

Placing a Graphic in Netscape Composer

It's good to know your HTML, but working with graphics is much easier in a WYSIWYG tool such as Netscape Composer. We recommend that you work in the tool, and then look at the underlying HTML to learn about it, rather than doing all your work directly in HTML.

To place a graphic in Netscape Composer and specify the graphic size, text flow, spacing, and border, if any, follow these steps:

1. **Open Netscape Composer.**

2. **Type in some text, or copy and paste it in.**

   It's much easier to experiment with placing a graphic if you have some text in your document.

3. **Place the cursor at the start of a line of text in your document. Then use the Insert⇨Image command to insert a GIF or JPEG image, as described in Chapter 9. Click OK to close the Image Properties dialog box.**

   If you don't have an image handy, you can find instructions on how to create images and sources for free images in Chapter 9.

   An example of how your document might look at this point is shown back in Figure 10-2.

Note that at this point the text is crowded right up against the graphic. The text doesn't all wrap around the graphic — only one line of text appears next to the graphic.

4. **Double-click the image to open the Image Properties dialog box. If the button to the left of the Image Preview area says More Properties, click it to show all the properties.**

Figure 10-3 shows how the dialog box appears at this point, with the image placed and with tabs available for changing the image's location, dimensions, appearance or linking characteristics.

Move the Image Properties dialog box to a spot on your screen so you can see both the image and the dialog box.

You don't have to specify the image's width and height in Netscape Composer. The program automatically adds the `WIDTH` and `HEIGHT` options to the `IMG` tag, or adds relevant style attributes to accomplish the same task, using the image's actual width and height. You should, however, add alternate text, using the option visible in the picture.

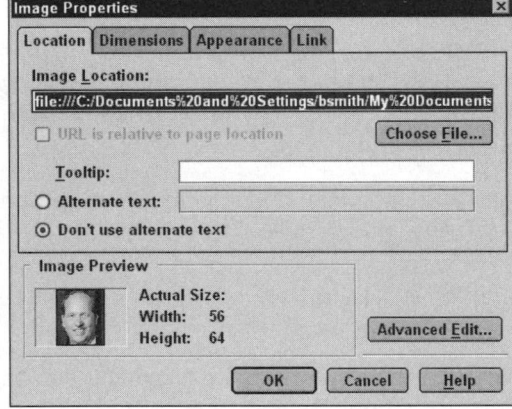

Figure 10-3:
The Image
Properties
dialog box
offers you
many
options.

5. **To scale the image to a larger or smaller size, click the Dimensions tab and then click the Custom Size radio button. In most cases, you will want to leave the Constrain checkbox checked. Change the Height or Width to the value you want.**

Clicking Custom Size allows you to change the image's height and width. By leaving the Constrain checkbox checked, you tell Composer to automatically keep the width and height scaled proportionally with the image's actual height and width.

The Image Preview doesn't change to reflect the dimensions you enter. Even if you clear the Constrain checkbox and enter a height twice as large as you did previously, and keep the width the same, the preview will not become tall and skinny to reflect the change. The Image Preview is actually an "image view" of the underlying image, not a preview of how it will look on your Web page. To see a true preview, simply close the dialog box at any point and the current values will be reflected in the image's appearance in the document window.

After changing any of the values in the Image Properties dialog box, click OK to close the dialog box and see what your page looks like with the new values. Then double-click the image to open the Image Properties dialog box again.

6. **Change the pull-down menu in the Align Text to Image area on the Appearance tab to reflect how you want text to flow around the image: A single line of text aligned to the top, center, or bottom of the image, or all of the text flowing to the left or right of the image.**

   If you want to create a caption next to the image, you'll want to use the At the Top, At the Center, or At the Bottom option, each of which aligns a single line of text beside the image accordingly. If you don't want captions, you have two choices. You can choose Wrap to the Right to keep the image on the left margin and wrap text to the right or you can choose Wrap to the Left to push the image to the right of the page and flow text down on its left.

7. **In the Spacing area on the Appearance tab, specify the number of pixels of blank area that you want around the image.**

   Unless you have a special reason to do otherwise, we suggest starting with the same amount of spacing for the Left and Right spacing and the Top and Bottom spacing. Four pixels is a good starting point. Fine-tune the numbers as needed to create the right look whenever you have your final text and images available.

8. **Still in the Spacing area, specify the size of the border that you want around the image.**

   A thin border around an image makes the image stand out much better from the surrounding white space and text. Try a 2-pixel-wide border to start, and then adjust it from there to get the look you want.

For consistency's sake, use the same spacing and border width around each of your images. You may need to experiment to find a set of values that works well for all your images, but the effort is worth it. Even minor inconsistencies of a pixel here or there are enough to throw off the overall appearance of your pages.

Placing a Graphic in HTML

Fine-tuning the positioning of graphics by using HTML directly is a frustrating exercise unless you're somewhat of an expert in Web design. If you're new to design work, be prepared to experiment. Luckily, experimenting is much easier using a tool such as Netscape Composer than it is with a text editing program such as Notepad. So we recommend that you use Netscape Composer, as described in the previous section, to place your graphic.

However, if you prefer to write the HTML in another HTML editor or Notepad, use the instructions in this section. Use the figures in the previous section to see how your pages should look as you experiment with different options.

To place a graphic in HTML and specify the graphic size, text flow, spacing, and border (if any), follow these steps:

1. **Open a document in a text editor. Save it with the extension .htm to make sure that it's treated as an HTML document.**

2. **Type in some text, or copy and paste it in.**

   It's much easier to experiment with placing a graphic if you have some text in your document.

3. **Insert an image into the middle of the text using the** IMG **tag. Add alternate text to explain what the image is.**

   The correct syntax to use is <IMG SRC=*url* ALT="*text*">, where *url* is a Web address and *text* is a brief description of the image. See Chapter 9 for details.

4. **Save your document and open it in a Web browser to see how it looks at this point.**

   Your document looks something like Figure 10-2, shown earlier in the chapter.

   Continue to save your document and look at it in your Web browser as you add tags and change options. This helps you see how the page looks after each adjustment you make.

   Click the Refresh or Reload button in your browser to update the Web page to reflect the most recently saved version of your document.

5. **Add the** WIDTH **and** HEIGHT **options to the** IMG **tag.**

   In most cases, set these options to the actual width and height of the image. If you want to change the size of the image, or to change its proportions, calculate the appropriate values for the WIDTH and HEIGHT options and enter them. (But see Figure 10-1 before changing the proportions.) Then review the result in a Web browser.

   The IMG tag now looks like this: <IMG SRC=*url* WIDTH=*xx* HEIGHT=*yy*>, where *xx* is the width, in pixels, and *yy* is the height, in pixels.

   Adding the WIDTH and HEIGHT options with the actual values of the image doesn't change the look of your page, but it does make it easy for a Web browser to load the rest of the page quickly around the image. Using different values will change the look of your page.

You can find the actual width and height of your image by right-clicking the image's icon. Right-click, choose Properties, and the image's width and height are displayed.

6. **To specify text wrapping, add the** ALIGN **option to the** IMG **tag.**

    The most commonly used options are RIGHT, to wrap text to the right of the image, and LEFT, to wrap text left of the image and move the image over to the right. Other options are TOP, CENTER, and BOTTOM. If you don't specify the ALIGN option then the default value, BOTTOM, is used. With this option, the text is shoved to the right and positioned at the bottom of the image, leaving an odd gap in most of the area next to the image. This is hardly ever what you want. Start with ALIGN=RIGHT, and change things around later if you want a different effect.

7. **To create white space around an image, add the** HSPACE **(for horizontal spacing) and** VSPACE **(for vertical spacing) options.**

    HSPACE creates an equal number of pixels of space to the left and right of the image; VSPACE creates an equal number of pixels of space above and below the image. Good settings to start with are HSPACE=4 VSPACE=4.

8. **To create a black border around the image, add the** BORDER **tag. A suitable value is** BORDER=2.

    If you've specified all the possible options, your tag now looks something like this:

    ```
    <IMG SRC=url ALT="text" WIDTH=xx HEIGHT=yy ALIGN=right
            HSPACE=4 VSPACE=4 BORDER=2>
    ```

For consistency's sake, use the same spacing and border width around each of your images. You may need to experiment to find a set of values that works well for all your images, but the effort is worth it. Even minor inconsistencies of a pixel here or there are enough to throw off the overall appearance of your page.

Chapter 11

Designing a Good-Looking Page

*O*ne of the trickiest issues in creating and publishing Web pages is creating and maintaining the overall look of each Web page. Some pages look great. Others look fine. Still others look hokey and amateurish. And how good a page looks varies considerably depending on who's looking — "beauty is in the eye of the beholder." Up to a point, anyway; some pages are so bad, or so good, that everyone agrees on them.

When you create your first Web page, as described in Part I of this book, it really doesn't matter how your page looks. You're just trying to have fun and get a little experience. But if you're creating a Web page a lot of people will be looking at, or if you're practicing to create a Web page for business or career use, you're going to want it to look good. And explaining how to make a Web page look good is hard.

The overall impression a Web page makes depends on many different factors — the balance of white space (empty space) to text and graphics, the size of text used, the font used, appropriate use of headings versus regular text, and appropriate use of bulleted and numbered lists, hyperlinks, and other eye-catching elements. Each of these factors has to be "right," but "right" is hard to define — you know it when you see it. All the choices you make have to work together as a whole.

It takes a professional to make a Web page look really good — so at the end of this chapter, we talk about how to get professional help for the look of your Web page. But it doesn't take a professional to make your Web page look pretty good — or at least to avoid having it be out-and-out ugly. We show you how to make sure your Web page looks good in this chapter.

Three Key Principles of Design

The design of a Web page can be most simply described as the look of the page and how it's perceived by the user — as attractive or unattractive, and as easy to use or difficult to use. Design is artistic and aesthetic; getting it right draws on people's creativity, and judging when it's right depends on people's individual taste. So there are no hard and fast rules that always yield a good-looking design. This fact drives some people crazy, but many of the most important things in life — like love, fine food, good wine, and good design — don't operate by specific rules.

In our years of work with the Web, we've learned many of the "tricks" of Web design. Instead of the specific and formal rules that professional Web designers follow, we have discovered that following general principles usually yields good results for smallish Web design projects. Of course, we do depend a great deal on existing professional models that most people agree look good, but at carefully chosen times, we like to break the rules. The design process is a challenge to anyone's sanity, but we feel that mixing and matching is the only way to consistently create designs that look good.

The design tips in this chapter are based on the authors' experience in designing and using many Web sites, not on formal design principles. Furthermore, our advice is just for people doing single Web pages and small Web sites of 5–10 Web pages — not large sites that have to be planned carefully from the beginning. All this means that our advice may be infuriating to professionals – but is likely to be very helpful to people just starting out. For detailed information about Web page and Web site design, we recommend *Web Design For Dummies* by Lisa Lopuck (Wiley).

The three most important principles for designing Web home pages and small Web sites are simplicity, predictability, and consistency. It's necessary to follow each principle in order to also follow the others. In the next few sections are a few pointers showing how to apply these principles.

Achieving simplicity

Simplicity is considered the hallmark of good design. The modern eye is trained to look for and appreciate simple, unornamented designs. Use the simplest design that accomplishes your task, and then figure out how to simplify it further. For Web pages, simplicity means using as few of everything — design elements, graphics, and text sizes — as reasonably possible.

Simplicity has specific advantages in Web design; in fact, the impact of time constraints and the differences among users' computer setups make simplicity a necessity. The fact that it takes time to download each element on a Web page means that a simply designed Web page usually loads faster than a complicated one, and users really like fast-loading pages. (Actually, they dislike slow-loading pages, but we'd rather describe the situation in a positive way.)

The differences among users' computer setups reward simplicity as well. One user can be looking at your Web page on a small screen with 256 colors; another can be looking at it on a large, high-resolution screen with thousands of colors. The simpler your Web page design, the more likely the page will look about the same on all the different computer setups out there.

To you as a novice Web page author, simplicity is especially important. You don't have the hard-earned experience of having tried many things that don't work. You also don't have the technical knowledge to always do things right when you're trying something new and complicated. The simpler you keep your design, the more likely you are not to mess up.

Simplicity is most important in *content pages,* Web pages where the user is reading an article or looking at a picture. The user doesn't want to be distracted from what he's doing. Figures 11-1 and Figure 11-2 show the first and second screenfuls of content for *Dreamweaver MX For Dummies,* mentioned earlier, on the For Dummies Web site. Notice how both Web pages allow you to focus on the content.

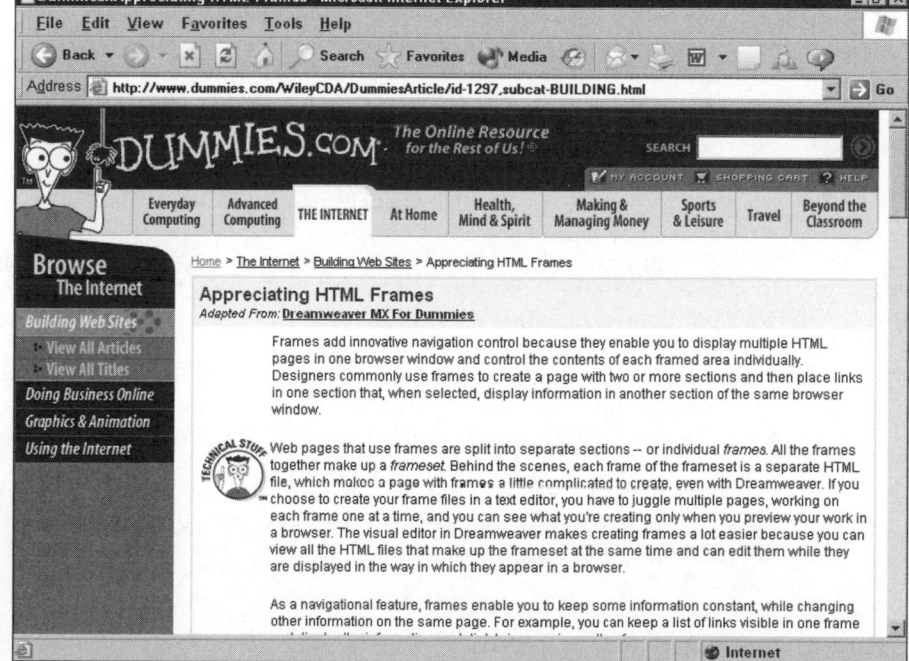

Figure 11-1:
The top of a Dummies content page is simple, offering tools, navigation, and content.

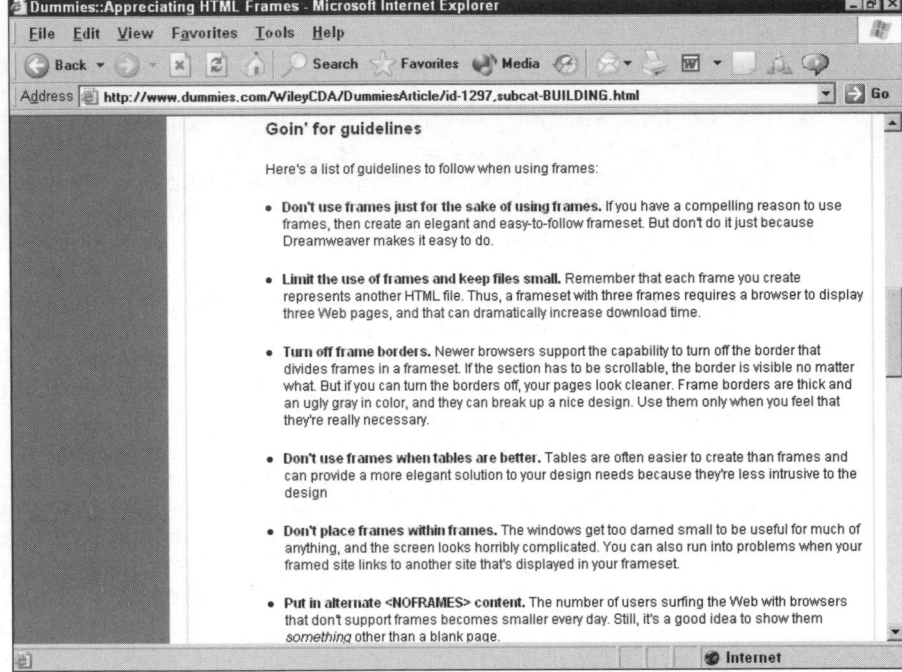

Goin' for guidelines

Here's a list of guidelines to follow when using frames:

- **Don't use frames just for the sake of using frames.** If you have a compelling reason to use frames, then create an elegant and easy-to-follow frameset. But don't do it just because Dreamweaver makes it easy to do.

- **Limit the use of frames and keep files small.** Remember that each frame you create represents another HTML file. Thus, a frameset with three frames requires a browser to display three Web pages, and that can dramatically increase download time.

- **Turn off frame borders.** Newer browsers support the capability to turn off the border that divides frames in a frameset. If the section has to be scrollable, the border is visible no matter what. But if you can turn the borders off, your pages look cleaner. Frame borders are thick and an ugly gray in color, and they can break up a nice design. Use them only when you feel that they're really necessary.

- **Don't use frames when tables are better.** Tables are often easier to create than frames and can provide a more elegant solution to your design needs because they're less intrusive to the design

- **Don't place frames within frames.** The windows get too darned small to be useful for much of anything, and the screen looks horribly complicated. You can also run into problems when your framed site links to another site that's displayed in your frameset.

- **Put in alternate <NOFRAMES> content.** The number of users surfing the Web with browsers that don't support frames becomes smaller every day. Still, it's a good idea to show them *something* other than a blank page.

Figure 11-2:
The body of a Dummies content page is even simpler — just content, thanks.

Producing predictability

Predictability means that the user can easily guess where things are on your Web page and how they work. In other words, one of your goals as you design your Web page is to achieve a sense of predictability of the content, layout functionality, and look of your page when it's compared to other, similar Web pages.

An important reason that the Web is so popular is that Web pages nearly all look and work alike. Web pages that go too far from the norm tend not to be very popular with users.

Part of the reason this book is called *Creating Web Pages For Dummies* and not *Creating Web Sites For Dummies* is that it's focused on people just starting out, who are likely to want to create a single Web page first, and then perhaps expand that page into a small site. But another reason is that users really do experience the Web as a bunch of individual Web pages. Many users aren't even aware, when they click a link to a different site, that they've left one site and gone to a different one. People really do experience the Web one Web page at a time.

To understand the value of predictability, imagine what a Web page with a newspaper article on it should look like. The first thing to catch your eye might be a picture — almost always one picture, if any. You'd also expect to see the headline describing the article and the reporter's byline.

You would expect to see some navigation at the top of the screen or along the left side. You'd expect a banner ad across the top (but you'd be pleasantly surprised if there wasn't one.) The left side would then be empty after the navigation was done. The right ride might be empty as well, or have some small ads.

On some sites you might see features, such as a button for e-mailing a copy of the article, somewhere on the first screen of the article. And you might also see a box with headlines for related articles. Figure 11-3 shows a sketch of what the major elements in an article page might look like.

Now imagine if one or more of these features was present but was implemented much differently than on other sites. For instance, imagine that the button for e-mailing the article was labeled "Transmit Content." You'd be frustrated and confused. The clever person who put an original label on the button hasn't impressed you — he or she has made the page harder to understand and use.

That, in a nutshell, is what predictability is about. For any Web page you create, find a few examples of pages on the Web that accomplish something similar to what you're trying to do. See whether your page is similar in content, layout, functionality, and (while you're at it) compare the simplicity of your design to the examples you've chosen (see "Achieving simplicity," earlier in this chapter). If your page is different, consider modifying the design to reduce or eliminate the differences. That's predictability.

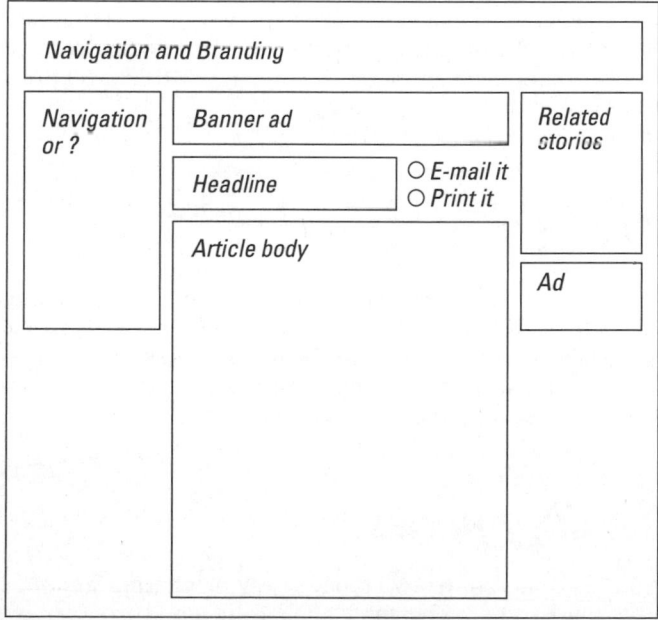

Figure 11-3:
Diagram of a typical article page.

Creating consistency

Just as every Web page you create should be predictable when compared to the other pages out there on the Web (See "Producing predictability," earlier in this chapter), each page should also be internally consistent. You shouldn't dramatically change fonts, text size, or layout style within a page.

If you create a multipage Web site (as described in Chapter 15), all the pages in the site should be consistent with each other as well. Do all you can to help users understand that they're visiting a single, unified Web site.

If your Web pages are simple, and if they're predictable to experienced Web users, then consistency becomes one of the easier principles to follow. Here are just a couple of ideas that can substantially improve the consistency of a small site:

- ✔ Use a repeated navigation block or graphic on each page in your Web site — always in the same position on each page.
- ✔ Use a consistent background color and foreground color, the same text size for body text, the same or similar image placements, and the same "voice" in the site's writing.

If you create a large Web site (over 20 pages or so), consistency becomes more difficult. The only foolproof way to maintain a consistent approach is to create a template for each of the different kinds of pages on your Web site: navigational pages, content pages (with and without images), forms pages, and so on. Then every page in your site is created from a template and then customized for the specific needs of that page. Most really large sites, such as Amazon.com, automatically "populate" templates with content drawn from a database to create individual Web pages.

Design Mistakes to Avoid

Simply cruise the Web — especially areas with lots of personal pages, like the GeoCities site or AOL's Hometown area — and you can find many examples of badly designed pages. But what is it that makes these pages bad? Of the many design mistakes you can make, three are common among new Web page creators: slow-loading pages, ugly color combinations, and small text.

Slow-loading pages

This is the number-one bane of Web page design, whether amateur or professional. People think they're designing a magazine and throw large, uncompressed graphics around, several per page. Then they add cute little design elements, each of which has to be sent as a separate file by the Web server. As each of the different elements comes in, the page design shifts and shimmies in a manner guaranteed to cause motion sickness. When a page of yours loads slowly, it's usually due to the fact you are committing one of two major errors.

- Error #1 involves a lack of care with one or two individual graphics. By keeping these graphics files large, you doom the whole page to slow loading. Use the techniques described in Chapter 10 to make your graphics small in their physical size as well as in their file size.

- Error #2 is to use graphics in a profligate manner in general. Highly designed pages can have lots of little graphical elements that cause many separate file transfers as the page loads. Unless the page is carefully designed, the page actually shifts a bit as each graphic comes in. The overall effect can be quite disconcerting.

Graphics not only can cause your page to load slowly — they also take a long time to create, tend to have copyright problems, and present challenging design and page layout issues. Keep the use of graphics on your page simple until you get really good at designing with graphics, or until you can get help from someone who has that talent themselves.

Ugly color combinations

Many Web page publishers don't much care if the color combinations they use are attractive or not. Others care, but can't critically appraise their own work and see how ugly and/or difficult to use the result is.

You may understand that certain color combinations can be ugly, but maybe it seems odd for us to say that bad colors can lead to difficult-to-use pages. The reason is that on the Web, color identifies hyperlinks, with unused links and recently used links having different colors. The standard colors for links are blue for unvisited links and purple for visited links. If you change these colors, your visitors have trouble identifying which links they've visited and which links they haven't. If you've read the section about creating predictability on your page, you are aware of just how major a sin this is!

If you simply must change the link colors, try to use color combinations that are analogous to the standard ones — a lighter, eye-catching color for unvisited links, and a dull color for visited ones. This is at least similar, conceptually, to the standard colors. Then test the design on a few people and see if they can quickly figure out which links are which.

Now, back to ugly. Just because the Web makes it possible to use various color combinations doesn't mean you should do so. Black text on a white or off-white background is what people are used to, and is always the safest choice. And with this combination, the standard link colors show up really well. You can use a graphical bar at some consistent location on the page to give your Web pages a colorful, graphical look without sacrificing predictability and readability within the body of each page.

A few other color combinations work fairly well, but many don't. Remember also that some users run their monitors in 256-color mode and that only 216 colors out of the 256 — the Web-safe color palette — are the same on PCs and Macs. So a color combination that looks good on your system may look poor on a system with fewer colors; likewise, colors that look good on a PC may not look so hot on a Mac. Use the Web-safe colors described in Chapter 9 to choose, or cruise the Web looking for an existing Web page that uses a good-looking Web-safe color combination; you can use the same combination for your own site. (This isn't stealing — there are only a few such useful combinations, so the person you're borrowing from didn't exactly invent the electric blender either.)

Small text (And large text, too)

A common mistake people make is to use small text on their Web pages. Small text does look kind of cool, and it allows you to pack in a lot of information. Because of these temptations, even large Web sites, such as early versions of the Microsoft site, have made this mistake. The trouble is that small text becomes *very small text* when viewed on a high-resolution monitor. So small, in fact, that many of the people who visit your Web site may not be able to easily read the text on your page.

Less common, but equally harmful, is text that's too large. You don't need to design Web pages with text that's readable from 20 feet away. Really. (People with true vision problems switch Windows and/or their browser to display text in extra-large size, so they have a way to read text that starts out normal size.) This looks awful, especially when viewed on a system with relatively low resolution, such as 800 x 600 resolution.

Both of these problems are made worse by the increasing tendency to embed much of a site's text in graphic images. This text always has a consistent look, because it is treated by the browser as a graphic image, but that look can easily be too small or large. When you save text as image files, the text can't be resized by the browser to accommodate different browser settings. So the user can't fix any problems they're having with graphically displayed text.

So what's "normal-size" text? Glad you asked. There's not one exact normal size, but there's a normal range. To find it, match the text size in your Web page to the text size in a few Web pages you like. Then ask several people — not all younger and hawk-eyed, nor all older and less visually acute — to tell you if they can easily read the text while sitting comfortably a couple of feet from the computer. If not, fix the problem before it becomes a burden for your Web site visitors.

Breaking the Rules Safely

A lot of the fun in creating your own Web page is doing what you want to do and not what someone else tells you. Yet you want your Web page to look good. How can you create a design that you like and that also looks good to other people?

Finding great home pages

Here are several places you can look to see how others have designed their home pages on the Web:

- **GeoCities:** As mentioned in Chapter 2, GeoCities is the top provider of home pages for the Web. From the GeoCities home page at `www.geocities.com`, you can access GeoCities Web pages in many different categories. However, there's no "best" or "highly rated" list to help you find the best Web pages. You're going to have to look at a lot of ugly ducklings before you find a swan.

- **Tripod:** Tripod is a free Web hosting company acquired by Lycos, a leading international Web portal. Visit Tripod at `www.tripod.com`. To see cool Lycos Web pages, look in the Member Spotlight area in the Member sites area. The Home and Family area is particularly relevant for personal home pages.

- **AngelFire:** AngelFire is the other free Web hosting company acquired by Lycos. You can find its home page at `www.angelfire.com`. Click the Cool Pages link on the left side of the home page to find links to top sites in various areas.

- **Hometown:** Hometown is the name of AOL's free Web page hosting site (see Chapter 3). You can use Hometown even if you're not an AOL member (although only members can use all of the AOL discussion areas and online help that make Hometown a real winner). The Hometown home page at `www.hometown.aol.com` has a list of the most popular categories, but you have to search all the home pages in a category to find the best ones.

- **Homestead and Bigstep:** Homestead and Bigstep no longer offer free personal home pages — they only offer business pages, and you have to pay for them. But because they offer a lot of support, they have some great Web pages, and each prominently features some of their customers' better work. Go to `www.homestead.com` and `www.bigstep.com` and look for customers' sites.

Getting design help from the pros

The best way to work with a Web graphic designer, while keeping your costs under control, is to create your Web site yourself first. Then bring in the designer just to improve the look of the site. Improving the look of your site might take the designer a few hours and cost you several hundred dollars. Money well spent if your Web site is going to be part of your career or your business.

The problem is that many of the people you talk to will be accustomed to doing the whole job of brainstorming your needs with you, creating content, revising it all to meet your needs, publishing the site, and then modifying it for you. This kind of project could cost you thousands of dollars — which you're going to avoid spending by doing nearly everything yourself for free using the information in this book. The one part where you might need help is in getting the look right, so do all the other steps yourself and then bring someone in just for the graphic design piece.

We suggest you follow this five-step process:

1. **Get your Web page up.**

   Include the content and images you want, as we describe in Part I of this book. Don't worry much about how it looks. Just do it!

2. **Find a model page or two that you like.**

   Look for pages that have a similar purpose and content. Make sure that they have a simple, attractive appearance. See the sidebar, "Finding great home pages," for places to look.

3. **Create a new, basic version of your Web page, using these models as your guide.**

   Get the major pieces — the main text, an image or two, and a list — in place first. Make this basic page look good.

4. **Add additional elements one at a time.**

   By working in this piecemeal fashion, you can prevent your page from becoming a hard-to-fix mess, while still indulging your own creativity.

5. **Publish the result and get comments.**

   Let some friends and colleagues see your newly published page, and ask them what they think. Let the site sit for a couple of days, and then take a fresh look at it yourself. Use your own fresh perspective and the comments you get to improve your page further.

You can repeat this process again and again as you improve your Web page and add new pages to create a full Web site. Work through these steps conscientiously and you may end up with some of the best-looking Web pages around.

Using Tables and Frames

Whether and how to use tables was, for a long time, one of the most controversial topics in Web page design (not exactly an area where controversies have earthshaking consequences, but we all need some excitement in our lives). The original purpose of tables was to allow Web designers to create tables of data (for instance, the monthly sales of several products).

Nowadays, people often use tables to manage the entire layout of a Web page. Designers have found that they can make the cells of a table very large and put large graphics or whole blocks of text in them. You can even automatically resize tables for to accommodate the various sizes of Web browser windows — at least, up to a point. We only touch on this advanced use of tables in this section.

Frames are more powerful layout devices than tables, but they have fallen into some disfavor. They allow separate parts of the Web browser window to be updated and scrolled separately. However, they produce odd effects; users seem to prefer one unified window to separate "panes" within a window. So we barely mention frames here or elsewhere in this book.

Creating simple tables

When used as intended, tables have rows and columns. For each spot where a row and column intersect, you have a table cell. Each cell can have its own formatting — the data in it can be aligned left, center, or right, formatted, and so on. Tables also have headers, in which you put the column headings, but no predefined row descriptions. You have to create those, if needed, by adding your own formatting.

Here's the HTML code for a simple table of this type:

```
<TABLE BORDER=2>
<TH><TD><B>Production (tons)</B></TD><TD><B>% of
          goal</B></TD></TH>
<TR><TD><I>North 40</I></TD><TD>87</TD><TD>102%</TD></TR>
<TR><TD><I>South 40</I></TD><TD>93</TD><TD>110%</TD></TR>
</TABLE>
```

Figure 11-4 shows how this simple table looks in HTML and when viewed in Internet Explorer.

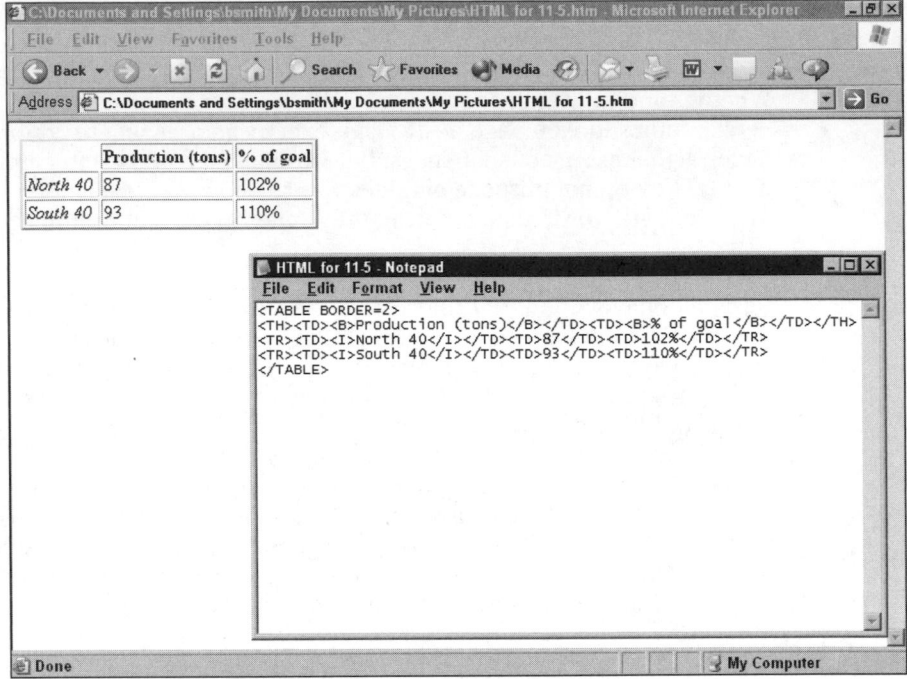

Figure 11-4:
A simple
Web table
and its
simple
HTML
source.

Here's what each part of the HTML code does:

> `<TABLE BORDER=2>`   The `TABLE` tag begins and ends the table. The `BORDER` attribute creates a 2-pixel-wide border around the table. Don't forget to include a border, so other text and graphics in your Web page don't crowd too close to the table.
>
> `<TH>, </TH>`   Begins and ends the table header. (Automatically leaves the first entry blank so rows can contain a row description.)
>
> `<TR>, </TR>`   Begins and ends the table row.
>
> `<TD>, </TD>`   Begins and ends the table data item.

So creating a table in HTML is fairly simple but also fairly tedious. You just create the rows and data items; if you get the data items right, the columns take care of themselves.

Getting the data items right can be a problem, though. To make your table look just right, you have to use a number of alignment and formatting options. Making mistakes becomes very easy, and updating the table's appearance becomes very hard. That's why so many people use an HTML editor like Composer to create and manage tables — and then, in some cases, do final tweaking in HTML to get them just right.

Tables weren't part of the original HTML standard; they were introduced in Netscape Navigator Version 1.1. As a result, some much older browsers don't support tables at all. (Tables are the main reason some Web pages still say "Best viewed with Netscape Navigator." For a while it was the only browser with table support.) Also, the official HTML standard and Navigator 1.1 used different versions of the same tags. Luckily, most browsers available today support both versions of table tags.

Using tables for layout purposes

When tables were added to HTML, Web designers quickly figured out how to take them to a whole other level. Imagine making a Web page one big table. Using HTML options, you can suppress the display of the table's cell borders. You can thus create a large, invisible grid into which you insert chunks of text and graphics. This allows you to create a layout with columns. You can also use tables in this fashion to make sure that a specific block of text stays next to a specific graphic, even if the user makes his Web text large or makes the window extra narrow.

Believe it or not, this whole table for layouts thing was a bit controversial at first. Why? Because there were some idealistic motives behind the original design of HTML, such as having Web pages be able to display on just about any screen. Table-based layouts, by contrast, only work well on screens of at least a certain minimum size, such as a PC screen rather than, say, a mobile phone screen. The controversy has now largely faded because the people who pay for Web site development demand that their sites look good on most of the PCs and Macs out there, and tables are just about the only way to create a complex design that looks good.

For your purposes, designing your own Web page, the key word here is "complex." There are so many different elements that you have to adjust in table-based page design that you need to invest a lot of time and energy to learn how to effectively use tables for layout purposes. And then a whole other set of issues arise about making sure your table-based page design works well on most or all of the current computer systems and Web browser setups that are in use.

Figure 11-5 shows the home page of Netsurfer Science, which uses tables to create a simple, clean layout. The column on the left is one big cell in a table; the content in the middle and right of the page is in another large cell. Use the <u>V</u>iew⇨Sour<u>c</u>e or similar command in your Web browser to view the underlying HTML source for this page to see how it's done.

To create your own tables, you can get started by using the Insert⇨Table command in Netscape Composer. However, you really need a more advanced tool to work effectively with tables in your Web pages — something like

Microsoft FrontPage or Dreamweaver, both of which give you more direct control over specific options. Of course, your other option is to start doing *a lot* of experimenting in HTML until you learn how to get things just how you want them.

For details on how to use tables for layout, start with this article: `www.anown site.com/web-design/html-tables.html`.

Friends don't let friends do frames

Frames, like tables, are a Netscape innovation. Frames divide a Web page into separate areas, which you can then update individually as needed. For example, you can click a link in a frame in the bottom half of a Web page and update it with new content while the other frame stays unchanged. This seems like a powerful capability. However, frames have proved to be less popular than tables.

Why are frames not as popular as tables? Well, frames are hard to create and manage, just like tables. But advanced Web authors are willing to do just about anything to make their Web pages more attractive and more useful, and tables help them do so. With frames, the trouble comes with the "useful" part; users have a hard time with framed Web pages.

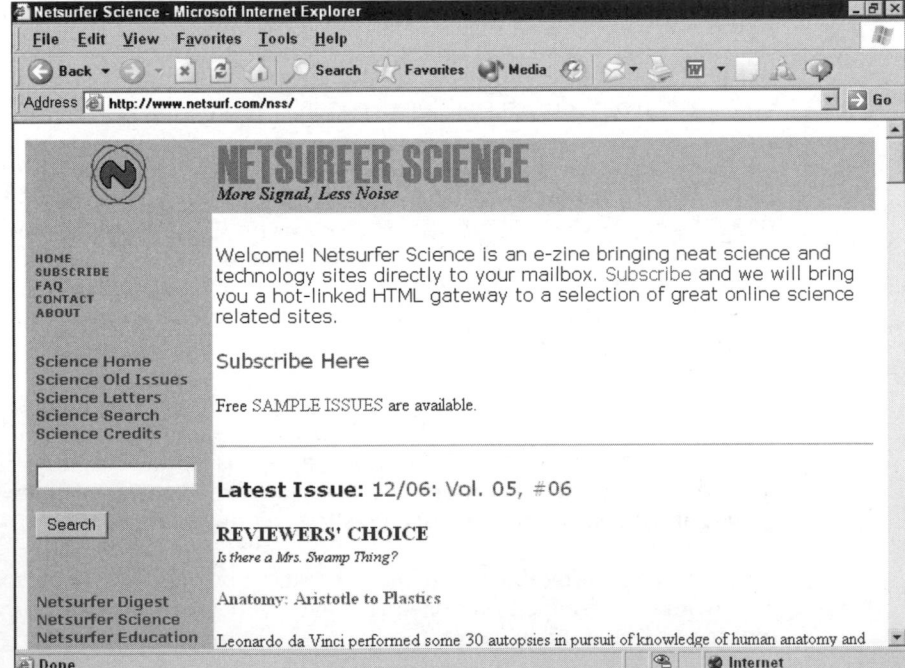

Figure 11-5:
Netsurfer Digest uses tables to organize content.

For example, when browsing a framed page, users sometimes have difficulty finding where the cursor is. If the user moves the scrollbar, which frame scrolls? Also, going forward and backward in a frame is different from going forward and backward in the overall Web page, so users may get lost easily. And printing a framed page properly requires extra steps – users often try to print the page and end up printing the contents of just one frame instead.

Finally, frames create a functional problem or two. When users resize a browser window, framed pages don't always resize correctly. And designing a framed page to work well for various monitor sizes is significantly harder than designing pages with tables embedded in them.

Usability tests have shown that users are confused by frames. Some highly controlled framed sites (for instance, those with only one scrollable window) give fairly good results. However, the main purpose of frames on such sites is to allow complex navigation, advertisements, or both to stay in the user's view at all times. Unless you have complicated navigational options that your users can't live without, or unless you have advertisers for your site whose dollars you can't live without, we recommend you avoid frames while creating your initial Web pages or simple Web site.

Still, framed pages can be useful to show complex sets of data and to support navigation. Because creating and managing the HTML for frames is even harder than for tables, we don't describe that process here.

Netscape Composer doesn't support frames. Use an advanced Web page tool such as Microsoft FrontPage or Macromedia Dreamweaver if you want to use frames in your pages. (Or look up the appropriate HTML tags in Appendix C and start experimenting!)

Chapter 12

Publishing Your Web Pages

. . . .

In This Chapter

▶ Getting Web server space

▶ Finding help for Web publishing

▶ Transferring your files to the Web server

▶ Putting your site to work

. . . .

*P*ublishing is the most exciting stage of creating your Web page or Web site. After all the fooling around with tools, HTML and all your images — and after figuring out what you want to say and how you want to say it, you can finally "go live," as they say in the business, and let the world see your creation.

Publishing on the Web can be straightforward if you're putting up a personal or topical home page that a few friends and/or coworkers see. But if you're creating a site for a business, or just creating a site that needs room to grow, publishing involves several steps.

The first step in publishing your Web page is to get Web server space. You have a lot of options here. Can you get free space or must you pay for it? Do you want your own domain name, so that your site has a simple URL (such as www.budsmith.net), or are you willing to let your site be a subdirectory in someone else's domain (such as www.geocities.com/budsmith)? You need to choose a server space provider that gives you reasonable pricing and support now plus room to grow later. Then you need to transfer your files to the site and check to see that your page really is online.

But you're not done yet. The whole purpose of getting your Web site online is for people to see it. With all the sites out there, you have to cut through the noise and get people to visit your site. After people see your site, you will want to know that they were there, so you need some kind of site statistics reporting. You also need to be able to receive and respond to feedback. Having all these things to think about reminds us of those U.S. Army ads — "It's not just a job, it's an adventure."

Packaged publishing

The easiest way to handle publishing your Web pages is to not handle it at all and to have it done for you. Easy-to-use Web page services such as GeoCities and AOL Hometown, described in Chapters 2 and 3, handle the publishing step for you — at least in the early stages. But as you build up your Web page, or create a multipage Web site, you need to start worrying about things like transferring files via FTP and so on. And you may want your own domain name or other advanced features that require you to find a new host for your Web pages. If publishing your Web site seems like a hassle, get started with an easy to use Web page service, then come back to this chapter when you need to take your site to the next level.

In this chapter, we cover the basic publishing steps — getting server space, transferring your files, and so on. These are the core steps that you need for either a single Web page or a multi-page Web site. In Chapter 15 we cover more advanced steps related to publishing, such as getting your own domain name and letting people know about your site.

After your site is up and publicized, you may expect to get a chance to relax. But then, while you cruise the Web, you might see something neat that you want to put into your own site. Or looking back at your own pages, you may suddenly discover a problem in the way you describe yourself, your company, or your interests. Or maybe you get a blizzard of e-mails asking a question that you thought you already answered on the site — or, worse, you get no feedback at all. Maybe it's time to fire up that HTML editor again.

Sorry to plug a book cowritten by one of the authors, but if you're in a hurry to create a Web site for a business, you may want to consult *Internet Marketing For Dummies,* by Frank Catalano and Bud Smith (Wiley). *Internet Marketing For Dummies* goes into more depth about business-related issues, such as how to register the right domain name, how to present your business online, and how to use other Internet services besides the Web as part of your marketing effort.

Getting Web Server Space

A *Web server* is a computer that's connected to the World Wide Web and runs special software that enables it to provide information to Web users. Hundreds of thousands of such servers are connected to the Web. You can have a lot of fun fooling around with a Web page that you create and store on your own computer. But only by placing your Web site's files on someone else's server — or by creating your own Web server with your site's files on it — can your site really be part of the World Wide Web.

You can easily get space on a Web server. For example, the free Web-based publishing services we describe in Chapters 2 and 3 all include free Web server space. You may have a friend or an affiliation with an organization that can lend you Web server space. These are all good options for a single Web home page or a small site.

If these options aren't available to you, though, or if real money is involved, things get tricky. When you create a site for a business or another kind of organization, most of the services we mention in the preceding paragraph don't give you free space. So if you're going to start paying for server space, you want to do some comparison shopping. And to do comparison shopping, you have to know what to compare.

America Online is the one major service that continues to allow free Web server space for businesses as well as individuals. See Chapter 3 for details.

Web hosting service features

A number of businesses and organizations offer Web hosting service — that is, space on their Web server for your Web site. Most of these organizations charge for this service, and fees vary. You should look at a number of concerns when choosing a Web hosting provider for your Web pages.

Focusing only on price when you compare Web hosting service providers is understandable. But you should look at many other factors that may actually be more important than the immediate cost:

- ✔ **Pricing structure:** Instead of focusing only on the charges for your initial, bare-bones site, consider also what providers charge you when your site grows larger and attracts a moderate number of visitors — say a few hundred or a few thousand a month. Some hosting providers charge a very low rate for your initial site but sock it to you when your needs grow.

- ✔ **Support:** We all need support of one kind or another, but excellent technical support for your Web publishing effort is one of the hardest — and most important — kinds of support to get. You need support for putting your pages onto the server, for answering questions about your site, and for solving problems about speedy access, uptime (how long the service is on the air trouble-free), and so on. Find out about the support providers offer for each type of Web hosting option that interests you. Ask other users of each service if they're able to get support fast when a problem comes up.

- ✔ **Web-related consulting services:** Some Web hosting providers, even those that offer some services for free, also offer other Web-related services that they charge for, such as hosting business sites or managing your site for you. What do the providers charge for these services? How well do they work? Most Web-related services are billed by the hour, but some service providers get things done better and faster than others. So a less expensive hourly rate may not mean a lower total bill at the end.

✔ **Site services:** Some Web hosting providers offer helpful services, such as counting the number of users who visit your site. Other providers allow *you* to create and run Common Gateway Interface (CGI) scripts that perform sophisticated functions, such as processing the data from an online form. Other Web hosting providers neither provide site services nor allow you to run CGIs. Look for a provider that does the simple stuff for you and supports you in doing the more complex functions yourself.

✔ **Domain name:** The *domain name* is the name of the server where your site resides, but clever providers can put multiple domain names on a single computer. This means that you can have your own domain name, even if you have a small site, as long as your Web hosting provider registers the name. Registering a domain name costs service providers anywhere from about $10 to about $30 per year. Expect your provider to pass this charge on to you, but don't let the provider charge you a great deal more. For more about having your own domain name, see Chapter 15.

Some Web hosting providers offer to register a domain name for you, but then retain ownership of the domain name themselves. This situation reminds us of those Peanuts cartoons in which Lucy sets up the football and then pulls it away when Charlie Brown runs up to kick it. Not owning your domain name free and clear can severely hamper your ability to move your site later.

Find out whether the Web hosting provider allows you to get your own domain name, either immediately or later. And if the provider does, ask for a clear, written statement that you own the domain name and can take your Web site to another host if you want to.

When you consider a Web hosting provider, consider in your evaluation the following factors:

✔ **Speed:** How fast can users access your Web site? How fast can users download files hosted on the site? You can ask, but you should also test. Try accessing some Web sites hosted by any service that you're considering and see how fast they are, especially at busy times of the day. Compare what you find to other Web sites.

✔ **Downtime:** Is the Web hosting service that you're considering ever "off the air"? You may think that downtime is rare, but even entire online services such as America Online have downtimes. Find out the track record for downtime of the Web hosting service that you're considering and compare that service's record with competitors.

✔ **Switchability:** Having the ability to switch Web hosting providers is crucial. With the right to switch, you can resolve any other problems. Without the right to switch, you may be unhappy with some key element of your Web site for a long time. Two things can keep you locked into an arrangement with a provider: contractual provisions and control of your domain name. Don't sign a contract that locks you in for more than a year, and don't let the Web hosting provider register your domain name for you unless the provider states, in writing, that you control your domain name and can take it elsewhere.

✔ **Viability:** Many Internet-related businesses have gone out of business. (Even giant firms collapse sometimes, like the energy giant Enron, but it seems that the Internet has had more than its share.) Make sure that your chosen provider has a track record and is of sufficient size to offer some assurance that it will be around for the long haul.

✔ **Reporting:** You really, really want your provider to offer basic reporting features, such as the number of visitors your site has each day, for free. Such features are rare but very valuable. This may be the critical factor in choosing between one provider and another.

✔ **Data transfer fees:** Another potential gotcha involves *data transfer fees*. When users look at a page on your site, all the data on that page is transferred to their machines. If users download files, more data is transferred. Many Web hosting services offer some free data transfer, but your costs can rise sharply if traffic at your site increases and data transfer rises above a minimal amount. Compare data-transfer pricing carefully.

✔ **Price:** If all other things are equal, price is the determining factor. But all other things are rarely equal. Consider other factors first, but don't let yourself get ripped off on the price you pay.

The key factors in choosing a Web hosting provider are the freedom to switch when you need to and having control of your domain name.

Options for Web server space

Now that you know what to look for in a host server, where can you find Web server space? Finding the right place for your Web site to be hosted is not an easy task. Major Web hosting options include sites that offer free server space, online service Web hosting options, Web hosting services, and a Web server of your own creation. Appendix B lists major Internet service providers; from their Web sites, you can find their current hosting options.

No matter what choice you make initially, be sure to keep your options open, because your needs may change rapidly as new Web hosting providers arise, your own knowledge grows, and the Web's role in business and in daily life increases.

What makes a Web server fast?

A Web server is usually rated by the number of *connections* — brief communication sessions between two machines — that it can handle in a given period of time. The number of connections that the server handles depends on how quickly the server establishes a connection, deciphers the request, sends the requested file, and terminates the connection. Most people assume that the most time-consuming step in this process is the speed with which files are transmitted. Surprise! When small files are transmitted, the bottleneck is usually not how fast the files are transmitted, but how quickly the server's hardware and software establish connections for each of the file transfers, and how fast the connections are terminated after the transfer is finished.

Engineers and various hangers-on, such as people who write computer-related books, like to call the cause of a bottleneck a *gating factor.* For example, the gating factor for completing this book on schedule is the speed at which the authors write. The gating factor in serving simple Web pages is often the speed with which the server can connect and disconnect, not the speed with which data can be sent over the wire.

In addition to the speed of connecting and disconnecting to other machines, the speed of the server's connection to the Internet makes a big difference, especially for larger files such as big graphic images. If you have a direct connection to the Internet (as you find at most large companies and most universities), your client-side connection may be even faster than the server's connection: Lots of personal and small business home pages are sitting on Web servers with nothing but a 56 Kbps modem connecting them to the Internet. So don't start cussing at your own modem when that full-color JPEG photograph of the winning Weimaraner takes forever to download; the problem may be at the other end.

Using free server space

You can get free server space for relatively small Web sites from several places. (See Chapters 2 and 3 for details.) These sites are great places to create small initial Web sites that help you learn about Web page design and construction. However, businesses generally can't use free server space for straightforward business promotion. (But you do see lots of not-so-straightforward promotions there!) Also, to get your own domain name, you either have to move to paid server space or create your own Web server.

If you have access to free server space through a friend or work, that's also a good place to get started. Be careful, though, that you don't violate any expectations that the people providing the space to you have about the content of your Web site.

As we mentioned in Chapter 11, Bigstep.com, a Web business, will help you create a starter business Web site for a moderate cost. Visit them at `www.bigstep.com`.

Using Internet service providers

Internet service providers (ISPs) may be best known for offering Web access, but many of them also offer a wide range of Web services, from consulting to hosting to programming and more. In fact, as larger players, such as AT&T and Earthlink, continue to establish their Web access business, the smaller ISPs that prosper will be those that move "upstream" into consulting and specialized hosting services. ISPs that are also traditional online services, like AOL and CompuServe, sometimes change their higher-level offerings as partnership opportunities change.

Some ISPs offer free Web page publishing services or free server space to customers, just like the major online services. They also offer varying levels of paid-for service. Compare major ISPs to see what they offer. If you already have Web access, don't stop checking. Many ISPs offer their extra-cost add-on services even to those who get their access elsewhere, and some ISPs may offer attractive bundles for access plus other services. You still have to be a customer to get that free server space deal, though.

Using paid-for server space

You can find thousands of Web hosting services out there. The providers vary tremendously in service, price, and competency. Some offer hosting only and charge you per stored or transferred megabyte. Others offer additional services, which may be billed separately or bundled with the "pure" hosting services in an overall fee. This business is changing and growing so rapidly that you need to exercise great care in the selection process to protect yourself. The largest service, Verio, which acquired the former leader Best Internet, is also considered among the best (no pun intended); you may want to start your search by checking on them at `www.verio.com`.

As the Romans figured out, just a few years before the Internet caught on, *caveat emptor* — let the buyer beware! Do your research! Check out "Web hosting service features," earlier in this chapter.

Creating your own Web server

Deciding whether to create your own Web server depends, as do many other choices about the Web, on what you want to accomplish and how much experience you have. If you've set up a Web server before or have a lot of computer and communications experience, setting up your own Web server may work out very well for you. If not, setting up a Web server may turn out to be an expensive nightmare — and slow to boot! (That's "slow as well," not slow to start up when you hit the On switch!)

Get it all in a cyberstore

An online store is a special kind of Web site that enables you to sell products online without any hassle. An online store operator may provide any or all of the following:

- ✔ Initial goal-setting for your Web site
- ✔ Creation of the Web page itself (expect to provide raw materials such as product or service descriptions, photographs, and price lists)
- ✔ Advertising and publicity
- ✔ Support for online sales

Yahoo!, eBay, and Amazon.com have cyberstore-type arrangements that you can use to get publicity for your online selling. Using the right cyberstore host can be a good way to get started on the Web, especially if you want to go from zero (no Web presence or expertise) to 60 (a robust Web presence with online transaction capabilities) in a few months. Expect to pay fixed monthly fees that amount to several hundred dollars a year. Cyberstores also collect a small share of transactions. Using a cyberstore gives you a chance to develop Web expertise so that you can eventually do more of the work yourself. (Make sure that your contract allows you to leave the cybermall quickly if you want to take over the whole job on your own.) For popular online store providers, see the following sites:

- ✔ `www.amazon.com`
- ✔ `www.ebay.com`
- ✔ `www.yahoo.com`

Many proponents of doing business on the Web are quick to suggest that you set up your own Web server, but we don't share that view. Unless you're an expert, we recommend that you start with a Web hosting provider of some kind. Then consider setting up your own server after you gain some experience and get to know some people who can help if problems arise.

Two things to remember: If you set up your own Web server, use a dedicated machine that isn't doing any other work. (If you follow this very good advice, you'll spend up to $1,000 or so before you store or serve a megabyte!) And be ready to devote time and energy to find out about the computer you're using, its Internet connection, and associated Web technologies so that you can set up your own server to meet your needs as effectively as a Web hosting service.

Hiring help

The *dot-bomb* phenomenon — the sudden crash of so many Internet businesses in 1999 through 2001 — made a lot of talented Web pros available. In addition, 10 years after the Web itself was invented, some of the amateurs are pretty good at what they do. So the odds of finding a good person to help you, either on a paid basis or just because he or she is a friend, is growing.

To find a good Web hosting provider — someone who can provide the Web hosting services we describe in the previous section — or get other help relating to getting your Web site up, we recommend the following steps:

✔ **Start small.** Asking the right questions to help you find a Web hosting provider or consultant is difficult if you have no Web publishing experience of your own. Start by creating a home page and then a small, special-purpose site of some kind before doing anything more robust. The experience will be valuable in finding a good hosting provider.

✔ **Figure out what services you need.** Are you going to create a simple site or a complex one? Do you want to create the site yourself and buy hosting services only, or do you want to contract out most of the work? List your needs, and then find someone who's well suited to fill them.

✔ **Investigate sites like your own.** Find Web sites that look like the kind you want to create. Ask the Webmasters how they got their sites up and running and what Web hosting providers they use. Ask others in your area about their Web sites and whether they're happy with the services they receive. When you consider a specific provider, check into a few of the sites that the provider hosts and ask customers whether they're happy. Talk to a couple of satisfied customers of consultants you're researching.

✔ **Go local.** One perk of hiring a local consultant is that you can meet with the consultant occasionally in person. (Even with all our technological aids, looking someone in the eye can contribute to better and deeper understanding. And sometimes a face-to-face meeting can lead you to find that you really dislike a person!) Although going local greatly restricts your choices, especially if you don't live in a big city, it may significantly improve your working relationship.

✔ **Be involved.** No consultant or service provider can do everything. You need to be very much involved in every step of the process, so plan to devote many hours to working with your consultant or service provider.

Is your site too cool?

What if your site is *too* successful? Believe it or not, the success of your site *can* be a problem. Many sites become overloaded when they catch on, rise high in the search rankings, are linked with a suddenly popular subject, are mentioned in the press, or receive other similar recognition. Be ready to upgrade your Web hosting provisions if your site suddenly gets popular. In particular, if you pay extra for transferred megabytes, make sure that you have a cap on how much you must pay if usage suddenly shoots up. If you don't have a cap, set up some method to track usage frequently or to receive an alert if usage shoots up. That way, you avoid a potentially nasty surprise on your bill.

Transferring Your Files

One of the really cool things about Web publishing is that you can set up, test, and modify a version of your Web site on your own machine. The problem is that, at some point, you have to transfer your files to the Web server. Until you become proficient at transferring files, you may have some anxious file-transferring moments. In this section, we try to eliminate some of the worry in getting your site online.

Arranging your files before transfer

Some of the most difficult things about creating, testing, and transferring your Web pages relate to directory structures. The problem is that a link from, say, your HTML-tagged text to a graphic has to specify what subfolder the graphics file is in. When you transfer your files to a different machine, the subfolders are likely to change, which breaks the link from your Web page to the graphics file. You can take steps, however, to keep your links from breaking when you transfer your Web files from your development machine to the Web server.

If your site has 20 files or fewer, here's a simple solution: Just put all your files in the same subfolder. That way, you only need to specify the filename, not the folder name — your links are that much simpler to access and maintain. And when you transfer files, you don't need to match up subfolder structures between machines. See Chapters 4 and 8 for details.

For sites with more than 20 or so files, use the simplest folder structure you can — only one level deep, if possible. (You don't need a separate subfolder for each of your 50 files, do you?) Also, create your links by using relative addressing. *Relative addressing*, described in Chapter 8, doesn't specify the entire pathname from the root folder downward, just the relative path from the file with the link embedded in it to the file with the link target. Relative addressing enables you to move folders and subfolders from one machine to another without having to change all the links between files.

Some people prefer to *zip* files (otherwise known as using a compression program, such as PKZIP) to keep file size small when transferring them online. Before you compress files, make sure that the recipient wants zipped files and that he or she can decompress (*unzip*) them. Also realize that the largest files in a Web site are usually GIF or JPEG graphics files. Because these files are compressed already, compression programs can't compact them much further. But a compression program can help you get all the files into a single package, with relative folder locations preserved.

As you can see, the underlying theme for anyone starting out is to *keep it simple*. After you have some initial successes under your belt, you can begin taking steps to organize your site better and to make it more convenient to manage and update.

Transferring your files with FTP

File Transfer Protocol (FTP) is an Internet service for transferring files between different machines. FTP helped make the Internet popular even before the World Wide Web caught on. FTP offers a relatively easy way to move files from one machine to another. Most Internet users rely on FTP to download files from an FTP host to the users' own machine; however, the user often starts the file transfer from a Web page, bypassing the details of FTP. When you publish your Web pages, your service provider may ask you to send files from your own machine to the host by using FTP. (You will probably be asked to "FTP the files to us.") If using FTP is a new operation for you, don't worry, it's not all that complex.

Dozens of FTP programs are available for Macintosh, Windows, and UNIX machines, and each program has its pluses and minuses. (The major online services also have facilities for uploading files, which we describe in the "Connecting to an FTP site" section that follows.) The most popular program we know of is WS_FTP Pro for Windows; Fetch is big on the Macintosh. You can find many free FTP clients on the Web. The steps we provide work with most popular FTP programs.

Many programs with FTP capability can download files from FTP sites but don't upload files to an FTP site. Make sure that your FTP program can *put* (write) as well as *get* (read) files. For a useful program, search for FTP on CINET's download site at www.download.com.

Connecting to an FTP site

The following steps specifically work with Fetch, the most popular Macintosh FTP program, shown in Figure 12-1. (Notice the little dog, probably a Scottie, running to fetch the file!) But the same steps generally apply to other FTP programs as well.

Figure 12-1: A fetching Mac FTP client.

Fetch: ftp.dartmouth.edu

Fetch — Copyright © 1994 Trustees of Dartmouth College — [Close Connection ⌘W]

fedjobs ▼

			Status
🗋 .cache	1K	Sep 14 09:28	Connected.
🗋 .cache+	3K	Sep 14 08:44	**File**
🗀 Disability	–	Aug 8 10:06	[Put File...]
🗀 DOD	–	Aug 7 09:47	
🗋 fedjobs.index	9K	Nov 20 10:44	[Get File...]
🗀 General	–	Aug 10 13:56	**Transfer**
🗀 Handbook	–	Aug 8 10:41	
🗀 Info	–	Jun 28 10:38	◉ Automatic
🗋 job_read.me	9K	Nov 20 10:45	○ Text
🗀 openings	–	Nov 16 09:51	○ Binary

2.1.2

Use these steps to transfer files to a Web site:

1. **Connect to the Internet.**

2. **Start your FTP program.**

3. **Enter the host name.**

   For a Web site, the FTP host name is often the same as the host name in the Web site's URL but with `ftp` in place of `www`; for example, if the Web site's URL is `www.mysite.com`, the host name is likely to be `ftp.my site.com`.

4. **Enter the user name.**

   Many sites allow you to enter `anonymous` as the user name, so you avoid having to enter a specific user name. (This capability is called, unsurprisingly, *anonymous FTP*.) Other sites give you a user name and password to use when uploading your Web files.

5. **Enter the password.**

   If you entered `anonymous` as the user name, enter nothing or your e-mail address as your password, as requested.

6. **Enter the directory that you want to put files in (that is, to write to).**

   You can also go to the correct directory after you connect, but the process is more convenient and less error-prone if you enter the correct directory first.

7. **Click OK to connect to the FTP site.**

   If you've done everything right and the site is up, your connection begins. Refer to Figure 12-1 for the dialog box that appears after you connect if using the Fetch FTP program.

Uploading your file(s) and disconnecting

Getting connected is half the battle, although we must admit that this process is hardly a fight. Writing your files is usually pretty easy. Here are the steps you must follow to complete the FTP process:

1. **Click the appropriate option for the file(s) that you want to write: Automatic, Text, or Binary.**

   For HTML files, use Text. For graphics and multimedia files, use Binary. For a combination of both types, either upload the types one at a time with the proper designation, or upload them together and choose Automatic; the server tries to figure out which is which.

   Until you have experience with a specific server, transfer files one at a time and specify the correct file type before each transfer.

2. **Click Put to write your file.**

   This option may be named "Send," "Upload," or something similar on other clients; to initiate the process, you may have to select the option from a menu rather than click a button.

3. **In the dialog box that appears, click the name of the file that you want to write and then click OK.**

   The file transfers. Repeat Steps 1 through 3 for each additional file that you need to transfer.

4. **When the transfer is complete, choose Quit (or Exit) from the File menu.**

Using an online service file transfer

In Chapter 3, we describe how to use the Web publishing programs on the major online services to create and publish a home page. However, the online services' Web facilities are flexible. You can create HTML-tagged text and graphics files with any tools and then upload the files to a server. The online service file transfer tools resemble FTP. Figure 12-2 shows the America Online file transfer program. Other file transfer programs are similar.

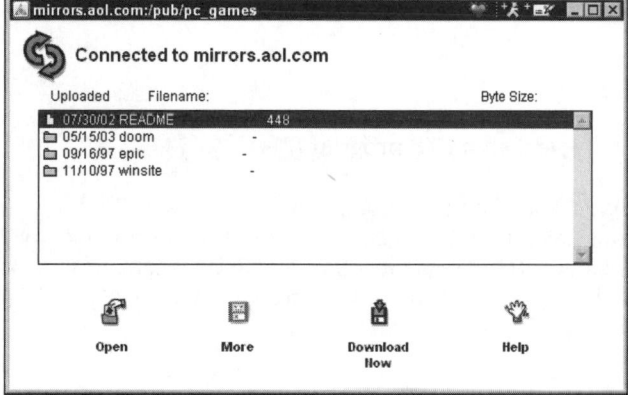

Figure 12-2:
File transfer that's not too AOL-ful.

Putting Your Site to Work

After you get your site up on the Web, you're probably too happy and relieved to worry about the site for awhile. But going live isn't an ending; it's really just the beginning of a whole new process. The following sections describe some initial steps to make your newly published site really stand out and accomplish your goals.

Testing your site

As soon as you get your site up, log on to it as a Web user. See if the site works. Test all links to make sure that they go where they should. Make sure that you can easily move between pages. Try accessing your site from a computer with a slow modem connection to see how usable the site is at slower speeds. Also try using your site in both the Netscape and Internet Explorer browsers. You can also test it in America Online's built-in browser, if you have access to AOL.

Also note how you would react if you were a new user. What does the site look like it's for? Does the site meet this expectation? Do you experience any difficulties or confusion in using it? This open-minded approach to your own site can help you quickly fix subtle problems that otherwise are hard to identify.

Testing your site can be a bit frustrating because you may find all sorts of things to fix, but if you follow through, you end up with a much better site. Be ready to take notes on your reactions from the moment you first log on to your site until the end of your visit — remembering first impressions later is difficult.

Use your browser's Print capability to print out all the pages in your Web site, and then put your notes right on the printout. Get feedback from anyone else who will take the time to look at your site. A printout enables you to easily keep track of your ideas as you go along and to make the right changes the first time.

Getting feedback on your site

Ask for feedback! You can put the request for feedback right in your Web site. You can also ask friends and colleagues to try the site and give you their honest opinions. Ask them some leading questions, such as "What do you think the site is for? How does it compare to other sites you've seen? What's the one thing you'd change about the site if you could?"

Part IV
Getting Interactive

The 5th Wave — By Rich Tennant

"See? I created a little felon figure that runs around our Web site hiding behind banner ads. On the last page, our logo puts him in a nonlethal choke hold and brings him back to the home page."

In this part . . .

Your users will enjoy seeing your Web pages, but they'll enjoy doing something with them even more. Use easily available online and offline tools to add animation, multimedia, and interactivity to your Web page. Use easy, free tools to create a Web log. Then make your Web page into a complete, multipage Web site.

Chapter 13

Adding Animation and Multimedia

Animation is a lot of fun — and it works well on the Web today because animation technology is so readily available to beginning Web page creators. Simple animations, called animated GIFs are easy to find, and you can put them on your Web site for free. If you're not interested in using someone else's creations on your Web page, it's not that much harder to create your own.

But there's more than just animation. Nowadays, you can incorporate audio, video, and other multimedia technology into your Web page design. This chapter introduces you to your multimedia options and gives you a heads up on some of the technological and legal pitfalls you face as you utilize these incredible innovations.

Getting your page right by using the basic Web ingredients of text and graphics is a real challenge but a lot of fun. Get the Web publishing basics down before you push forward into the realm of multimedia. And, note the problems that you can run into when using multimedia, as described in the next section. However, if you're adventurous, you can use the information that follows to add exciting multimedia flavorings to your Web pages.

Understanding Multimedia Pitfalls

Multimedia is a somewhat different beast. Audio works fairly well on the Web today. Animated GIFs are readily available and easy to incorporate in your Web page, as are audio files. The MP3 standard has revolutionized the availability and usability of music on the Web. (Unfortunately, however, MP3 has also caused the greatest challenge to copyright laws in years.) And full-motion video, however, is yet *another* kettle of fish.

How TV beats PC

As an entertainment transmission system, TV beats the PC hands down. The "user experience" of watching *Why Animals Attack Scary Police Videos* far surpasses — from a technical point of view, anyway — the best of Web multimedia.

Why? Just do the math. A typical text-only Web page takes about 2KB (kilobytes, or thousands of bytes) of storage space. Say you're willing to make the user wait one second to see a page. So the minimum bandwidth needed for effectively transmitting text Web pages through the Internet — from the server, across the Internet backbone, and all the way down to your PC — is 2KB in a second, which is 16 Kbps (kilobits per second; 8 bits are in a byte). A 56K modem is about three times faster than this, so you're in good shape for text-only Web pages.

Now add graphics. Major Web sites try to keep their total "page weight" under 50KB for fast viewing. 50KB (kilobytes) equals 400Kb (kilobits). So to experience good response times for typical Web pages, you need a 400Kb connection — about as fast as a DSL connection or a well-managed corporate network. So you're pushing the limits of the technology available to a typical user if you want to see today's typical Web pages at a reasonable speed.

Now look at multimedia. A typical TV displays 30 frames per second at roughly 560 x 420-pixel resolution, or over 200,000 pixels. That's 6MB (megabytes, or — at 8 bits in a byte — 48

Megabits, per second, more than 100 times the speed of a DSL connection. (Remember, 8 bits in a byte.) And that's just the picture — no sound! Not even a cable modem, on a good day and with none of your neighbors on with you to share the cable line to your home, can hope to deliver this. Neither can most corporate networks; the Internet backbone would get overcrowded very quickly with TV transmission added in. Displaying multimedia as good as an uncompressed TV broadcast is really beyond the capability of the worldwide Internet or of the connections to your home.

To work around these problems, all sorts of tricks are needed. Compression makes sound files — and short video clips using very small image sizes — ready for Internet downloading and use. Streaming technology, running on a server, can dole out multimedia packets — again, for a small image — at a rate that the user's system can handle. And creative people work hard behind the scenes to try to extract acceptable quality from the highly compressed multimedia files they have to work with.

Do-it-yourself Web authors, though, are generally the kind of people who enjoy a challenge. Multimedia on the Web is in the same early stages as the Web itself was only a few years ago. There are technical difficulties, but interest and use are growing. Use the information in this chapter to get started now while it's still early.

The Web has the potential to be the ultimate video network. There are just three little problems — the solutions to which will take many years to be realized:

   ✔ **Problem #1: Bandwidth.** The Web needs much more bandwidth for multimedia capabilities to grow. Video clips today are limited to tiny windows — much smaller than a regular TV picture, let alone HDTV and other high-resolution standards. It isn't just the thin 56K connection to a typical home PC that's a problem. Corporate networks and the entire global Internet structure are not nearly ready yet for full-screen, full-motion video.

✔ **Problem #2: Creative capability.** It takes scores of people to put on a typical TV show, or run a radio station day and night, from video and/or sound people to editors to on-air talent. When you create your own multimedia, you're taking on — or arranging for someone else to perform — many of these jobs yourself.

✔ **Problem #3: Copyright.** All great artists borrow, but multimedia files are highly protected by copyright. Borrowing others' work and combining it with your own can get you in trouble. And just plain taking other people's work and distributing it as your own — well, that's certainly a problem. Be very careful to only distribute original work that you create, or others' work that you have written permission to use.

Overall, however, the opportunity is tremendous. Multimedia — from the simplest animation or sound clip to a full-screen, surround-sound movie — can be much more engaging than static text and graphics. And solutions that allow you to add low-bandwidth multimedia to your Web page are becoming more readily available.

So expect to see and hear more and more multimedia on the Web — and to be able to include it, where appropriate, in your own Web pages right away.

Animating Your GIFs

Using animated GIFs is the simplest, cheapest way to liven up your Web page with multimedia. It's worth trying to create animated GIFs and host them on your Web page even if your real goal is to add other multimedia files to your site — the experience you get with animated GIFs will help you with any other multimedia efforts you make.

Most people know that a movie is simply a series of still pictures. An *animated GIF* is like a short movie — anywhere from a pair, up to a couple of dozen GIF images that, when displayed in sequence, create the illusion of motion. Think of an old-fashioned flip book; you flip through the pages, and the drawings on each page seem to come alive as a single, moving image.

The big advantage to animated GIFs is that there's no special software needed to host them on your Web server, nor to play them on the user's machine. You don't have to have any special artistic talent or pay anyone a licensing fee. And if you don't want to take the time to create your own animated GIF image, there are literally thousands available for free on the Web.

There are many ways you can create GIF animations and deploy them on your site. Not all of the things you can do are obvious:

- **Buttons and icons:** Buttons and icons on your Web site are intended to get users' attention and help them navigate. Animating them increases their effectiveness even further. Animated buttons and icons are freely available in many places on the Web.

- **Initial letters:** A "drop cap" is a big capital letter used to add an eye-catching beginning to an article (see the first letter of the first word of this chapter for an example). An animated drop cap is even more eye-catching! (Or distracting, depending on how you look at it — no pun intended.)

- **Humanicons:** You can use animated images of people as human icons, or "humanicons." Images of people are very attention-getting. Drawn images are pretty compelling. Photographs are *very* compelling. See the sidebar, "Photo-animated GIFs," for details.

- **Product shots:** You can use drawn or photographic product images to bring attention to your products and give visitors an experience — they feel like they are picking the product up and looking at it.

- **Advertising:** You can use any or all of these ideas to advertise on your site. You can use traditional, paid advertising, or internal "advertising" for whatever links on your site you want people to click most.

- **Pure creativity:** You can come up with things that no one has ever thought of before. Hamster Dance, a briefly famous Web phenomenon, was a page full of animated GIFs of hamsters and other rodent-like animals doing a Macarena-type dance. (For a look at the original Hamster Dance see `accpc.com/hamsterdance.html`.) Come up with your own ideas!

It's easy to overuse animated GIFs. The same icon that looks cute the first time someone comes to your site might be annoying by the fifth time. Deploy animated GIFs anywhere on your site that they make sense, but don't hesitate to remove some if the effect becomes a bit overwhelming.

Finding animated GIFs

The easiest way to get started with using animated GIF files in your Web pages is to use files that have already been created. You can find animated GIF files ready to plug into your Web page at a number of sites on the Web.

Smaller sites with fewer files are more likely to make the files available for no obligation on your part. Larger sites with large file libraries are more likely to want something from you in exchange. You can use a search engine to look up the term "animated GIF" and find both kinds of sites.

Photo-animated GIFs

Apple QuickTime VR — VR is short for Virtual Reality — is a technology that uses images to create 3D objects and 3D interactive scenes on the Web. You can create a similar effect with animated GIFs.

To create an animated image of a product or other object — even a person's head — take a series of digital photographs of any "thing" from, say, 8 or 16 different, equally spaced angles. Use a photo-editing program like Adobe Photoshop to make each image as small as possible. Then combine the images, in order, into an animated GIF, as explained in this chapter. The resulting animation is called an *object,* or *object movie.* The effect is amazingly detailed and realistic.

Less obvious in their usefulness, but perhaps even more interesting, are animated scene shots. To create one of these, stand with your camera in an open area — hopefully an interesting one — and take a series of shots at evenly spaced angles, gathering 8, 16, or some other even number of shots. As with objects, make the images as small as you can, then combine them into an animated GIF. The resulting image — called a *panorama* — gives the impression that the user is inside a scene, looking around.

Like any other creative enterprise, you can put as much time into animated GIFs in general, and photo-animated GIFs in particular, as you're willing to spend. A few people have even made a living at interactive photography.

One leading site for animated GIFs is Animation Factory, at `www.animfactory.com` (see Figure 13-1). You can use any of their 3,000 free animations on any personal Web page, as long as you're not doing so for profit. All Animation Factory asks is that you include a link to the Animation Factory Web site.

Although you can buy a membership to a premium site that gets you access to over thousands of animations, with no requirement that you link to anyone's site, we suggest that you try the free ones first. Free animation categories include buttons, text, people, events, computers, and many more.

Another big GIF site is 2Cool Animations at `gifanimations.com`. This site is a little less polished than Animation Factory, but everything on it — including 20,000 graphics files — is free. You can't use the animations for business purposes, though.

Use these sites, and others that you find on your own, as resources for animated GIF files. And have fun!

Think before you link! It might seem tempting to link to a cool GIF animation or other illustration on the Web. When you link directly to a GIF file on someone else's Web site, the GIF appears on your Web page as if it belongs there. Two problems: It's bad for the owner of the other Web site, and it's bad for you. The owner has to pay for all the resources needed to serve up the animated GIF file. And you have to worry about the owner moving the file and "breaking" your Web page! (A malicious site owner could even replace an image you like with one you don't like. How'd you like someone visiting your Web page to see an animated obscene gesture where they expected to see dancing hamsters?) And finally, you may be breaking copyright law by making someone else's work appear within your Web site.

Adding animated GIFs to your Web page

To add an animated GIF to your Web page, use the same steps you'd use when adding any other GIF to your Web page. In straight HTML, you use the image tag (img). For instance, to show an animated GIF called peace.gif, the syntax would be something like this:

```
<IMG SRC="peace.gif" HEIGHT=40 WIDTH=40 ALT="Peace,
         people!">.
```

For more about the img tag, see Chapter 9.

Figure 13-1:
Animation Factory has thousands of free GIF animations.

In adding animated GIFs to your Web page, you need to keep a few things in mind, before and after adding the file:

- ✓ **File size:** File size is a concern with all graphics files, and much more so with animated GIFs. Because every frame of the animation is a separate graphics file, it's easy to have an animated GIF be hundreds of KB in size — and therefore take over a minute for users with modems to download. In most cases, it ain't worth it! You must either reduce the size of the file by editing each frame in the animation — thus reducing the total number of frames — or put the animation on a separate page and label the links to it with a warning about the file size.

- ✓ **Playback speed:** Car companies always say "your mileage may vary." The same is true of animated GIFs. The user's Internet connection speed affects how long it takes the animated GIF to start moving, and the speed of his or her computer and graphics subsystem may affect how quickly the animation runs. Try your animation on some different setups to make sure it runs and looks the way you want it to.

- ✓ **Fun factor:** Keep updating and moving your animated GIFs around on your Web page so that they don't wear out their welcome with your frequent visitors. If you're getting tired of your animated GIFs, chances are your users are too.

Creating an animated GIF

You need a special program to create an animated GIF, unless you want to use a resource editor to directly edit the contents of the GIF graphics file. Luckily, we've been able to include a trial version of one of the leading GIF animation programs, Ulead GIF Animator, on the *Creating Web Pages For Dummies* CD-ROM.

Use the user manual included with the program if you need help setting it up or need more details on how to use the program. But here is a set of simplified steps to help you get your first animation done:

1. **Install Ulead GIF Animator on your machine.**

   Use the instructions on the CD-ROM to get the file installed.

2. **Create a few GIF images for your animation.**

   Use the instructions in Chapter 9 to create a few GIF images in sequence. Make sure the images are all the same size.

   If you're at a loss for ideas, a short series of photographs of someone turning his head produces an interesting, if somewhat spooky, effect.

3. **Start Ulead GIF Animator.**

4. **In the Startup Wizard dialog, click Close to close the dialog box. Then use the File⇨New command to open a new file.**

   You'll be asked to specify the canvas size; an object on a canvas is shown in Figure 13-2.

5. **Enter the Width and Height of your images in the dialog box to set the canvas size to the size of your images. Click OK to accept the changes.**

6. **In the Frame Panel at the bottom of the screen, click the Add Frame button to add a frame. Then click the frame to select it. Press the Ins key to insert an image into the selected frame. In the Add Image dialog box that appears, select the image that appears in the frame.**

   Add each of the frames for your animation, in order.

7. **Click the Optimize tab to optimize your animation.**

   GIF Animator is able to remove duplicated information from successive frames, reducing the size of each frame and the total file size of the animation.

8. **Click File⇨Save to save your animation. Choose GIF as the file format from the pull-down menu, and then save your file.**

9. **Insert your animation as a GIF file in a Web page on your hard disk and test it. Then publish your Web page to the Web and test again.**

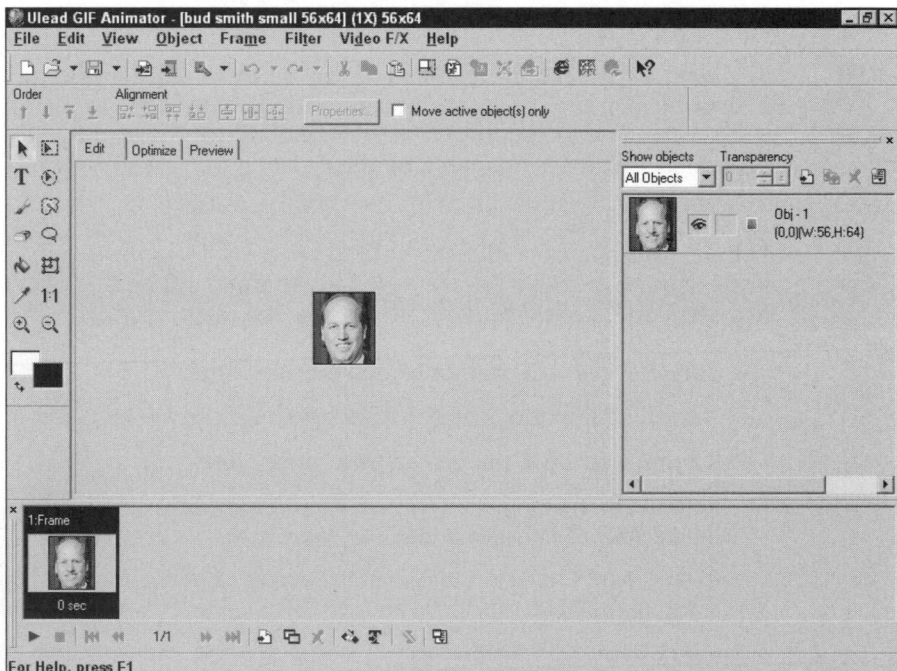

Figure 13-2:
GIF
Animator
will get you
shakin'.

GIF Animator has a vast number of options beyond those used in this example (the user manual goes into detail about each option). However, the process above is a good quick-and-dirty way to get your animation ready for publishing on the Web.

If you like GIF Animator and you're interested in doing more with graphics in your Web pages, Ulead has a number of other graphics-related tools that might help. Many are available in free trial versions, which is a great way to get started with new software. If you're interested, check out their offerings at www.ulead.com.

The M- (for Multimedia) Files

In the early days of the Web, people downloaded multimedia files, saved them to disk, and then started up a special player to view the files. Now, people embed multimedia files in Web pages and users view them "in place," with very little waiting, by using multimedia players such as Windows Media Player, RealPlayer, and Apple QuickTime. Macromedia Flash is also used to control multimedia playback.

Using multimedia causes some of the same problems as using graphics files, only more so. Many users don't have the right players for viewing multimedia and don't know how to get the players and set them up when needed. The players themselves can cause annoying problems — like system crashes, frequent alerts about necessary updates, and annoying promotional e-mail.

If a user doesn't have the right multimedia player (or worse, doesn't know whether he or she has the right multimedia player) that can be a tremendous source of frustration. More frustrating still is the effort to download and install the right multimedia player. If you use multimedia files on your Web site, make sure to add information to the Web page that tells users what player each file requires. You should also provide a link to a site where users can download the correct player.

Performance is also a problem. Waiting as long as several minutes to download a small-sized, brief video clip is frustrating. And the sound quality of many video clips is poor. Test their quality before making files available.

However, when you get multimedia working right, they can spice up a Web site like nothing else. Just look at the tremendous popularity of the MP3 format for transmitting music over the Web. Operating at nearly the level of quality of FM radio, MP3 files have spawned a whole culture of music trading and sharing on the Net. (Unfortunately, at this point much of the sharing is of MP3 files of copyrighted songs that can't legally be published or downloaded for free on the Net.)

The secret to MP3 is the widespread use of compression technology that makes relatively small files with quality near what people are used to hearing (FM radio). It will take a new generation of compression technology to create movies anywhere near as good as TV. At that point, expect an explosion of movies and TV shows on the Net that will rival the MP3 phenomenon in importance.

For now, the most important players for Web multimedia are

- **Real Networks RealPlayer:** RealPlayer is a plug-in for real-time playback of audio and video files that works pretty darn well. The user of a RealAudio-enhanced Web site typically clicks a link to get an audio or a video clip. A reasonably brief pause ensues while an initial part of the file downloads, and then sound or a video clip starts playing. The file is *streamed* in real time, meaning that no big file is stored on the user's hard disk. (Streaming also means that a faster Internet connection produces better sound quality.) See the sidebar, "I stream, you stream?" for details.

- **Windows Media Player:** Microsoft is trying to take back the multimedia player lead from Real with its own, similar offering. Windows Media Player supports most of the same formats as RealPlayer and comes bundled with just about every PC. However, RealPlayer is now moving ahead with deals with Apple for QuickTime interoperability, so Windows Media Player may still be playing catch-up for awhile.

- **Apple QuickTime:** QuickTime is Apple's multimedia technology that has become the industry standard for video editing and high-quality video playback on computers. QuickTime VR is an offshoot of QuickTime that creates high-resolution virtual reality panoramas and objects. Most QuickTime content is not streamed; users have to wait until some or the entire file downloads before it will play back. Although this reduces immediacy, it allows improved quality and greater flexibility for the user.

  The QuickTime player comes bundled with many computers and supports all kinds of multimedia formats, including animation, sound, QuickTime VR, and QuickTime video clips. A large percentage of the movie files on the Web are QuickTime files. QuickTime is easy to use in your Web page, and no licensing or server fees are involved. Newer versions of QuickTime support streaming, so expect to see more streamed QuickTime content over time.

- **Macromedia ShockWave/Flash:** The ShockWave plug-in allows presentations and experiences created in Macromedia Director to be played back over the Web. Figuring out Director is no mean feat, but luckily you don't need to understand Director in order to use the powerful ShockWave tool, which delivers multimedia experiences over the Web. Flash is a simple format for delivering animations in your Web page and is rapidly becoming popular. If you are a Director user, or want to become one, or if you're interested in Flash, run, don't walk, to the Macromedia Web site to get more info about ShockWave and Flash.

I stream, you stream?

You can find two flavors of video files. (We'll just assume sound is included.) The first type is *streaming* video. Streaming video is a lot like a TV/VCR combo with a very, very small screen — you click the Go button and, after a few seconds' wait, you start seeing video. Users can pause, rewind, or fast-forward. Streaming video files are experienced by the user with minimal hassles, assuming that the user has the correct player installed.

Streaming video files require special software on the Web server to synchronize the transmission and reception of each frame in the video file. Usually, it costs money to either buy the software or to rent space on a server that supports streaming. For instance, the low-end version of RealNetworks' streaming server costs just under $2,000 at this writing.

The second type is a *downloaded* video file, for which some or the entire movie clip must be downloaded to the user's computer before the video can be seen. Downloaded movie files make the user wait longer but are easier for you to manage — with either type of file, you don't need special software on your Web site. However, you may have to pay your Web host extra for the many megabytes of data that must be sent to support even moderate numbers of users of video clips.

But just because it can be prohibitively expensive to host your own streaming video files doesn't mean you can't add video-related content to your Web page. Just create external links to other peoples' clips! (Do make clear that you're linking so that you don't run into the problem of making someone else's work appear to be your own.) If you have a particular interest, an index of current, interesting video clips in your area is bound to be interesting and valuable to your users. Include brief summaries or reviews, and you'll save your site visitors a lot of wasted time.

To find out more about how to use multimedia on the Web, start by checking out the following URLs:

```
www.real.com
www.microsoft.com
www.apple.com/quicktime
www.macromedia.com
```

Adding a QuickTime Video File

Many different multimedia formats exist, each with its own strengths and weaknesses. But no other multimedia format is as widely accepted, capable, or supported by so many different multimedia and Web page creation tools as QuickTime. Adding multimedia to your Web page is easy with QuickTime, and using QuickTime-based multimedia is likely to be easy for your users as well. Here are the necessary elements for a successful QuickTime Web publishing experience:

- ✔ **Multimedia content:** You need a QuickTime multimedia file to put in your page. Dozens of multimedia tools create QuickTime multimedia; for starters, use one someone else has created and that's available for free re-use. When you're ready to create your own, look for tools at `www.apple.com/quicktime`.

- ✔ **HTML commands:** Some Web tools support embedding of QuickTime content directly. But unless you have such a tool, you need to write HTML commands to embed QuickTime content. Luckily, the commands are simple; an example follows shortly.

- ✔ **QuickTime and the QuickTime plug-in:** You and your users need the latest version of QuickTime and the QuickTime player. (Many versions of QuickTime include QuickTime VR support as well, adding virtual reality to what you can do with QuickTime.) Many of your users may have the latest version of QuickTime, but many may not. To help your users get updated, provide a link to the QuickTime Web page at `www.apple.com/quicktime`.

QuickTime is a big program! Users who don't already have QuickTime on their machines have to download it from the Web, and several megabytes is a lot to ask your users to download. However, doing so gives them a lot of capability. Be aware that you may get some questions and complaints about the download hassle.

You don't have to pay fees or sign special licenses before using QuickTime, as you do with competing technologies. From a business point of view, using QuickTime is as easy as putting a GIF or JPEG image in your Web page. To see some new QuickTime clips, visit `www.apple.com/hardware/ads/`.

For more information, visit the QuickTime VR home page and the Berkeley Macintosh User's group QuickTime authoring site at the following Web URLs:

```
www.apple.com/quicktime/qtvr
www.judyandrobert.com/quicktime/
```

Here are the steps to add a QuickTime movie to your Web page:

1. **Install QuickTime and the QuickTime plug-in on your own machine.**

   To download these files, go to the QuickTime software page at `www.apple.com/quicktime`.

2. **Create or obtain a QuickTime movie — animation, sound, video, or VR.**

   Use a Web search engine to search for "free QuickTime," or visit sites (especially U.S. Government sites such as `eosweb.larc.nasa.gov/ EDDOCS/Teacher_Notes/erbe_video.html`) to find a clip you can use with minimal or no restrictions.

3. **Embed the movie in your Web page. (If you're using Netscape Composer, click the <HTML> Source tab at the bottom of the page so you can add the following HTML tag directly.)**

   Use the `embed` HTML command. In its basic form, for a file named `file.mov` in the same folder as the Web page, it's very simple:

   ```
   <embed src="file.mov">
   ```

   You have additional options when you use the `embed` command with the QuickTime plug-in; for details, see the QuickTime Web page (in particular, visit `www.apple.com/quicktime/tools_tips/tutorials/ activex.html`). But try the simple command shown here first to make sure that you don't accidentally introduce a problem when you try to add options.

4. **Test it on your own machine.**

   Test the Web page by opening it in Internet Explorer and seeing if the movie acts properly. Then test in Netscape Navigator.

5. **Upload the changed Web page and the QuickTime file to the Web and test, as described in Chapter 12.**

   Congratulations — you're a multimedia Web publisher!

Adding an MP3 Audio File

MP3 audio files bring with them many questions. The quality of the audio is just okay, and many of the files are illegal copies. They are, however, extremely popular, and a whole industry of sites — even new playback devices — has sprung up around MP3 and related formats.

Creating MP3 files is a lot of work, and you need to search the Web for the right tools and resources to do it. Or you can search for a license-free MP3 file. When you have an MP3 file — fully legal ones are easy to find — it's a snap to put one on your Web page. Just follow these instructions:

1. **Get an MP3 file.**

   Just search the Web using any search engine; it won't take long.

2. **Link to the file from your Web page.**

   ```
   Use the <a> (for anchor) HTML command. Creating a
   link for an MP3 file on another Web server is as
   simple as it for any Web page:
   <a href="http://artists.iuma.com/site-bin/
   mp3gen/23182/IUMA/Bands/AbunoahIII/audio/
   AbunoahIII_-_Clay_Jar.mp3">A Christian MP3
   file</a>.
   ```

   The file here is just one example. Many thousands more are out on
   the Web.

3. **Test the link and the file on your own machine.**

   Test the MP3 file by opening it from the Web page and playing it back.

4. **Upload the changed Web page and the MP3 file to the Web, as
   described in Chapter 12, and test.**

   Congratulations — you're a Net DJ!

Chapter 14

Adding More Interactivity

. . . .

In This Chapter

▶ Adding a site counter, guestbook, and form to your page

▶ Incorporating CGIs

▶ Programming your pages

▶ Going beyond HTML

. . . .

*I*nteractivity is what distinguishes the best Web sites from the rest. In years of work creating and deploying Web sites, we have seen that many of the best sites are those at which users enter data and then can come back to add to it, manage it, or see if someone else has reacted to it.

E-mail is a good example of this kind of interaction. You struggle over what to say. You send your message out to one person, or two, or dozens. Then you invest countless hours replying to the replies, checking if everyone who was meant to get your message actually did, even phoning or meeting with people to follow up. Web sites that can capture the same kind of interactivity do very well.

But interactivity is much harder to add to your Web site, and to manage, than "brochureware" — a Web site that simply displays your message, however well-written and laid out, to the world. There are real technical barriers to interactive sites because you need sophisticated databases to store and update data so that it can be accessed by scores or thousands of people. The same Web hosting providers who are happy to give you a free or low-cost basic Web site are much less likely to want to help you create and maintain fancy databases.

Luckily, you can get started simply. In this chapter we introduce you to easy-to-add interactive features, such as site counters and guestbooks that many hosting providers offer for free. If not, you can get these features for free — or at least, for the cost of including an ad on your site — from several independent sources. We then go on to introduce you to advanced features like CGI scripting and ActiveX programming that you may not tackle soon, but will at least want to understand for future reference.

Interactivity Made Easy

There are several forms of interactivity for your Web page that have been canned and made easy for you to implement. Among the interactive features you may want to add to your Web page are

✔ **Site counters:** A *site counter* counts the number of times a Web page has been accessed and displays the count on the Web page. Site counters let you — and your Web site visitors — know how many times the page has been accessed. You may want to add a site counter to your Web page; if you have a multipage Web site, you may even want a site counter on each page.

✔ **Guestbooks:** A *guestbook* allows Web site visitors to leave comments. Guestbooks can be a lot of fun; they can even allow people a way to get to know each other through your site. Imagine a family site where everyone signs in and leaves a "Happy Holidays" message for each other.

✔ **Forms:** A *form* allows the user to enter data using entry boxes, pull-down menus, checkboxes, and so on. Creating a form using HTML commands isn't the hard part; unfortunately you need a computer program, running on a Web server, to handle the resulting data. The computer program accesses the data using something called a CGI, or Common Gateway Interface.

A message board, or forum, is like a guestbook, but with much more flexibility. Users can post messages, reply to one anothers' messages, start new topics, and more. Setting up and managing a message board requires a lot of work — after all, you don't want your friends and family to see a rude message some idiot left, do you? But if you're willing to do the maintenance work, having a message board can be very rewarding as well. To try using a free message board service, visit www.amazingforums.com.

Each of these forms of interactivity needs some cooperation from the Web server that's hosting your page, or from some other Web server. Why is that, you wonder? Well, think about it a bit.

When you have a site counter on your Web page, the counter goes up by 1 every time the page is displayed. (Actually, the counter goes up by 1 every time the *counter* is displayed. If the user visits your Web page, then clicks away before the part of the page with the counter on it is displayed, the counter doesn't go up.) How does this happen?

When the counter file is requested by some HTML code in your Web page, it reads a database to find out how many times the request has been made in the past. That's the visit count that it displays. A program notes the request. It updates a database with a request to add 1 to the number of times the file has been accessed. The next time the counter is requested, the number for it to display is 1 higher. All of this takes a bit of computer programming.

The same is true for guestbooks — data is being stored somewhere, updated with new additions, and displayed on request. Any time data is being stored and modified, some kind of computer programming is involved. Sometimes you can use a canned, prewritten program to do the work. However, someone still had to write and test the program, and it still has to run every time the functionality is used.

Computer programs are dangerous! They can, unless carefully prevented from doing so, read and write data — which is great when it's done right, but is disastrous when done wrong. (Just think of computer viruses for an example of a computer program doing the wrong thing.) The same people who will happily host your Web page on their server for free, or at a small price, will suddenly become very unhappy if you try to run your program on their server. The interactive features you incorporate into your page, even simple ones like site counters and guestbooks, are carefully managed by the administrators of Web servers. Ordinary people often aren't allowed to put their own programs to support these features on their host's Web server.

Using site counters

A site counter is a graphic that goes on your Web page, just like any other GIF image, but it has a rather magical property: It displays the current count of the number of pages your Web page has been displayed. (Of course, if you want a lot of visitors and you're only getting a few, that property might not seem so magical.)

A site counter is valuable if you care about how many visits your site is getting — information that's really nice to know if you've created a site for fun, and vital to know if you've created a site for business purposes.

Your access to site counters depends on where your Web page is hosted:

- **Yahoo! GeoCities pages:** For GeoCities users, Yahoo! hosts your Web pages and the counter software. The same people who host your Web page run the program and database that support the counter, so you don't have to do anything tricky. Start by creating your Web page on Yahoo! GeoCities, as described in Chapter 2. Then follow the instructions at geocities.yahoo.com to add a site counter to your site. Figure 14-1 shows the various counter styles available from GeoCities.

- **AOL Member pages:** As on GeoCities, if you create your Web page at members.aol.com, as described in Chapter 3, you can use the built-in Web counters there. Just follow AOL's instructions.

- **Other hosts:** If you have your site hosted by another free or paid Web pages service, or by an ISP other than AOL, you may have access to a free Web site counter feature. If so, use it, as described by your Web page's host. Otherwise, see the next bullet.

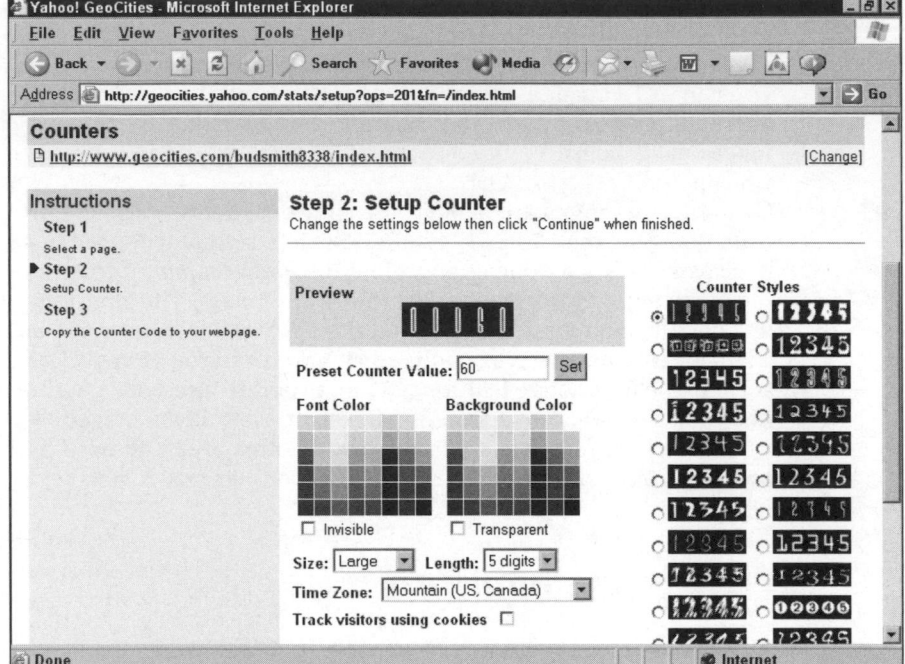

Figure 14-1:
GeoCities
makes your
pages
count.

✔ **Free Web-based service:** Several "free" Web-based services provide counters for users. (We say "free" in quotes because many of them require you to include an ad or link to their server, though they don't charge money.) One good one is at `www.bcentral.com/products/fc`. Check it out, or search for other free Web-based counter services on the Web.

✔ **Run your own server:** You can run your own Web server software on your own computer over your own Internet connection. Then you can create and run any computer program on the server that you want! This is a much more difficult approach than we recommend in this book, but if you want to do a lot with your site, having this degree of control may be worth it. The book _Building a Web Site For Dummies,_ by David A. Crowder and Rhonda Crowder (Wiley) has the instructions and software — including CGIs — that you need to get started.

Adding guestbooks

A guestbook is a place on your page or site where visitors can leave comments. If you get a lot of activity in your guestbook, users will return to your site more often to see what's new and to leave additional comments; eventually, new users will visit and return to check the guestbook. As you can see, a guestbook can be great for making your site more interesting and increasing traffic to it.

As with site counters, a guestbook requires that a program run on a Web server somewhere, store the data that users enter in it, and display the data when needed. Also as with site counters, your access to guest counter functionality depends on which type of service provider hosts your Web page:

- ✔ **Yahoo! GeoCities pages and AOL Member pages:** If you create your Web page at `geocities.yahoo.com`, as described in Chapter 2, you can use the built-in guestbook there. Same thing if you create your Web page at `members.aol.com`, as described in Chapter 3. With the same people supporting your Web page and your guestbook, you just need to follow the on-site instructions and everything will work.

- ✔ **Other hosts:** For other hosts, check to see if you have access to a free guestbook feature. If not, use a free Web-based service, as described in the next bullet.

- ✔ **Free Web-based service:** There are a few Web-based services that support a guestbook. They may be truly free, free with the caveat that you display an ad or link on your page, or require a fee for use. You can find an ad-based or paid guestbook at `guestbook.mycomputer.com`.

- ✔ **Run your own server:** You can run guestbooks all day and all night if you take on the challenge of running your own Web server. The aforementioned *Building a Web Site For Dummies,* by David A. Crowder and Rhonda Crowder (Wiley) will help you get started.

A chat room can be even more fun than a guestbook. To learn about a good one that you can try, go to `www.icq.com/ircqnet`.

Incorporating forms and CGIs

A *form* is just what the name implies: a place where a user can enter data, such as name, e-mail address, and other contact information. Figure 14-2 shows a simple form used by Netsurfer Digest for signing up subscribers.

Forms have been around for years, and most books about using HTML describe them. Getting data from users via forms is pretty easy. What happens after that is more complicated.

Processing the data from a form requires one or more computer programs. A common way to handle data is to use a CGI script and an application. A *CGI script,* sometimes simply called a CGI, is a Common Gateway Interface script — a program that sends the data to an application that you create. The CGI script runs on the server that hosts your Web page. CGI scripts are different on NT, UNIX, and Macintosh. Many CGI scripts are written in the C programming language or PERL, a cross-platform scripting language.

To run a CGI script, you need the permission of the *sysop* (system operator) responsible for the server that hosts your Web page. Sysops are paid to protect their systems from harm, so getting your sysop to run an unknown program on his or her precious server may not be possible. Many Web hosts, including Yahoo! GeoCities (see Chapter 2) and AOL (see Chapter 3), have prepackaged forms or CGI packages that handle common tasks such as counting visitors, allowing users to register, and more. Finding and using one of these prewritten packages is a good intermediate step toward creating your own CGI scripts and applications.

For basic information about CGI scripting, check out the online tutorial, CGI Programming 101, at `www.cgi101.com/class/`.

Programming Your Pages

You can do an awful lot on the Web with simple text and graphics, and adding interactive features such as a counter or guestbook extends your powers even further. However, to really do business on the Web and support interactivity, you need to consider doing some programming.

Web programming is a complicated topic that is beyond the scope of this book. However, you may want to experiment with programming on your own.

For a long time, a big advantage of living in certain areas was the improved access such places had to large and specialty bookstores. For example, when the early editions of this book came out, both authors lived in Silicon Valley, home to the excellent Computer Literacy bookstores — which gave the authors a leg up over people living elsewhere. Now, through the Web, most people can find whatever books they need. And recently, the Computer Literacy bookstores have gone out of business!

To find computer books, you can start by looking at the following URLs:

```
www.amazon.com
www.bn.com
www.booksmatter.com
```

You may also be interested in online courses on these and other topics. To see what's available from EducationToGo, an industry leader, check out `www.educationtogo.com`.

JavaScript

JavaScript is a very popular and widely used scripting language that gives you increased control over your Web pages without true programming. You can learn quite a bit by simply searching online for the word JavaScript. To go further requires more books, more training, and more work. Want to read *JavaScript For Dummies,* 3rd Edition, by Emily A. Vander Veer (Wiley), anyone?

ActiveX

ActiveX is technology from Microsoft that allows Microsoft Visual Basic programs to work with the Web. The good news is that ActiveX enables you to do some pretty amazing things. The bad news is that it has had serious security problems, doesn't work well on the Macintosh, and doesn't work on UNIX. However, if you are willing to do Windows-only Web work and want more information on ActiveX, you can start at Microsoft's .NET site at `www.microsoft.com/net`.

Also, see Appendix D and the *resource.htm* file on the CD-ROM that comes with this book for pointers to more information about ActiveX.

Many, many resources

There are many resources on the Web for learning advanced topics such as those described here. However, if you're trying to get a good overview, it can be worthwhile to go to one or two major resources, where the different pieces tie together in an understandable way. Try these resources to get started:

```
www.about.com
builder.cnet.com
www.webmonkey.com
```

Database interactivity

Tying your Web site to a database is a way to supercharge it beyond anything we demonstrate in this book. Technologies whose names you may have heard or seen within a Web page URL, such as Active Server Pages (ASP) and PHP (PHP: Hypertext Preprocessor), are used for this purpose. Some free hosting services enable you to set up your own database and tie it to your Web site. One of them, from a Web hosting company called Brinkster, Inc., is at www.brinkster.com.

Going beyond HTML

Although the simplicity and flexibility of HTML have been essential to the success of the Web, HTML does, of course, have limitations. Two major languages, Dynamic HTML (DHTML) and XML (eXtensible Markup Language), address many of the limitations. Most, but not all, users have browsers that support these technologies.

Style sheets — Cascading onto the Web

Cascading Style Sheets, commonly known as CSS, is the name of a standard for defining formatting within Web pages. You can use CSS to quickly change the look of a Web page — or a whole series of Web pages.

Unfortunately, CSS was developed so quickly that in its early days browser support was inconsistent and buggy. Now, you can use CSS with good results across the great majority of browsers currently in use.

However, there are still enough users out there with no CSS support, or inconsistent CSS support, to make deploying it a bit tricky. Get your Web pages looking and working right without CSS before you consider learning more about, and using, this powerful standard.

HTML gets Dynamic

Dynamic HTML, or DHTML for short, is an extension of HTML that allows multiple layers of information to be sent to the user during a server connection. The user only sees some of the information at first. Additional information can be unveiled as time passes or as the user undertakes different actions, all without having to reconnect to the server. For instance, this capability allows a Web page to change its appearance based on options the user selects, all without having to download more data from the server.

Only the 4.0 and later versions of Netscape Navigator and Microsoft Internet Explorer support any of these Dynamic HTML features, which leaves out users of older browsers. Even though most users have browsers new enough to support it, DHTML is not yet widely used on the Web.

XML x-es out HTML

HTML is a subset of an overall standard called *Standard Generalized Markup Language,* or SGML. (We bet the people who created SGML didn't know what would happen with their invention!) XML, or e*X*tensible *M*arkup *L*anguage, is a superset of HTML, which has been created within the overall SGML standard. XML allows complex data structures to be built into a Web page.

For example, with XML authors can create database applications and deliver them across the Web. XML is being deployed first on intranets and extranets — shared networks used by business partners — because that way organizations can ensure that all Web authors and users use the same XML definitions. If you're responsible for intranet- or extranet-related activity, keep an eye on this one.

The Web enters the twenty-first century

Because of its flexible nature, the Web has the theoretical capability to support almost anything that can be done or imagined on a computer. As the connection speed available to the average user improves, as more technology is used in advanced Web pages, and as users move up to more capable browsers, more and more will be possible. The trick is not to chase down any of the new pathways before they settle down into widely used standards. Develop your skills in the key areas that make the Web useful, productive, interesting, and fun today, and most importantly, that will make your Web page attractive to your target users. Using the capabilities of today's mainstream Web is the best way to prepare yourself to take advantage of the advanced Web that will be here the day after tomorrow.

Chapter 15

Creating a Full Web Site

So far, this book has focused on creating individual, separate Web home pages. In this chapter we tell you how to tie several different Web pages together into a multipage Web site. However, it's good to keep your focus on each individual Web page even as you combine them all together.

Users of your site are always able to leave for any other site or page on the Web. If you make sure every Web page you put up is interesting, fun, and attractive, as described throughout this book, you'll end up with a strong Web site.

The terms Web page and Web site are used very similarly. In this book we use the term *Web page* to refer to a single Web page consisting of an HTML document and the graphics that go with it. We use the term *Web site* to refer to an area on the Web consisting of multiple Web pages tied together by shared navigation.

Creating Your Web Pages

It's typical, when designing a Web site, to use a top-down approach and to start by thinking a lot about navigation, organization, navigation, and so on. (We mention navigation twice because it's such a big concern when you're creating a large Web site.) But for a small Web site, we say go from the bottom up — building the site from carefully crafted individual pages.

Your approach to creating Web pages for a small Web site should be similar to your approach to creating a single Web home page. Each page should stand alone as a worthwhile place for your Web visitors to spend time, learn something, or have some fun.

Getting your pages right

Think of each Web page as a separate "information asset." Why would people want to come to your Web page? What would they take away from having seen it? Is there anything about your page that might make people come back, or want to encourage someone else to visit? Most of us have enough to say to easily create a single Web home page that our friends, family, and colleagues find interesting. But it takes extra work to make each Web page in a multipage site valuable to people.

One of the best ways to create a strong Web site is to first create each Web page separately. Make sure that each page has the information you want, that it downloads in a reasonable amount of time, that all the links work, and that the page looks good. Then use the information in this chapter to add navigation and make your Web pages into a unified Web site.

What about consistency? Consistency is important within a Web site, but not that difficult to achieve if your site is only a few pages to perhaps a dozen pages in size. Use the same background color, text color, font, and text size throughout your pages. If you use standard HTML headers, bulleted and numbered lists, and small images to break up your text, your pages will have a consistent appearance.

Figure 15-1 shows a Web page from within the Netsurfer Science Web site created and managed by one of the coauthors (Bebak). Note how the page uses a simple design, which is repeated throughout the site. (Visit the Netsurfer pages at `www.netsurf.com` to see for yourself.) The Netsurfer Science site is a good example of the effectiveness of simple, clean design across a Web site.

In addition to a standardized design across pages, the other elements that make a site consistent are predictable, understandable Web page addresses and repeated navigational elements throughout the site. The next section explains how to achieve these qualities in your site.

You may want to take the design consistency of your Web site to another level by adding repeated graphical elements and a strong, consistent approach to layout across all your Web pages. This is the approach taken by the pros. We suggest that, unless you have some design experience, you first create the site's pages and navigation. Then work on improving the overall design after the site is up and working. (This is also the approach taken by the pros!)

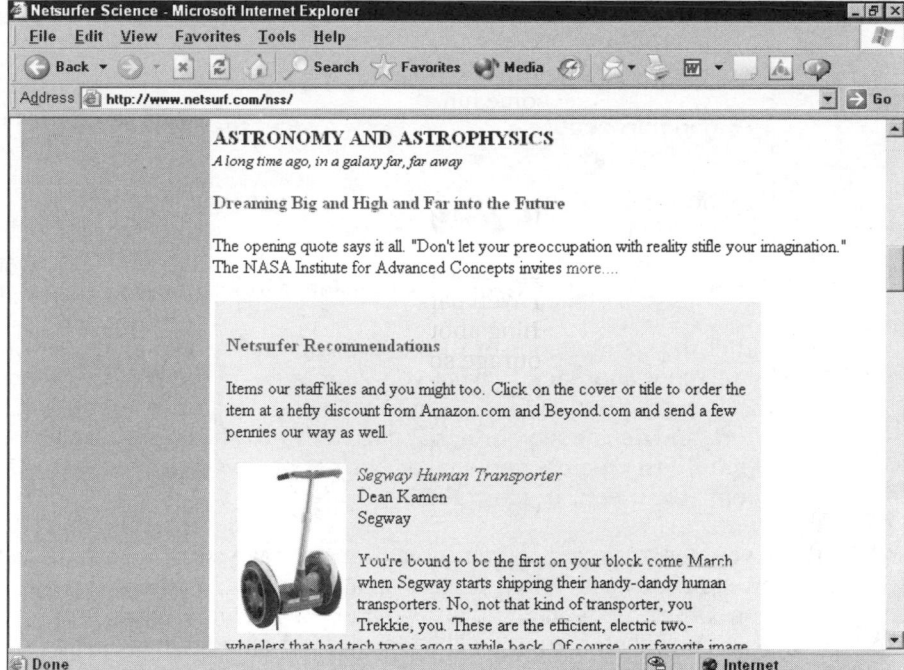

Figure 15-1:
Netsurfer
Science has
a clean,
simple
design.

Planning versus pushing ahead

You can take two approaches to your role as a Web site publisher: the spontaneous approach favored by someone like Captain Kirk, the risk-taking leader of the Starship *Enterprise* in the original Star Trek TV series and movies, or the careful approach favored by the more logical Mr. Spock. The spontaneous Captain Kirk approach can be summarized in the well-known Nike slogan "Just do it." You can get a simple site up on the Web with just a little more work than doing a single Web page.

If you're trying for a more complex Web site, such as a Web site for your business, you'll want to take a more careful approach. In contrast to Captain Kirk's quick-and-dirty approach, Mr. Spock's more logical method requires you to do the following:

✔ Set goals for your Web site.

✔ Plan the contents of your site to meet those goals.

✔ Create a *storyboard* of your site — a sketch of each page, or at least of the most important pages — that specifies what will go on each Web page and how you want the pages to fit together.

- ✔ Compare your planned site to similar or competing sites and revise your plans accordingly.

- ✔ Create your site on your own machine first and test it thoroughly.

- ✔ Carefully choose a Web service provider that will do the best job of hosting your site.

- ✔ Get your site up on the Web and begin an ongoing cycle of testing and revision.

Whew! That's a lot of Tribble — we mean, a lot of trouble!

Either the spontaneous or the careful approach is just fine, but you should match your approach to what you want to do on the Web. We recommend that you try the spontaneous approach first. Don't put out a great deal of effort, and don't use your initial page to try to start a Web-based business empire. Just create a personal or business home page that says something about you or your organization.

If you don't own or run your organization, make sure that you have the permission you need before putting up a Web site that represents the organization. Otherwise, you could find yourself on an unexpected, rapid transition off your current career path. (The Monster job search database at `www.monster.com` is a good example of a fun Web site — and is a great help in looking for a new job!)

If that one page is all you ever publish on the Web, that's fine. A lot of the fun of being on the Web is seeing the Web pages created by individuals who are just trying to have fun and share their interests. Whether you go on to create a Web presence for a business or even create a Web-based business of your own, the experience that you get when you "just do it" may prove invaluable. Table 1-1 suggests when to use the careful versus the spontaneous approach to Web publishing.

Table 15-1	The Kirk (Spontaneous) and Spock (Careful) Approaches to Web Publishing				
	Have Fun	*Learn Now for Advanced Work Later*	*Small Biz Web Presence*	*Larger Biz Web Presence*	*Web-Based Business*
Spontaneous	X	X	X		
Careful			X	X	X

Planning your Web site

The only tools you need for this part of the Web publishing process are Web access, for doing research, and either a word processing and drawing program, or a pencil and paper — whichever is more comfortable — for sketching your plans and taking notes. A few extra hours upfront can save you a great deal of time later and help you produce a better Web page; yet the planning step is the most frequently overlooked part of the Web publishing process. To plan your Web site, follow these steps:

1. **Determine the purpose of your site.**

   Decide which type of site you want to create: personal, topical, commercial, or comical. (We could also call the last two "business" and "entertainment," but those don't sound as nice together.)

   After you decide what type of site you want, research existing sites; then research other media that serve the same purpose (magazines, brochures — even television). Ask yourself what it is about your material, or about the Web, that makes the Web a good way to get your material out. Think some more about your own needs and interests. Then write a few goals for your initial site and for later versions of it.

2. **Decide on the structure of your site and the layout of your pages.**

   The structure of your site can help guide visitors to the parts that interest them most. A great layout of your site's Web pages can make the pages more useful, more interesting, or more entertaining, depending on their purpose. Here are a few general rules:

   • Decide how many pages to have and how they link to each other.

   • Put the purpose of your site near the top of your home page.

   • Indicate the purpose of each additional page near the top of that page.

   • Use headers, bullets, icons, and other graphical or emphasis elements to highlight key points.

   • Think about what graphics you need. Start the process of generating or obtaining them.

   • Use summary elements, such as a site map and a Frequently Asked Questions (FAQ) page.

   • Put navigational elements — links from your home page to other pages in your site, and from other pages back to the home page — in a consistent spot at the top or bottom of each page.

3. Decide which links to include.

A Web page that has no links is generally pretty boring. You already decided in Step 2 which links to include between the pages in your site. Now think about which links to include from your pages out to other sites. Which links make sense? Which links are fun? Use Web search engines such as Google (www.google.com) to search the Web and find suitable links (see Figure 15-2). Then check the links and cut the list down to the personally significant ones, not just a laundry list (unless you're making a list of laundries). Create a place to save links that you run into while using the Web so that they're readily available when you make updates to your pages.

Now think some more. Do the links that you're including fit the purpose of your page? How can you organize them? Should you group sets of key links together? Are some of the links repetitive or superfluous? Getting your links right makes your site more useful. And although no one likes to be left behind, which is what happens to you when people click an outbound link in one of your pages, a good set of links can, paradoxically, make users more likely to return to your site in the future.

Make sure to check your external links frequently — otherwise, you can soon have several broken links on your site.

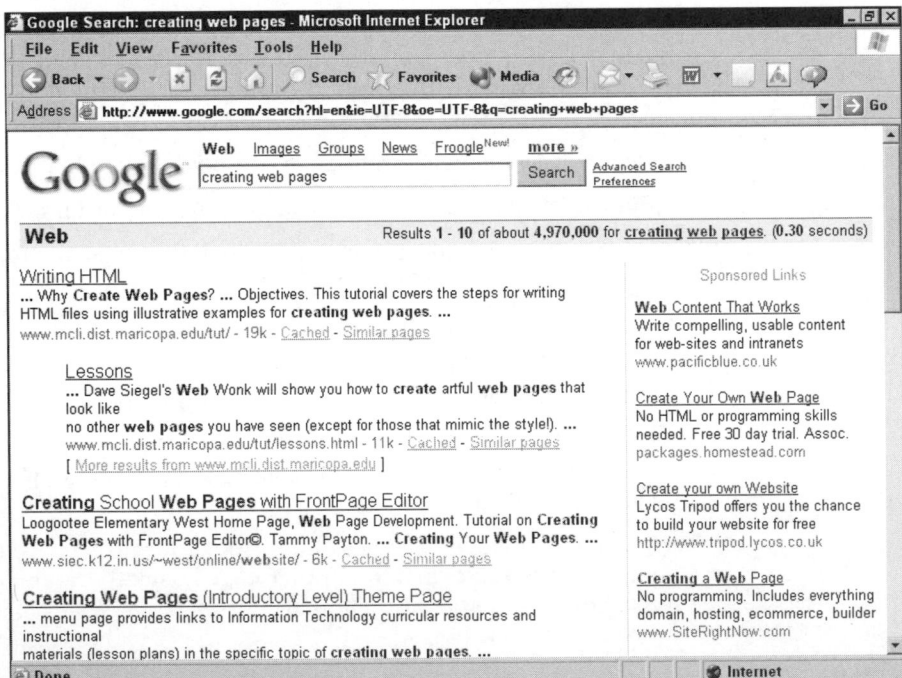

Figure 15-2: Don't get all Google-eyed while searching.

Creating the content

Creating content is the part of the Web publishing process where tools come in. You need tools to create HTML-tagged text (or a word processing program or text editor if you want to work in HTML directly) and graphics tools to create graphics and convert them to one of the common Web formats, GIF or JPEG. (Yes, you can use other file formats for Web graphics, but, as we say in Chapter 9, GIF and JPEG are the only formats that are widely supported by all browsers.) For simple sites, one person can do all the work (but it *is* a lot of work); for creating and maintaining larger sites, you need a team of people, often including consultants who have HTML expertise and other skills.

Follow these general steps to create content for your Web site:

1. **Type up the text for your pages.**

   The best thing to do here, if you're new to Web publishing, is to work in a word processing program without putting in HTML tags, at least at first. That way you can use a familiar tool to get the text right. You can achieve much more precise formatting in a word processing program than you can in a Web page.

   Don't forget to run the spell checker!

Consider using non-English Web pages

One of the most limiting factors to the spread of the World Wide Web is that it's largely in English. This situation is changing: already, many larger sites, such as the Yahoo! Web Directory, offer their services in several languages. But the amount of non-English content is small compared to the size of the Web.

To create Web pages, you need to know enough English to figure out and use HTML and Web tools. But what about your audience?

First, find out how many people in your target audience speak a specific language and how many of them have access to the Web. Then consider the cost of translating your content into each language that you're interested in. Compare that cost to the size of the potential audience.

Be optimistic; having native-language content distinguishes your site. At this point in the Web's development, you're better off having the Web's best list of movies in Farsi (Iran's predominant language) than yet another list of movies in English because your site will be a standout.

At the least, if you have printed materials already translated into other languages, either put those materials on the Web or publicize them on your site. In some languages and some areas of information needs, using non-English languages on the Web offers the same kind of ground-floor opportunity that the Web as a whole offered when its popularity started about ten years ago.

If you've already created a Web home page in HTML or a Web editing tool such as Netscape Composer, as we describe throughout the book, then you can use the same techniques for your Web site.

You may want to consider going an extra step and creating a dummy of your Web site — pun intended — in your word processing program before you commit to HTML. Making a *dummy* (a printer's term for a mock-up of a printed page) is a good way to plan what's on each page, and you can insert graphics and simulate links by underlining text and changing the color of fonts. Compare your model to relevant Web sites you admire and see what changes you want to make.

2. **Convert the content to HTML.**

   Next, you need to convert the content to HTML. You can add the HTML tags yourself (see Chapter 4), use HTML conversion capabilities built into your word processing program, or use a Web page editor (like Netscape Composer, first described in Chapter 5). You may well end up using a combination of conversion methods for new content and for files that you use or adapt from various sources.

Read Chapter 4 to find out how HTML works. Even if you use a Web authoring tool to create your Web page and don't put in the HTML tags yourself, knowing what is (*and isn't*) possible in basic HTML saves a great deal of time and effort in the overall publishing process.

3. **Create the graphical elements in your pages.**

   Graphical elements often take a long time to create, so start early. They include not just photos and computer-generated images but also mastheads, separator bars, and icons.

4. **Incorporate any multimedia that you want to add.**

   This is also the time to create multimedia elements, such as sounds or video clips, if you really want to push the envelope. We cover these elements in Chapter 13.

5. **Add navigation and test it.**

   As we describe later in this chapter, you have to add navigation to make your separate Web pages into a site. Then you'll be ready for the next step — publishing your site!

Publishing your Web site

Publishing your site — either on an intranet or on the open World Wide Web — is the most exciting part of the Web publishing process. (But watch out! Your excitement may quickly turn to anxiety as you think of people actually looking at your carefully crafted baby.) For this part of the process, you don't need any tools, except possibly an FTP (File Transfer Protocol) program to move your files to the Web server (as described in Chapter 12). Usually, whoever is providing your Web hosting service supports this process.

First, bring the elements of your site together, then test it on your local machine, and finally publish it! Here are the steps for publishing (or updating) your site:

1. **Put it all together and test it.**

   Check to make sure that you have all the content and links in the places that you want them and then test each Web page and the entire site. On your own machine, you can use a Web browser not just to see what your pages look like, but also to follow links from your site to other sites. Then you can use the Back button on your browser to return to your own site, on your own machine. (The only thing missing is that the people who eventually surf your site can't get to it until it's actually published on a Web server.)

2. **Put your content on a Web server.**

   This is where it gets real. After you get your pages on the server, as described in Chapter 12, test them again. Especially, test all the links to make sure that they really go somewhere; remember, nothing is more frustrating than clicking a broken link.

3. **Publicize your site.**

   Get some users onto your site. Tell your friends, use Web resources, and, especially, get related Web sites to put in links to your site. Offer some kind of reward for feedback on your site — even if it's just taking that person's site off your "bad Web pages" list! (For more detail on this part of the process, see the section "Getting the Word Out" later in this chapter.)

4. **Bask in the glory of being a Web publisher.**

   Having a Web site up and running is something to be proud of. Sit and enjoy it for awhile.

After you get your site on the Web, you'll experience a brief moment of elation — and then one of concern — as you think of all the things you wanted to do with the site before you ran out of time. Then you'll click around your site and realize that something doesn't look quite as good as you wanted. You may compare your site with others and decide to add new features. Back to square one!

Stumbling blocks on the Web

For all its great characteristics, the Web has some problems that you're more likely to run into when you're creating a full Web site than when you're just publishing a single Web page. Among these issues:

- **Differences in browsers:** Different browsers, such as different versions of Internet Explorer or Netscape Navigator, display the same HTML tags differently. And some browsers support newer or nonstandard tags, so pages displayed in them look better — or at least different — than they look on other browsers. This inconsistency can drive you to distraction. Use basic tools and keep your site simple until you learn your way around some of these concerns.

✔ **Faster and slower connections:** Some users have fast network connections to the Web, whereas many home users dawdle along at 28.8 Kbps — 10 times slower than a typical corporate connection. So a graphics-rich page that comes up fast on one machine downloads *very s-l-o-w-l-y* on another. See Chapter 9 for information on how to keep your graphic file sizes small and Chapter 11 for information on how to keep your overall page size small.

✔ **Those darn users:** Users have different screen sizes, and they can reconfigure their browsers to use different fonts, different window sizes, and so on. So even users who connect to the Web through the same network and run the same browser can see the same Web page quite differently. Chapter 11 has details.

✔ **Getting on a server:** For your Web pages to show up on the Web, they have to be on a Web server. This means that you have to find either a volunteer or a vendor with a Web server and some hard disk space to spare. Luckily, space for a small Web site is usually either free or cheap (ahem, inexpensive), but finding the right server space and getting your files to the server can be a hassle. You can find out more in Chapter 12.

Page description languages

HTML is not a *page description language* — that is, a specification for exactly how your text and graphics should look when they're displayed or printed. But Adobe Acrobat *is* a page description language, by far the most widely used on the Web.

So if you want to put up a formatted page that keeps its look, feel, fonts, and more (regardless of the user's computer settings), use Acrobat. You can put the page up on the Web so that it looks exactly like a printed version. The problem: Users have to download a special viewer for your information, Acrobat Reader; most users are likely to have it, but a few may not. (So

expect a few technical support calls from users who can't figure out what to do if they need to download Acrobat Reader.) *Time* magazine is among the big "names" who have adopted Acrobat, and many organizations use PDF files internally.

To bypass this potential problem, Acrobat is now supported by a plug-in for Microsoft Internet Explorer and Netscape Navigator. Many computers ship with a version of Acrobat Reader already installed. For more information, see the following URL:

`www.adobe.com/prodindex/acrobat`

The first three problems are related to inconsistencies in the Web, and you may have run into them as a user looking at different Web pages. Now that you're a beginning Web publisher, the answer to all these problems is the same: Keep it simple! In this book, we use simple Web page layouts and stick almost completely to the basic HTML features available in all browsers to help you avoid these problems.

The problem of getting your Web page on the server is a little different — the kind of hurdle that can stop neophytes cold, but one that experienced users clear with ease. In Part I of this book and in Chapter 12, we show you enough varied server solutions to meet any needs — and some of the solutions are even free!

Creating Navigation

Navigation is what helps users find their way around your Web site. If you have previously put up a single Web home page and are now expanding to a multi-page site, creating navigation is a new challenge for you. But using navigation isn't. Every time you visit a major Web site, you encounter carefully designed navigation. Luckily, for a small site, consistent navigation is easy to achieve.

Arranging your pages

Arranging your Web pages in your Web site is most like creating a very small newspaper. You divide your Web pages up into a few sections, perhaps three to seven. Each section of your Web site is like a section of a newspaper, and should include one or several Web pages that fit within the theme of the section.

The home page of your site is kind of like the front page of a newspaper, and somewhat like the table of contents in a magazine. The home page grabs people's attention with one or a few elements that are interesting in and of themselves; it also serves as a guide to what's inside the rest of the site.

Take your Web pages — you may want to print them out for this exercise — and arrange them into sections. Be a little creative. If you have two pages in a section, you may want to combine them into a single page (to eliminate the need for navigation in that section), or rearrange them into three pages (to have more than one other page within the section to navigate to).

The original Web site for Zanzara, a Web usability company, can be found at www.zanzara.com/old. It's a good example of simple, consistent navigation for a small site. Most of the sections have a single page. A few have a front page to the section that links to one or two additional pages that give further details. Figure 15-3 is a chart showing the layout of the site.

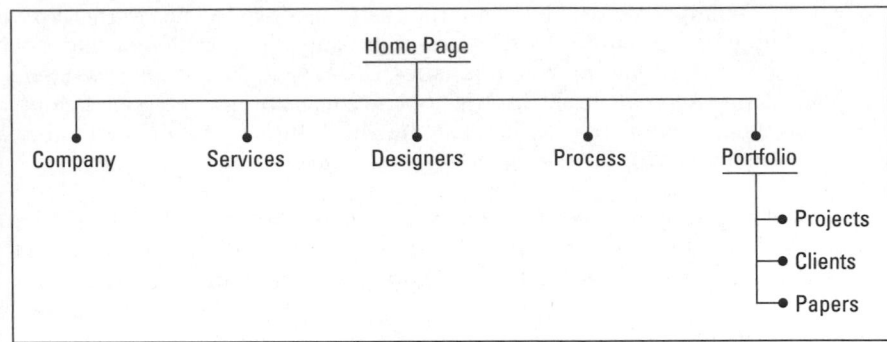

Figure 15-3:
The original
Zanzara site
has a simple
layout.

Getting the addresses right

One major navigational element is easy to achieve: consistent Web addresses for your Web pages. For a small Web site, you want to have an understandable URL for the site, a few major sections, and then one or a few Web pages within each section.

Say your Web site is within the Yahoo! GeoCities site and is mainly focused on rotifers, small creatures made up of a few hundred cells. You've cleverly created the user ID `rotifers` in GeoCities, and the home page of your site is at `www.geocities.com/rotifers`.

Now you're going to create a multipage Web site. You decide to redo your home page to make it a site home page, and have four sections to your site:

- ✔ About Rotifers: Text pages
- ✔ Roti-Photos: Image pages
- ✔ Web Resources: Text pages
- ✔ About Me: Text with an image

With this arrangement, you can isolate the bulk of the photos, which tend to download slowly, onto pages where people should reasonably expect a slow download. Visitors to your site can get the basic information about rotifers and about you from the text-intensive pages, without a long wait, and they can visit the photo-intensive pages when they're ready to take their time.

Further, you decide that About Rotifers will be a single page of text, Roti-Photos will be several pages with one photo each, Web Resources will be a single page of Web links, and About Me will be two pages: a text-intensive page with a small photo of you, and a copy of your résumé on its own page.

Given these decisions, a list of possible choices for the Web addresses for your photos might be:

```
www.geocities.com/rotifers/index.htm
```

```
www.geocities.com/rotifers/aboutrotifers/index.htm
```

```
www.geocities.com/rotifers/photos/index.htm
```

```
www.geocities.com/rotifers/photos/photo1.htm
```

```
www.geocities.com/rotifers/photos/photo2.htm
```

```
www.geocities.com/rotifers/photos/photo3.htm
```

```
www.geocities.com/rotifers/photos/photo4.htm
```

```
www.geocities.com/rotifers/resources/index.htm
```

```
www.geocities.com/rotifers/aboutme/index.htm
```

```
www.geocities.com/rotifers/aboutme/resume.htm
```

To make these URLs work, you'll need to put the files in folders that match the hierarchy that you want to have, so you'll need a main folder enclosing all the other files and folders. Within the main folder (`www.geocities.com/rotifers`) you will have the `index.htm` file for the site's home page, plus any photos that will display on that Web page, plus folders for the other pages. The folders at that level will be `aboutrotifers`, `photos`, `resources`, and `aboutme`. Each folder will then contain the `index.htm` file for that part of the site, plus any HTML files for additional pages in that section, and the photos needed for that section of your Web site.

If you want to keep all your files in a single folder, just use filenames to achieve the same effect. For instance, call the HTML file that displays the first photograph `photos-photo1.htm`, the second photograph `photos photo2.htm`, and so on.

Having your site organized well, with understandable URLs, makes life easier for users. Many users look at URLs to see where they are in a site. And users frequently write down or e-mail URLs to bring a page to the attention of others.

Many large Web sites have abandoned the convenience (for users) of having easy-to-understand URLs, in favor of the convenience (for them) of using a database to store all the content in the site. Each new Web page is displayed as a result of a database call, with the parameters for the database call placed in the URL. For instance, here's a (slightly disguised) URL from a search engine:

```
http://dir.saltavista.com/search?pg=dir&tp=Entertainment/Musi
        c&crid=317855
```

Users would be happier with something like:

```
http://dir.saltavista.com/Entertainment/Music
```

Some companies do cover up the database call with an understandable URL like the one immediately above, but most don't. If you provide a sensible set of URLs for your Web pages, you'll be ahead of most of the big fish.

Creating a navigation bar

Consistent navigation is key to a good-looking Web site. Follow these steps to create consistent navigation:

1. **Type in some text, or copy and paste it in.**

   It's much easier to experiment with placing a graphic if you have some text in your document.

2. **Decide on the sections of your site.**

   Decide on the major sections of your site, as described in the previous section of this book.

3. **Create a set of navigation links.**

   Navigation links consist of a set of words, linked to the major sections of your site, and usually separated by the horizontal bar character (|) on your keyboard. (You may not know about this character now, but you will after you create your navigation links!) A typical set of navigation links looks something like this:

   ```
   Home | About Rotifers | Roti-Photos | Web Resources |
       About Me
   ```

   You can create a set of navigation links in Netscape Communicator or other Web page creation tools by typing in text and then assigning a link to the name of each section. In HTML, use code something like the following:

   ```
   <A HREF="index.htm">Home</A> | <A
           HREF="aboutroti.htm">About Rotifers</A> |<A
           HREF="photos.htm">Roti-Photos</A> |<A
           HREF="resources.htm">Web Resources</A> |<A
           HREF="aboutme.htm">About Me</A>
   ```

Testing navigation

Always carefully test the navigation on your site. Test every link, on every page, at least twice: Once, after you create the site on your own computer, and again, after you publish your site to the Web. It's very common for links to stop working — to "break" — right after you publish your site to the Web, so be ready to quickly fix any problems.

A nice trick for making your navigation bar more useful is to create a new version of it for each page, keeping all the text the same but removing the hypertext link for the current page. For instance, if the user is looking at the About Me page, the words About Me in the navigation bar shouldn't be hyperlinked. That way, users can always figure out where they are.

4. **Add the set of navigation links to the same spot — usually centered, at the top or bottom of the page — on each page in your Web site.**

If you want to have a graphical navigation bar, use a graphics program to create the image you want to use. Then use Netscape Composer or another Web page creation program to create the image map that goes with it. Alternatively, you can use a group of small graphics in a table. Use the navigation bar at the top of each page; keep the navigation links at the bottom, so users have a choice.

Getting the Word Out

Getting people to come to your site can be very easy, or very difficult. The main thing that makes it seem hard to get traffic is your own set of expectations. If you expect huge numbers of visitors (a rarity, especially at first) or huge volumes of online sales (an even bigger rarity) without doing a lot of work, you're bound to be disappointed. But if you set your expectations at a reasonable level and use several different techniques to get people to come to your site, you're likely to meet your goals.

Publicize your site

After your site is up and tested, publicize it. The amount and type of publicity you need depends upon your goals for the site. If you are trying to impress press and analysts, issue a press release. If you are publicizing a personal site, you may find that telling friends and family about it is sufficient. If you are trying to give customers another avenue for communicating with you, put your URL on stationery, business cards, and advertisements. If you are trying to sell on the Web, put ads on other Web sites that attract your prospective customers. Tailor your publicity strategy to your goals.

There's an old saying that "you have to spend money to make money." Contrary to popular belief, this saying is just as true on the Web as it is anywhere else. You can do a tremendous amount with a personal, hobby, or group Web site while spending little or no money and only a moderate amount of time. But don't expect to make money from your Web site unless you're willing to spend money — or enormous amounts of time, remembering that "time is money" — creating, marketing, and updating it.

Playing the name game

One of the best ways to get people to remember your site is to get your own *domain name.* A domain name is the first part of a Web address, usually not including the `www.` at the start. For example, `yahoo.com` and `whitehouse.gov` are domain names. What people use to reach you is the *Web address* or *URL* (Uniform Resource Locator), which is just a standardized, or uniform, way of finding resources such as Web servers and files on the Internet.

`www.smithtires.com` is much easier to remember — and much more impressive — than `www.geocities.com/smithtires`. In the first case, the domain name is `smithtires.com`; in the second case, it's `geocities.com`. Clearly, an individual might plausibly own the first domain name; the second is owned by Yahoo!, one of the busiest sites on the Web.

You can get a domain name in one of several ways, but the most popular way is to go to the Network Solutions Web site at `www.networksolutions.com`. Network Solutions charges less than $40 a year for a license for a name. The Network Solutions Web site makes it easy to try different domain names to see what's available. (It also gives you the ability to build a Web site hosted by Network Solutions for a reasonable, but not insignificant, fee.) You can also purchase your domain name, often for a higher fee, through a Web hosting company such as GeoCities or AOL.

We recommend that you follow a little bit of a process for deciding on your domain name. Come up with a list of desired domain names. Then check on the Network Solutions Web site to see which ones are available. When a domain name is not available, the Network Solutions Web site suggests similar names that are available — and, the whole process might give you new ideas. Write down the best of those as well. Then check your top three to five names with a few friends or colleagues for their reactions and ideas.

Go through this process a couple of times, and give yourself a day or so to think about your final candidate before finally purchasing a domain name. Getting a name is so easy that it's all too easy to end up buying three names before you finally end up with the one you really want.

The first and most important place to publicize your site is on the Web itself. Your basic goal is to get as many links as possible to your site from What's New lists, What's Cool lists, and especially directories or pages that are specific to the interests your site addresses. Find pages with a similar purpose and trade pointers from their site to yours and from your site to theirs.

The Web publicity picture changes all the time, so the best place to go for information is any of several Web sites with publicity info and pointers:

```
www.cyberwave.com/ppoint2.html
www.netbusiness.com
www.bcentral.com
```

These sites give you information on how to get your pages publicized on popular sites such as the Yahoo! What's New page. (See Figure 15-4 for an example.) You can find this page at `dir.yahoo.com/new`.

You should also use non-Web means of publicizing your site. Put out a press release — but be sure to wait until your site's really ready, not full of Under Construction signs. Many companies proudly include their Web site URLs on business cards, stationery, print ads, and even television ads. You've invested a lot in your Web site — now's the time to benefit from your efforts.

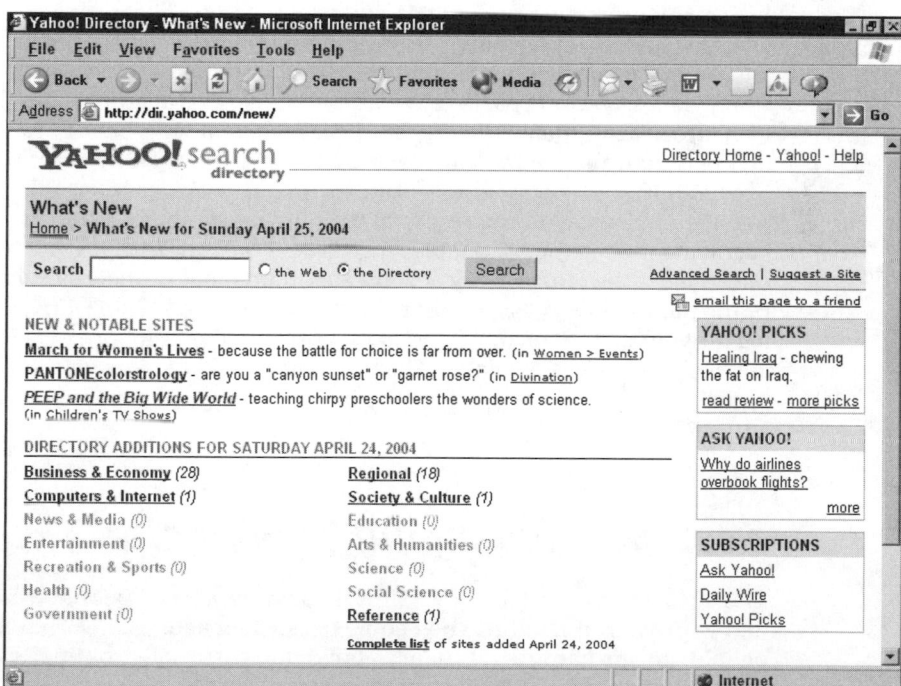

Figure 15-4:
Yahoo! for
new stuff.

What about hiring out your Web work?

Getting help in creating your Web site is often a good idea. Use this book to learn enough about Web publishing so you can communicate effectively with a consultant, and so you can do some of the work yourself. Then find someone to help. Bigstep, at www.bigstep.com, is a service that helps individuals achieve their Web site goals — inexpensively. For a more customized approach, hire your own consultant. eLance, at www.elance.com, is a good place to start looking.

If you work in a large organization, you or your boss may consider hiring out all the Web work for your company. This is a bad idea. Although using consultants to help introduce and use new technology is a good idea, developing a reasonable amount of expertise in-house is an even better idea. So don't hire out the entire process; have a mix of employees and contractors working on your company's Web site. A good way for you to get the necessary experience to be a useful member of such a team is to create one or two small Web sites yourself, as described in this book.

Count your blessings — and your users

For Web pages in general, and for business Web pages in particular, knowing how many users visit your site is important. If you are creating a business site, you need to establish goals for the number of users who visit your site and for the number who take specified actions, such as downloading software, visiting various parts of the site, or buying products. Set goals and then measure against them. Microsoft's Bcentral site at www.bcentral.com includes many useful tools for Web traffic measurement.

Among the things you can track are the number of e-mails you receive from users and the number of people who register on your site (if you support that option). But the most widely accepted measurement of success is *page views,* or the number of pages that users have visited on your site. Obtain the server log for your site from your Internet service provider and pore over it, or obtain any reports that are available. Many Web hosting providers give you a monthly report, or at least let you access the log files from your site for your own review and analysis.

Keep people coming to your site

The missing link for many Web sites is *return visitors* — people who have visited your Web site before, then come back again and again. Given how busy people are, it's hard to get them to build into their daily routines visits to your site.

One of the best ways to get people to come back to your Web site is through e-mail. For a personal site, send your friends and family e-mail when you put something new on the site. For a business site, plan on adding something new at least once a month. Then tell people about it using your customer and partner e-mail list — a list that, as a businessperson, you'll put time and money into expanding and maintaining. (And a list that you'll use wisely by asking permission before sending mass e-mails to people.)

Be sure to give users a place to see the progress of your Web site and find out about your plans for it. Some sites have a "What's New" page to describe recent additions; such a page is also a good place to describe your plans for the site's expansion. Avoid giving specific dates unless you're very sure of them. Be sure to convey excitement about what you already have up and what you're planning to add, not embarrassment about what's missing.

Chapter 16

Becoming a Wizard with Blogs

A *blog* — the name is short for Web log — is a wonderful thing; an online journal of a person's thoughts, experiences, and interests. Kept up to date, a blog can help users move with the writer through space — well, Web space, anyway — and time.

In a sense, any site can be used as a blog. Just create a new page on your site and write your thoughts for the day. Include links to any site that you visited and want to share with others. Especially, link to any blog that you find interesting.

Then, a day or two later, add another chunk of text — put the new content on top, pushing your previous work down the page a bit. In your new content, refer to your earlier posting wherever necessary — and, of course, refer to other Web sites and blogs you visit.

Over time, your burgeoning blog may develop into an appealing take on your life and interests — or preoccupations — or even obsessions. You may find that you need to split up the blog among multiple pages, and change your links to fit. Your blog may even get linked to by other *bloggers* (people who keep blogs) and begin to develop a following of your own.

The Wonderful World of Blogs

Blogging is not just another tool for generating Web content. Even though it's relatively new, blogging has developed such a following that many people spend hours a day perusing others' blogs and commenting on them as they add to their own. There's even a special word for all this: the *blogosphere*, the world of comments about blogs and blogging.

Many blogs are focused on the Web itself or on technical matters relating to computers — different types of computers, different operating systems and so on. But many of the most interesting are deeply personal. One blog that's a mix of the two is from, the famous, or infamous, Dave Winer, a talented creator and marketer of software who also happens to be a top-notch complainer. You can find his blog at `www.scripting.com`, which is also a great site for blogging information and tools.

Blogs have even had a big influence on politics. Remember Howard Dean, the former governor of Vermont who was the leading Democratic presidential candidate in late 2003 and early 2004? His blog was one of the leading tools of his campaign. Through it, people felt they came to know him quickly and well — and wanted to join him in changing the world of politics.

Both Dave Winer and Howard Dean are known for being, well, intense characters — and other people who are into blogging can be very intense about it as well. They tend to talk a lot about blogging and about related topics such as content syndication, collaboration, and online communities. You'll run into this if you search around the Web for blogs and conversations about them (mostly found in other blogs, of course.)

One site that is, essentially, a big blog — but doesn't shout too much about it — is our very own Netsurfer site, created by one of the authors (Arthur Bebak). Netsurfer shows that people were using blogging on the Web before the term, or any special software, was invented.

Netsurfer hosts a series of online magazines, or e-zines, each of which includes a brief description of interesting news and a link to a site for more information. It's updated constantly — and the results are sent to users via e-mail. Figure 16-1 shows a typical page from the Netsurfer site.

Finding blogs to read

To find some blogs yourself, you can simply do a Web search using "blogs" as the search word. You're likely to run into a lot of stories about blogs and some technically oriented blogs before you find personal or interesting blogs.

For instance, in a recent search about blogging, we quickly found a story on a sex-related blog that got a U.S. Senate aide in trouble, a Bill Gates speech about blogging, and some blogging software — but none of the quirky, interesting, if sometimes self-obsessed content that has made blogging a phenomenon.

Here are some list sites that give you a quick peek at what other bloggers are doing:

✔ `top-blogs.com`: A blog listing with a nice mix of personal and political blogs — as well as adult-oriented blogs

✔ `blogarama.com`: A directory of blogs, by category

✔ `weblogs.com`: Some blogs aren't updated much; this list shows only recently updated blogs

Finding software for blogging

Later in this chapter we show you how to use Blogger, owned by Google. Blogger is one of the easiest and best blogging tools out there — but it's far from being the only tool in town to suit your blogging fancy.

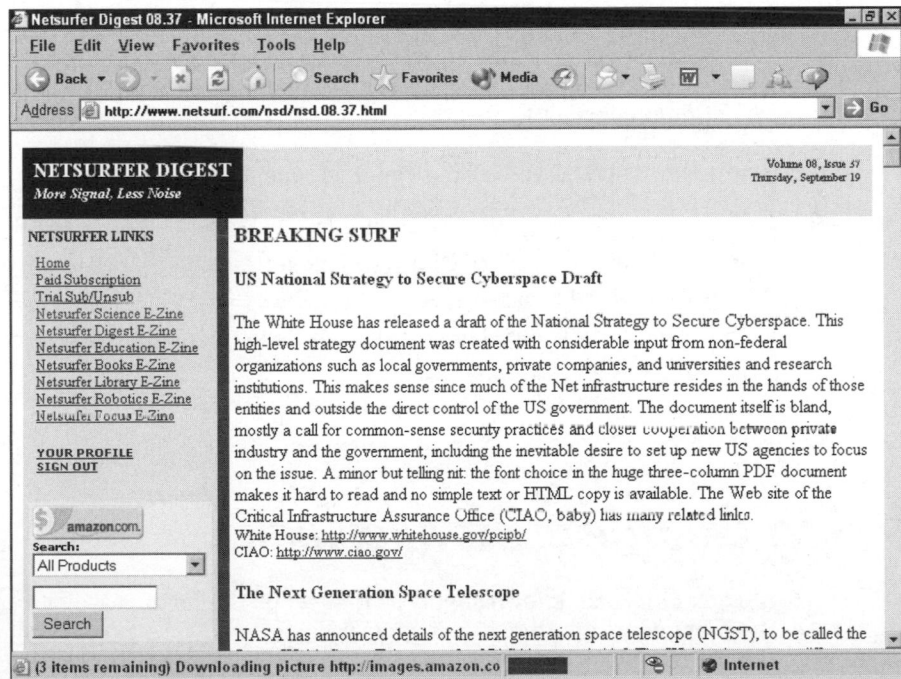

Figure 16-1: Netsurfer was blogging from the beginning.

Committing to a blog

A blog takes more commitment than a Web site. The reason is simple — the diary, or "log," aspect of a blog. An ordinary Web site can still be interesting and useful if it's not updated for awhile. A blog, by contrast, is valuable precisely because it contains the latest information on a given topic — whether the topic is software, politics, or the daily musings of a bored teenager.

You'll see, as you search through various blogs, that many are started, gain an interesting slant or approach, start to gain regular visitors and fans — and are then abandoned. It's very frustrating to start to read an interesting blog, only to see that postings slow down, and then stop completely.

Another thing you may notice is a lot of personal information in blogs. Many bloggers willingly sacrifice some degree of privacy to participate in the blogosphere — but you may want to think twice before following their lead.

So if you're not sure a blog is what you want to do, consider creating a regular Web site first. You can then put the skills you gain creating your initial Web site to good use in creating the world's greatest blog — when you're ready to put in the time to maintain it.

Be warned, we can't promise that you will ever want to stop blogging once you start. Blogging can be an art form, so if you want to know more about blogs and get your own blog started, there are several top blogging resources you should check out:

- ✔ `blogs.com`: Home for the TypePad Web logging service
- ✔ `diaryland.com`: Easy, easy, easy is Diaryland's claim to fame
- ✔ `hometown.aol.com`: AOL's Web logging service — free to all, even non-AOL members
- ✔ `livejournal.com`: LiveJournal and its users emphasize the community aspect of blogs
- ✔ `moveabletype.org`: quite technical, quite powerful

Using Google's Blogger.com

Blogger.com, also known simply as Blogger, is the leading blogging site, with the most users and the widest name recognition. The site was acquired by Google in 2003 when Google bought Pyra Labs, the creators of Blogger. At the time it was acquired, Pyra Labs had just six employees — but over a million registered users for its blogging-oriented Web sites.

The great thing about Google acquiring Blogger is that it gives ordinary folks — that's you — some reassurance that the site will be around for the long term. Many Web sites have come and gone, and Blogger wasn't immune to those pressures. Google is a profitable Web business, so the chances are increased that Blogger will go on and on.

As GeoCities does with free Web sites (see Chapter 2), Blogger makes you pay for your free blog by having advertising hosted on your page. It's a relatively small price to pay for a very good service. However, you may want to consider a paid service, such as Radio Userland (`www.userland.com`), if you want an ad-free site.

All blogs that you set up through the setup process described here are hosted on blogspot.com and have similar URL. If you want to have your site hosted elsewhere, use the advanced blog setup at `www.blogger.com/adv-create-blog.g`. You will need details such as the FTP server to use; get help from the site host if you need it.

Setting up your blog

Since its acquisition by the megalith Google, Blogger has obtained the resources to make blogging easier and faster without quickly pushing its users into paying for services. At this writing, Blogger has just updated its interface to make creating an initial blog even easier — a perfect fit with the purpose of this book. Follow these steps to get started:

1. **Go to** `www.blogger.com`.

   The Blogger site appears, as shown in Figure 16-2.

   If you look closely at the Blogger home page, you'll see a link to BlogThis, a way to quickly comment on any Web page. Don't worry about this for now — we'll describe it later.

2. **Click the orange arrow to "Create Your Blog now."**

   The Create an Account page appears, as shown in Figure 16-3. Read carefully; just about everything you enter is very important to your blogging happiness.

3. **Choose a user name.**

   Your proposed user name is your sign-on name for Blogger; only you will see it. Because Blogger is so popular, it's quite likely that most of the convenient or funny user names that you might think of, such as "budsmith" or "blogguy" are already taken. Choose something you'll find easy to remember, but be ready to enter a second choice if your first choice is already taken.

Figure 16-2:
Blogger
welcomes
you.

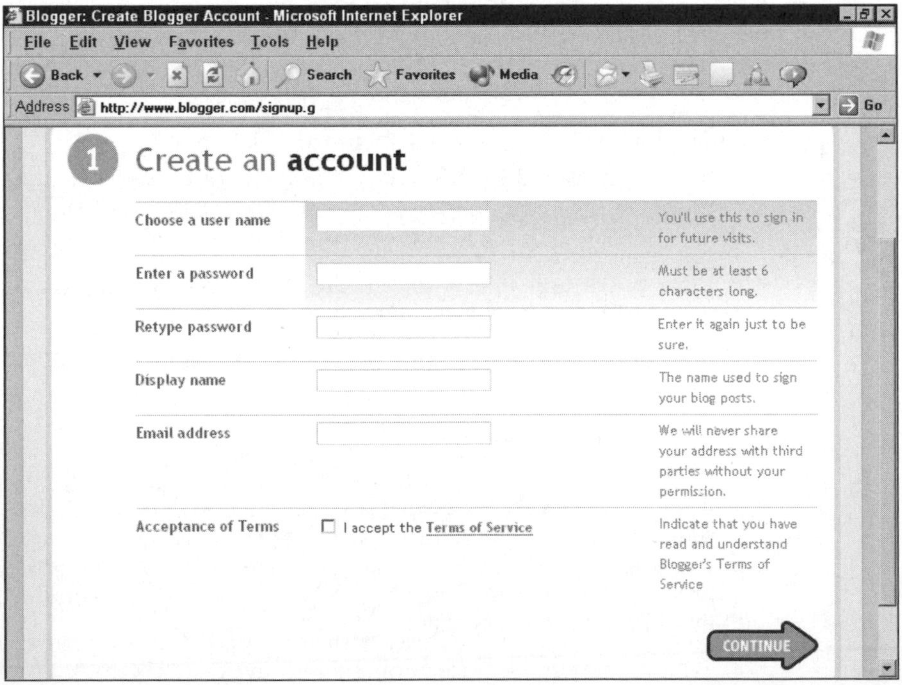

Figure 16-3:
Getting
started with
a Blogger
account
is easy.

4. Enter your password, and then retype your password.

Unlike your user name, you can enter any password you like — it doesn't matter if someone else has the same one. Just make sure your password is both easy to remember and hard for someone else to guess.

It might seem like your password is pretty unimportant because your blog is going to be immediately posted on the Web anyway. This is true, but that's not the point. The point is that if someone guesses your user name and password, he can post on your blog, and people will think the postings are from you — which could get pretty embarrassing!

5. Enter your display name.

You may be tempted to enter your full name here, but with the increasing power of the Internet, it's quite likely that someone who has your full name can find your address, phone number, e-mail address, and so on. Consider using a display name that doesn't give away your complete real name.

Think a bit about your display name; if your blog might cover personal or serious topics, for instance, don't choose a really silly one. (A posting from "wild&crazyguy" about being injured in a traffic accident, for instance, might be a bit disconcerting to your blog visitors.) You may also want your display name to relate in some way to your blog title and blog address; see steps 9 and 10 for details.

6. Enter your e-mail address.

Blogger — and Google, the site's owner — promise not to share your e-mail address with third parties without your permission. That's good, but remember that the marketing folks at Blogger and Google might find an awful lot of reasons to e-mail you themselves!

7. Click the Terms of Service link.

Before you click to put a check mark (indicating that you agree with Blogger's terms), click the Terms of Service link to make sure that you actually do agree.

The Terms of Service appear in a new window, so don't worry about losing the data you've already entered.

You should always inspect the terms of service for a Web site if you're going to enter personal information on it, such as your e-mail address. This is especially true with a blogging site because by nature blogs require you to put so much data into the service, some of which may be personal. (Some blogs are embarrassingly personal!) Blogger and Google, as a public company, may be more trustworthy than most — but you should still see what you're getting into.

Courts take Terms of Service seriously — after you agree to them, you're bound by them, whether you've read them or not. Some unscrupulous companies have gotten away with some pretty shady scams this way — and even big, respectable companies have used them to protect themselves from angry users. So give the Terms of Service the once-over.

8. **Click the checkbox to accept the Terms of Service, and then click the Continue arrow.**

   If you see a new screen called 2 Name your blog (see Figure 16-4), go to the next step. If you see the same screen as before, with an error message, do the following.

   The error message is most likely to be a caution sign and a warning: "Sorry, this username is not available." If so, enter a new user name and re-enter your password in both blank areas below it. Then click the Continue arrow.

   After your username is accepted, the Name Your Blog screen appears.

9. **In the Name Your Blog screen, enter the title for your blog.**

   You can give your blog any title you want, but give your decision some thought. Ideally, the title should be rare or even unique; should sum up what's different and special about your blog; and should relate to the blog address you'll give it in the next step, which also needs to be unique.

   For instance, if you're creating a blog in support of a book about creating Web pages, you might call it Creating Web Pages Web Log.

Figure 16-4:
Name your blog.

10. **Enter the blog address, the first part of the URL for your blog.**

    Enter the first part of the blog address for your blog. This portion of the address will be used by Blogger to form the first part of your URL for your blog. For instance, if you enter **caveboy4** in the blog address spot, your URL will be `caveboy4.blogspot.com`.

    As with your username, your Blog address must be unique — if someone else has it already, you won't get it. Believe us — most of the good addresses are taken! So think carefully about a display name (see step 5), blog title and blog address that work together and are unique, so as to pass muster.

    Google can help you find interesting blogs on Blogger.com — or other interesting content on other interesting sites. If you search for "site:blogspot.com caveboy", for instance, you're likely to find most of the blogs on Blogger.com that have "caveboy" in their content somewhere. (We say "most of" because Google doesn't index sites instantly, so you may not be able to find something that's moved recently or that has otherwise escaped Google's attentions.)

11. **Click the Continue arrow.**

    If you see a new screen called 3 Choose a template (see Figure 16-5), go to the next step. If you see the same screen as before with an error message do the following.

    The error message is most likely to be a caution sign and a warning: "Sorry, this blog address is not available." If so, enter a new blog address. Then click the Continue arrow. When your blog address is accepted, you see the Choose a Template screen.

12. **Choose a template.**

    You'll see a dozen or so templates to choose from — different looks for your blog. Choose one that fits the way you want your site to appear. Click the image of any of the templates to see a larger preview appear in a pop-up window.

    It might be tempting to rush this part of the process — especially since Blogger allows you to change your template (by editing the page's HTML) or substitute a different template later, without losing any of your content.

    Before you click Continue in the next step, be sure to check all your choices; your blog will be created instantly, you won't have a chance to review your choices first.

13. **When you've made your choice of template, think about whether you're happy with all the choices you've made so far. If you're happy, and ready to create your blog, click Continue.**

    Your blog is created!

Figure 16-5:
Showcase
your blog in
a template.

14. **Click the Start Posting button to open your blog so you can start adding content to it. When your blog appears, save the URL in your Favorites list.**

   In Internet Explorer, click Ctrl+D to add the current page to your Favorites.

Adding content to your blog

Adding content to your blog is easy — but doing it just the way you want it can be hard. Not all the options you're used to having for text formatting in, say, a word-processor, are available with the Blogger software. You have to experiment to find out what you can and can't do.

From this point, your choices as to what to do, and in what order, are nearly infinite. You may want to create posts right away; you may want to understand everything about your blog page before creating any content, let alone telling anyone where to find it.

To accommodate all the different approaches you can take, the following sections give highlights of each page you use to edit your blog. Read each section briefly — then roll up your sleeves and go experiment, that's what Blogger is there for!

Posting and formatting

The Posting page (see Figure 16-6) is where you create the posts that appear on your site. You can always edit, delete, or rearrange posts later, but it all starts here.

To reach the Posting page from the Dashboard, simply click the link to your page; then click the Create link.

The Posting page allows you to enter plain text and format it using four simple options:

- **Bold:** Makes the text you select bold, as you would guess. You'll see the HTML tags ⟨B⟩ and ⟨/B⟩ surround the text, indicating that bolding is beginning (⟨B⟩) and ending ⟨/B⟩). Don't overuse bold text because it looks like you're shouting.

- **Italics:** Also obvious — makes text italic. The HTML tags ⟨I⟩ and ⟨/I⟩ surround the text to indicate the beginning and end of italicization. Don't overuse italic text because it makes the text harder to read onscreen. (Printed italic text is much easier to read than onscreen italic text.)

- **Link:** Here's where you link text to a Web address — a big part of the original purpose of blogging. To use this, highlight the text that you want to have linked, and then click the Globe-and-Chain icon. You'll have the opportunity to link the text. To delete the link, delete the linked text.

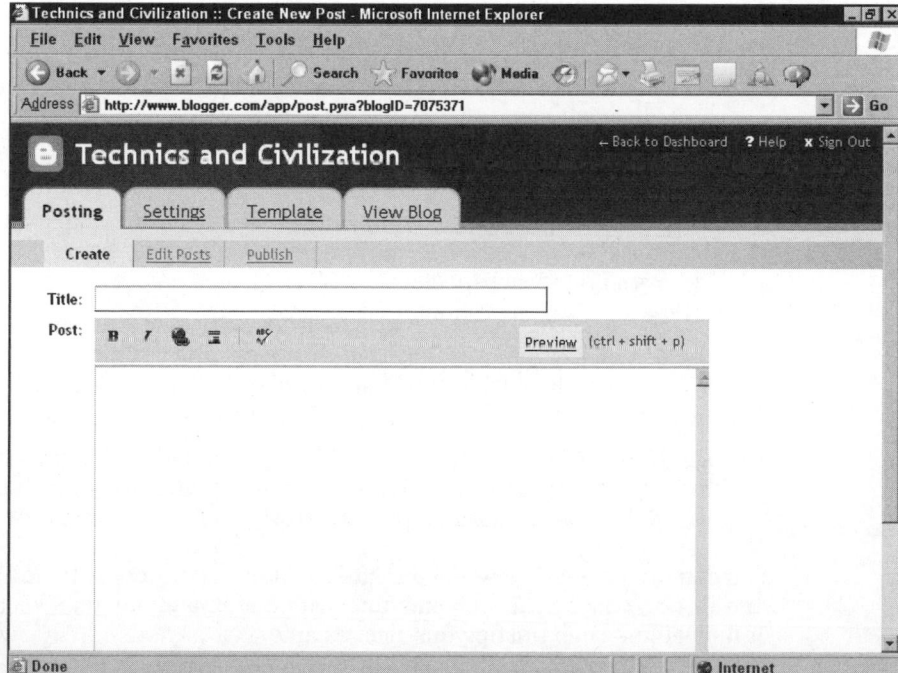

Figure 16-6:
Post to
your host.

Make the linked text short, but at the same time ensure that the user will be able to tell what they'll get when they click the link. It's extremely annoying to see a link called <u>My Favorite Dummies Book</u>, for instance, and click it only to find that the link is to the overall Dummies site, not a description of the specific book.

✔ **Blockquote:** This option reformats text so that it's indented and in a different font — a good choice when you're quoting text from elsewhere. Make sure to let your Web visitors know where such text is from, and don't use paragraphs and paragraphs of it — you may be violating copyright laws if you overdo it.

You also have the option of spell-checking your content — a capability added since Google purchased Blogger, and for which those of us with bad spelling can be grateful.

Using other Blogger options

In addition to posting — which, we hope, you'll spend the majority of your time doing — Blogger offers many other options. Highlights include

✔ **View Blog:** This option simply pops up a new window with your blog in it. Don't simply use this option to view your site after you make changes — you may also want to use this option to see what's currently on your site as you're writing new posts.

✔ **Settings:** Settings allows you to change options in separate pages devoted to Basic, Publishing, Formatting, Comments, Archiving, Site Feed, E-mail, and Members options. Carefully check out and test these options; they support powerful capabilities such as posting to your blog by e-mail.

✔ **Template:** Here's where you can see the HTML code for your template — and change it any way you'd like, for better or worse. It requires real HTML skill to navigate through and change the code so that it looks exactly as you want it to.

Don't be afraid to ask someone for help if you know a skilled person. You can also choose a different pre-existing template here, for which you won't need any special skill.

✔ **Dashboard:** This is the screen you'll see when you sign in to Blogger in the future. It's your starting point for managing your site. See Figure 16-7 for an example of what the Dashboard looked like for a given user — okay, one of the authors — on a given day.

✔ **BlogThis!:** Add an icon to your Web browser's toolbar allowing you to quickly add a post to your blog that refers to the site you're visiting in the Web browser at that moment. Wow!

You can do a great deal with your site — allow other people to add comments to it or not, change the look and functioning of it, and much more. Have fun with it — and keep posting to it every day or two.

Figure 16-7:
Use your blogging dashboard to gel started.

There are many options for including blogging capability in a full Web site, but one of the easiest is just to use Blogger for blogging, and then copy and paste the "best of your blog" onto your full Web site — at GeoCities or any-where else.

When you have your blog up and running, let people know! Let them add comments if you like. That way your humble little blog can begin to be the center of a new online community — yours!

Part V
The Part of Tens

The 5th Wave   By Rich Tennant

"Well, it's not quite done. I've animated the gurgling spit sink and the rotating Novocaine syringe, but I still have to add the high-speed whining-drill audio track."

In this part . . .

Our Top Tens tell you the do's and don'ts of creating Web pages so you can look like a pro your first time out on the Web.

Chapter 17

Ten Web Publishing DO's

Mr. Do-Bee was a star of the *Romper Room* TV show of the 1960s — kind of a Teletubby with wings. He was famous for words of wisdom that began, "Mr. Do-Bee says . . ."

Well, if Mr. Do-Bee were a Web author, here are ten things he would definitely do.

DO Think About Your Target Audience

Who is your Web site targeting? A little thought along these lines can make your pages much more appealing to your visitors. Before you begin creating your Web site, choose the right look and feel and a style of presentation that is appropriate for your audience.

Include links that *your visitors* find interesting, not just the ones that *you* find interesting — unless that's the point of your page, of course.

In addition to using good sites as models (see the following "DO"), research other media, such as newspapers and magazines (check the articles and the ads) that have an audience similar to yours, to find good and bad examples.

DO Use Good Sites as Models

To say that there are many good sites out there on the Web is to make a huge understatement. Therefore, it is also an understatement to suggest that ignoring those good examples when designing your own site is "not the best idea." Take a look around and find the designs that work. Many top-rated sites have settled on relatively simple designs. Think about why each design you like works well. Is it

- The use of color and the layout of the Web page?
- The fact that the site loads quickly?
- The well-organized content?

Note what works and why, and then strive to duplicate that effect in your own Web pages. Look for conventions in presenting information that Web users have grown accustomed to, neat design ideas, and various types of content. You'll be surprised by how many ideas you get from this huge reservoir of Web expertise — the Web itself.

DO Get Permission for Content

You can easily peek at the HTML source of any Web page, and that's a good way to figure out new design techniques. But you can also easily grab any content that exists on the Web, even privately owned content that belongs to others. However, the fact that you can easily grab others' content does *not* make doing so right or legal. It's also not necessary.

You can find a great deal of public domain content, and getting permission to use some private content is not all that hard to do. If a Web page doesn't explicitly say that its content can be freely borrowed, assume that it's copyrighted or otherwise protected, which means you should ask before borrowing any of it. Many people are happy to let you use their content as long as you provide proper attribution and reciprocal links so that they can gain exposure to new

Web users who will visit your pages. In the process, you may just gain new friends or business contacts, as well as avoid legal problems down the road. (And in case you get tempted to borrow quietly, keep in mind that word of unethical practices gets around quickly on this amazing global network.)

DO Use Links to Outside Sites

No matter how great your content is, you're wasting the most important feature of the Web if you don't include links to sites outside your own. No matter what your topic, you can find complementary sites out there. Giving your visitors links to those sites is not only courteous — it's the foundation on which the Web was founded.

If you research your links carefully and organize them well, your links can be a valuable resource for others. In your own Web surfing, you've probably found that one of the best experiences on the Web is the serendipity of stumbling upon some cool site that you had no idea existed. Give your visitors that same experience. Point them to the outside world. That's why it's the Web and not the Pit.

DO Use Graphics and Multimedia

A prime attraction of the Web is that it's designed to present graphical information; yet there are still many beginning Web authors who are intimidated by graphics and shy away from using them. Include pictures, icons, bars and graphical menus in your Web page. Go ahead, try out transparent GIFs. Multimedia is a great addition, too; one or two sound files, a QuickTime movie, even a simple animated GIF can really liven up a site.

The bottom line is that sites that carefully use graphics and multimedia are much more interesting than purely text-oriented ones. Give it a go. (But be prudent; see Chapter 18 for a complementary DON'T.)

DO Think Before You Create

A surprising number of people just jump in and start throwing around text and HTML tags with no clue about where they're going or what they want to accomplish. That approach is fine if you just want to play around; in fact, that approach can be a lot of fun. But if you want to make a good impression on the Web, sitting down and thinking about a few things ahead of time really pays off.

Sketch your ideas on paper. Then describe them to someone else and ask for feedback. This prep work forces you to consider things that you may not think about otherwise:

- ✔ Page layout
- ✔ Graphic design
- ✔ Relationship between pages
- ✔ Target audience
- ✔ Content structure
- ✔ Link grouping

All these issues and more, when properly considered and acted on, can make your site a first-class Net surfing experience.

DO Ask for Feedback

Put your e-mail address on your home page and ask for comments. You'll be amazed by what people say about your pages. (Some of the comments may even be complimentary!) People who have never before seen your site can offer a good, fresh perspective and give you feedback on things that you may not have thought about.

Everyone can benefit from outside input. Criticism by your prospective audience is not only useful, it's also educational. You can learn a lot about what people expect and want. Criticism can't hurt anything but your pride, and listening to it almost always improves your site.

DO Test Your Pages

Testing your pages is easy. You probably don't write a memo without spell-checking it. Similarly, you should not put up your Web pages without testing them. That means looking at your pages on your own machine before testing them on the Web — follow links, see how graphics and text fit together, and so on. Also, looking at your pages in different browsers doesn't hurt. If you can't do it, ask a friend or even a stranger to help. And, again, don't forget to spell check your pages.

DO Publicize Your Site

Nothing is more frustrating than putting up a site that no one visits. Fortunately, publicizing your site is not hard. Add your site to the popular indexes, for example, through the excellent Submit-It site at www.submit it.com. (Like many other such services, the Submit-It site charges a fee.)

You can also post to appropriate Usenet newsgroups, put out a press release, send e-mail to friends and business contacts, or shout from the rooftops.

DO Update Your Site

A static site is a boring site. True, it works for some purposes, but in general, if you want people to continually revisit your site, you must keep it updated. The best sites are those that continually provide new and interesting content. Include pointers to information that's frequently updated, like "Thought for the day" or "Links to new, cool sites." Let users know how often to expect updates and be sure to showcase new content. A "New" icon next to recently added or updated content can work wonders.

Chapter 18

Ten Web Publishing DON'Ts

*T*hose of us who remember Mr. Do-Bee, who we mentioned at the start of Chapter 17, also probably remember Bozo the Clown, another TV character. (Ever hear people say, "What a bozo?") When someone did something wrong it was a "Bozo no-no." Don't-don't do these no-no's.

DON'T Limit Your Audience

Be careful when designing your pages not to inadvertently limit your audience by using some oddball feature that can't be accessed by large numbers of people who use different Web browsers.

Stick to basic HTML through HTML Version 4.0. Think twice before using HTML frames, Java programs, or ActiveX programs — some people won't be able to access Web pages with these features. Warn people if you use non-standard features. Often, providing alternative pages, such as text-only versions of your pages, is worthwhile.

Don't feel as though you should limit your Web page, however, if using non-standard features and software is important to your goals for the page. Include links to the software that works with your pages — a link to the QuickTime site if you host QuickTime movies or a link to the RealAudio site if you include RealAudio sound, for example.

Many features of Microsoft FrontPage only work if hosted on servers that support FrontPage extensions. Other FrontPage features only work if the user is running Microsoft's Internet Explorer browser. Test your pages with a wide range of browsers and browser versions if you are using FrontPage to create your pages.

DON'T Break Netiquette Rules

Using poor *netiquette* — the etiquette, or "Miss Manners" rule book, of the Internet — is easy to do, and it can bring you a lot of negative attention. If you make any serious offenses against good Internet practices, your Web service provider's server may remove your pages. And you can even get into legal problems.

Avoid the following dubious practices:

✔ *Spamming,* or sending unwanted e-mail to publicize your site or sell things

✔ *Flaming,* or being fervently disparaging of other people or other Web pages

✔ Posting offensive material on your page without some kind of warning label

Netiquette is an amorphous and evolving area of online behavior, so you may want to join a Web-oriented newsgroup where you can ask questions before publishing. Also, check out this site for in-depth info:

```
www.albion.com/netiquette/corerules.html
```

DON'T "Borrow" Content without Asking

Make sure that content you get from the Web to use on your own Web page is labeled as being freely available for reuse, or else get permission to reuse it.

Many people are quite happy to help if you ask nicely and credit their work. The best part is that you make some good contacts with other interesting people. You also keep the law on your side.

DON'T Abuse Graphics and Multimedia

The biggest mistake that beginning Web authors — and some experts — make is overusing graphics on a page. Keep in mind that not everyone has a cable modem or DSL connection wired directly to his or her home PC; the majority of folks around the world receive Web pages via a more limited 56K or slower modem. Keep your page size, including both text and graphics, under 50K. Here are ways that you can keep down your page size without sacrificing design flexibility:

- ✔ Convert photos to JPEG format.
- ✔ Use simple icons and banners — images without very many colors or complex textures — in GIF format.
- ✔ Lay out your site to limit the amount of graphics on any one page; add pages if you need to display more graphics.
- ✔ Use thumbnail icons to give access to larger images.

All these strategies make your pages smaller and faster for others to download. Your Websurfers will thank you.

DON'T Forget ALT Text and Text Versions of Menus

One beginners' mistake is not offering text versions of menus needed because some people turn off graphics when surfing the Net. Who would turn off graphics, you ask?

Many home users turn off graphics to speed things along, downloading only the graphics that they really need. Some people pay a high hourly rate for their Internet access, especially in much of the non-Western world, and turn off graphics to save money on their connection time. Others may be looking at your Web page through a palmtop computer or Web-enabled cell phone with limited or no graphics capability. And some people who are visually impaired use the Web with software that translates text — but not graphics — into spoken words.

If your navigation bar or other menu-type items are in graphical form, provide a text version as well, as we show in Chapter 15. Always use ALT text to provide text equivalents to your graphics, as we describe in Chapter 9. Using ALT text is easy to do and makes it easier for all those people to access your content.

DON'T Forget the Basics

Your site may be the greatest thing since sliced bread, but if you forget to include contact information for yourself in the site, how will you find out that you misspelled "bureaucracy" all over the place? Similarly, you won't get many orders for your spiffy new widget if you put the ordering information five levels down in a Web page called "Fruit Bat Guano Statistics — 1776."

More basics:

✔ Include your e-mail address on your Web page.

✔ Include a copyright notice.

✔ If you create a Web site of more than 5–7 pages, add a site map.

✔ Give credit where credit is due.

✔ Make the important info prominent.

✔ Be ready to revise, based on user feedback.

DON'T Start by Setting Up Your Own Web Server

You can find so-called "easy-to-use" Web server packages on the market, and Web server capability is being built into many Macs and PCs. But even with these efforts, buying, setting up, and maintaining a Web server can become the most expensive, most complicated, and most frustrating part of Web publishing. Luckily, you can put your content on someone else's Web server using the free services we describe in this book, or you can use an inexpensive paid service, while you figure out the other tricks of the trade. Then, as your knowledge and experience grow, consider setting up your own Web server.

DON'T Make Your Site Hard to Navigate

Beginners often organize their pages so that their sites are hard to navigate. If your site has more than 5–7 pages, you should put some thought into how your visitors navigate it. Nobody likes wandering from link to link with no idea what is where. Likewise, users don't want to follow ten links to find one piece of information.

Keep the relationship between your pages simple. Make clear which links are internal to your own site and which go out to other sites. Provide a site map or a common menu. And make navigation work consistently throughout the site.

DON'T Forget the "World" in World Wide Web

Remember that your Web pages are available and accessible to the whole world. Think a bit about the foreign audience. Is including content in multiple languages? Do you use colloquialisms that may not be understood by international Net surfers? How do your pages look to your overseas colleagues who view them through a slow transoceanic Net link? Will your humorous or risqué content offend someone in another country or culture?

When you become a Web publisher, you also become a global citizen, and your Web pages play on a global stage. Think through the accessibility and meaning of your pages in advance.

DON'T Be Afraid to Find Out More

Web publishing is not rocket science. It *is* computer science, but it's relatively easy computer science. You're not trying to land the space shuttle here — and chances are, lives are not at stake. After you have your site working the way you want it to, experiment. Try weird things. Ask for feedback. Never be afraid to figure out complex and hard stuff. (It's only complex and hard because you don't understand it yet!)

You can find so much neat stuff out there that can make your Web publishing efforts even more exciting — JavaScript, multimedia, new browsers and publishing tools, Net-based games, and online business infrastructure. All this new stuff is understandable and usable by normal folks like you. Don't be intimidated. You can use all of it. (If you've come this far, you've got what it takes!)

Part VI
Appendixes

In this part . . .

This part includes appendixes that are a bridge to a wide range of different kinds of resources, including Web publishing definitions, Internet service providers, HTML tag definitions, and online developer resources.

Appendix A
Web Words Worth Knowing

*T*his glossary defines important terms used in this book. To see where a term is used in the book, check the index.

56K. The name of a faster standard for Internet access that is now used by most new modems. 56K is nearly twice as fast as the previous standards, 28.8 Kbps and 33.6 Kbps. However, online access speeds are actually limited by U.S. government regulation to a top speed of about 53 Kbps, and your 56K modem may not even achieve that speed reliably, depending on the quality of the connection you get when you dial in.

absolute address. A description of a file's location that starts with the machine name or disk name on which the file is located. See also *pathname* and *relative address.*

anchor. One end of a link between two files. When you look at a Web page, the underlined, colored text that you see is an anchor at one end of a hypertext link. Clicking the text brings up another Web page, which is the anchor at the other end of the link.

animated GIF. A GIF graphic that includes several slightly different images in sequence. Browsers that support animated GIFs display the graphics one at a time to create an animation.

attribute. In HTML, an attribute is a qualifier added within an HTML tag. The attribute modifies the tag's purpose. For example, in the tag `<IMG SRC="budpic.jpg">`, the attribute is `SRC` (short for "source"). See also *tag.*

broadband. Any kind of fast Internet access, whether by cable modem, DSL, or other connection significantly faster than the 56K top speed of a modem. Broadband connections are typically "always on" and do not require dialing in.

browser. A program used to look at World Wide Web documents. Mosaic was the first popular browser, followed by Netscape Navigator; Microsoft Internet Explorer is the current market leader.

bulleted list. See *unordered list.*

cable modem. A form of broadband access to the Internet that uses a cable TV connection. If the local cable company that serves your house offers this service, it's worth a look.

clickable image map. A graphic that includes areas called *hot spots*, which, when clicked, take you to different Web pages or different locations within a Web page. Some large Web sites use clickable image maps on their home pages to entice the user to move farther into the site.

Common Gateway Interface script (CGI script). A kind of program often used to transfer data from an HTML form to an application. The CGI script runs on the server that hosts the Web page with the form. See also *form*.

definition list. A type of HTML list in which terms occupy a column on the left side of the screen and definitions occupy a wider column on the right side.

domain name. A name that represents a Web site to the outside world. In the United States, the domain name can end in `.com` (for businesses), `.edu` (for educational institutions), `.org` (for nonprofit organizations), or the prestigious `.net` (for organizations that are part of the structure of the Web itself). Newly added suffixes, which haven't necessarily caught on yet, include `.biz` and `.firm`. When visiting a domain that was created for an organization outside the U.S., you may see different suffixes that have been added to represent a country or region. For example, `.uk` signifies that the domain was created for the United Kingdom. The part of the domain that precedes the suffix, such as `stanford` in `stanford.edu`, is either the name of the group that puts up the Web site, or a name that attracts people to the site. Domain names can start with `www` if desired, but it's not necessary.

DSL. Digital Subscriber Line, a type of *broadband* Internet access that uses a phone line. Not available in some areas, but worth serious consideration if it's available to you.

electronic mail (e-mail). A message sent over a network from one computer user to another computer user. The most popular service on the Internet. Used as a noun ("I just got an e-mail") and a verb ("E-mail me on that, will you?"). Also used as singular ("I just deleted an e-mail") and plural ("I just deleted all my e-mail").

File Transfer Protocol (FTP). An Internet service for transferring files between different machines, including those that run different operating systems.

firewall. Hardware, software, or a combination that protects a network from unauthorized access while allowing authorized access.

form. An HTML-defined way to specify text boxes and pull-down menus to enable users of a Web page to enter data. The data from the form must be processed on the Web server by a program such as a *CGI script*.

freeware. Software that can be used for free, though often with a license that contains some restrictions on its use. See also *shareware*.

Graphic Interchange Format (GIF). Can be pronounced "jiff" or (our preference) "giff." A format for encoding images, such as computer-generated art, for transfer among machines. GIF format is the most popular means for storing images for transfer over the Internet and is supported by all graphical Web browsers. An image stored in GIF format is often referred to as "a GIF." See also *transparent GIF.*

Graphical User Interface (GUI). Software that enables users to interact with a computer by using a mouse and keyboard to manipulate images and menus on the computer's screen. The Windows and Macintosh user interfaces are both examples of GUIs.

hexadecimal. What the witch did to her accountant so that her tax bill would be more favorable. More commonly, a way of counting that uses 16 "digits," 0–9 plus A–F, instead of the 10 digits that common decimal numbering uses. Hexadecimal numbers are often used to describe values stored inside a computer.

In hexadecimal numbering, 0–9 have their normal values, but A represents 10, B represents 11, and so on through F, which represents 15. Place values are also different; each successive place represents the next greater power of 16. For example, 2F in hexadecimal translates to 47 in decimal; the 2 represents two 16s, and the F represents fifteen 1s.

hit. This is what you hope your Web site will become. Also, a successful connection, file transfer, and disconnection between a Web client and a Web server. Accessing a single, text-only page generates one hit; accessing a single page with three graphics on it generates four hits. Hits can be counted fairly easily and are a crude measure of the popularity of a Web site. When you see a site that advertises "a million hits a week," remember that the number of hits may be many times greater than the number of different people who visited. See also *Web client* and *Web server.*

home page. A Web page that you intend users to come to directly. If a Web site has multiple pages, the home page usually serves as the front door to the rest of your site, and the guide to all the other pages housed there.

HTML 4.0. Currently the most broadly used version of *Hypertext Markup Language*. All browsers available today support this version of HTML, though different browsers may interpret some tags differently.

Hypertext Markup Language (HTML). The language used to annotate or *mark up* text documents so that they can be formatted appropriately and linked to other documents for use on the World Wide Web.

Hypertext Transfer Protocol (HTTP). The agreed-upon format for exchanging messages among World Wide Web servers and between Web servers and clients.

image map. See *clickable image map.*

Integrated Services Digital Network (ISDN). A special type of phone line available to many businesses and homes. ISDN is a *broadband* connection option that supports faster transmission of data than standard phone lines.

Internet. The hardware and software that together support the interconnection of most existing computer networks, allowing a computer anywhere in the world to communicate with any other computer that's also connected to the Internet. The Internet supports a variety of services, including the World Wide Web.

Internet Protocol (IP). The networking specification that underlies the Internet. IP's most important feature is its support for routing of the packets — small chunks of information that make up a communication — across multiple connections to the final destination.

Internet service provider (ISP). An Internet service provider offers connections to the Internet and support for Internet services such as the World Wide Web.

intranet. An internal network used for distributing information broadly within an organization, but not to the general public. Many intranets work just like the Internet and World Wide Web, only on a smaller scale.

Java. A programming language that supports the creation of distributed programs, called *applets,* whose functionality can be easily and flexibly split between a client computer and the server that it's connected to. Java provides a way for the Web to support easy sharing of programs and data. Java has become less widely used within Web pages, but it is widely used on Web servers and corporate networks.

Joint Photographic Experts Group (JPEG). A format for storing compressed images. JPEG images were once supported by helper applications but are now directly supported by nearly all browsers. JPEG is the best format for most photographs.

link. A connection between two documents on the Web, usually specified by an *anchor* in an HTML document.

mirroring. Keeping a copy of data on additional servers to make data available more quickly and to a greater number of simultaneous users.

multimedia. Literally means "many media," and in this sense, a Web page with graphics has multimedia. However, multimedia is usually understood to mean either more than two types of media or, alternatively, time-based media such as animation, sound, or video and space-based media such as 3-D and virtual reality. On the Web, multimedia is also used to mean any extension of the Web beyond the basics of text, hyperlinks, GIF graphics, and JPEG graphics.

newsgroup. An ongoing exchange of electronic messages about a specific topic, such as pets, restaurants, or Web authoring. To access newsgroups, users must use special software called news reader software, which is available on the Web and also included as a feature of current browsers.

numbered list. See *ordered list.*

online service. Also referred to as a "traditional" or "proprietary" online service to differentiate from the Internet, which is seen as an "open" online service. Traditional online services, such as America Online and CompuServe, package access and content into a single branded product. The Internet and the Web have eroded the boundaries between online services by allowing cross-service functionality, such as e-mail between subscribers of different online services. The online service providers are further eroding these boundaries by offering Internet access, Web access, and Web authoring support.

ordered list. A numbered list. A type of HTML list in which each item is given a number, in sequence, when the list displays. The author of the list can rearrange the items as needed, and the numbers adjust accordingly because the numbers are assigned only when the list appears on-screen.

page description language. A defined format for specifying the appearance of a document when displayed or printed. Adobe's PostScript, used by many programs and in many laser printers, is a page description language, not a structural markup language such as HTML or SGML.

pathname. A description of the location of a file. Pathnames can be specified by absolute addressing or relative addressing.

plug-in. A small program that works with a Web browser to allow multimedia files to be displayed in a Web page, or that otherwise extends the capabilities of the browser.

protocol. A format for exchanging data, such as *FTP.*

QuickTime. A multiplatform standard from Apple Computer, Inc., for multimedia. See also *multimedia, QuickTime plug-in,* and *QuickTime VR.*

QuickTime plug-in. A plug-in for Netscape Navigator and Microsoft Internet Explorer that supports user interaction with QuickTime and QuickTime VR content embedded in a Web page. See also *QuickTime* and *QuickTime VR*.

QuickTime VR. A multiplatform standard for image-based virtual reality. See also *QuickTime* and *QuickTime plug-in*.

relative address. The path from a base document, such as an HTML document, to another document on the same computer, such as another Web page on the same site. See also *pathname* and *absolute address*.

shareware. Software that can be used for free for a limited period of time, after which the user is requested (though usually not forced) to pay a fee for continued use. See *freeware*.

shrink-wrapped software. No, this is not software developed and packaged by psychiatrists. Actually, shrink-wrapped software is just software that is sold as a product and packaged in a box, with the user paying upfront before taking possession of the software. See also *freeware* and *shareware*.

site management. Capabilities in a Web authoring package that help authors work on characteristics of an entire Web site, instead of just one page at a time. Site-management capabilities include the ability to easily manage links between Web pages (such as offering notification when links are no longer functional), the capacity to spell-check, and the ability to easily search and replace across an entire site.

standard. An agreed-upon way to do something, such as building a computer system (for example, the IBM-compatible standard) or exchanging data (for example, the ASCII standard). Many different standards exist, ranging from those created by a single manufacturer for its own purposes (the DOS standard) to those created by internationally recognized standards bodies such as ISO (the International Standards Organization). In other words, in computing, the definition of standard is not very standard.

Standard Generalized Markup Language (SGML). A full-featured specification for describing the content and structure of documents but not their exact appearance when displayed. HTML is a subset of SGML.

syntax. A fee paid for moral or legal violations — no, wait, that's a "sin tax." A syntax is the ordering of the elements in a language or protocol, such as HTML.

system operator (sysop). Pronounced "siss-op." A person responsible for some part of the operations of a computer system, including online services. A sysop's responsibilities can vary from the technical, such as backing up a computer hard drive, to the nontechnical, such as monitoring a newsgroup for inappropriate or irrelevant content and removing it if found.

tag. Part of an HTML document that contains information besides the actual document content, such as formatting information or an anchor. For example, the <B> tag starts bolding the characters that follow it, and the </B> tag ends bolding. So to make a word or phrase bold, surround it with the <B> and </B> tags.

text editor. A program that allows text to be entered and edited but not formatted for display. Text editors save their files without proprietary formatting information, so the files are portable across different application programs and different computer systems. Examples are Notepad (Windows), BBEdit (Macintosh), and vi (UNIX).

thumbnail. A small graphical image that serves as a preview of a larger image.

Transmission Control Protocol/Internet Protocol (TCP/IP). A communications *protocol* that was developed under contract from the U.S. Department of Defense in the 1970s to connect different systems and different networks. TCP/IP is the protocol on which the Internet is based.

transparent GIF. A file stored in Graphic Interchange Format and modified so that the area around the objects of interest is assigned the color transparent. This capability makes the rectangular frame around the objects seem to disappear so that the graphic appears to float over the page on which it appears.

Uniform Resource Locator (URL). A specification for identifying any file on the Internet. The URL is made up of the name of the protocol by which the file should be accessed, the name of the server that the file is stored on, and the pathname of the file on the server. Here is a sample URL for an HTML file named MyCruise, to be accessed by using the Web protocol http, which is stored on a server called www.bigweb.com in the Travel directory:

```
http://www.bigweb.com/Travel/MyCruise.html
```

If no filename is given at the end of the path, a default file, typically index.htm or index.html, is returned.

unordered list. A bulleted list. A type of HTML list in which each item is displayed next to a symbol such as a bullet.

Web authoring. Creating documents for use on the World Wide Web. Web authoring includes creating text documents with HTML tags, as well as creating or obtaining suitable graphics and, in many cases, multimedia files.

Web browser. See *browser*.

Web client. A computer that connects to the World Wide Web and downloads Web pages and other data from it.

Web page. A text document that uses HTML tags to specify formatting and links from the document to other documents and to graphics and multi-media files.

Web publishing. The entire process of creating and maintaining a Web site, from creating text documents with HTML tags and graphics, to putting the documents on a server, to revising the documents over time.

Web server. A computer that connects to the World Wide Web and hosts HTML-tagged text documents, graphics, and multimedia files to be down-loaded by *Web clients*.

Web site. One or more linked Web pages accessed through a *home page*. The URL of the home page is made available to users on other Web sites, and often through other advertising and marketing means as well.

word processor. A program for creating and editing text files with formatting. Files created by a word processor contain formatting codes and cannot be used on the Web unless specifically saved in *text-only* or *plain-text* format, without the proprietary codes that word processors embed in the file to indicate formatting.

World Wide Web (also known as the Web). An Internet service that provides files from servers linked by *Hypertext Transfer Protocol* (HTTP). The Web specification allows formatted text and graphics to be viewed directly by a Web browser and allows other kinds of files to be opened separately by helper applications specified in the Web browser's setup. After e-mail, the Web is the most popular Internet service, partly because it can also be used to access other Internet services, such as newsgroups and FTP.

Appendix B

Internet Service Providers

● ●

*O*ne of the best resources for Internet service providers is on the Web itself at

```
www.boardwatch.com
```

You can log on to ISPWorld to get a directory of local *Internet service providers* (ISPs) in any part of the United States or Canada. Local providers sometimes offer the best access, but, of course, the level of service you get varies from one provider to another.

Another great source for Internet access providers is Yahoo!; check out the following navigation path:

```
www.yahoo.com>Business_and_Economy>Business_to_Business>
         Communications_and_Networking>Internet_and_World_
         Wide_Web>Network_Service_Providers>Internet_
         Service_Providers_(ISPs)
```

Typing out this long address is worth it; Yahoo! provides links to regional, national, and international ISPs, as well as links to other ISP directories online.

For your browsing pleasure — in the old-fashioned, analog sense of the word "browsing" — here's a brief list of some of the top national Web service providers. This list is U.S.-centric; if you live elsewhere or travel, check online sources, or check with the providers listed in this appendix to see which can meet your needs.

America Online

Tyson's Corner, VA
800-827-6364

```
www.aol.com
```

AT&T WorldNet

Basking Ridge, NJ
800-967-5363

```
www.att.net
```

CompuServe

(owned by America Online)
Columbus, OH
800-848-8990

```
www.compuserve.com
```

Earthlink

Atlanta, GA
800-890-6356

```
www.earthlink.com
```

The Microsoft Network

Redmond, WA
800-635-7019

```
www.msn.com
```

MCI

Ashburn, VA
800-644-6397

```
consumer.mci.com
```

WorldCom

Clinton, MS
800-967-5326

```
www.worldcom.com
```

Appendix C

A Quick Guide to HTML Tags

● ●

One of the best resources on the Web is *The Bare Bones Guide to HTML.* At this writing, this excellent reference lists nearly all the tags in the most widely supported version of HTML, Version 4.0, plus Netscape extensions. Unless otherwise noted, HTML tags are compatible with later HTML versions. This site was developed and is maintained by Kevin Werbach, a Harvard Law School graduate and former FCC attorney in Washington who has invested a lot of time and thought into Web authoring. You can find out an awful lot about Web authoring from the thoughts, resources, and examples on Kevin's home page at www.werbach.com.

The Bare Bones Guide lists tags from the different versions of HTML with notes describing which version of HTML a given tag supports. We thought splitting out the HTML tags into separate tables by the version of HTML they support would help you.

In the version of *The Bare Bones Guide* in this book, we include only HTML tags from HTML versions through Version 4.0. For frames only, we use HTML 4.0 tags; see Table C-26 at the end of this chapter. We do this because these tags are the most commonly used by the broad range of Web pages and Web browsers out there. The online version of *The Bare Bones Guide to HTML* lists tags up to the current version of the HTML standard at the time that you access the site.

The original *The Bare Bones Guide to HTML,* from which we adapted this version, is copyrighted ©1995-2000 to Kevin Werbach. You can reproduce the original, as long as you include this statement:

Copyright ©1995-2000 Kevin Werbach. Distribution is permitted, as long as there is no charge and this document is included without alteration in its entirety. This Guide is not a product of Bare Bones Software. More information is available at http://werbach.com/barebones.

Note: *The Bare Bones Guide to HTML* is not affiliated with Bare Bones Software, makers of the BBEdit text editor for the Macintosh (www.barebones.com).

Twenty-two world languages in *The Bare Bones Guide*

Online, you find versions of *The Bare Bones Guide* in English in plain text, formatted text, and table versions, as well as translations into 21 additional languages: Chinese (two versions), Danish, Dutch, Estonian, Finnish, French, German, Hebrew, Icelandic, Indonesian, Italian, Japanese, Korean, Norwegian, Portuguese, Romanian, Russian (three versions), Slovenian, Spanish, Swedish, and Turkish.

Versions of HTML

The tags in this table are part of the HTML 4.0 standard and are supported by all up-to-date browsers. So if you aren't worried about ancient history — in Web terms, that's anything that happened more than a year ago — and aren't worried about the stubborn few users of your Web pages who may still have old browsers, you can ignore this section and go straight to the tables. But if you really want to know the details, read on.

The versions of HTML we describe in this appendix are

- **HTML 2.0:** All browsers available today support this basic version of HTML. However, some tags are interpreted differently by different browsers. For example, a top-level heading, marked by an <H1> tag, may be formatted somewhat differently in different browsers.

- **Netscape Navigator 1.0, 1.1:** These early versions of Netscape Navigator fueled the first huge surge in the growth of the Web. These were the first browsers to provide support for centered text, floating graphics, and colored text and backgrounds by using new "extensions" to HTML 2.0. Other browsers and HTML 3.2 have adopted many of the features and new tags introduced by Netscape in Netscape Navigator 1.0 and 1.1.

- **HTML 3.2:** This is a widely supported version of the HTML standard. Many of the ideas originally included in the HTML 3.0 proposal, such as tables and paragraph alignment, were first supported by Netscape Navigator 1.0 and 1.1.

- **Netscape Navigator 2.0:** This years-old used version of Netscape Navigator implements a few minor features, plus a major one: frames, which are specific areas within the browser window that contain different content and can be updated separately.

✔ **HTML 4.0 and later browser versions:** HTML 4.0 is the latest standardized version of HTML. It includes some features that were introduced
by Microsoft and Netscape in their own browsers. However, HTML 4.0
includes some complex features that are not consistently implemented
in current browser versions.

Over time, browsers are updated and improved to support a wider range of
tags. However, some users still have the old version of their browser. So don't
assume that just because a new version of a browser supports specific tags,
all users of that browser will upgrade and gain the ability to view those tags
correctly.

How to Use This Appendix

To use this appendix when creating your own pages, start with the first table, a
basic list of HTML 2.0– and HTML 3.2–compliant tags that work with almost any
browser. If you use only the tags in this list, your pages will be as widely usable
as possible. Then you can selectively spice up your pages by using tags from
the different sets of HTML extensions listed in the later tables. You can also use
this list to create separate versions of your pages: one version for all browsers
and another for browsers that support the specific extensions that you use.

This appendix includes HTML tags that we did not discuss in the text of
this book. To find out more about a specific tag, experiment with it in your
Web text and your browser. If you need more information than you can get
by experimenting, buy a more advanced book on HTML, such as *HTML 4
For Dummies,* 4th Edition, by Ed Tittel et al (Wiley).

Reading the Tables

Within the tables you may see some tags that are not preceded by a dash,
followed by tags preceded by a dash, such as

Tag Name	Tag	Notes
Preformatted	`<PRE></PRE>`	Display text spacing as-is
- Width	`<PRE WIDTH=?></PRE>`	Width in characters

The tags with descriptions that start with a dash are actually options within
other tags. These optional tags modify the effect of the tag that they appear
with. You will always see the option listed with the tag that it modifies, so that
you can see how to use it in your own HTML-tagged text.

The use of the dash symbol to indicate optional tags and other symbols in the tables are described in the following table.

Note: In order to align columns correctly, some tags are broken. At the points that these tags break, we placed a downward, left-curving arrow (↵) to indicate the break.

Table C-1	Symbols Used in the Tables
Symbol	**Meaning**
URL	URL of an external file (or just filename if in the same directory)
?	Arbitrary number (for example, `<H?>` means `<H1>`, `<H2>`, `<H3>`, and so on)
%	Arbitrary percentage (for example, `<HR WIDTH=%>` means `<HR WIDTH=50%>`, and so on)
***	Arbitrary text (for example, `ALT="***"` means fill in with text)
$$$$$$	Arbitrary hexadecimal number* (for example, `BGCOLOR="#$$$$$$"` means `BGCOLOR="#00FF1C"`, and so on)
|	Alternatives (for example, `ALIGN=LEFT|RIGHT|CENTER` means pick one of these)
- *Option*	An option within a tag

For an explanation of hexadecimal numbering, see Appendix A.

Widely Supported Tags

The following tags are in the HTML 2.0 or 3.2 specifications and should work in all browsers.

Table C-2	Generally All HTML Documents Should Have These Tags	
Tag Name	**Tag**	**Notes**
Document Type	`<HTML></HTML>`	Beginning and end of file
Title	`<TITLE></TITLE>`	Must be in header
Header	`<HEAD></HEAD>`	Descriptive info, such as title
Body	`<BODY></BODY>`	Bulk of the page

Table C-3	Structural Definition: Appearance Controlled by the Browser's Preferences	
Tag Name	**Tag**	**Notes**
Heading	`<H?></H?>`	The HTML 2.0 specification defines six levels
Block Quote	`<BLOCKQUOTE>`	Usually indented `</BLOCKQUOTE>`
Emphasis	`<EM></EM>`	Usually displayed as italic
Strong Emphasis	`<STRONG></STRONG>`	Usually displayed as bold
Citation	`<CITE></CITE>`	Usually italics
Code	`<CODE></CODE>`	For source code listings
Sample Output	`<SAMP></SAMP>`	
Keyboard Input	`<KBD></KBD>`	
Variable	`<VAR></VAR>`	
Author's Address	`<ADDRESS></ADDRESS>`	

Table C-4	Presentation Formatting: Author Specifies Text Appearance	
Tag Name	**Tag**	**Notes**
Bold	`<B></B>`	
Italic	`<I></I>`	
Typewriter	`<TT></TT>`	Displayed in a monospaced font
Preformatted	`<PRE></PRE>`	Displays text spacing as-is
- Width	`<PRE WIDTH=?> /PRE>`	Width in characters

Table C-5	Links and Graphics	
Tag Name	**Tag**	**Notes**
Link	`<A HREF="URL"></A>`	
Link to Target	`<A HREF="URL#***"></A>`	If in another document
	`<A HREF="#***"></A>`	If in current document

(continued)

Table C-5 *(continued)*

Tag Name	Tag	Notes
Define Target	`<A NAME="***"></A>`	
Display Image	`<IMG SRC="URL">`	
- Alignment	`<IMG SRC="URL" ALIGN ⟳ =TOP|BOTTOM|MIDDLE| ⟳ RIGHT|LEFT>`	HTML 3.2 only
- Alternate	`<IMG SRC="URL" ALT="***">`	
- Imagemap	`<IMG SRC="URL" ISMAP>`	Requires a script

Table C-6		Dividers
Tag Name	*Tag*	*Notes*
Paragraph	`<P>`	See Table C-14 for more info
Line Break	` `	A single carriage return
Horizontal Rule	`<HR>`	HTML 3.2 only

Table C-7		Lists: Can Be Nested
Tag Name	*Tag*	*Notes*
Unordered List	`<UL><LI></UL>`	`<LI>` before each list item
Ordered List	`<OL><LI></OL>`	`<LI>` before each list item
Definition List	`<DL><DT><DD></DL>`	`<DT>` = term, `<DD>` = definition

Table C-8		Special Characters: Must All Be Lowercase
Tag Name	*Tag*	*Notes*
Special Character	`&#?;`	Where ? is the ISO 8859-1 code for the character
`<`	`&lt;`	
`>`	`&gt;`	
`&`	`&amp;`	
`"`	`&quot;`	

Tag Name	Tag	Notes
Registered TM	`&reg;`	
Copyright	`&copy;`	

See a complete list of special characters at `www.bbsinc.com/symbol.html`.

Table C-9   Forms: Generally Require a Script on Your Server

Tag Name	Tag	Notes
Define Form	`<FORM ACTION=⤶ "URL" METHOD=GET|⤶ POST></FORM>`	
Input Field	`<INPUT TYPE="TEXT|⤶ PASSWORD|CHECKBOX|⤶ RADIO|IMAGE|HIDDEN|⤶ SUBMIT|RESET">`	
- Field Name	`<INPUT NAME="***">`	
- Field Value	`<INPUT VALUE="***">`	
- Checked?	`<INPUT CHECKED>`	Check boxes and radio buttons
- Field Size	`<INPUT SIZE=?>`	In characters
- Max Length	`<INPUT MAXLENGTH=?>`	In characters
Selection List	`<SELECT></SELECT>`	
- Name of List	`<SELECT NAME="***"> ⤶ </SELECT>`	
- # of Options	`<SELECT SIZE=?> ⤶ </SELECT>`	
- Multiple Choice	`<SELECT MULTIPLE>`	Can select more than one
Option	`<OPTION>`	Items that can be selected
- Default Option	`<OPTION SELECTED>`	
Input Box Size	`<TEXTAREA ROWS=? COLS=?>⤶ </TEXTAREA>`	
- Name of Box	`<TEXTAREA NAME="***">ccc ⤶ </TEXTAREA>`	

Table C-10	Miscellaneous	
Tag Name	**Tag**	**Notes**
Comment	`<!-- *** -->`	Not displayed by the browser

Prologue	`<!DOCTYPE HTML↪`
	`PUBLIC " -//IETF//↪`
	`DTD HTML 2.0//EN">`	

URL of This File	`<BASE HREF="URL">`	Must be in header
Relationship	`<LINK REV="***"↪` `REL= "***" HREF="URL">`	In header
Meta Information	`<META>`	Must be in header

Other Widely Used Tags

These tags work with nearly all the browsers currently in use. For a frequently updated list of widely used tags, see *The Bare Bones Guide to HTML* at the URL listed at the beginning of this chapter.

Table C-11	Structural Definition: Appearance Controlled by the Browser's Preferences	
Tag Name	**Tag**	**Notes**
- Align Heading	`<H? ALIGN=LEFT|↪` `CENTER| RIGHT></H?>`	HTML 3.2 Option within the HTML 2.0–compliant Heading tag
Division	`<DIV></DIV>`	HTML 3.2

- Align Division	`<DIV ALIGN=LEFT|↪`
	`RIGHT| CENTER|↪`
	`JUSTIFY></DIV>`
		HTML 3.2

Large Font Size	`<BIG></BIG>`	HTML 3.2
Small Font Size	`<SMALL></SMALL>`	HTML 3.2

Table C-12	Presentation Formatting: Author Specifies Text Appearance	
Tag Name	*Tag*	*Notes*
Subscript	`<SUB></SUB>`	HTML 2.0
Superscript	`<SUP></SUP>`	HTML 2.0
Center	`<CENTER></CENTER>`	Netscape 1.0. widely implemented; for both text and images

Table C-13	Links and Graphics	
Tag Name	*Tag*	*Notes*
Dimensions	`<IMG SRC="URL"↵ WIDTH= "?" HEIGHT=↵ "?">`	HTML 3.2. Image width and height in pixels

Table C-14	Dividers	
Tag Name	*Tag*	*Notes*
Paragraph	`<P></P>`	HTML 3.2. Paragraph tag, `<P>`, redefined as a container tag, `</P>` is optional
- Align Text	`<P ALIGN=LEFT|↵ CENTER|RIGHT|↵ JUSTIFY></P>`	HTML 3.2
- No Line Breaks	`<P NOWRAP></P>`	Internet Explorer only

Table C-15	Backgrounds and Colors	
Tag Name	*Tag*	*Notes*
Tiled Background	`<BODY BACKGROUND=↵ "URL">`	HTML 3.2
Background Color	`<BODY BGCOLOR=↵ "#$$$$$$">`	HTML 3.2. Color order, red/green/blue

(continued)

Table C-15 *(continued)*

Tag Name	Tag	Notes
Text Color	`<BODY TEXT=↩ "#$$$$$$">`	HTML 3.2. Color order, red/green/blue
Link Color	`<BODY LINK=↩ "#$$$$$$">`	HTML 3.2. Color order, red/green/blue
Active Link	`<BODY ALINK=↩ "#$$$$$$">`	HTML 3.2. Color order, red/green/blue
Visited Link	`<BODY VLINK=↩ "#$$$$$$">`	HTML 3.2. Color order, red/green/blue

You can find more info at `www.werbach.com/web/wwwhelp.html`.

Table C-16   **Tables**

Tag Name	Tag	Notes
Define Table	`<TABLE></TABLE>`	HTML 3.2
- Table Border	`<TABLE BORDER>↩ </TABLE>`	HTML 3.2. Either on or off
- Table Border	`<TABLE BORDER=?>↩ </TABLE>`	HTML 3.2. Can set the border width in pixels
- Cell Spacing	`<TABLE CELLSPACING=?>`	HTML 3.2
- Cell Padding	`<TABLE CELLPADDING=?>`	HTML 3.2
- Desired Width	`<TABLE WIDTH=?>`	HTML 3.2. In pixels
- Width Percent	`<TABLE WIDTH=%>`	HTML 3.2 Percentage of page
Table Row	`<TR></TR>`	HTML 3.2
- Alignment	`<TR ALIGN=LEFT|RIGHT|↩ CENTER|JUSTIFY VALIGN= TOP|↩ MIDDLE|BOTTOM>`	HTML 3.2
Table Cell	`<TD></TD>`	HTML 3.2. Must appear within table rows

Tag Name	Tag	Notes
- Alignment	`<TD ALIGN=LEFT|`↵`RIGHT| CENTER`↵`VALIGN=TOP|MIDDLE|`↵`BOTTOM>`	HTML 3.2
- No Line Breaks	`<TD NOWRAP>`	HTML 3.2
- Columns to Span	`<TD COLSPAN=?>`	HTML 3.2
- Rows to Span	`<TD ROWSPAN=?>`	HTML 3.2
- Desired Width	`<TD WIDTH=?>`	HTML 3.2. In pixels
- Width Percent	`<TD WIDTH=%>`	HTML 3.2 Percentage of table
- Desired Height	`<TD HEIGHT=?>`	HTML 3.2. In pixels
- Height Percent	`<TD HEIGHT=%>`	HTML 3.2 Percentage of page
Table Header	`<TH></TH>`	HTML 3.2. Same as data, except bold centered
- Alignment	`<TH ALIGN=LEFT|RIGHT|`↵`CENTER|JUSTIFY|CHAR.`↵`VALIGN=TOP|`↵`MIDDLE|BOTTOM>`	HTML 3.2
- No Line Breaks	`<TH NOWRAP>`	HTML 3.2
- Columns to Span	`<TH COLSPAN=?>`	HTML 3.2
- Rows to Span	`<TH ROWSPAN=?>`	HTML 3.2
- Desired Width	`<TH WIDTH=?>`	HTML 3.2. In pixels
- Width Percent	`<TH WIDTH=%>`	HTML 3.2. Percentage of table
- Desired Height	`<TH HEIGHT=?>`	HTML 3.2. In pixels
- Height Percent	`<TH HEIGHT=%>`	HTML 3.2. Percentage of page
Table Caption	`<CAPTION></CAPTION>`	HTML 3.2
- Alignment	`<CAPTION ALIGN=TOP|`↵`BOTTOM>`	HTML 3.2. Above/below table

Table C-17	Miscellaneous	
Tag Name	*Tag*	*Notes*
Script	`<SCRIPT></SCRIPT>`	
- Location	`<SCRIPT SRC="URL"></SCRIPT>`	
- Type	`<SCRIPT TYPE="***"></SCRIPT>`	
- Language	`<SCRIPT LANGUAGE="***"></SCRIPT>`	
Java Applet	`<APPLET>`	HTML 3.2
- Applet Name	`<APPLET NAME="***">`	HTML 3.2
- Alternate Text	`<APPLET ALT="***">`	HTML 3.2
- Applet Code Location	`<APPLET CODE="URL">`	HTML 3.2
- Code Base Directory	`<APPLET CODEBASE="URL">`	HTML 3.2
- Applet Window Height	`<APPLET HEIGHT=?>`	HTML 3.2. In pixels
- Width	`<APPLET WIDTH=?>`	HTML 3.2. In pixels
- Horizontal Offset	`<APPLET HSPACE=?>`	HTML 3.2. In pixels
- Vertical Offset	`<APPLET VSPACE=?>`	HTML 3.2. In pixels
- Alignment	`<APPLET ALIGN=[left| right|top| middle|bottom]>`	HTML 3.2
Applet Parameter	`<PARAM>`	HTML 3.2
- Parameter Name, Value	`<PARAM NAME="applet name", VALUE=" parameter value">`	HTML 3.2
3.2 Prologue	`<!DOCTYPE HTML PUBLIC"- //W3C//DTD HTML3.2 FINAL//EN">`	HTML 3.2

Less Frequently Used Tags

Some Netscape Navigator-only tags were slow to be adopted by non-Netscape browsers. However, most of these tags can be used with up-to-date browsers. HTML 4.0-specific tags are only supported by relatively recent browsers.

Table C-18	Structural Definition: Appearance Controlled by the Browser's Preferences	
Tag Name	*Tag*	*Notes*
Defined Content	`<SPAN></SPAN>`	HTML 4.0
Quote	`<Q></Q>`	HTML 4.0. For short quotations
- Citation	`<Q CITE="URL"></Q>`	HTML 4.0
Insert	`<INS></INS>`	HTML 4.0. Marks additions in a new version
- Time of Change	`<INS DATETIME=":::"></INS>`	HTML 4.0
- Comments	`<INS CITE="URL"></INS>`	HTML 4.0
Delete	`<DEL></DEL>`	HTML 4.0. Marks deletions in a new version
- Time of Change	`<DEL DATETIME=":::"></DEL>`	HTML 4.0
- Comments	`<DEL CITE="URL"></DEL>`	HTML 4.0
Acronym	`<ACRONYM></ACRONYM>`	HTML 4.0
Abbreviation	`<ABBR></ABBR>`	HTML 4.0

Table C-19	Presentation Formatting: Author Specifies Text Appearance	
Tag Name	*Tag*	*Notes*
Blinking	`<BLINK></BLINK>`	Navigator 1.0. Most derided tag ever
Font Size	`<FONT SIZE=?> </FONT>`	HTML 3.2. Ranges from 1–7

(continued)

Table C-19 *(continued)*

Tag Name	Tag	Notes
Change Font Size	`<FONT SIZE=+|-?>↵ </FONT>`	HTML 3.2
Base Font Size	`<BASEFONT SIZE=?>`	HTML 3.2. From 1-7; default is 3
Font Color	`<FONT COLOR=↵ "#$$$$$$"> </FONT>`	HTML 3.2
Underline	`<U></U>`	HTML 2.0
Strikeout	`<S></S>`	HTML 2.0
Select Font	`<FONT FACE="***"></FONT>`	HTML 4.0

Table C-20   Links, Graphics, and Sounds

Tag Name	Tag	Notes
- Target Window	`<A HREF="URL"↵ TARGET="***"></A>`	HTML 4.0
Action on Click	`<A HREF="URL"↵ ONCLICK="***"></A>`	HTML 4.0
Mouseover Action	`<A HREF="URL"↵ ONMOUSEOVER="***"></A>`	HTML 4.0
Mouseover Action	`<A HREF="URL"↵ ONMOUSEOUT="***"></A>`	HTML 4.0
- Alignment	`<IMG SRC="URL"↵ ALIGN= LEFT|RIGHT|↵ TEXTTOP|ABSMIDDLE|↵ BASELINE| ABSBOTTOM>`	Navigator 1.0. Option within the HTML 2.0–compliant Display Image tag
- Image Map	`<IMG SRC="URL"↵ USEMAP="URL">`	HTML 3.2. Option within the HTML 2.0–compliant Display Image tag
- Map	`<MAP NAME="***">↵ </MAP>`	HTML 3.2. Describes the map. Option within the HTML 2.0–compliant Display Image tag
- Section	`<AREA SHAPE="RECT"↵ COORDS="#,#,#,"HREF=↵ "URL"|NOHREF>`	HTML 3.2. Option within the HTML 2.0–compliant Display Image tag

Tag Name	Tag	Notes
- Border	`<IMG SRC="URL"`↪ `BORDER=?>`	HTML 3.2
Runaround Space	`<IMG SRC="URL"`↪ `HSPACE= ? VSPACE=?>`	HTML 3.2. In pixels
Low-Res Proxy	`<IMG SRC="URL"`↪ `LOWSRC= "URL">`	
N1.1 Client Pull	`<META HTTP-EQUIV=`↪ `"Refresh" CONTENT=`↪ `"?; URL=URL">`	HTML 2.0
Embed Object	`<EMBED SRC="URL">`	Navigator 2.0. Insert object into page
- Object Size	`<EMBED SRC="URL"`↪ `IDTH ="?" HEIGHT=`↪ `"?">`	Navigator 2.0, Internet Explorer
Object	`<OBJECT></OBJECT>`	Navigator 4.0
Parameters	`<PARAM>`	Navigator 4.0

Table C-21		Dividers
Tag Name	**Tag**	**Notes**
- Clear Text Wrap	`<BR CLEAR=LEFT|`↪ `RIGHT|ALL>`	HTML 3.2. Option within the HTML 2.0– HTML 2.0–compliant Line Break tag
- Alignment	`<HR ALIGN=LEFT|`↪ `RIGHT|CENTER>`	HTML 3.2. Option within the HTML 2.0– compliant Horizontal Rule tag
- Thickness	`<HR SIZE=?>`	HTML 3.2. In pixels. Option within the HTML 2.0–compliant Horizontal Rule tag
- Width	`<HR WIDTH=?%>`	HTML 3.2. In pixels. Option within the HTML 2.0–compliant Horizontal Rule tag
- Width Percent	`<HR WIDTH=?%>`	HTML 3.2. As a percentage of page width. Option within the HTML 2.0– compliant Horizontal Rule tag
- Solid Line	`<HR NOSHADE>`	HTML 3.2. Without the 3-D cutout look. Option within the HTML 2.0–compliant Horizontal Rule tag
No Break	`<NOBR></NOBR>`	Navigator 1.0. Prevents line breaks
Word Break	`<WBR>`	Navigator 1.0. Where to break a line if needed

Table C-22   **Lists: Can Be Nested**

Tag Name	Tag	Notes
- Bullet Type	`<UL TYPE=DISC| CIRCLE| SQUARE>`	HTML 3.2. For the whole list. Option within the HTML 2.0–compliant Unordered List tag
	`<LI TYPE=DISC| CIRCLE| SQUARE>`	HTML 3.2. This and subsequent list items. Option within the HTML 2.0–compliant Unordered List tag
- Numbering Type	`<OL TYPE=A|a|I|i|1>`	HTML 3.2. This and subsequent list items. Option within the HTML 2.0–compliant Ordered List tag
	`<LI TYPE=A|a|I|i|1>`	HTML 3.2. This and subsequent list items. Option within the HTML 2.0–compliant Ordered List tag
- Starting Number	`<OL START=?>`	HTML 3.2
- Count	`<OL VALUE=?>`	HTML 3.2 For the whole list. Option within the HTML 2.0–compliant Ordered List tag

Table C-23   **Backgrounds and Colors**

Tag Name	Tag	Notes
N1.1 Active Link	`<BODY ALINK= "#$$$$$$">`	HTML 3.2

You can find more info at `werbach.com/web/wwwhelp.html#color`.

Table C-24   **Forms: Generally Require a CGI Script on Your Server**

Tag Name	Tag	Notes
- File Upload	`<FORM ENCTYPE= "multi part/form- data"></FORM>`	HTML 4.0
- Wrap Text	`<TEXTAREA WRAP=OFF| VIRTUAL|PHYSICAL> </TEXTAREA>`	HTML 2.0
Button	`<BUTTON></BUTTON>`	HTML 4.0

Tag Name	Tag	Notes
- Button Name	`<BUTTON NAME="****">` `</BUTTON>`	HTML 4.0

- Button Type	`<BUTTON`
	`TYPE="SUBMIT|`
	`RESET|BUTTON">`
	`</BUTTON>`
		HTML 4.0

- Default Value	`<BUTTON VALUE="****">` `</BUTTON>`	HTML 4.0
Label	`<LABEL></LABEL>`	HTML 4.0
- Item Labelled	`<LABEL FOR="****">` `</LABEL>`	HTML 4.0
Option Group	`<OPTGROUP LABEL="****">` `</OPTGROUP>`	HTML 4.0
Group Elements	`<FIELDSET></FIELDSET>`	HTML 4.0
Legend	`<LEGEND></LEGEND>`	HTML 4.0. Caption for fieldsets

- Alignment	`<LEGEND`
	`ALIGN="TOP|`
	`BOTTOM|LEFT|`
	`RIGHT"></LEGEND>`
		HTML 4.0

Table C-25	Tables	
Tag Name	**Tag**	**Notes**
- Table Alignment	`<TABLE ALIGN=LEFT|` `RIGHT|CENTER>`	HTML 4.0
- Table Color	`<TABLE BGCOLOR="$$$$$$">` `</TABLE>`	HTML 4.0

- Table Frame	`<TABLE FRAME=VOID|`
	`ABOVE|BELOW|HSIDES|`
	`LHS|RHS|VSIDES|BOX|`
	`BORDER></TABLE>`
		HTML 4.0

- Table Rules	`<TABLE RULES=NONE|GROUPS|` `ROWS|COLS|ALL></TABLE>`	HTML 4.0
- Desired Width	`<TD WIDTH=?>`	HTML 4.0. In pixels

(continued)

Table C-25 *(continued)*

Tag Name	Tag	Notes
- Cell Color	`<TD BGCOLOR="#$$$$$$">`	HTML 4.0
- Desired Width	`<TH WIDTH=?>`	HTML 4.0. In pixels
- Cell Color	`<TH BGCOLOR="#$$$$$$">`	HTML 4.0
Table Body	`<TBODY>`	HTML 4.0
Table Footer	`<TFOOT></TFOOT>`	HTML 4.0. Must come before `<THEAD>`
Table Header	`<THEAD></THEAD>`	HTML 4.0
Column	`<COL></COL>`	HTML 4.0. Groups column attributes
- Columns Spanned	`<COL SPAN=?></COL>`	HTML 4.0
- Column Width	`<COL WIDTH=?></COL>`	HTML 4.0
- Width Percent	`<COL WIDTH="%"></COL>`	HTML 4.0
Group columns	`<COLGROUP></COLGROUP>`	HTML 4.0. Groups column structure
- Columns Spanned	`<COLGROUP SPAN=?>` `</COLGROUP>`	HTML 4.0
- Group Width	`<COLGROUP WIDTH=?>` `</COLGROUP>`	HTML 4.0
- Width Percent	`<COLGROUP WIDTH="%">` `</COLGROUP>`	HTML 4.0

Table C-26   **Frames: Define and Manipulate Specific Regions of the Screen**

Tag Name	Tag	Notes
Frame Document	`<FRAMESET></FRAMESET>`	HTML 4.0. Instead of `<BODY>`
- Row Heights	`<FRAMESET ROWS=` `#,#,#,> </FRAMESET>`	HTML 4.0. Pixels or percent
- Row Heights	`<FRAMESET ROWS=*>` `</FRAMESET>`	HTML 4.0. * = relative size
- Column Widths	`<FRAMESET COLS=` `#,#,#,> </FRAMESET>`	HTML 4.0. Pixels or percent

Tag Name	Tag	Notes
- Column Widths	`<FRAMESET COLS=*>↩` `</FRAMESET>`	HTML 4.0. * = relative size
- Borders	`<FRAMESET FRAMEBORDER="yes|no"↩` `</FRAMESET>`	HTML 4.0
- Border Width	`<FRAMESET BORDER=?↩` `</FRAMESET>`	HTML 4.0
- Border Color	`<FRAMESET BORDERCOLOR="******"↩` `</FRAMESET>`	HTML 4.0
Define Frame	`<FRAME>`	HTML 4.0. Contents of an individual frame
- Display Document	`<FRAME SRC="URL">`	HTML 4.0

- Frame Name	`<FRAME NAME="***"|↩`
	`_blank |_self|↩`
	`_parent|_top>`
		HTML 4.0

- Margin Width	`<FRAME MARGINWIDTH=?>`	HTML 4.0. Left and right margins
- Margin Height	`<FRAME↩MARGINHEIGHT=?>`	HTML 4.0. Top and bottom margins
- Scroll bar?	`<FRAME SCROLLING=↩` `"YES |NO|AUTO">`	HTML 4.0
- Not Resizable	`<FRAME NORESIZE>`	HTML 4.0
Borders	`<FRAME FRAMEBORDER="yes|no">`	HTML 4.0
Border Color	`<FRAME BORDERCOLOR="#$$$$$$">`	HTML 4.0
Inline Frame	`<IFRAME></IFRAME>`	HTML 4.0. Takes same attributes as FRAME
Dimensions	`<IFRAME WIDTH=? HEIGHT=?>` `</IFRAME>`	HTML 4.0
Dimensions	`<IFRAME WIDTH="%" HEIGHT="%">` `</IFRAME>`	HTML 4.0
Unframed Content	`<NOFRAMES></NOFRAMES>`	HTML 4.0 For non-frames browsers

Note: Frame tags introduced prior to HTML 4.0 are not supported by all browsers.

Table C-27	Miscellaneous	
Tag Name	*Tag*	*Notes*
- Prompt	`<ISINDEX PROMPT=`↵`"***">`	HTML 2.0. Text to prompt input
Base Window Name	`<BASE TARGET="***">`	HTML 2.0. Must be in header
Other Content	`<NOSCRIPT></NOSCRIPT>`	HTML 4.0. If scripts not supported
Base Window Name	`<BASE TARGET="***">`	HTML 4.0. Must be in header
Bidirect Off	`<BDO DIR=LTR|RTL></BDO>`	HTML 4.0. For certain character sets

Appendix D

Using Resource.htm

A great many resources are available online for Web developers of all skill levels. On the CD-ROM enclosed with this book, you can find a file called `Resource.htm`. To use this file, start your browser and then use the Open command from the File menu to open the `Resource.htm` Web page. You can find it on the CD-ROM.

In `Resource.htm`, you find links to numerous sources of Web authoring information and links to sites that support some of the more popular Web software packages. The CD-ROM includes some of those packages, but it is always a good idea to check the support sites for the latest upgrades and bug fixes. The following is a short description of the key Web sites and software packages that you can access via this resource page. Note that some of the resources will lead you to more advanced Web page creation topics not covered in this book, such as CSS, XML, and Java.

General Web Developer Resources

Probably the most useful sources of Web information are the excellent World Wide Web FAQ files by Thomas Boutell. The files are brimming with answers to many questions about the Web and contain numerous links to a variety of sites that provide further information or support for Web and Internet-related software. These files are an excellent starting point for any would-be Web author and Net surfer.

✔ World Wide Web FAQs

```
www.boutell.com/newfaq/
```

The indispensable Yahoo! Index has a superb collection of links to just about every Web and Internet-related topic under the sun. We saved you the trouble of searching and provide a link to the Yahoo! World Wide Web section directly. The topic selection is vast and comprehensive.

✔ Yahoo! World Wide Web Resources

```
http://dir.yahoo.com/computers_and_internet/internet/
       world_wide_web/
```

For more advanced topics and resources specifically related to Web authoring, check out the following sites:

- ✔ O'Reilly Network

  `www.oreillynet.com/`

- ✔ The Web Developer's Virtual Library

  `www.wdvl.com/`

- ✔ Webdeveloper.com

  `www.webdeveloper.com/`

Three special topic resources are always in high demand. A great basic HTML tutorial can be found at the NCSA Beginner's Guide to HTML site. The WWW Security FAQ covers various aspects of maintaining secure Web sites and writing secure Web scripts. Finally the GIF-related site teaches you all you need to know about creating transparent, interlaced, and animated GIFs.

- ✔ NCSA Beginner's Guide to HTML

  `www.ncsa.uiuc.edu/general/internet/www/`

- ✔ The World Wide Web Security FAQ

  `www.w3.org/Security/Faq/`

- ✔ GIF Animation on the WWW

  `members.aol.com/royalef/gifanim.htm`

Microsoft Windows Web Resources

In this section, you can find a number of sites that deal specifically with Microsoft Windows Internet and Web software. You find browsers, Web page creation tools, file viewers, specialized network clients, helper applications, and even various system administration utilities. And if you want to keep up with the daily deluge of Windows software releases, try Version Tracker. If you're looking for just the right Windows netsurfing tool, these sites are the place to start:

- ✔ Download.com

  `www.download.com/`

- ✔ ZDNet Downloads

  `http://downloads-zdnet.com.com/`

   ✔ Tucows Software Library

   `www.tucows.com/`

   ✔ Version Tracker for Windows

   `www.versiontracker.com/windows/`

Microsoft Windows Software

The `Resource.htm` Web page on your CD-ROM contains links to support sites for a variety of software programs that make life easier for the Web developer. You can find some of these programs on the enclosed CD-ROM (see Appendix E for a list). Others are freely available online either as shareware, freeware, or demo versions.

Your `Resource.htm` Web page offers links to a number of Web browsers and HTML editors. Other goodies include Mapedit the elegant image map editor, several image editing programs including the excellent PaintShop Pro paint program, image animation programs, an HTML syntax checker, software to add special effects to your Web pages, as well as several other generally useful Web page utilities. We also include the FeedDemon RSS Reader, a program, which will allow you to read syndicated news, feeds from your favorite Web logs or online news sites. If you need support or updates to any of the packages on the CD-ROM the `Resource.htm` file links you directly to the software Web sites.

Macintosh Web Resources

This section contains Macintosh-oriented sites. For general Web authoring resources, nothing beats the ULTIMATE Macintosh Web site ("Still the BIGGEST, UGLIEST, and MOST USEFUL Macintosh Page on the Web . . ."). Version Tracker keeps you up-to-date on the latest Mac software releases. MacUpdate and the Info-Mac HyperArchive are large repositories of Mac software. Finally, MacTech magazine is a great resource for serious Mac-oriented Web developers.

   ✔ ULTIMATE Macintosh

   `http://ultimatemac.com/`

   ✔ Version Tracker for Mac OS X

   `www.versiontracker.com/macosx/`

   ✔ MacUpdate

   `www.macupdate.com/`

✔ Info-Mac HyperArchive

```
http://hyperarchive.lcs.mit.edu/hyperarchive.html
```

✔ MacTech

```
http://mactech.com/
```

Macintosh Web Software

We include a number of Mac Internet software packages, such as the Mozilla suite of Web browsers and mail clients, and the Opera Web browser. For HTML and Web site editing we have Macromedia Dreamweaver, a sophisticated Web site creation tool, and BBEdit, the first rate HTML and text editing package. GraphicConverter and Mapedit will help you with your image manipulating needs, while NetNewsWire will allow you to easily read syndicated news feeds from your favorite Web logs or online news sites.

Web Logs

As you learn in Chapter 16, Web logs (or *blogs*) are regularly updated online journals whose content can range from diary-like entries, to lists of interesting Web links, to collections of photos, or even music files. That chapter also shows you how to create your own Web log very easily through the online hosting service provided by Google's Blogger.com. (Other blogging services include TypePad and LiveJournal.)

Alternatively, if you have access to a Web hosting service that allows you to install your own software, you can install powerful stand-alone blogging programs such as Radio UserLand, Movable Type or the open source WordPress. Because you can find a vast number of online resources devoted to Web logs, we don't have space to include all of them in this brief write-up; make sure to check `Resource.htm` for the full list.

✔ Google's Blogger.com

```
www.blogger.com/
```

✔ LiveJournal

```
www.livejournal.com/
```

✔ TypePad

```
http://typepad.com/
```

- ✔ Movable Type

  `www.movabletype.org/`

- ✔ Userland

  `www.userland.com/`

- ✔ WordPress

  `www.wordpress.org/`

Cascading Style Sheets

Cascading Style Sheets (often abbreviated as CSS) is a standard for specifying style (such as fonts, colors, and spacing) in Web documents. This standard makes it very easy to manage a consistent look and feel for a large Web site, and is used extensively in many sophisticated sites. Because CSS gives Web designers such great control over the appearance of a Web page, it is the modern technology of choice for advanced Web site designs. CSS is not that far removed from making simple HTML Web pages, so after you've mastered this book you may want to check out some of these Web resources, or read Damon Dean's book *Cascading Style Sheets For Dummies* (Wiley).

- ✔ W3C Cascading Stylesheet Web pages

  `www.w3.org/style/css/`

- ✔ Web Design Group Guide to Cascading Style Sheets

  `www.htmlhelp.com/reference/css/`

- ✔ CSS School

  `www.w3schools.com/css/`

RSS, Atom, and Content Syndication

Content syndication is a set of very simple technologies that allow you to share your Web pages, particularly Web logs, with other Web sites. Why's this a big deal? Many Web sites (such as blogs and online news sites) change often. To let the world keep up with their changes, these types of sites make their content available in a special format called RSS (Really Simple Syndication). Some use a related, newer format called Atom.

RSS and Atom *feeds,* as they are known, can be easily parsed by software and can then be automatically formatted and displayed on other Web pages or in special news readers such as FeedDemon and NetNewsWire, both of which are included on your CD-ROM. These Web sites teach you what you need to know about RSS, Atom, and content syndication in general.

- ✔ Mark Pilgrim's "What is RSS?"

  `www.xml.com/pub/a/2002/12/18/dive-into-xml.html`
- ✔ RSS and Content Syndication at About.com

  `http://weblogs.about.com/od/rssandcontentsyndication/`
- ✔ RSS 2.0 Specification

  `http://blogs.law.harvard.edu/tech/rss`
- ✔ Atom Syndication Format

  `www.atomenabled.org/`

Perl

Perl is an immensely powerful and flexible scripting language widely used by system administrators and Web developers. If you want to delve into the creation of more sophisticated Web-based applications, you can take advantage of a huge base of existing programs and tools written in Perl. The key sites for Perl include the Perl.com Web site, and the Perl Mongers ("The Perl advocacy people") users group Web site. The Comprehensive Perl Archive Network (CPAN) lets you tap the power of a worldwide Perl developer community through thousands of pre-built applications and modules. Finally, the Perl Journal is a great resource for advanced Perl programmers.

- ✔ Perl.com

  `www.perl.com/`
- ✔ Perl Mongers

  `www.perl.org/`
- ✔ CPAN — Comprehensive Perl Archive Network

  `www.cpan.org/`
- ✔ The Perl Journal

  `www.tpj.com/`

Java

Java is the sophisticated programming language of choice for creating interactive Web applications. These sites contain a plethora of information about Java, with both developer resources and numerous sample applications.

- ✔ The official Sun Java Site

  `http://java.sun.com/`

- ✔ Developer.com Gamelan Java Site

  `www.developer.com/java/`

- ✔ Yahoo! Java Resources

  `http://dir.yahoo.com/computers_and_internet/programming_`
  `         and_development/languages/java/`

- ✔ Java FAQ Archives

  `www-net.com/java/faq/`

JavaScript

JavaScript (no relation to Java, despite the similar name) is a scripting language that is built into Web browsers. It lets Web page authors create more interactive Web pages by using the built-in browser features running on the Net surfer's computer. Just about every sophisticated Web site uses JavaScript in some fashion. The JavaScript FAQ Knowledge Base at irt.org and the IDM JavaScript FAQ can answer all your questions, while the Internet.com JavaScript site offers plenty of examples to work with. Finally, there's always the Yahoo!'s JavaScript resources listing for in-depth explorations of the language.

- ✔ JavaScript FAQ Knowledge Base

  `http://developer.irt.org/script/script.htm`

- ✔ IDM JavaScript FAQ

  `www.intranetjournal.com/faq/js-faq.shtml`

- ✔ JavaScript at Internet.com

  `http://javascript.internet.com/`

- ✔ Yahoo! JavaScript Resources

  `http://dir.yahoo.com/computers_and_internet/programming_`
  `         and_development/languages/javascript/`

XML

XML (Extensible Markup Language) is a method of marking up content using tags that look very similar to HTML tags. What's nice about XML is that anybody can define a standard set of XML tags in a very structured way so that others can use them. This allows content to be easily interchanged and displayed on all sorts of devices. The official keeper of the XML standard is the World Wide Web Consortium (W3C), and the XML tutorial offered at its Web site is a great place to start if you want to learn about the topic. Numerous commercial Web sites cover the rapidly growing XML technology beat, the best of which we list here.

✔ XML Tutorial

    www.w3schools.com/xml/default.asp

✔ W3C Extensible Markup Language (XML)

    www.w3.org/xml/

✔ The XML Cover Pages

    http://xml.coverpages.org/xml.html

✔ XML.org The XML Industry Portal

    www.xml.org/

✔ XML.com

    http://xml.com/

✔ IBM XML Zone

    www.ibm.com/developerworks/xml/

ActiveX

ActiveX is Microsoft's answer to Java for Web interactivity. ActiveX enables programmers to extend the Web to do a great deal more with many different kinds of data than plain old HTML. Even so, not many developers work with ActiveX these days, despite Microsoft's strong efforts to make it popular.

✔ Microsoft ActiveX site

    http://www.microsoft.com/com/tech/Activex.asp

✔ Download.com ActiveX site

    http://download.com.com/2001-2206-0.html

✔ Yahoo! ActiveX Resources

    http://dir.yahoo.com/computers_and_internet/programming_
        and_development/languages/activex/

Microsoft .NET

We must mention Microsoft's .NET initiative. Simply put, .NET technology allows applications to communicate and share data over the Internet using XML technology, regardless of operating system or programming language. Think of it as a sophisticated extension of the World Wide Web. While the topic is fairly advanced for beginning Web page creators, it is worth knowing about as you continue your Web education. The Microsoft .NET Web site has a very readable explanation and links to numerous developer resources.

✔ Microsoft .NET Web pages

```
www.microsoft.com/net/
```

USENET Newsgroups

Whatever your Internet or Web-related passion, you are sure to find others with the same interests on Usenet. In the `Resource.htm` file on the accompanying CD-ROM we include an extensive selection of newsgroups dealing with various aspects of Web page creation. Here you can ask and answer questions, debate, and participate in standard-setting projects. You can access newsgroups in two ways. Your ISP may make a Usenet NNTP server available for your use, in which case you can subscribe to newsgroups using software such as the built-in Mozilla mail and news reader. Alternatively, you can read newsgroups on the Web through the Google Groups server. Though in recent years Usenet newsgroups have increasingly succumbed to being overrun by spam, many of the technical groups are still an excellent resource for communicating with the Web developer community. Give them a try.

✔ Google Usenet Groups

```
http://groups.google.com/
```

Appendix E

About the CD-ROM

System Requirements

Make sure that your computer meets the minimum system requirements shown in the following list. If your computer doesn't match up to most of these requirements, you may have problems using the software and files on the CD. For the latest and greatest information, please refer to the ReadMe file located at the root of the CD-ROM.

- A PC with a 1GHz or faster processor; or a Macintosh with a 1GHz Power PC or faster processor.

- Microsoft Windows XP or later; or Mac OS X or later.

- At least 256MB of total RAM installed on your computer; for best performance, we recommend at least 512MB or more.

- A CD-ROM drive.

- A sound card for PCs; Mac OS computers have built-in sound support.

- A monitor capable of displaying at least 256 colors.

- A modem with a speed of at least 56.6 Kbps; for best performance, we recommend a DSL or cable modem broadband Internet connection.

Using the CD with Microsoft Windows

To install from the CD to your hard drive, follow these steps:

1. **Insert the CD into your computer's CD-ROM drive.**

   A window appears with the following options: HTML Interface, Browse CD, and Exit.

2. **Click the Start button and choose Run from the menu.**

3. **In the dialog box that appears, type** d:\Start.htm.

   Replace *d* with the proper drive letter for your CD-ROM if it uses a different letter. (If you don't know the letter, double-click My Computer on your desktop and see what letter is listed for your CD-ROM drive.)

   Your browser opens, and the license agreement is displayed. If you don't have a browser, Microsoft Internet Explorer and Netscape Communicator are included on the CD.

4. **Read through the license agreement, nod your head, and click the Agree button if you want to use the CD.**

   After you click Agree, you're taken to the Main menu, where you can browse through the contents of the CD.

5. **To navigate within the interface, click a topic of interest to take you to an explanation of the files on the CD and how to use or install them.**

6. **To install software from the CD, simply click the software name.**

   You'll see two options: to run or open the file from the current location or to save the file to your hard drive. Choose to run or open the file from its current location, and the installation procedure continues. When you finish using the interface, close your browser as usual.

Note: We have included an "easy install" in these HTML pages. If your browser supports installations from within it, go ahead and click the links of the program names you see. You'll see two options: Run the File from the Current Location and Save the File to Your Hard Drive. Choose to Run the File from the Current Location and the installation procedure will continue. A Security Warning dialog box appears. Click Yes to continue the installation.

Using the CD with Mac OS

To install items from the CD to your hard drive, follow these steps:

1. **Insert the CD into your computer's CD-ROM drive.**

   In a moment, an icon representing the CD you just inserted appears on your Mac desktop. Chances are, the icon looks like a CD-ROM.

2. **Double-click the CD icon to show the CD's contents.**

3. **Double-click** `start.htm` **to open your browser and display the license agreement.**

   If your browser doesn't open automatically, open it as you normally would by choosing File⇨Open File (in Internet Explorer) or File⇨Open⇨Location in Netscape (in Netscape Navigator) and select *Creating Web Pages FD*. The license agreement appears.

4. **Read through the license agreement, nod your head, and click the Accept button if you want to use the CD.**

   After you click Accept, you're taken to the Main menu. This is where you can browse through the contents of the CD.

5. **To navigate within the interface, click any topic of interest and you're taken to an explanation of the files on the CD and how to use or install them.**

6. **To install software from the CD, simply click the software name.**

What You'll Find on the CD

The following sections are arranged by category and provide a summary of the software and other goodies you'll find on the CD. If you need help with installing the items provided on the CD, refer back to the installation instructions in the preceding section.

Shareware programs are fully functional, free, trial versions of copyrighted programs. If you like particular programs, register with their authors for a nominal fee and receive licenses, enhanced versions, and technical support. Freeware programs are free, copyrighted games, applications, and utilities. You can copy them to as many PCs as you like for free but they offer no technical support. GNU software is governed by its own license, which is included inside the folder of the GNU software. There are no restrictions on distribution of GNU software. See the GNU license at the root of the CD for more details. Trial, demo, or evaluation versions of software are usually limited either by time or functionality (such as not letting you save a project after you create it).

A Quick Overview

This book includes a CD-ROM with a variety of PC and Macintosh programs and demos that you will find useful while creating your Web pages. You can use some of these programs for one of the most important tasks in Web authoring: using HTML tags to create the text file that will be seen by users as a Web page.

The programs on the CD are either free, try before you buy, or demo versions. Some of the programs are HTML focused, and others hide the HTML tags and give you a more intuitive interface to work with. Still others enable you to do more advanced things with your Web pages, such as create graphics, create fancy text effects, or check your HTML tags for correctness.

While all the programs on the CD-ROM are free in their current form, some require you to pay a fee to get a fully functional version by registering the program. Other programs are functional and ready to go "as is," with no payment required.

The HTML file "**Resource.htm**" contained on your CD-ROM has links to numerous online resources, including links to program home pages, which you will find useful as you create your Web pages. You can read more about this file in Appendix E.

In this appendix, you will find a brief description of the contents of the *Creating Web Pages For Dummies* CD-ROM. Each program listing also includes a pointer to the URL of the program's Web site where you can check for the latest upgrade and support information. Have fun!

Resources

Resource.htm, from Arthur and Bud, your humble authors.

For Windows and Mac OS. This is probably the most useful file on your CD-ROM. This HTML file contains links to many great Internet resources of use to the Web page creator. To use this file productively, you'll need an Internet connection and a Web browser installed on your computer. You will find links to all sorts of HTML and image editing tools, to sources of information, and to Usenet newsgroups dealing with the Web. To use this file, simply open it in your browser using the File⇨Open menu.

You can find the **Resource.htm** file on the CD-ROM in the *Author* folder within your *Creating Web Pages For Dummies* folder if you choose to install these files on your computer. Keep this file handy, you'll use it often.

HTML Editors

BBEdit, from Bare Bones Software

For Mac OS. BBEdit is one of the oldest, best known, and best loved text and HTML editors for the Macintosh. In addition to being a first rate HTML editor, BBEdit also contains a huge toolkit of features for manipulating text in every imaginable way. Incidentally, Bare Bones has a great motto: "Software That Doesn't Suck." We totally agree.

```
www.barebones.com/products/bbedit/index.shtml
```

Dreamweaver MX 2004, from Macromedia

For Windows and Mac. Dreamweaver is a serious, award-winning professional Web page authoring program. It has many advanced features, such as support for the CSS standards and the ability to build in Flash graphics on your Web pages. Dreamweaver is a great product to move to after you've mastered the simple Web page design techniques in this book. This is a trial version of this sophisticated and popular program.

```
www.macromedia.com/software/dreamweaver/
```

HotDog Professional HTML Editor, from Sausage Software

For Windows. The HotDog HTML Editor from Sausage Software is a fast, flexible, and user-friendly HTML editor that has been getting rave reviews on the Net for many years. With its advanced document navigation features and support for advanced Web standards it is the perfect choice for managing Web sites with large amounts of content.

```
www.sausagetools.com/hotdog-professional.html
```

HotDog PageWiz, from Sausage Software

For Windows. HotDog PageWiz is a great choice if you want to create fast, straightforward Web pages. It comes with 10 templates allowing you to whip up a Web page in 4 simple steps. Once you have the basics, the integrated editor allows you to tweak your HTML and instantly see what the changes will look like. Great choice for speedy, simple Web page creation.

```
www.sausagetools.com/hotdog-pagewiz.html
```

NoteTab Lite Editor, from Fookes Software

For Windows. This nifty little HTML editor has won a raft of awards over the years. It's billed as the ultimate free Notepad replacement and a handy HTML editor. It can handle a heap of files with an easy to use tabbed interface, search files, strip HTML tags, and format text quickly. And you certainly can't argue with the price — it's free! If you find yourself editing HTML files with Windows Notepad, consider adding this little gem to your desktop.

```
www.notetab.com/ntl.php
```

Web Weaver and Web Weaver EZ HTML Editors, from McWeb Software

For Windows. Another pair of very easy to use HTML editors. WebWeaver has numerous wizards to make creating Web pages quite easy. Its freeware, cousin WebWeaver EZ, is a visual what-you-see-is-what-you-get Web page creation tool that allows you to avoid dealing with HTML code altogether.

```
www.mcwebsoftware.com/webweav.asp
```

```
www.mcwebsoftware.com/wwez/
```

Graphical tools

Easy Thumbnails, from Fookes Software

For Windows. One of the most useful graphical tools for any Web designer is a program, which produces small thumbnail images from big graphic files. A program like Easy Thumbnails is indispensable if you want to create any sort of image catalog on your Web page. It automatically handles many graphic formats, has a simple user interface, rotates images, and adjusts their contrast, brightness, sharpness, and quality. No Web page author should be without it.

```
www.fookes.com/ezthumbs/index.php
```

GraphicConverter, from Lemke Software

For MacOS. GraphicConverter is a Macintosh shareware program that converts pictures to various formats. It imports about 175 different formats, and outputs about 75 formats. GraphicConverter also contains features that you can use for image manipulation. If you're using a Mac, GraphicConverter is a very useful utility for manipulating the images you'll use in your Web Pages.

```
www.lemkesoft.de/en/graphcon.htm
```

Jasc PaintShop Pro and Jasc Animation Shop, from Jasc Software

For Windows. Paint Shop Pro is a powerful and easy-to-use image viewing, editing, and conversion program, which also happens to include many sophisticated drawing and painting tools. This evaluation version will give you an idea of its power. Paint Shop Pro contains features normally found in programs hundreds of dollars more expensive than this. This version includes features which are specifically useful to Web page creators, such as the ability to optimize graphics for the Web and sharing your photos online. A great value for your money, this may be the only paint/graphics program you'll ever need. Also from Jasc is Animation Shop, a nifty little program which allows you to create image animations, Web banners, and image transitions which you can insert in your Web pages.

```
www.jasc.com/products/paintshoppro/
```

```
www.jasc.com/products/animationshop/
```

Ulead GIF Animator, from Ulead Systems

For Windows. A fast and powerful GIF animation program that will help you add some motion to your Web pages and graphics. This is a fully functional trial version. As an added bonus the program can be used to add animation to Flash (tm) Web sites or to Microsoft Power Point presentation. A good, versatile, GIF animation tool.

```
www.ulead.com/ga/runme.htm
```

Ulead Photo Impact, from Ulead Systems

For Windows. Photo Impact is a graphics program specifically designed for working with digital photographs. If you want to prepare photos for the Web then this is the software package to use. It includes numerous features for tweaking the look and feel of digital photographs, tools for optimizing photos for Web display, special effects filters, and even tools to help you lay out your photo Web pages. Great choice if you have a digital camera.

```
www.ulead.com/pi/runme.htm
```

Web page utilities

CSE HTML Validator Lite, and CSE HTML Validator, from AI Internet Solutions

For Windows. CSE HTML Validator is a powerful, easy-to-use, and user-configurable HTML syntax checker. After you create your Web pages, simply run them through the Validator, and it will tell you if you have any errors in your HTML. Validator Lite is the perfect choice for the beginner HTML coder, while the Pro version has more support for advanced features such as XHTML and checking large numbers of files at once. No Web page author should be without a good syntax checker, and either of these programs will do the job admirably.

```
www.htmlvalidator.com/lite/
```

```
www.htmlvalidator.com/
```

J-Perk, from McWeb Software

For Windows. J-Perk is a kitchen sink collection of tools that let you create all sorts of neat special effects on your Web pages. Effects you can create include animations, photo slide shows, text transitions, background effects, news tickers, scrolling credits, pull down menus, and much more. The list of tools is very impressive, and the software is very easy to use.

```
www.mcwebsoftware.com/j-perk/default.asp
```

Mapedit, from Boutell.com

For Windows and Mac OS. Mapedit is an elegant utility for creating image maps for Web pages. An image map is simply a picture that can have clickable image areas linked to other Web pages. You can find out more about Mapedit and image maps by visiting the Mapedit Web site.

```
www.boutell.com/mapedit/
```

Text Effects, from Blaiz Enterprises

For Windows. Text Effects allows you to create very nice 3D, multicolor, shaded, or rotating text for that special Web image, greeting card, or logo. A nice way to add some excitement to your Web site.

```
www.blaiz.net/TE.HTM
```

Other Internet Tools

FeedDemon, from Bradbury Software

For Windows. FeedDemon is a program which lets you read thousands of news feeds from online news sites and Web logs which syndicate their content using RSS. See the **Resource.htm** file on your CD-ROM for links to more information about RSS and content syndication in general. FeedDemon comes pre-configured with many popular news feeds already set up, allows you to search news feeds, and can even alert you when new feeds match your keyword selections.

```
www.bradsoft.com/feeddemon/index.asp
```

Mozilla, from Mozilla.org

For Windows and Mac. Mozilla is the famous open source Internet software bundle, the main rival to Microsoft's Internet Explorer. The Mozilla package on the CD-ROM is best known for its Web browser, but the package also includes a terrific HTML authoring tool, a sophisticated e-mail client notable for its spam filters, and a chat client compatible with all the major Instant Messaging networks.

```
www.mozilla.org/products/mozilla1.x/
```

Mozilla Firefox, from Mozilla.org

For Windows and Mac. This is the next generation open source Web browser from Mozilla.org. Whereas the Mozilla software suite is kind of like the kitchen sink of Internet tools, Firefox is strictly just a Web browser. It's small, fast, secure, fully compliant with modern Web standards, and full of features, which make Web browsing a real pleasure.

```
www.mozilla.org/products/firefox
```

Mozilla Thunderbird, from Mozilla.org

For Windows and Mac. Thunderbird is the Mozilla project's stand-alone mail and newsgroup client. It has many advanced features, which make reading and sorting e-mail highly configurable and useful. Thunderbird is also notable for its advanced spam filtering features. On top of all that, you can also use it to read Usenet newsgroups.

```
www.mozilla.org/products/thunderbird
```

NetNewsWire Lite, from Ranchero Software

For Mac OS. NetNewsWire is an easy-to-use RSS Web newsreader for the Mac. The Web is full of news sites and Web logs which syndicate their content using RSS standards. See the Resource.htm file on your CD-ROM for links to more information about RSS and content syndication in general. NetNewsWire can fetch and display news from thousands of different Web sites and Web logs, making it quick and easy to keep up with the latest news. The freeware NetNewsWire Lite version on your CD-ROM is a slightly limited edition of the fully functional NetNewsWire, but is still a very usable way to keep up with online news feeds.

```
Ranchero.com/netnewswire
```

Troubleshooting

We tried our best to compile programs that work on most computers with the minimum system requirements. Alas, your computer may differ, and some programs may not work properly for some reason.

The two likeliest problems are that you don't have enough memory (RAM) for the programs you want to use, or you have other programs running that are affecting installation or running of a program. If you get an error message such as `Not enough memory` or `Setup cannot continue`, try one or more of the following suggestions and then try using the software again:

- ✔ **Turn off any antivirus software running on your computer.** Installation programs sometimes mimic virus activity and may make your computer incorrectly believe that it's being infected by a virus.

- ✔ **Close all running programs.** The more programs you have running, the less memory is available to other programs. Installation programs typically update files and programs; so if you keep other programs running, installation may not work properly.

- ✔ **Have your local computer store add more RAM to your computer.** This is, admittedly, a drastic and somewhat expensive step. However, if you have a Windows 95 PC or a Mac OS computer with a PowerPC chip, adding more memory can really help the speed of your computer and allow more programs to run at the same time. This may include closing the CD interface and running a product's installation program from Windows Explorer.

If you still have trouble with the CD-ROM, please call the Wiley Product Technical Support phone number: (800) 762-2974. Outside the United States, call (317) 572-3994. You can also contact Wiley Product Technical Support through the Internet at: `www.wiley.com/techsupport`. Wiley Publishing will provide technical support only for installation and other general quality control items; for technical support on the applications themselves, consult the program's vendor or author.

To place additional orders or to request information about other Wiley products, please call (800) 225-5945.

Index

• *H* •

Wiley Publishing, Inc.
End-User License Agreement

5. **Limited Warranty.**

   (a) WPI warrants that the Software and Software Media are free from defects in materials and workmanship under normal use for a period of sixty (60) days from the date of purchase of this Book. If WPI receives notification within the warranty period of defects in materials or workmanship, WPI will replace the defective Software Media.

   (b) WPI AND THE AUTHOR(S) OF THE BOOK DISCLAIM ALL OTHER WARRANTIES, EXPRESS OR IMPLIED, INCLUDING WITHOUT LIMITATION IMPLIED WARRANTIES OF MERCHANTABILITY AND FITNESS FOR A PARTICULAR PURPOSE, WITH RESPECT TO THE SOFTWARE, THE PROGRAMS, THE SOURCE CODE CONTAINED THEREIN, AND/OR THE TECHNIQUES DESCRIBED IN THIS BOOK. WPI DOES NOT WARRANT THAT THE FUNCTIONS CONTAINED IN THE SOFTWARE WILL MEET YOUR REQUIREMENTS OR THAT THE OPERATION OF THE SOFTWARE WILL BE ERROR FREE.

   (c) This limited warranty gives you specific legal rights, and you may have other rights that vary from jurisdiction to jurisdiction.

6. **Remedies.**

   (a) WPI's entire liability and your exclusive remedy for defects in materials and workmanship shall be limited to replacement of the Software Media, which may be returned to WPI with a copy of your receipt at the following address: Software Media Fulfillment Department, Attn.: *Creating Web Pages For Dummies,* 7th Edition, Wiley Publishing, Inc., 10475 Crosspoint Blvd., Indianapolis, IN 46256, or call 1-800-762-2974. Please allow four to six weeks for delivery. This Limited Warranty is void if failure of the Software Media has resulted from accident, abuse, or misapplication. Any replacement Software Media will be warranted for the remainder of the original warranty period or thirty (30) days, whichever is longer.

   (b) In no event shall WPI or the author be liable for any damages whatsoever (including without limitation damages for loss of business profits, business interruption, loss of business information, or any other pecuniary loss) arising from the use of or inability to use the Book or the Software, even if WPI has been advised of the possibility of such damages.

   (c) Because some jurisdictions do not allow the exclusion or limitation of liability for consequential or incidental damages, the above limitation or exclusion may not apply to you.

7. **U.S. Government Restricted Rights.** Use, duplication, or disclosure of the Software for or on behalf of the United States of America, its agencies and/or instrumentalities "U.S. Government" is subject to restrictions as stated in paragraph (c)(1)(ii) of the Rights in Technical Data and Computer Software clause of DFARS 252.227-7013, or subparagraphs (c) (1) and (2) of the Commercial Computer Software - Restricted Rights clause at FAR 52.227-19, and in similar clauses in the NASA FAR supplement, as applicable.

8. **General.** This Agreement constitutes the entire understanding of the parties and revokes and supersedes all prior agreements, oral or written, between them and may not be modified or amended except in a writing signed by both parties hereto that specifically refers to this Agreement. This Agreement shall take precedence over any other documents that may be in conflict herewith. If any one or more provisions contained in this Agreement are held by any court or tribunal to be invalid, illegal, or otherwise unenforceable, each and every other provision shall remain in full force and effect.

FOR DUMMIES®

The easy way to get more done and have more fun

⸺RSONAL FINANCE & BUSINESS

Investing FOR DUMMIES

0-7645-2431-3

Home Buying FOR DUMMIES

0-7645-5331-3

Grant Writing FOR DUMMIES

0-7645-5307-0

Also available:

Accounting For Dummies
(0-7645-5314-3)

Business Plans Kit For Dummies
(0-7645-5365-8)

Managing For Dummies
(1-5688-4858-7)

Mutual Funds For Dummies
(0-7645-5329-1)

QuickBooks All-in-One Desk Reference For Dummies
(0-7645-1963-8)

Resumes For Dummies
(0-7645-5471-9)

Small Business Kit For Dummies
(0-7645-5093-4)

Starting an eBay Business For Dummies
(0-7645-1547-0)

Taxes For Dummies 2003
(0-7645-5475-1)

⸺OME, GARDEN, FOOD & WINE

Feng Shui FOR DUMMIES

0-7645-5295-3

Gardening FOR DUMMIES

0-7645-5130-2

Cooking FOR DUMMIES

0-7645-5250-3

Also available:

Bartending For Dummies
(0-7645-5051-9)

Christmas Cooking For Dummies
(0-7645-5407-7)

Cookies For Dummies
(0-7645-5390-9)

Diabetes Cookbook For Dummies
(0-7645-5230-9)

Grilling For Dummies
(0-7645-5076-4)

Home Maintenance For Dummies
(0-7645-5215-5)

Slow Cookers For Dummies
(0-7645-5240-6)

Wine For Dummies
(0-7645-5114-0)

⸺TNESS, SPORTS, HOBBIES & PETS

Fitness FOR DUMMIES

0-7645-5167-1

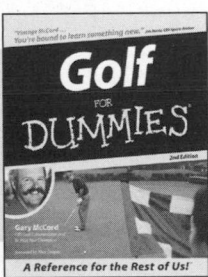

Golf FOR DUMMIES

0-7645-5146-9

Guitar FOR DUMMIES

0-7645-5106-X

Also available:

Cats For Dummies
(0-7645-5275-9)

Chess For Dummies
(0-7645-5003-9)

Dog Training For Dummies
(0-7645-5286-4)

Labrador Retrievers For Dummies
(0-7645-5281-3)

Martial Arts For Dummies
(0-7645-5358-5)

Piano For Dummies
(0-7645-5105-1)

Pilates For Dummies
(0-7645-5397-6)

Power Yoga For Dummies
(0-7645-5342-9)

Puppies For Dummies
(0-7645-5255-4)

Quilting For Dummies
(0-7645-5118-3)

Rock Guitar For Dummies
(0-7645-5356-9)

Weight Training For Dummies
(0-7645-5168-X)

⸺vailable wherever books are sold.
⸺o to www.dummies.com or call 1-877-762-2974 to order direct

WILEY

FOR DUMMIES®

A world of resources to help you grow

TRAVEL

0-7645-5453-0

0-7645-5438-7

0-7645-5444-1

Also available:

America's National Parks For Dummies
(0-7645-6204-5)

Caribbean For Dummies
(0-7645-5445-X)

Cruise Vacations For Dummies 2003
(0-7645-5459-X)

Europe For Dummies
(0-7645-5456-5)

Ireland For Dummies
(0-7645-6199-5)

France For Dummies
(0-7645-6292-4)

Las Vegas For Dummies
(0-7645-5448-4)

London For Dummies
(0-7645-5416-6)

Mexico's Beach Resorts For Dummies
(0-7645-6262-2)

Paris For Dummies
(0-7645-5494-8)

RV Vacations For Dummies
(0-7645-5443-3)

EDUCATION & TEST PREPARATION

0-7645-5194-9

0-7645-5325-9

0-7645-5249-X

Also available:

The ACT For Dummies
(0-7645-5210-4)

Chemistry For Dummies
(0-7645-5430-1)

English Grammar For Dummies
(0-7645-5322-4)

French For Dummies
(0-7645-5193-0)

GMAT For Dummies
(0-7645-5251-1)

Inglés Para Dummies
(0-7645-5427-1)

Italian For Dummies
(0-7645-5196-5)

Research Papers For Dummies
(0-7645-5426-3)

SAT I For Dummies
(0-7645-5472-7)

U.S. History For Dummies
(0-7645-5249-X)

World History For Dummies
(0-7645-5242-2)

HEALTH, SELF-HELP & SPIRITUALITY

0-7645-5154-X

0-7645-5302-X

0-7645-5418-2

Also available:

The Bible For Dummies
(0-7645-5296-1)

Controlling Cholesterol For Dummies
(0-7645-5440-9)

Dating For Dummies
(0-7645-5072-1)

Dieting For Dummies
(0-7645-5126-4)

High Blood Pressure For Dummies
(0-7645-5424-7)

Judaism For Dummies
(0-7645-5299-6)

Menopause For Dummies
(0-7645-5458-1)

Nutrition For Dummies
(0-7645-5180-9)

Potty Training For Dummies
(0-7645-5417-4)

Pregnancy For Dummies
(0-7645-5074-8)

Rekindling Romance For Dummies
(0-7645-5303-8)

Religion For Dummies
(0-7645-5264-3)

Available wherever books are sold. Go to www.dummies.com or call 1-877-762-2974 to order direct